CASES TO ACCOMPANY
CONTEMPORARY
STRATEGY ANALYSIS

SIXTH EDITION

CASES TO ACCOMPANY CONTEMPORARY STRATEGY ANALYSIS

SIXTH EDITION

ROBERT M. GRANT

John Wiley and Sons Editorial Offices
John Wiley & Sons Inc., 111 River Street, Hoboken, NJ 07030, USA
Jossey-Bass, 989 Market Street, San Francisco, CA 94103-1741, USA
Wiley-VCH Verlag GmbH, Boschstr. 12, D-69469 Weinheim, Germany
John Wiley & Sons Australia Ltd, 42 Mc Dougall Street, Milton, Queensland 4064, Australia
John Wiley & Sons (Asia) Pte, 2 Clementi Loop #02-01, Jin Xing Distripark, Singapore 129809
John Wiley & Sons Canada Ltd, 6045 Freemont Blvd, Missisauga, ONT, L5R 4J3
Wiley also publishes its books in a variety of electronic formats. Some content that appears in
print may not be available in electronic books.

First published as *Cases in Contemporary Strategy Analysis* 1996 by Blackwell Publishers Ltd,
second edition published 1999, third edition published 2003, published as *Cases to Accompany
Contemporary Strategy Analysis*, fifth edition 2005, sixth edition published 2008 by Blackwell
Publishing Ltd. Reprinted September 2008, January 2009.

Library of Congress Cataloguing-in-Publication Data
Grant, Robert M., 1948–
    Cases to accompany Contemporary strategy analysis/ Robert M. Grant—6th ed.
        p. cm.
    Includes bibliographical references.
    ISBN 978-1-4051-6310-1 (paperback : alk.paper)
1. Strategic planning-Case studies.   2. Decision making- Case studies.   I. Grant, Robert M.,
1984– Contemporary strategy analysis.   II. Title.

    HD30.28.G716 2008
    658.4′012—dc22

                                                                            2007008013

A catalogue record for this title is available from the British Library.
ISBN: 978-1-4051-6310-1 (Paperback)

Set in 10/12pt Classical Garamond by Graphicraft Limited, Hong Kong.
Printed and bound in the United Kingdom by TJ International, Padstow, Cornwall.

This book is printed on acid-free paper.

Email (for orders and customer service enquiries): cs-books@wiley.co.uk
Visit our Home Page on www.wiley.com

CONTENTS

Madonna Ciccone has been one of the world's leading female entertainers for more than two decades. Madonna shows an inexhaustible capacity to defy changes in style and her own aging by continually reinventing herself. What can we learn from Madonna's remarkable career about the nature of strategy and the foundations of success?

In February 1999 Ng Kwan Cheong took over as the seventh CEO of Laura Ashley Holdings since the death of its founder in 1985. During this period, the company's performance had been mostly downhill. Cheong faced a critical situation: despite several years of cost cutting and restructuring, sales were declining and operating losses were mounting. Cheong must determine the sources of Laura Ashley's problems, and determine what can be done to stem the losses and protect the interests of Laura Ashley's long-suffering shareholders. The case tests your ability to diagnose the sources of a company's performance problems and use that diagnosis as the basis for a turnaround plan.

The period 2005–7 saw a remarkable revival in the fortunes of the US airline industry. Was the return to profitability a temporary blip, or was a fundamental shift in economics of the industry taking place? The case calls for an analysis of the reasons for the intense price competition and appalling profit record of the industry for most of the past 30 years, the reasons for the recent upturn, and the prospects for the future.

Ford Motor Company is experiencing one of the most difficult periods of its 100-year history. In 2006 it posted a $12.7 billion loss, raising questions about survival. Ford's ability to survive the next five years depends critically on the state of the world automobile industry. The case asks you to advise Ford's new CEO, Alan Mulally, in predicting competition and profitability in the industry based on an analysis of changes in industry structure – the number of competitors, demand growth, investment in new capacity, product differentiation, and a number of other factors. The case shows how internationalization and maturity in an industry can combine to create intensely competitive conditions that make it difficult for companies to cover their cost of capital. The case also raises the issue of why it is that some companies (Toyota, BMW) are much more profitable than others (Ford, GM, Volkswagen, Fiat) – this calls for an analysis of key success factors in the industry.

Raisio, a long-established grain-milling and vegetable oil company, has become the darling of the Helsinki stock market as a result of an innovatory food ingredient, stanol ester, which reduces cholesterol levels in the human body. Its margarine *Benecol*, which includes stanol ester, has become a runaway success in Finland. The question presented by the [A] case is: how should Raisio exploit its innovation on the world market? The [B] case takes up the story two years later when Raisio's global partnership with Johnson & Johnson is encountering difficulties and Raisio is now meeting competition from Unilever. The case addresses the problems of managing innovation when the market for the new product is evolving quickly.

In 2006, the battle for the latest generation of video game consoles (the seventh since the industry's inception in the early 1970s) began in earnest. Since the exit of Sega, the industry comprised three players: Sony, Microsoft, and Nintendo. Despite Sony's huge installed base from its earlier PS2, the market was more open than it had been for many years. Microsoft had a first-mover advantage in the new generation, while Nintendo relied on its reputation and its innovative controller for its Wii machine. The case provides a history of competition in the industry and requires an analysis of key success factors in this winner-take-all industry. However, the dynamics of competition are changing – the balance of power between hardware and software suppliers has shifted, online game playing has grown, and video game consoles are becoming multifunctional home entertainment devices. These changes have important implications for network effects and the basis of competitive advantage. Given the changing dynamics of competition and the differential strengths and weaknesses of the three players, what strategies should Sony, Microsoft, and Nintendo deploy in their quest for market leadership?

Eni's metamorphosis from a widely diversified, inefficient, state-owned corporation to a highly profitable, shareholder-owned, international energy major is a fascinating tale of corporate transformation led by two exceptional CEOs: Franco Bernabè and Vittorio Mincato. Yet, despite Eni's outstanding operational and financial performance, it faces important questions of corporate strategy. Which businesses should it include within its corporate portfolio? How should it allocate its investment budget between them? What geographical scope is appropriate for the company? What is the scope for managing linkages between Eni's different businesses? Answering these questions requires analysis of the determinants of profitability in the oil and gas sector, and an assessment of Eni's resources and capabilities relative to other integrated energy majors.

During the 1950s and 1960s, Unilever subsidiary Birds Eye Foods used a strategy of vertical integration to develop and dominate the British frozen food industry. Birds Eye invested heavily in a national network of cold stores and refrigerated trucks, while securing supplies of fresh produce through contracts with growers and fishing boats. As the industry developed, Birds Eye lost market share to competitors that concentrated on a few stages of the value chain, outsourcing most other activities. As the industry evolved, the competitive advantages that Birds Eye had derived from vertical integration were transformed into disadvantages. The case requires analysis of Birds Eye's vertical integration decisions during the industry's early stages, and the reasons for the declining benefits of vertical integration as the industry grew in size and complexity.

six years as CEO and sheds light on the complex task of creating value through managing the linkages between different businesses within a large diversified corporation.

Under the leadership of its founders Roger Sant and Dennis Bakke, AES was like no other company in the electricity generation industry. It was committed to social responsibility and providing fun for employees. Its radical management system was described as "empowerment gone mad." During 2002, external events – Enron, the California power crisis, falling wholesale prices, and political and economic difficulties in Latin America, Pakistan, and Eastern Europe – brought AES to the brink of collapse. CEO Bakke was ousted and AES reverted to a more traditional management style. The case raises questions over the potential for radical new approaches to strategic management – in particular, the limits of decentralization and self-organization. Does the durability of traditional approaches to management and the failure of most experiments in radical organizational innovation reflect the superiority of conventional hierarchies, or are they the result of pressures for conformity exercised by the financial markets and the business sector in general? Given growing demands for social and environmental responsibility, the need for creativity, and individuals' quests for meaning in their lives, is there scope for new approaches to strategy, organization, and leadership?

PREFACE

This edition of *Cases to Accompany* Contemporary Strategy Analysis, *Sixth Edition* represents an ongoing commitment to examining the concepts and techniques of business strategy analysis in the context of real business situations.

The cases have been written to accompany the sixth edition of my *Contemporary Strategy Analysis* textbook (also published by Blackwell Publishing). Each case presents issues that illuminate the ideas, concepts, and analytical techniques contained in one or more chapters of the textbook. Most important, the cases promote deep learning by students of strategic management by requiring the application of these concepts, techniques, and frameworks to the subject matter of the cases. To achieve this, the cases are focused closely around the material in the textbook chapters. For example:

- Case 1 (*Madonna*) offers an opportunity to explore some of the key themes of Chapter 1 of the textbook – namely, the nature of strategy as a dynamic, emergent phenomenon – and consider the factors that makes such a strategy successful (in terms of delivering outstanding performance).

- Case 2 (*Laura Ashley*) is a vehicle for deploying the tools of performance diagnosis outlined in Chapter 2 of the textbook, and illuminates the potential for integrating financial and strategic analysis.

- Cases 3 and 4 (*The US Airline Industry* and *Ford and the World Automobile Industry*) are industry cases suitable for the application of the tools of industry and competitive analysis outlined in Chapters 3 and 4 of the textbook (especially the Porter "five forces of competition" framework).

- Cases 5, 6, and 7 (*Wal-Mart Stores Inc.*, *Manchester United*, and *Eastman Kodak* each focus on the analysis of resources and capabilities outlined in Chapter 5 of the textbook.

Similarly, with all the other cases in the book, each case has been designed to illustrate and apply the tools in one or more of the textbook's chapters – right through to the last case about AES, which explores the new approaches to strategic management discussed in the final chapter of the textbook.

Most of the cases in this collection refer to recent situations. However, no matter how up to date at the time of writing, by the time the book reaches the reader, the case situations will be history. Teaching cases that refer to the recent past rather than to the present inevitably involves some loss of immediacy and taming of uncertainty. The challenge for students and their instructors is to address the business situation as it existed at the time of the case. The key issue here is not to let hindsight cloud learning. For example, by the end of 2007, it will probably be evident whether Sony, Microsoft, or Nintendo will be the market leader in the new generation of video game consoles. If we are to use this case to develop our skills of strategic analysis and strategic decision making, we need to disregard the events of 2007 and ask: Given what we knew in January 2007 about this industry and the decisions and characteristics of the leading firms, how is the market likely to develop and what strategies should each of the three contenders adopt?

The majority of the cases outline situations where decision making is required: What can Laura Ashley's CEO do to improve the company's dire performance? How can Wal-Mart sustain its competitive advantage in discount retailing? How can Nintendo survive against Microsoft and Sony in the video game industry? However, the key learning is not about decision making, it is about analyzing and gaining insight into the business situation in which strategic decisions are taken. Indeed, some cases have a much weaker decision focus. The Harley-Davidson case is primarily concerned with gaining understanding of the brilliance of Harley's strategy in terms of its close fit with Harley's resources and capabilities and its development of differentiation advantage. The Kodak case is primarily about gaining understanding of how difficult it is to develop the new organizational capabilities needed to adjust to a radical technological shift within one's core business.

By being more focused than the typical strategy cases, these cases are typically shorter than most business strategy cases (notably those from Harvard Business School). Brevity also limits the amount of information that is supplied to students. Does this mean that students should seek out additional information? Preferably not – the cases provide all the data needed to identify and analyze the key issues. More data permits more detailed analysis, but at the cost of slowing and overloading the decision process. For most companies, strategic decisions must be taken with only a fraction of the relevant information available – events are moving too quickly to allow the luxury of extensive, in-depth research.

We hope you will find the cases instructive and enjoyable. The process of case development is continuous, so please check the Blackwell website for new and updated cases. The website also offers teaching notes for instructors and guidance on the textbook study questions.

I shall appreciate any comments and suggestions that you have – including offers of new cases.

Robert Grant (grantr@georgetown.edu)

ACKNOWLEDGMENTS

The author and publisher gratefully acknowledge the permission granted to reproduce the copyright material in this book:

Case 2. Extract from "Giving Laura Ashley a Yank" *Business Week* May 27, 1997. p. 147. Copyright © 1997 by *Business Week*. Reprinted by permission from *Business Week*.

Tables 5.1, 5.5 and Appendix. Extracts taken from walmartstores.com. Used with permission of Wal-Mart Corporate Communications.

Case 8. Extract from M. Moody-Stuart, Changes in Shell's organization: comments to the Shell Global Leadership Conference, London, December 10, 1998. Used with permission of Shell International Exploration & Production B.V.

Case 8. Extract from Martin van den Bergh "Strengthening the portfolio." Shell press release, April 3, 2000. Used with permission of Shell International Exploration & Production B.V.

Table 13.4. From C. Baden Fuller, *Rising Concentration: The UK Grocery Trade 1970–82*, London Business School, 1984. © 1984 by C. Baden Fuller. Reprinted by permission of the author.

Case 14. This case draws extensively on M. L. Taylor, G. M. Puia, K. Ramaya, and M. Gengelback, "Outback Steakhouse Goes International," in A. A. Thompson and A. J. Strickland, *Strategic Management: Concepts and Cases*, 11th edn. (New York: McGraw-Hill 1999). Copyright © 1997 by case authors and North American Case Research Association. Used with permission of Marilyn L. Taylor.

Case 14. Extracts from Chris T. Sullivan, "A Stake in the Business," *Harvard Business Review* (September 2005). Copyright © 2005 by the Harvard Business School Publishing Corporation; all rights reserved. Reprinted with permission from *Harvard Business Review*.

Figure 16.1 "Virgin Group of Companies"; table 16.1 "Main businesses within the Virgin group"; and 16.1 "Main businesses within the Virgin group" taken from www.virgin.com – Virgin Management Company.

Case 17. Extracts from Noel Tichy and Ram Charan, "Speed, simplicity, and self-confidence: an interview with Jack Welch," *Harvard Business Review*, September–October 1989. Copyright © 1989 by the Harvard Business School Publishing Corporation; all rights reserved. Reprinted with permission from *Harvard Business Review*.

Case 19. Table 19.5 and extracts from Appendix B "What made AES different" in Dennis W. Bakke, "Joy at Work" (PVG, 2005). © 2005 by Dennis W. Bakke. Reprinted by permission of www.dennis.bakke.com

Madonna

The Struggle

In July 1977, shortly before her 19th birthday, Madonna Louise Ciccone arrived in New York City with $35 in her pocket. She had left Ann Arbor where she was majoring in dance at the University of Michigan. Madonna was raised in the suburbs of Detroit. The third of eight children, her mother had died when she was 6 years old. Her prospects in the world of show business looked poor. Apart from her training in dance, she had little musical background and no contacts.

Life in New York was a struggle. "I worked at Dunkin' Donuts, I worked at Burger King, I worked at Amy's. I had a lot of jobs that lasted one day. I always talked back to people and they'd fire me. I was a coat-check girl at the Russian Tea Room. I worked at a health club once a week."[1] She spent a few months training with the Alvin Ailey Dance Theater and had a succession of modeling engagements for photographers and artists. During 1979, Madonna began to explore New York's music and acting scenes. With new boyfriend Dan Gilroy, his brother Ed, and bassist Angie Smit, "Breakfast Club" was formed, with Madonna sharing vocals and drums with Dan. For 6 months Madonna was dancer and backup singer to French singing star Patrick Hernandez, during which time she performed in Paris and around Europe and North Africa. In August 1979, Madonna was offered the lead role in underground movie director Stephen Lewicki's low-budget film *A Certain Sacrifice* – she was paid $100.

After breaking up with Dan Gilroy, Madonna renewed her effort to form a band. She invited her former Michigan boyfriend, Steve Bray, to New York. They moved into the Music Building – a converted 12-story building crammed with studios, rehearsal rooms, and striving, impoverished young bands. Together they worked on writing songs and developing their sound. The resulting rock band, "Emmy," made little impression, but Madonna maintained a continuous stream of calls to managers, agents, record companies, and club owners. Camille

Barbone offered a management contract – but only for Madonna. However, Barbone was unable to deliver success fast enough for Madonna and after 18 months Madonna fired her.

Finding a Sound, Finding a Style

During 1981, Madonna's music and image moved in a new direction. Influenced by the emerging dance scene in New York, Madonna moved increasingly from Pretenders/Pat Benatar rock to the dance music that was sweeping New York clubs. In addition to working with Steve Bray to develop songs and mix demo tapes, she worked on her image – a form of glam-grunge that featured multilayered, multi-colored combinations of thrift-store clothing together with scarves and junk jewelry. She adopted "Boy Toy" as her "tag name" and prominently displayed it on her belt buckle. It was a look that she would continue to develop with the help of jewelry designer Maripole. Her trademark look of messy, badly dyed hair, neon rubber bracelets, black lace bras, white lace gloves, and chunky belt buckles would soon be seen on teenage girls throughout the world.

Madonna was quick to recognize the commercial implications of the new musical wave – it was the dance clubs that were key inroads and the DJs who were the key gatekeepers. Armed with her demo tapes, Madonna and her friends increasingly frequented the hottest dance clubs where they would make a splash with their flamboyant clothing and provocative dancing. At Danceteria, one of the staff referred to her as a "heat-seeking missile targeting the hottest DJs." There she attracted the attention of DJ Mark Kamins who introduced her to Mike Rosenblatt and Seymour Stein of Sire Records, a division of Warner Records. A recording contract and $5,000 were soon hers.

The first release was a 12-inch single with different versions of *Everybody* on each side. The record gained extensive dance-club play. Madonna began working on her first album. Although she had promised both longtime friend and music collaborator Steve Bray and DJ Mark Kamins the job of producer, she dumped both in favor of Warner Records' house producer, Reggie Lucas. Together with Warner Records' national dance promoter, Bobby Shaw, Madonna began a relentless round of courting DJs and pushing her record for play time. Central to the promotion plan was New York's hottest DJ, John "Jellybean" Benitez, who Madonna began dating in November 1982.

Her second single, *Burning Up*, with *Physical Attraction* (written by Reggie Lewis) on the B-side, was released in March 1983. It too was a dance-club hit and bounded up the dance charts to number three. With the attention and resources of Warner Brothers and a network of DJs, Madonna had most of the pieces she needed in place – but not quite. Early in 1983 she flew to Los Angeles to visit Freddie DeMann, then manager of megastar Michael Jackson. DeMann remembers the meeting vividly: "I was knocked off my feet. I've never met a more physical human being in my life." In a short time DeMann dropped Michael Jackson in favor of managing Madonna.

Breakthrough

The album *Madonna* was released in July 1983. By the end of 1983, the record was climbing the US album charts supported by the success of single release *Holiday*. In April 1984, another single release from the album, *Borderline*, became Madonna's first top-ten hit. At Madonna's national TV debut on *American Bandstand*, presenter Dick Clark asked her, "What do you really want to do when you grow up?" "Rule the world," she replied.

Within little more than a year Madonna was part-way there. The fall of 1984 saw Madonna filming in *Desperately Seeking Susan*. Although initially hired as support for the movie's star, Rosanna Arquette, Madonna progressively hijacked the movie. By the time the shooting was complete, it was essentially a movie about Madonna playing herself, wearing her own style of clothes, and featuring her own music. Its release coincided with a surge of Madonna-mania. Her second album, *Like a Virgin*, had gone triple-platinum (over 3 million copies sold) in February 1985, while the singles charts featured a succession of individual tracks from the album. Madonna's first concert tour was a sell-out. Her marriage to bad-boy actor Sean Penn on August 16, 1985 further reinforced her celebrity status. When Madonna took up residence in Los Angeles during 1985, she was already a star and seldom far from the popular press headlines.

Fame, Fortune, Notoriety

During the next two decades, little would come between Madonna and her quest for fame. Between 1986 and 1990, she released six albums. The 16 single releases from these albums gave her a near-continuous presence in the charts, including a remarkable seven number-one hits.[2] In the process, Madonna rejected the industry's conventional wisdom of "Find a winning formula and stick to it." Madonna's career was a continuous experimentation with new musical ideas and new images, and a constant quest for new heights of fame and acclaim. Having established herself as the queen of popular music, Madonna did not stop there. By the end of the 1980s she was destined to be "the most famous woman on the planet."

Madonna in Charge

Madonna's struggle for fame revealed a drive, determination, and appetite for hard work that would characterize her whole career. "I'm tough, I'm ambitious, and I know exactly what I want – and if that makes me a bitch, that's okay," she told the London *News of the World* newspaper in 1985. On the set of *Desperately Seeking Susan* she maintained a blistering pace. "During the shoot we'd often get home at 11:00 or 12:00 at night and have to be back at 6:00 or 7:00 the next morning. Half the time the driver would pick up Madonna at her health club. She'd get up at 4:30 in the morning to work out first."[3]

There was never any doubt as to who was in charge of managing and developing Madonna's career. While Madonna relied on some of the best minds and strongest companies in the entertainment business, there was never any ambiguity as to who was calling the shots. In addition to Freddie DeMann as manager, Madonna hired top lawyer Paul Schindler to represent her business deals. Her swift exit from her marriage with Sean Penn further emphasized her unwillingness to allow messy personal relationships to compromise her career goals. When it came to her third album – *True Blue*, released in June 1986 – Madonna insisted on being co-producer.

The best evidence of her hands-on management style is the documentary of her 1990 "Blonde Ambition" tour, *Truth or Dare*. The tour itself was a masterpiece of the pop concert as multimedia show embracing music, dance, and theater. The tour's planning began in September 1989. Madonna was involved in every aspect of the show's design and planning, including auditioning dancers and musicians, planning, costume design, and choice of themes. For example, Madonna worked closely with Jean-Paul Gaultier on the metallic, cone-breasted costumes that became one of the tour's most vivid images. On the tour itself, the *Truth or Dare* movie revealed Madonna as both creative director and operations supremo. In addition to her obsessive attention to every detail of the show's production, she was the undisputed organizational leader responsible for building team spirit among the diverse group of dancers, musicians, choreographers, and technicians; motivating the troupe when times were tough; resolving disputes between her fractious and highly strung male dancers; and establishing the highest standards of commitment and effort.

The "Blonde Ambition" tour in the summer of 1990 marked new heights of international obsession with Madonna. The tour coincided with the release of *Dick Tracy*, the Disney movie that was a vehicle for the high-profile lovers, Madonna and Warren Beatty. The film did much to rectify a string of Hollywood flops and scathing reviews of Madonna's own acting capabilities. Madonna's portrayal of Breathless Mahoney exuded her natural talents for style and seductiveness and became her biggest box office hit to date. At the annual MTV Music Awards on September 4, Madonna yet again stole the show with a version of her *Vogue* single in which she portrayed French queen, Marie Antoinette.

Fame and Controversy

From her initial launch into stardom, Madonna's fame was tinged with notoriety. From the early days of her singing career, her overt sexuality was reinforced by her "Boy Toy" moniker. This combined with her sexually audacious, expletive-laced talk and use of crucifixes as items of jewelry raised disquiet within conservative and religious circles. Madonna's explanation only added fuel to the fire: "Crucifixes are sexy because there's a naked man on them." With every video and interview, Madonna pushed a little harder against the boundaries of acceptable language, behavior, and imagery. Her *Like a Prayer* album, released in March 1989, proved to be a landmark in this process.

Pepsi Cola saw the opportunity to piggy-back on the surge of Madonna-mania by making an advertising video based on the album's title track *Like a Prayer*. What Pepsi had not taken into account was that Madonna was making her own music video of *Like a Prayer* to accompany the launch of the record. The day after the first broadcast of the Pepsi commercial, Madonna's own *Like a Prayer* video appeared on MTV. The video was a stunning mixture of sex and religion that featured Madonna dancing in front of burning crosses, making love on an altar, and revealing stigmata on her hands. The video outraged many Christian groups and the American Family Association threatened to boycott Pepsi products. Pepsi pulled its Madonna commercial, leaving Madonna with her $5 million fee from Pepsi.

The explicit sexuality of the "Blonde Ambition" tour and its mixing of sexual and religious imagery resulted in Madonna achieving new heights of controversy – and public awareness. In Toronto, city authorities threatened to cancel the show. The Vatican condemned the show as "blasphemous." Her *Justify My Love* video released in November 1990 set a new record for Madonna – it was banned by MTV on the basis of its inclusion of homosexuality, voyeurism, nudity, sado-masochism, and oral sex. Again, Madonna was quick to turn controversy into profit: as soon as MTV refused to air *Justify My Love*, the video was rush released for retail sale. The publicity generated helped the *Justify My Love* single to the top of the charts.

During the early 1990s, Madonna continued to break new ground in sexual explicitness. Her photographic "art" book *Sex* featured Madonna in an array of sexual poses. The book itself introduced several marketing and design innovations from its unusual size (14 by 11 inches), its stainless steel covers and spiral binding, its sale in sealed wrapping, and its inclusion of Madonna's latest CD, *Erotica*. And it was a smash hit. Despite its high price ($49.95 for 120 pages) the book sold half a million copies in its first week. The record too went beyond any of Madonna's prior albums in terms of the sexually explicit content of its lyrics and supporting videos.

Evita

While Madonna has been compared to previous superstars and goddesses of sex and glamour – Greta Garbo, Marilyn Monroe, Mae West, Brigitte Bardot – she has gone further in creating a persona that transcends her work as an entertainer. All the prior-mentioned female superstars were defined by their movie roles. The same is true of the big names in popular music, from Lena Horne to Janet Jackson – all have been famous primarily for their music. Madonna achieved a status that was no longer defined by her work. By the 1990s, Madonna was no longer famous as a rock singer or an actress – she was famous for being Madonna. For the next decade she worked to reinforce this status. Strategically, superstar status has much to commend it. Joining the pantheon of superstars acts as insulation from comparison with lesser mortals. As her website proclaims, she is "icon, artist, provocateur, diva, and mogul."

In her acting roles the key was to take roles that were primarily vehicles for Madonna to be Madonna. Her successes in *Desperately Seeking Susan* and *Dick Tracy* were the result of roles where Madonna could be herself. However, both these roles were to be eclipsed by Madonna's portrayal of Eva Peron in the movie version of the Andrew Lloyd Webber musical *Evita*. Madonna had coveted the role for years and mounted a vigorous campaign to gain the support of director Alan Parker and Argentine President Carlos Menem. While in previous roles Madonna had been able to use her talents as a singer, a poser, a sharp talker, and a seductress, in *Evita* Madonna could present her own life. Like Madonna, Evita had working class origins, a burning ambition, and had used sex and shrewd judgment to become a legend in her time. The film, released in December 1996, was a huge commercial and critical success. As *Q* magazine's Paul Du Noyer remarked, "If ever there was an ideal vehicle for Madonna's dream of transcendent stardom, this must be it."[4]

Motherhood, and More

During most of the filming of *Evita*, Madonna was coping with her pregnancy. On October 14, 1996, she gave birth to Lourdes Maria Ciccone Leon at the Good Samaritan Hospital in Los Angeles. The baby's father was Carlos Leon, Madonna's personal trainer.

In terms of her life, image, and career, motherhood was a major discontinuity for Madonna. The press began reporting a host of lifestyle changes: Madonna abandoned pumping iron in favor of yoga, she had begun to study Kabbalah ("A mystical inter-pretation of the Old Testament," she explained), she developed a closer circle of women friends, she spent increasing amounts of time writing music, she became less available to the media. Her interviews were amazingly devoid of sex, expletives, and shock value. "I think [motherhood] made me face up to my more feminine side. I had a much more masculine view of the world. What I missed and longed for was that unconditional love that a mother gives you. And so, having my daughter is the same kind of thing. It's like that first, true, pure, unconditional love."[5]

The clearest revelation of these changes was in Madonna's new album, *Ray of Light*, which was unlike any previous Madonna album. Working with William Orbit, the album incorporated a host of new influences: electronic music; traditional Indian music; Madonna's musings on the troubles of the world and the hollowness of fame; reflections on her own emotional development and her unhappy childhood. In per-forming tracks from the album both on TV and on video, Madonna revealed a series of entirely new looks including Madonna as goth-girl (black hair, black clothes, black nail polish), Madonna as Shiva (multi-armed with henna tattoos on her hands), Madonna as geisha (straight black hair, kimono, and white makeup).

The new persona was the most ambitious and risky reinvention of Madonna's career, insofar as it was the first that was not founded on sexuality and sexual aggression. Yet this transformation was met with no loss of popularity or worldwide acclaim. *Ray of Light* hit number two on the album charts and went triple-platinum on the basis of US sales alone, and at the MTV Video Music Awards she walked away with a total of six awards followed by three Grammy Awards.

Madonna as Investor and Business Manager

Not only did Madonna maintain control over her own content, she increasingly wanted a cut in distribution too. In April 1992 she signed a $60 million deal with Time Warner, Inc. The joint venture, Maverick Records, was a music production com-pany (together with TV, video, and music publishing wings) that was to provide a vehicle for Madonna's creative and promotional talent. Warner Records provided dis-tribution. Although Madonna remained contracted to Warner Records for her own recordings, Maverick offered an avenue for her to develop and promote other singers and musicians.

During the late 1990s her efforts became increasingly focused towards identifying and nurturing emerging young singers and musicians, relying upon her creative and promotional intuition and experience, the wealth of talented specialists and media moguls who were part of her personal networks, and, above all, her ability to open any door in the business. Among Maverick's early signings was Canadian singer/songwriter Alanis Morissette, whose *Jagged Little Pill* album sold over 30 million copies. Through Madonna's links with director Mike Myers, Maverick released the soundtrack for the Austin Powers movie *The Spy Who Shagged Me*. Other Maverick artists included William Orbit, Prodigy, the Deftones, and Michelle Branch. Madonna also teamed up with British comedian Sacha Baron Cohen (of Ali G and Borat fame) and helped his US launch.

Madonna's interest in new musicians and in developing and producing their music was linked closely to her own widening musical interests. Her involvement with William Orbit on *Ray of Light* was followed by increased interest both in electronic and world music, including collaboration with the French electro-boffin, Mirwais.

Twenty-First Century Madonna

During the new millennium, neither Madonna's career nor her command over media attention showed much sign of flagging. In 2000 Madonna set up home in London with a new partner, the actor and director Guy Ritchie. In August, shortly before her 42nd birthday, Madonna gave birth to her second child, Rocco. In the following month, her new album, *Music*, was released. The album was an immediate hit, topping the album charts within two weeks. In October, the *Music* single from the album became her 12th number-one single in the US. On December 22, Madonna and Ritchie were married at Dornoch Castle in Scotland.

After an eight-year lapse, 2001 marked Madonna's return to concert touring. The "Drowned World" tour opened in Europe with shows in Barcelona and Milan followed by a run of shows at London's Earls Court before moving on to its US leg. The "Re-invention" tour of 2004 and "Confessions" tour of 2006 were similar successes. The "Confessions" tour grossed $195 million – more than for any other concert tour by a female artist. Observations of Madonna's audiences for her shows confirmed her ability to recruit whole new generations of fans, many of whom had not been born when she recorded her debut album.

With the 20th anniversary of Madonna's first album release, she celebrated the occasion by topping the album charts in March 2003 with her new release *American Life*. Her subsequent album, *Confessions on a Dance Floor*, released in November 2005, also topped the US and UK charts.

Outside of music her artistic efforts met less success. Her 2002 London stage performance in the leading role of the comedy *Up for Grabs* and her *Swept Away* movie co-starring with Guy Ritchie were both panned by the critics. These set-backs did little to dent Madonna's entry into new fields. During 2003 she published the first two in a series of children's books. The first, *The English Roses*, was printed in 42 languages and launched in 100 countries. As part of a deal with The Gap in which Madonna promoted Gap clothing, the book was distributed through Gap stores.

Unchanged throughout was Madonna's ability to court controversy and attract media attention. During October 2006, the world's tabloid newspapers were dominated by news that Madonna was adopting a 13-month-old boy, David Banda, from an orphange in Malawi. Despite donating $4 million to the care of orphans in Malawi, Madonna soon became immersed in a media war over "cash for babies" and "one law for the rich; another for the poor."

Appendix
Madonna's Biographical Timeline

1958:   Born August 16 in Bay City, Michigan to Sylvio Ciccone (design engineer for Chrysler and General Motors) and Madonna Ciccone.
1964:   Mother dies of breast cancer.
1973:   Starts at Rochester Adams High School.
1976:   Freshman at University of Michigan, Ann Arbor; majoring in dance.
1977:   July: arrives in New York City with $35.
        September: begins training with Alvin Ailey Dance Theater.
1979:   Flies to Paris, becomes backup singer for Patrick Hernandez.
        Joins Dan and Ed Gilroy to form "Breakfast Club."
        Lands part of Bruna in underground movie *A Certain Sacrifice*.

1980:   Forms rock band "Emmy" with Steve Bray.
1982:   Establishes friendship with DJ Mark Kamins.
Signs recording contract with Sire Records (division of Warner Brothers).
First record release, *Everybody*, enters dance charts.
Begins dating DJ John "Jellybean" Benitez.
1983:   Second single, *Burning Up/Physical Attraction*, reaches No. 3 in dance charts.
Release of first record album, *Madonna*.
Persuades Freddie DeMann (Michael Jackson's manager) to become her manager.
Appears in the movie *Vision Quest*.
1984:   TV appearance on *American Bandstand*.
Appears and performs on annual MTV Awards.
Release of second record album *Like A Virgin* (produced by Niles Rodgers); sells 7 million copies worldwide.
Begins work on major studio movie *Desperately Seeking Susan*.
1985:   "Virgin" tour opens April 10 in Seattle.
Signs merchandising deal for official Madonna Boy-Toy clothing designs.
Appears in *Live Aid* charity concert (London/Philadelphia, July 13).
Marries Sean Penn.
1986:   Releases *True Blue* album.
Shoots *Shanghai Surprise* with Sean Penn.
Establishes her own film production company, Siren Productions, backed by Universal Studios.
1987:   "Who's That Girl" tour opens Osaka, Japan on June 14; closes in Turin, Italy. *Who's That Girl* album and film also released.
1989:   Divorce with Sean Penn (January 10).
Signs $5 million contract with Pepsi to produce video commercial based upon *Like A Prayer*. Pepsi pulls its commercial after just one showing.
Releases *Like A Prayer* album.
Plays Breathless Mahoney in *Dick Tracy*, co-starring with Warren Beatty.
Begins affair with Warren Beatty.
1990:   Album releases: *I'm Breathless* and *The Immaculate Collection*.
"Blonde Ambition" world concert tour kicks off in Tokyo, April 13. Shows in Toronto and Italy threatened with closure because of their explicit sexual content.
MTV refuses to screen Madonna's *Justify My Love* video.
1991:   *Truth or Dare* documentary of "Blonde Ambition" tour is released.
Appears in Woody Allen's *Shadows and Fog*.
1992:   Grammy Award: Best Music Video (Long Form), *Madonna: Blonde Ambition World Tour Live*.
Release of photographic book *Sex*: sells 500,000 copies in first week; tops *New York Times* best-seller list.
Release of feature movie, *A League of Their Own*.
Madonna signs deal with Time Warner to create Maverick, her own record label.
1993:   Movie releases: *Body Of Evidence* and *Dangerous Game*.
1994:   *Bedtime Stories* album released.
1995:   Releases *Something to Remember* album.
Movie releases include *Blue In The Face* and *Four Rooms*.
1996:   Release of *Evita* in which Madonna plays Eva Peron. Wins Golden Globe Award for Best Actress in a Motion Picture (Musical or Comedy).
Also release of the movie *Girl 6*.
Gives birth to Lourdes Maria Ciccone Leon, October 14; father is Carlos Leon.
1997:   Release of *Ray of Light* album, which in 1998 wins three Grammy Awards in the categories Dance Recording, Pop Album, and Music Video, and six MTV Video Music Awards.

1999: Grammy Award for *Beautiful Stranger* – best song written for a motion picture, television or other visual media (shared with William Orbit).

Release of movie *The Next Best Thing*.

2000: Son, Rocco Ritchie born August 11, 2000; father is actor/director Guy Ritchie.

Release of new album, *Music*. Sells 2.9 million copies in US alone.

Wins WIPO arbitration to gain control of Madonna.com domain name.

Marries Guy Ritchie at Dornoch Castle, Scotland.

2001: July–Sept. "Drowned World" concert tour (kicks off in Europe prior to US).

2002: US release of movie *Swept Away* – goes direct to video in UK.

Lead role in London stage comedy *Up for Grabs*.

2003: Release of *American Life* album.

Publication of children's books *The English Roses* and *Mr Peabody's Apples*.

Stirs controversy at MTV Music Awards by kissing Britney Spears.

2004: Sells shares in Maverick to Time Warner.

"Re-invention" world tour grosses over $100 million.

2005: Releases new album, *Confessions on a Dance Floor*.

2006: "Confessions" world tour opens May 21 in LA; closes Sept. 21 in Tokyo.

Adopts David Banda, a one-year-old orphan from Malawi, amidst criticism from aid agencies and children's charities.

Notes

1 Mark Bego, *Madonna: Bionde Ambition*, Cooper Square, New York, 2000, p. 46.

2 Her Billboard number ones during 1986–90 were: *Live to Tell* (1986), *Papa Don't Preach* (1986), *Open Your Heart* (1986), *Who's that Girl* (1987), *Like a Prayer* (1988), *Vogue* (1990), *Justify my Love* (1990).

3 Carl Arrington, "Madonna," *People*, March 11, 1985.

4 "Commanding" (Review of Evita), *Q*, December 1996.

5 Mary Murphy, "Madonna Confidential," *TV Guide*, April 11–17, 1998.

Laura Ashley Holdings plc: The Battle for Survival

On February 1, 1999 Ng Kwan Cheong took over as chief executive of Laura Ashley Holdings. Cheong was the company's seventh CEO since the death of Laura Ashley in 1985. Indeed, the longevity of Laura Ashley CEOs was shortening. John James was CEO from 1976 to 1990, Jim Maxmin from 1991 to 1993, A. Schouten from 1993 to 1995, Ann Iverson from 1995 to 1997, David Hoare from 1997 to 1998, while Cheong's immediate predecessor, Victoria Egan, had held the job a mere 5 months.

Top management turmoil coincided with a downward spiral for the company. In the financial year ended January 31, 1999, sales were down 17% on the previous year, and the bottom line showed a net loss of £33 million. Ng Kwan Cheong was one of the senior management team of MUI Asia Group – a diversified Malaysian corporation that acquired 40% of Laura Ashley's equity in May 1998. He had been chief executive of MUI's retailing arm, Metrojaya Berhad, as well as holding board positions with several other Malaysian companies. However, despite considerable senior management experience as well as familiarity with the UK (Cheong was a graduate of Middlesex University), little in his prior career could have prepared him for the situation at Laura Ashley. Despite a succession of restructurings and strategy redirections since 1990, the company continued to bleed cash – cash outflow from operations was £11.4 million during the most recent financial year and MUI's cash injection of £43.5 million had been absorbed by debt repayment and covering operating losses. Many outside observers wondered whether there was any future for this icon of the 1970s, or whether Laura Ashley Holdings would follow its founder to the grave.

The History

Development of the Business, 1953–1985

Bernard and Laura Ashley began designing and printing scarves and tablemats in their flat in Pimlico, London in 1953.[1] The products combined Laura's interest in color and design with Bernard's expertise in printing and dyeing. The product range was extended to include Victorian-styled aprons and linen kitchen towels. Laura's designs drew upon British traditional country styles, patterns, and colors. The designs were mainly floral, and the colors predominantly pastel. They sold mainly to department stores such as John Lewis, Heals, and Peter Jones. In 1957 the Ashleys opened a showroom in London, and in 1961 they transferred their production operations to a disused railway station at Carno, Wales, using a flatbed printing process designed by Bernard.

The popularity of Laura's first dress designs encouraged the Ashleys to open a London retail store in Pelham Street, South Kensington in 1968. Although sales were initially slow, advertisements on the London Underground stimulated a surge of interest in Laura Ashley's dresses and fabrics. Throughout the early 1970s, the reaction against modernism, pop art, and other trends of the 1960s rekindled a strong interest in the rural English styles and traditions of the Victorian and Edwardian eras. Laura Ashley's positioning between English bourgeois tradition and hippie abandon, and her ability to evoke nostalgia for the comfort and simplicity of pre-industrial Britain placed her styles in the vanguard of contemporary fashion. During the early 1970s Laura Ashley expanded the company's product range from furnishing fabrics, clothes, and housewares into wallpaper and house paints. What Laura Ashley offered was a coordinated approach to home décor and clothing with a perfect matching of designs and colors across fabrics, wallpapers, paints, and ceramic tiles.

The company expanded internationally with shops in Geneva, Paris, Amsterdam, and Düsseldorf. In Canada, Australia, and Japan licenses were sold to local companies to open Laura Ashley stores. In 1974 Laura Ashley entered the US, initially by licensing McCall's Patterns of New York to distribute its fabrics, and then with an office and retail store in San Francisco.

The business was highly vertically integrated. By the beginning of the 1980s, almost all products were designed by a design team led by Laura and her son Nick (who became design director in 1982) and 85% of all products were manufactured either in the company's own plants or by subcontractors. The majority of sales were through Laura Ashley retail stores. The company became expert in the fast, flexible production of quality fabrics manufactured in small runs. By the early 1980s there were eight garment assembly plants close to Carno in Wales, a fabric plant in Dublin, and two plants in England making home furnishing products and made-to-measure curtains and blinds. Distribution from plants and warehouses to retail stores was done by the company's own transport division. Products for the North American stores were airfreighted weekly; others were manufactured under contract at a plant in Kentucky.

The distinctive design of Laura Ashley products was extended to the retail stores. The dark-green Laura Ashley storefronts were clearly recognizable in the high street, and the interiors with their wooden fittings projected an image of quality and homeliness. The company was an early adopter of electronic point-of-sale systems, which linked retail sales to inventory planning, distribution, and production planning. Laura Ashley also offered mail order sales.

The family ownership and management of the group was reflected in relationships with employees. There was a cooperative, non-hierarchical working environment with a high level of job security and generous employee benefits.

Continued growth encouraged the adoption of a divisional structure: in addition to design and production divisions, retailing was organized around separate divisions for the UK, Continental Europe, North America, and Asia-Pacific.

In November 1985, the company went public. The offer for 23% of Laura Ashley Holdings plc was oversubscribed 34 times. Just 1 month before the public offering, Laura Ashley died after a fall in her home. *The Economist* wrote:

> *Her popularity lay in the taste she stamped on her international empire, not so much for the elegance and smartness as for the prettiness and comfort. Nobody was intimidated by the look or price of a Laura Ashley design. Her home furnishings offered a cheap and feminine alternative to the drab, the posh, and the sternly post-war Habitat Scandinavian. She made it possible to look smart without paying Liberty prices. Her company's success has been the acceptable face of British capitalism in the past two decades. She was deputy chairman to her husband and her power has been considerable. She prized the loyalty of her staff and cared for their welfare.*

Expansion, 1986–1989

Fueled with capital from the public offering, Laura Ashley Holdings launched a new phase of its growth. Between 1986 and 1989 a series of acquisitions extended the product range and geographical scope of the company. These included Sandringham Leather Goods Ltd, Bryant of Scotland (a knitwear company), Willis and Geiger (a US outdoor clothing company with both production facilities and retail outlets), and Penhaligons (an old-established producer of perfumes and toiletries).

The company also continued its internal expansion. In 1985 a 135,000 square foot textile factory in Wales was completed. This increased the company's production capacity by 50%. The new capacity was supported by heavy investment in a new computer-aided design system, computerized fabric-cutting equipment, and a computerized material-handling system.

Emerging Problems, 1990–1991

The expansion of the late 1980s was followed by a deteriorating bottom line as the UK recession of 1989–92 coincided with a series of internal difficulties. Problems included:

- massive overproduction of Laura Ashley catalogs in 1989;
- losses at the Willis and Geiger subsidiary;
- delivery of the 1989 autumn range to the retail stores was 3 months late;
- manufacturing costs rose with the appreciation of the pound sterling;
- rising interest rates boosted borrowing costs;
- exceptional charges were incurred from the sale or closure of non-core businesses, including Penhaligons, Bryant of Scotland, Sandringham Leather Goods, and the Units chain of stores;
- the closure or sale of several production plants.

As the company shifted from expansion to retrenchment, it simultaneously searched for a new design look that would be faithful to Laura Ashley values while appealing to the 1990s consumer. Table 2.1 shows financial performance during the 1990s.

The Iverson Era

In June 1995, Ann Iverson was appointed Laura Ashley's chief executive. Iverson was one of the most sought-after executives in the retail sector after a successful retailing career on both sides of the Atlantic. She had been a vice president at Bloomingdale's, the US department store, a senior vice president at Bonwit Teller, CEO of Kay-Bee Toys, and had led the turnaround of Mothercare, the British mother and baby chain. With an annual salary of £883,000, Iverson became one of the highest paid retail executives in Britain.

Iverson moved quickly to restructure Laura Ashley's manufacturing, purchasing, and merchandising. Processes were redesigned, decision making was centralized, international procedures were standardized, unprofitable businesses sold, smaller shops closed, and cost controls tightened. In March 1996, Iverson outlined her strategy for the future (see Exhibit 2.1).

Iverson's first year at Laura Ashley was hailed by investors and industry observers as the long-awaited turnaround in the fortunes of the beleaguered group. *Business Week* enthused:

> *Since becoming CEO of Laura Ashley Holdings, plc last July, Ann Iverson has replaced most of top management, cut the payroll, slashed costs, and unveiled an aggressive expansion plan in the US. "I'm the kind of person who has a steamroller behind her back," says Iverson, 52, who was recruited when shareholders were getting fed up. Now the market's applauding. On April 18, the company reported pretax income of $15.6 million for 1995, compared with a $46.5 million loss a year before. Since Iverson's appointment, Laura Ashley's stock has more than doubled . . . [but] no one knows yet if Iverson can solve the biggest problem: the apparel line with its signature floral prints and long, girlish dresses, is deeply unfashionable in the minimalist 1990s. . . . Iverson acknowledges that the company's Victorian look is dated, but cites recent research showing that the brand could appeal to 19 million women in America and Britain. She hopes the new designer she lured from Carole Little, Basha Cohen, will help freshen the line, but still keep the flowing romantic look. More important, she is betting that home furnishings will boost sales. The company's wallpaper, bedspreads, linens and curtains have proven much more resistant to fashion's whims than the frocks have.[2]*

Even long-serving Laura Ashley executives were heartened by Iverson's clarity of vision and effective leadership. Visiting the first of the new-style, large-format Laura Ashley stores in the US (in North Carolina), Sir Bernard Ashley commented, "I almost cried, it was so marvelous."

During 1996, the company's capital expenditures increased as the number of stores and their average size increased. (Table 2.2 shows the expansion in US retail floor space.) However, any prospects of the new strategy delivering improved sale profit performance soon evaporated. Despite the emphasis on expansion in the US, North

TABLE 2.1 Laura Ashley Holdings plc: summary of selected financial data, 1989–1999 (£ million)

	Financial year to January 31										
	1999	1998	1997	1996	1995	1994	1993	1992	1991	1990	1989
Turnover	288.3	344.9	327.6	336.6	322.6	300.4	247.8	262.8	328.1	296.6	252.4
Operating (loss)/profit before exceptional items	(15.2)	(23.6)	14.8	9.1	4.1	2.3	1.1	(0.6)	3.4	6.1	23.6
Exceptional operating costs	(2.9)	(12.4)	(0.4)	0.1	(33.4)	–	–	–	–	–	–
Operating (loss)/profit	(16.6)	(36.0)	14.4	9.2	(29.3)	2.3	1.1	(0.6)	3.4	6.1	23.6
Income from associated cos.	(0.2)	0.5	2.1	2.0	1.5	1.8	1.5	1.9	0.1	(0.2)	42.0
Exceptional items	(13.8)	(11.4)	0.4	–	(1.0)	–	–	(8.1)	(2.6)	(3.1)	–
Net interest payable	(1.3)	(2.4)	(0.7)	(0.9)	(1.8)	(1.1)	(0.8)	(2.3)	(12.4)	(8.6)	(5.0)
(Loss)/profit before taxation	(31.9)	(49.3)	16.2	10.3	(30.6)	3.0	1.8	(9.1)	(11.5)	(4.7)	20.3
Taxation	(1.1)	–	(6.1)	(3.3)	(0.9)	(1.9)	(1.0)	–	2.5	(2.1)	(7.1)
(Loss)/profit after taxation	(33.0)	(49.3)	10.1	7.0	(31.5)	1.1	0.8	(9.1)	(9.0)	(6.8)	13.1
Dividends	–	–	(2.4)	(1.2)	–	(0.2)	(0.1)	(0.1)	(0.1)	(1.7)	(4.7)
Retained (loss)/profit	(33.0)	(49.3)	7.7	5.8	(31.5)	0.9	0.7	(9.2)	(9.1)	(9.8)	8.4
Fixed assets	22.0	42.2	49.5	45.2	48.3	71.7	66.3	60.5	67.1	81.5	80.2
Net current assets	36.7	27.6	49.7	27.0	43.7	50.2	53.9	52.8	66.9	n.a.	n.a.
Long-term creditors	(0.9)	(30.4)	(21.8)	(0.9)	(15.0)	(35.1)	(34.4)	(28.0)	(41.4)	3.5	44.7
Provisions for liabilities/charges	(27.4)	(19.7)	(7.3)	(8.3)	(21.3)	(0.7)	(0.3)	(0.5)	(0.4)	2.9	2.2
Net assets	30.4	19.7	70.1	63.0	55.7	86.1	85.5	84.8	92.2	72.9	79.8
Share capital	19.9	11.9	11.9	11.8	11.7	11.7	11.7	11.7	11.7	10.0	10.0
Reserves	10.5	7.8	58.2	51.2	44.0	74.4	73.8	73.1	80.5	n.a.	n.a.
Equity shareholders' funds	30.4	19.7	70.1	63.0	55.7	86.1	85.5	84.8	92.2	72.9	79.8
Employees											
Total	3,634	3,657	4,104	4,173	4,430	n.a.	n.a.	n.a.	7,800	8,350	8,100
Manufacturing	582	617	859	1,019	1,010	n.a.	n.a.	n.a.	n.a.	n.a.	n.a.
Retail	2,452	2,415	2,592	2,459	2,639	n.a.	n.a.	n.a.	n.a.	n.a.	n.a.
Administrative	600	625	653	695	781	n.a.	n.a.	n.a.	n.a.	n.a.	n.a.

n.a. = not available.

SOURCE: LAURA ASHLEY HOLDINGS PLC, ANNUAL REPORTS.

EXHIBIT 2.1

Ann Iverson's Strategy

I was delighted to become Group Chief Executive in June 1995 because I saw a retail business that could be fixed and also a brilliant brand with great potential. However, it was a time of great unrest for the organization, as it was showing no signs of improvement or turnaround.

The restructuring program announced last year was needed for the business. With that said, there were many business issues this program did not address. It only looked at overhead costs, it had no retail focus, it identified no change to our business processes and nothing was mentioned about sales growth and improving gross margins. All of these elements are vital to the turnaround of this business and if not addressed could allow history to repeat itself.

When I joined the business I had many impressions that needed validation. I reacted from three different points of reference: as a customer, as a non-executive and finally as the new Group Chief Executive. I saw a business not led by a single point of view; we had multi-design, multi-buying, multi-merchandising and even multi-catalogues.

In other words, each market or business category was defining what they thought the Laura Ashley brand was all about. As you and I know, every successful brand has a single message consistently delivered to their customer. That was not the case at Laura Ashley.

I also found serious supply chain inefficiencies and, most importantly, shops that were too small to show the extensive range in garments and home furnishings. There were also no clear lines of accountability, which is an unproductive and demotivating culture to have. It doesn't allow hardworking people to really know what

their job is, how they are going to be measured and where to go for answers.

So in my first three months we set about making things right. We consolidated design, buying and merchandising, the pivotal areas of our business, into our Fulham office.

We began the necessary changes in the buying process, reducing the width of the product ranges by 25% and also developing a common catalogue worldwide. We delivered the head count reduction that was identified in the restructuring program, changed and eliminated tasks and put the right structure in place. Simply said, we set about establishing a retail culture.

Additionally, I identified six key initiatives which were critical to the consolidation and turnaround of the Group. They have proved to be exactly the right priorities to have aggressively focused on for the second half of the financial year.

These initiatives are ongoing and I would like to describe them:

● *Product ranges and gross margins*. Improvement of product ranges and gross margins are the most important for topline growth. The key to this is modernizing the fashion offer in garments and expanding our strengths in home furnishings. The improved product offer in fashion will increase sales and reduce mark-downs and is absolutely essential for repositioning this international lifestyle brand. The home furnishings ranges are already very strong and offer the greatest opportunity for growth. They must be expanded, however, to reflect the developments in the market sector and realize the strength of the Laura Ashley brand.

- *Supply chain*. Development of efficient product sourcing is critical in achieving supply chain improvement. This will be accomplished by developing and working closely with our suppliers so they are more reactive to the needs of the business.

- *Manufacturing review*. A total review of manufacturing continues, within the context of the overall supply chain, focusing primarily on home furnishings where we produce 80% of our own product. It is essential that we ensure our factories are competitive as a supplier to a worldwide retailer.

- *Distribution*. In the area of distribution, our costs are well above industry standards. Work is being done to reduce these costs and we will begin to see these reductions coming through in the next financial year. We will strive to achieve best practice industry standards in this important supply chain category.

- *Shop portfolio*. The assessment of our shop portfolio with regard to both location and shop size is underway. Increasing the size of our shops is absolutely necessary to remain competitive in today's retail environment.

- *The US market*. This market should be our greatest vehicle for topline growth and profit improvement. Our brand values, reaffirmed through customer research,

show a potential audience of over 19 million female shoppers. But our shops are too small to even begin presenting the width of the range that supports customer perception and demand. We have started to change this and have already opened the first of our new shops, much larger in format, positioned in premier locations.

The strategy of the Laura Ashley brand is already clearly defined. We are the quintessential English company with a timelessness and spirit understood and embraced worldwide. Our research supports the brand values our customer identifies with: love of flowers, family, romanticism, freedom and simplicity and the tradition which directly relates to the enduring brand qualities and its uniqueness.

In the past the business has talked too much about strategy and not about results. It is time we delivered to our customers and shareholders. As a retailer I see clearly what needs to be done and how to do it.

The way forward continues to be about focus and implementation of the key initiatives which are fundamental to the Company's turn-around. Additionally, we have identified two new initiatives, namely: to establish an appropriate infrastructure for licensing, franchising and wholesaling and to build a new mail order business.

Source: "Chief Executive's Statement," *Laura Ashley Holdings plc Annual Report 1996*, London 1996.

American sales fell during 1996. Then, in the spring of 1997, problems of poor co-ordination caused losses to mount. Overoptimistic sales projections for garments resulted in excessive inventories, while in home furnishings demand was also weak. Clearance sales during spring and early summer devastated margins. Table 2.3 shows sales by region.

In April 1996, John Thornton, a senior partner at Goldman Sachs, succeeded Lord Hooson as Chairman of the Board, and in November 1997, Ann Iverson was replaced

SOURCE: LAURA ASHLEY HOLDINGS PLC, ANNUAL REPORTS 1996–9.

TABLE 2.2 Laura Ashley Holdings plc: retail stores and floor space

Financial year to January 31:	Number of stores				Square footage (000s)			
	1999	1998	1997	1996	1999	1998	1997	1996
UK	234	237	189	174	587	561.5	441.8	394.1
North America	106	132	155	168	301	379.3	349.6	276.8
Continental Europe	69	72	74	76	112	114.1	115.9	117.7
Total	409	441	418	418	1,000	1,054.9	907.3	788.6

TABLE 2.3 Laura Ashley Holdings plc: sales by product group and by region (£ million)

	UK and Ireland	North America	Continental Europe
Year to 1.31.99			
Garments	70.0	37.1	19.4
Furnishings	85.4	25.9	21.1
Year to 1.31.98			
Garments	85.9	57.0	23.0
Furnishings	90.0	34.5	24.7
Year to 1.31.97			
Garments	82.3	49.7	21.7
Furnishings	76.9	34.5	24.1
Year to 1.31.96			
Garments	80.8	60.1	28.6
Furnishings	67.4	35.9	31.9
Year to 1.31.95			
Garments	78.3	61.8	27.2
Furnishings	59.9	36.6	30.1

SOURCE: LAURA ASHLEY HOLDINGS PLC, ANNUAL REPORTS 1996–9.

as CEO by David Hoare, formerly a partner with Bain & Company and chief executive of the conglomerate Cope Allman plc.

Retrenchment: November 1997–April 1998

Almost immediately, David Hoare began undoing much of the previous strategy. Plans for new stores were pruned and several existing stores were closed. Attention was focused on cost reduction, particularly on reducing inventory. To staunch losses and raise finance, several manufacturing plants were sold, and a 13% stake in Laura Ashley Japan Ltd. was sold to Laura Ashley's Japanese partner Jusco for £9.5 million.

In March 1998, David Hoare reported on his progress since September 1997 and on his plans for the future (see Exhibit 2.2).

EXHIBIT 2.2

David Hoare's Three-Phase Strategy

I am pleased to have joined Laura Ashley in September 1997. I am well aware that over the past 12 years, since flotation, Laura Ashley's financial performance has been most disappointing. A number of serious problems face our business and need to be addressed. However, we have an opportunity to build a successful business on the back of a strong international brand.

Key Problems Facing Laura Ashley

- *Complexity of the Business*. Laura Ashley is too complex for a business of its size. We attempt to be experts in design, manufacturing, distribution, retailing in 13 countries, franchising, licensing and mail order. Our management information systems are outdated and our cost base is too high. We have not been sufficiently focused on our core competencies of brand management and retailing.

- *Garment Design*. Over the past three years, the garment range has been repositioned towards the High Street and a younger market. However, it has been taken too quickly and too far in this most competitive sector of the market. We have confused our loyal customers and not attracted sufficient new ones.

- *North American Expansion*. In 1996, we operated 168 stores in North America, with an average size of 1,600 sq. ft. This small-store format was not profitable. Over the past two years our North American store portfolio was restructured by closing 68 smaller stores and opening 32 larger stores (5,000 sq. ft.) in prestige mall locations. Store merchandising was centralized in

London. This program was implemented rapidly without sufficient planning and knowledge of market conditions and with an inadequate supply chain. Costs, particularly rents, have increased whilst sales have not grown significantly.

Overall, these problems led to a shortfall in sales against expectations and excess stocks in both garments and home furnishings, across all markets, which was cleared throughout the year with heavy discounting. As a result, gross profit margins reduced by 10% from 48% to 38% on sales of £345 million, a £34 million adverse gross profit variance. In addition, operating costs rose by 8% or £11.5 million, principally due to a 16% increase in floor space in North America and the UK. As a result, we have reported an operating loss before exceptional items and tax of £25.5 million for 1997/98 against £16.2 million profit last year. In addition, exceptional charges of £23.8 million have been taken mainly to restructure our North American and manufacturing business.

Recovery Program

Whilst it is clear that we have had a number of significant problems at Laura Ashley, and that it will take time to fix them, it is also clear that there are great opportunities for our business. Laura Ashley is one of the best known international brand names, representing the quintessential English country lifestyle. We trade in 34 countries, in over 550 owned and franchised stores. We have a base of loyal customers who, though disappointed in the recent past, will return provided we can develop products and services that meet their aspirations.

In order to tackle our current problems and take advantage of the significant opportunities, we have put in place a three-phase recovery plan to be implemented over the next five years.

- ● *Phase I. Stabilize the Business*
  - – stop significant new store development
  - – rebuild the senior management team
  - – generate cash by reducing stocks and selling non-core assets
  - – raise additional finance
- ● *Phase II. Improve the Profitability of the Business*
  - – return to full price retailing
  - – redesign the product to meet the wishes of our core customers
  - – fix the North American retail business
  - – reduce business complexity and costs
  - – invest in systems
- ● *Phase III. Grow the Business*
  - – focus on core competence of brand management
  - – build our brand internationally with new products, new distribution channels and new partners

Phase I

In late 1997 and into 1998 good progress was made to stabilize the business. Store expansion was stopped, and we refocused on managing the existing business. Our worsening trading position in the autumn of 1997 required us to renegotiate with our banks. They supported us with a 15 month £170m bank facility through to April 1999. Cash outflow was minimized by reducing year end stock by 32% from £93 million to £63 million. In addition, following the year end, we announced the sale of part of our shareholding in our Japanese licensee, Laura Ashley Japan, to Jusco, the majority owner . . . in a transaction which realized aggregate gross proceeds of 9.5 million pounds. The transaction included a revision of the terms of the license agreement between us.

Phase II

Progress has also been made in improving the profits of the existing business. Following our January 1998 end of year sale, we returned to more normal full price retailing with occasional marketing promotions. We recognize that our garment range has moved too far towards the High Street and a younger market and has lost an element of its Laura Ashley signature. We are redesigning our product range, which, because of lead times, will be only partly evident in our Autumn/Winter 1998 collection. More substantial change will be seen in Spring/Summer 1999.

North America remains a major challenge. Our business there has suffered disproportionately from the problems affecting the Group. The product range was not right, the large-stores format did not work and the complexity of the business led to severe supply problems. Significant losses were incurred. However, research shows that there is a major opportunity in North America for lifestyle brands aimed at discerning 30–50 year old customers, and we believe that our quintessential English country brand can succeed in this market.

In order to fix our North American business . . . a decisive program of restructuring, cost reduction, store closures and carefully targeted new investment will be required. As part of this program, we intend to close a number of larger stores while investing in information systems, store refurbishment and brand development.

Throughout the Group, our overheads are too high, partly as a result of the complexity of the business and partly due to the weakness of our systems which require significant investment. Some steps have been taken to reduce costs but greater progress will need to be made in 1998.

As a first step to simplifying our business we announced, in January 1998, our intention to sell our manufacturing operations with a continuing supply agreement.

Phase III

We have significant opportunities to expand our franchise, license and wholesale activities internationally. In 1997/98 we opened 22 new franchised stores. In addition, we continue to expand our range of licensed products. However, we will pursue this expansion program only once we are satisfied that we have the right product, service and infrastructure to give the required levels of support.

Equity

In the light of last year's results, the investment need in North America, the opportunities in the rest of the business and the current levels of debt, we have added additional equity capital essential to improve the financial stability and operational health of the Group. On 17 April 1998 we announced that we intend to raise new equity of £43.7 million net in a subscription by the Malayan United Industries Group. The Board believes that raising this new equity is essential in order to implement the recovery plan.

Source: Extracts from the "Chief Executive's Statement," *Laura Ashley Holdings plc Annual Report 1998*, London 1998.

By the end of 1997, Laura Ashley's need for new financing became increasingly evident. Debt had more than doubled to £30.6 million and renegotiation of the company's bank facility had resulted in an agreement that Laura Ashley could use within the business the £9.5 million received from the sale of shares in Laura Ashley Japan, but could not draw further on its banking facility, and nor could it use funds from outside of North America to fund continued losses within North America.

MUI to the Rescue

In April 1998, the Board agreed to increase the issued equity of Laura Ashley Holdings and to sell the new equity to the MUI Group, a diversified Malaysian group with interests in retailing, hotels and resorts, food and confectionery, cement and building materials, real estate, and financial services. After the equity sale, MUI would own 40% of Laura Ashley's equity and would appoint four board members. Mrs Victoria Egan, president of MUI's retail subsidiary in the Philippines, would become chief executive and Mr Paul Ng Tuand an Tee, executive director of Metrojaya, would become President of Laura Ashley North America.

The £43.5 million that the equity sale would raise (net of expenses) put Laura Ashley on a sounder financial footing. Extensive restructuring and repositioning were needed, especially in North America. (Tables 2.4 and 2.5 show the deteriorating financial performance of the North American business, while table 2.6 shows performance by business segment.) The North America recovery program would require about £20 million (mainly for store closures) and £6.5 million was needed to upgrade its logistics and information systems. The Board agreed with its banks to reduce its existing £50 million revolving credit facility to £35 million by the end of 1998.

TABLE 2.4 Laura Ashley Holdings plc: retail sales and contribution by geographical segment (£ million)

	UK and Ireland	North America	Continental Europe	Total retail
Turnover				
Year to Jan. 31, 1999	155.4	63.0	40.5	258.9
Year to Jan. 31, 1998	175.9	91.5	47.7	315.1
Year to Jan. 31, 1997	159.2	84.2	45.8	289.2
Contribution				
Year to Jan. 31, 1999	15.0	(7.1)	6.9	14.8
Year to Jan. 31, 1998	14.9	(12.9)	7.3	9.3
Year to Jan. 31, 1997	24.5	7.6	10.7	42.8

TABLE 2.5 Laura Ashley Holdings plc: sales, profit, and net assets by geographical segment (£ million)

	Year to 1.31.99	Year to 1.31.98	Year to 1.31.97	Year to 1.31.96	Year to 1.31.95
Sales.					
UK and Ireland	176.1	197.2	175.1	160.0	145.2
North America	68.2	96.4	92.7	104.6	107.0
Continental Europe	42.5	50.2	57.7	65.8	57.4
Other	1.5	1.1	1.1	1.3	0.9
Profit before tax (after exceptionals):					
UK and Ireland	(21.7)	(12.6)	8.6	(0.5)	(29.5)
North America	(20.0)	(29.4)	3.3	1.7	(1.2)
Continental Europe	10.7	(7.8)	1.4	5.6	(0.8)
Other	(0.9)	0.5	3.2	3.5	1.6
Net assets:					
UK and Ireland	(3.6)	16.0	25.7	15.4	14.1
North America	(5.6)	(18.6)	11.4	13.3	14.3
Continental Europe	38.0	19.9	29.2	32.5	26.4
Other	1.6	2.4	2.3	1.8	0.9

Victoria Egan's approach was to continue with the three-phase strategy developed by the previous CEO with a particular emphasis on reducing losses, restructuring the North American business, and disposing of assets. In August 1998, a reorganization plan was announced, involving the creation of three profit centers: Europe, North America, and Franchising. A £2.5 million provision was made to cover the redundancy costs associated with this reorganization. However, during 1998, the business continued to deteriorate – especially in the US. (Tables 2.4 to 2.6 show financial performance by region and business segment.) Although inventories were reduced and the costs of closing US large-format stores remained within budget, sales were sharply

TABLE 2.6 Laura Ashley Holdings plc: sales, contribution, and net assets by business segment (£ million)

	Year to 1.31.99	Year to 1.31.98	Year to 1.31.97
Turnover:			
Retail	258.9	315.1	289.2
Non-retail	29.4	29.8	22.9
Contribution:			
Retail	14.8	9.3	42.8
Non-retail	7.8	7.6	12.1
Net assets:			
Retail	14.6	(0.6)	40.7
Non-retail	15.8	20.3	27.9

Retail includes Laura Ashley managed retail stores and mail order. Non-retail includes wholesale, licensing, franchising, and manufacturing.

lower than the year-ago period. The half-yearly results (to August 1, 1998) were greeted with a fall in Laura Ashley's share price to 17 pence – an all-time low.

February 1999

As he prepared for his first board meeting as group chief executive of Laura Ashley Holdings, Ng Kwan Cheong reviewed the company's financial statements for the financial year ended January 31, 1999 (see Appendix). His immediate concerns were for Laura Ashley's cash position. MUI had pumped £43.5 million into Laura Ashley in order to underpin its recovery program. This sum, plus the £7.9 million profit from the sale of 13% of Laura Ashley Japan, had been eaten up by debt repayment, restructuring and closure costs, and continuing operating losses. With continuing operating losses together with the need to close unprofitable stores, and refurbish profitable stores, Laura Ashley would need to find new sources of finance during the coming financial year. Given the weakness of Laura Ashley's balance sheet and the continuing cash drain, it was unlikely that the banks would be willing to lend. It seemed as though the parent company, MUI, was the only possible source of additional funding. With Chairman John Thornton stepping down to become president and chief operating officer of Goldman Sachs, and MUI's Khoo Kay Peng taking over his position and chairmanship of Laura Ashley, this might be an opportune moment to press MUI for additional funding.

But did it make sense for MUI to continue to invest in Laura Ashley? Despite an improvement in margins, sales had continued to decline. Did a profitable market exist for Laura Ashley products? If so, was this market primarily within Britain, or did it extend overseas? And how could Laura Ashley best access and develop this market?

Appendix

TABLE 2.A1 Laura Ashley Holdings plc: profit and loss statement (£ million)

	Year to 1.31.99	Year to 1.31.98	Year to 1.31.97
Turnover	288.3	344.9	327.6
Cost of sales	(159.9)	(214.0)	(168.9)
Gross profit	128.4	130.9	158.7
Operating expenses	(146.5)	(166.9)	(144.3)
Other operating income	1.5	–	–
Operating profit/(loss)	(16.6)	(36.0)	(14.4)
Share of operating (loss)/profit of associate cos.	(0.2)	0.5	2.1
Profit on sale of investment in associate	7.5	–	–
Profit on sale of freehold property	2.0	–	–
Amounts written-off investment	–	(2.4)	–
Provision for disposal of businesses	(23.3)	(9.0)	–
(Loss)/profit on ordinary activities before interest	(30.6)	(46.9)	16.9
Net interest payable	1.3	2.4	0.7
(Loss)/profit on ordinary activities before taxation	(31.9)	(49.3)	16.2
Taxation on (loss)/profit on ordinary activities	(1.1)	0.0	6.1
(Loss)/profit on ordinary activities after tax	(33.0)	(49.3)	16.2
Dividend	0.0	0.0	2.4
Retained (loss)/profit for the period	(33.0)	(49.3)	7.7

SOURCE: LAURA ASHLEY HOLDINGS PLC, ANNUAL REPORTS 1997–9.

TABLE 2.A2 Laura Ashley Holdings plc: balance sheet (£ million)

	At 1.31.99	At 1.31.98	At 1.31.97
Fixed assets			
Tangible fixed assets	19.5	38.9	44.0
Investment in associated undertaking	1.7	2.5	2.2
Own shares	0.8	0.8	3.3
Total	22.0	42.2	49.5
Current assets			
Stocks (inventories)	56.4	63.2	93.1
Debtors	19.7	21.2	24.4
Short-term deposits and cash	8.4	10.2	6.2
Total	84.5	94.6	123.7

TABLE 2.A2 *continued*

	At 1.31.99	At 1.31.98	At 1.31.97
Creditors: amounts due within one year			
Borrowings	0.1	9.9	0.0
Trade and other creditors	47.7	57.1	72.6
Total	47.8	67.0	74.0
Net current assets	36.7	27.6	49.7
Total assets less current liabilities	58.7	69.8	99.2
Creditors: amounts due after one year			
Borrowings	0.0	29.2	21.0
Trade and other creditors	0.9	1.2	0.8
Total	0.9	30.4	21.8
Provisions for liabilities and charges	27.4	19.7	7.3
Net assets	30.4	19.7	70.1
Capital and reserves			
Share capital	19.9	11.9	11.9
Share premium account	87.1	51.6	51.5
Profit and loss account	(76.6)	(43.8)	6.7
Equity shareholders' funds	30.4	19.7	70.1
Ordinary shares issued (millions)	398	236	236

SOURCE: LAURA ASHLEY HOLDINGS PLC, ANNUAL REPORTS 1997–9.

TABLE 2.A3 Laura Ashley Holdings plc: cash flow statement (£ million)

	Year to 1.31.99	Year to 1.31.98	Year to 1.31.97
Net cash flow from operating activities	(11.4)	5.2	(0.7)
Returns on investments and servicing of finance:			
Interest received	0.5	1.2	0.8
Interest paid	(1.6)	(3.3)	(1.2)
Interest element of lease payments	(0.2)	(0.3)	(0.3)
Dividends received from associates	0.1	0.2	0.1
Net cash outflow for returns on investments and the servicing of finance	(1.3)	(2.2)	(0.6)
Tax paid	(1.6)	(5.5)	(1.5)
Capital expenditure and financial investment:			
Acquisition of tangible fixed assets	(3.9)	(9.6)	(14.2)
Disposal of tangible fixed assets	4.6	0.1	0.2
Net cash flow for capital investment	0.7	(9.5)	(14.0)
Acquisitions and disposals	7.9	–	–
Equity dividends paid	–	(1.4)	(2.1)
Net cash outflow before financing	(5.6)	(13.4)	(13.8)

TABLE 2.A3 *continued*

SOURCE: LAURA ASHLEY HOLDINGS PLC, ANNUAL REPORTS 1997–9.

	Year to 1.31.99	Year to 1.31.98	Year to 1.31.97
Financing:			
Issue of ordinary share capital	44.6	0.1	1.4
Expenses of share issue	(1.1)	–	–
Settlement of currency swaps	–	0.5	4.0
Loans taken out	–	18.1	21.0
Repayment of loans	(39.0)	–	(5.0)
Capital element of lease payments	(0.8)	(0.9)	(1.2)
Net cash inflow from financing	3.7	17.8	20.2
Increase in cash	(1.9)	4.4	1.4

TABLE 2.A4 Financial ratios: Laura Ashley compared with other clothing retailers

SOURCE: LAURA ASHLEY HOLDINGS PLC, ANNUAL REPORTS 1997–9.

	Laura Ashley	Talbots	Next plc	Ann Taylor Stores	The Limited	Monsoon plc
Sales ($, m.)	478	1,142	2,041	912	9,347	212
Gross profit margin (%)	44.4	34.4	30.1	48.8	32.1	61.0
SGA/Sales (%)	50.8	28.5	17.6	38.4	24.6	45.0
Operating margin (%)	(5.8)	5.9	12.7	10.4	7.5	15.1
Net profit margin (%)	(11.5)	3.2	10.0	14.3	22.0	9.9
Inventory turns*	5.1	6.6	8.7	6.6	7.6	10.2
Total asset turns*	2.7	1.7	1.5	1.2	2.8	2.5
Current ratio*	1.8	2.4	1.8	2.3	1.0	1.3
ROE (%)*	(108.6)	9.1	22.8	7.9	72.0	47.5

*Based on balance sheet values.

Notes

1 This section draws upon "Laura Ashley: History," Laura Ashley Holdings plc; and J. L. Heath, *Laura Ashley Holdings PLC (A) and (B)*, European Case Clearing House, 1991.

2 "Giving Laura Ashley a Yank," *Business Week*, May 27, 1997, p. 147.

The US Airline Industry in 2007

Here's a list of 129 airlines that in the past 20 years filed for bankruptcy. Continental was smart enough to make that list twice. As of 1992, in fact – though the picture would have improved since then – the money that had been made since the dawn of aviation by all of this country's airline companies was zero. Absolutely zero.

Sizing all this up, I like to think that if I'd been at Kitty Hawk in 1903 when Orville Wright took off, I would have been farsighted enough, and public-spirited enough – I owed this to future capitalists – to shoot him down. I mean, Karl Marx couldn't have done as much damage to capitalists as Orville did.

WARREN BUFFETT, CHAIRMAN, BERKSHIRE HATHAWAY

As they returned to work at the beginning of January 2007, the senior executives of America's leading airlines experienced a feeling of optimism and *joie de vivre* that had been largely absent for most of the previous six years.

Between 2001 and 2005, the industry had been ravaged by the horror of September 11, 2001 and the raft of new security measures that followed in its wake, by a tripling in the price of jet fuel, and by unprecedented competitive pressures from a new generation of low-cost airlines. During this period, the industry racked up losses of $35 billion and four of America's six biggest airlines were forced into Chapter 11 bankruptcy.

Yet, 2006 appeared to be a turning point. For the first time since 2000 the industry made a profit (albeit a small one), while only two of the leading carriers reported losses (see table 3.1). United Airlines followed US Airlines out of bankruptcy, leaving only Delta and Northwestern still in Chapter 11. Even the

TABLE 3.1 Revenues, profits, and employment of the seven largest US airlines

	Revenue		Net income		Return on assets*		Employees	
	2006 $ billion	2005 $ billion	2006 $ million	2005 $ million	2006 (%)	2005 (%)	2006	2002
AMR	22.6	20.7	231	(861)	3.6	(3.2)	86,800	109,500
UAL	19.3	17.4	22,868	(21,176)	1.8	(4.1)	57,000	72,000
Delta	17.2	16.2	(6,203)	(3,818)	0.3	(10.0)	55,700	76,100
Northwest	12.6	12.3	(2,855)	(2,533)	5.6	(7.0)	32,460	44,300
Continental	13.1	11.2	343	(68)	4.1	(0.4)	42,200	43,900
US Airways Group	11.6	5.1	304	(537)	9.7	(3.1)	12,100	46,600
Southwest	9.1	7.6	499	548	7.0	5.8	31,729	33,700
TOTAL	105.5	90.5	15,187	(28,445)	n.a.	n.a.	317,989	426,100

* Return on assets = Pre-tax operating income/Total assets; n.a. = not applicable.

SOURCES: 10-K REPORTS.

battered stocks of the airline companies were experiencing revival. The AMEX Airline Index had hit a high for the year in December 2006, while the stock prices of AMR (the parent of American), Continental Airlines, and US Airlines Group had all more than doubled since the beginning of the year. Stock market interest in the sector had been stimulated by the prospects for a new round of consolidation in the industry. The merger of US Airlines Group and America West Airlines at the end of 2005 was followed by a hostile bid by the newly merged company for Delta Airlines in November 2006. Responding to news of the bid, United's CFO, Jack Brace, told investment analysts: "We think consolidation is good for the industry, and if it makes sense for us to participate, we will. Consolidation is a natural phase for the evolution of an industry as mature as ours." Brace believed that the domestic airline industry would consolidate around two to four legacy network carriers, with three being the most likely number. This would help limit seat capacity and provide more pricing power to the airlines.

Among industry executives and investment analysts, opinions on the prospects for the US airline industry were mixed. Some pointed to a new climate of realism and financial prudence in the industry. After more than five years of struggle, the major carriers had done much to get costs under control. They had confronted the labor unions and gained substantial concessions on pay, benefits, and working practices. They had gained efficiency benefits from outsourcing and better use of IT, and retired many of their fuel-inefficient older planes.

Others were less sanguine. The problems of the airline industry could not be attributed just to 9/11 and high fuel prices. For decades the industry had generated poor returns on the capital invested in it – not just in the US, but in other countries too. Nor could poor industry performance be attributed to inept management. It was notable that, while the "legacy carriers" (the major, established network operators) had cut costs and eliminated losses, many of the low-cost carriers were beginning to struggle. Jet Blue and Air Tran were both barely profitable during 2006. "We've been here before, many times," observed one industry veteran, "Just when the industry seems to be climbing out of the mire, the industry's dire economics reassert themselves."

From Regulation to Competition

The history of the US airline industry breaks into two main phases: the period of regulation up until 1978, and the period of deregulation since then.

The Airlines Under Regulation (Pre-1978)

The first scheduled airline services began in the 1920s – primarily for carrying mail rather than passengers. By the early 1930s, transcontinental routes were controlled by three airlines: United Airlines in the north, American Airlines in the south, and TWA through the middle. New entry and growing competition (notably from Delta and Continental) led to the threat of instability in the industry, and in 1938 Congress established the Civil Aeronautics Board (CAB) with authority to administer the structure of the industry and competition within it. The CAB awarded interstate routes to the existing 23 airlines, established safety guidelines priorities, and strict rules for passenger fares, airmail rates, route entry and exit, mergers and acquisitions, and interfirm agreements. Fares were set by CAB on the basis of cost plus a reasonable rate of return. The outcome was an ossification of industry structure – despite more than 80 applications, not a single new carrier was approved between 1938 and 1978. Instead, new entrants set up as local carriers offering intrastate routes.

Rapid expansion of the industry after World War II and a wave of technological innovations – notably the jet – led to increasing concerns over airline safety and the establishment of the Federal Aviation Administration to regulate airline safety.

During the 1970s, a major shift occurred in political opinion as increasing support for economic liberalism resulted in demands for less government regulation and greater reliance on market forces. Political arguments for deregulation were supported by new developments in economics. The case for regulation had been based traditionally on arguments about "natural monopoly" – competitive markets were impossible in industries where scale economies and network effects were important. During the early 1970s, the *theory of contestable markets* was developed. The main argument was that industries did not need to be competitively structured in order to result in competitive outcomes. So long as barriers to entry and exit were low, then the potential for "hit and run" entry would cause established firms to charge competitive prices and earn competitive rates of return. The outcome was the Airline Deregulation Act which, in October 1978, abolished the CAB and inaugurated a new era of competition in the airline industry.

The Impact of Deregulation

The elimination of restrictions over domestic routes and schedules and over domestic fares resulted in a wave of new entrants and an upsurge in price competition. By 1980, 20 new carriers – including People Express, Air Florida, and Midway – had set up.

TABLE 3.2 Financial and operating data for the US airline industry, 1978–2006

	Available seat miles (billions)	Load factor (%)	Breakeven load factor (%)	Operating revenue ($ billion)	Net income ($ million)	Operating margin (%)	Net margin (%)	Rate of return on investment[a] (%)
1978	369	61.5	57.4	22.9	1,197	6.0	5.2	13.3
1979	416	63.0	62.5	27.2	347	0.7	1.3	6.5
1980	433	59.0	59.1	33.7	17	(0.7)	0.1	5.3
1981	425	58.6	59.2	36.7	(301)	(1.2)	(0.8)	4.7
1982	440	59.0	60.0	36.4	(916)	(2.0)	(2.5)	2.1
1983	465	60.7	60.1	39.0	(188)	0.8	0.5	6.0
1984	515	59.2	56.3	43.8	825	4.9	1.9	9.9
1985	548	61.4	59.7	46.7	863	3.1	1.8	9.6
1986	607	60.3	58.7	50.5	(235)	2.6	(0.5)	4.9
1987	649	62.4	59.6	57.0	593	4.3	1.0	7.2
1988	677	62.5	58.9	64.6	1,686	5.4	2.6	10.8
1989	684	63.2	61.6	69.3	128	2.6	0.2	6.3
1990	733	62.4	64.0	76.1	(3,921)	(2.5)	(5.1)	(6.0)
1991	715	62.6	64.1	75.2	(1,940)	(2.4)	(2.6)	(0.5)
1992	753	63.6	65.6	78.1	(4,791)	(3.1)	(3.1)	(9.3)
1993	771	63.5	62.4	83.8	(2,136)	1.7	1.7	(0.4)
1994	784	66.2	66.8	88.3	(344)	3.0	(0.4)	5.2
1995	807	67.0	64.9	94.6	2,314	6.2	2.4	11.9
1996	835	69.3	66.9	101.9	2,804	6.1	2.8	11.5
1997	861	70.3	65.0	109.6	5,168	7.8	4.7	14.7
1998	874	70.7	66.7	113.5	4,903	8.2	4.3	12.0
1999	918	71.0	66.4	119.0	5,360	7.0	4.5	11.1
2000	957	71.2	70.2	130.8	2,486	5.3	2.0	6.4
2001	923	69.1	77.0	115.4	(8,275)	(5.4)	(8.9)	(6.5)
2002	833	70.3	84.1	107.0	(11,295)	(8.0)	(10.6)	(9.6)
2003	894	72.4	86.0	115.9	(3,625)	(1.9)	(3.1)	(0.3)
2004	971	75.5	90.2	134.5	(7,643)	(1.1)	(5.7)	(5.8)
2005	1,002	77.6	91.8	150.8	(5,673)	(0.2)	(3.8)	(3.4)
2006	1,006	79.2	89.6	160.0[e]	2,500[e]	3.6[e]	1.6[e]	4.9[e]

[a] Net income *plus* Interest expense *as a percentage of* Shareholders' equity *plus* Long-term debt.
[e] Estimated.

SOURCES: AIR TRANSPORT ASSOCIATION, *ANNUAL ECONOMIC REPORTS* (VARIOUS YEARS); BUREAU OF TRANSPORTATION STATISTICS.

Deregulation was quickly followed by the oil shock of 1979, the onset of worldwide recession, and the air traffic controllers' strike of 1981. During 1978–82, the industry incurred massive losses (see table 3.2), causing widespread bankruptcy (between 1978 and 1988 over 150 carriers went bust) and a wave of mergers and acquisitions. By 1982, expansion had resumed and during the rest of the 1980s and into the 1990s mileage flown grew at a trend rate of 4% per annum. At the same time, competition and the quest for efficiency resulted in a continuous decline in real prices (see table 3.3)

TABLE 3.3 The falling price of air travel: revenue per passenger seat mile (cents)

	1960	1965	1970	1975	1980	1985	1990	1995	2000	2005
At nominal prices	6.1	6.1	6.0	7.7	11.5	12.2	13.4	13.5	14.6	12.3
At constant 1984 prices	20.3	19.4	15.4	14.3	14.0	11.3	10.2	8.9	8.5	6.3

SOURCE: BUREAU OF TRANSPORTATION STATISTICS.

Firm Strategy and Industry Evolution After Deregulation

Changes in the structure of the airline industry during the 1980s and 1990s were primarily a result of the strategies of the airlines as they sought to adjust to the new conditions of competition in the industry and gain competitive advantage.

Route Strategies: The Hub-and-Spoke System

During the 1980s the major airlines reorganized their route maps. A system of predominantly point-to-point routes was replaced by one where each airline concentrated its routes on a few major airports linked by frequent services using large aircraft, with smaller, nearby airports connected to these hubs by shorter routes using smaller aircraft. This "hub-and-spoke" system offered two major benefits:

- It allowed greater efficiency through reducing the total number of routes needed to link a finite number of cities within a network and concentrating traveler and maintenance facilities in fewer locations. It permitted the use of larger, more cost-efficient aircraft for interhub travel. The efficiency benefits of the hub-and-spoke system were reinforced by scheduling flights such that incoming short-haul arrivals were concentrated at particular times to allow passengers to be pooled for the longer haul flights on large aircraft.

- It allowed major carriers to establish dominance in major regional markets and on particular routes. In effect, the major airlines became more geographically differentiated in their route offerings. Table 3.4 shows cities where a single airline held a dominant local market share. The hub-and-spoke system also created a barrier to the entry of new carriers who often found it difficult to obtain gates and landing slots at the major hubs.

The hub-and-spoke networks of the major airlines were extended by establishing alliances with local ("commuter") airlines. Thus, American Eagle, United Express, and Delta Shuttle were franchise systems established by AMR, UAL, and Delta respectively, whereby commuter airlines used the reservation and ticketing systems of the major airlines and coordinated their operations and marketing policies with those of their bigger partners.

Mergers

New entry during the period of deregulation had reduced seller concentration in the industry (see table 3.5). However, the desire of the leading companies to build

TABLE 3.4 Local market share of largest airline for selected US cities (by number of passengers), 2005

City	Airline	Share of passengers (%)
Dallas-Forth Worth	American	72
Miami	American	68
Minneapolis-St. Paul	Northwestern	65
Detroit	Northwestern	61
Houston	Continental	61
Altanta	Delta	58
Charlotte	US Airways	55
Baltimore	Southwest	53
Newark	Continental	52
San Francisco	United	44
Denver	United	44
Cincinnati	Delta	39

SOURCE: BUREAU OF TRANSPORTATION STATISTICS.

TABLE 3.5 Concentration in the US airline industry

Year	Four-firm concentration ratio	Year	Four-firm concentration ratio
1935	88%	1982	54.2%
1939	82%	1987	64.8%
1949	70%	1990	61.5%
1954	71%	1999	66.4%
1977	56.2%	2002	71.0%
		2005	55.4%

Notes The four-firm concentration ratio measures the share of the industry's passenger-miles accounted for by the four largest companies. During 1935–54, the four biggest companies were United, American, TWA, and Eastern. During 1982–2005, the four biggest companies were American, United, Delta, and Northwest.

SOURCE: US DEPT. OF TRANSPORT.

national (and international) route networks encouraged a wave of mergers and acquisitions in the industry – many of which were facilitated by the financial troubles that beset several leading airlines. Consolidation would have gone further without government intervention on antitrust grounds – the proposed merger between United and US Airways was halted in 2001. Figure 3.1 shows some of the main mergers and acquisitions. During 2002–5, concentration declined as a result of capacity reduction by the major bankrupt airlines (United, Delta, and Northwest) and market share gains by low-cost carriers.

FIGURE 3.1 Consolidation in the US airline industry after deregulation

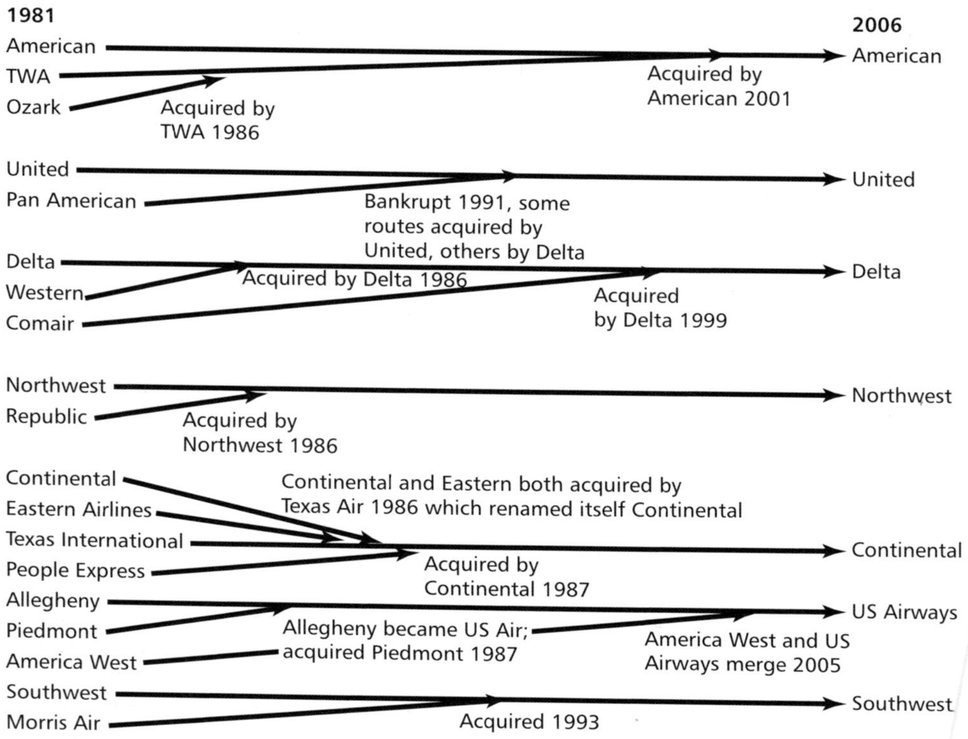

SOURCE: UPDATED FROM S. BORENSTEIN, "THE EVOLUTION OF US AIRLINE COMPETITION," *JOURNAL OF ECONOMIC PERSPECTIVES*, VOL. 6, NO. 2, 1992, P. 48.

1981 — **2006**

American → American

TWA — Acquired by American 2001

Ozark — Acquired by TWA 1986

United → United

Pan American — Bankrupt 1991, some routes acquired by United, others by Delta

Delta — Acquired by Delta 1986 → Delta

Western — Acquired by Delta 1999

Comair

Northwest → Northwest

Republic — Acquired by Northwest 1986

Continental — Continental and Eastern both acquired by Texas Air 1986 which renamed itself Continental

Eastern Airlines

Texas International → Continental

People Express — Acquired by Continental 1987

Allegheny — Allegheny became US Air; acquired Piedmont 1987 → US Airways

Piedmont

America West — America West and US Airways merge 2005

Southwest → Southwest

Morris Air — Acquired 1993

Prices and Costs

The growth of competition in the post-deregulation era was most apparent in the prices of air tickets. Price cuts were instigated either by established airlines suffering from weak revenues and excess capacity and eager for cash flow, or by low-cost carriers. The new, low-cost entrants played a critical role in stimulating the price wars that came to characterize competition after deregulation. People Express, Braniff, New York Air, and Southwest all sought aggressive expansion through rock bottom fares made possible by highly efficient cost structures and a bare-bones service (the low-cost carriers economized on in-flight meals, entertainment, and baggage handling). Although most of the low-cost newcomers failed during the early years of airline deregulation, new entrants continued to appear throughout the 1980s and 1990s.

In response to the price initiatives of the low-cost airlines, the major carriers sought to cut prices selectively. Fare structures became increasingly complex as airlines sought to separate price-sensitive leisure customers from price-inelastic business travelers. As a result, fare bands widened: advanced purchased economy fares with Saturday night stays were as little as 10% of the first-class fare for the same journey.

Price cuts were also selective by route. Typically the major airlines offered low prices on those routes where they faced competition from low-cost rivals. Southwest, the biggest and most successful of the economy carriers, complained continually of predatory price cuts by its larger rivals. However, the ability of the major airlines to compete against the budget airlines was limited by the majors' cost structures – in particular, restrictive labor agreements, infrastructure, and commitment to extensive route networks. Hence, to meet the competition of low-cost newcomers, several of the majors set up new subsidiaries to imitate the strategies and cost structures of the budget airlines. These included: Continental's Continental Lite (1994), UAL's "Shuttle by United" (1995), Delta's Song (1993), and United's Ted (1994). By 2007, only the United offshoot, Ted, was still in operation.

During the crisis years of 2001–5, the major airlines made strenuous efforts to cut costs. Union contracts were renegotiated, inefficient working practices terminated, unprofitable routes abandoned, and employment numbers reduced. Nevertheless, the budget airlines still maintained a substantial cost advantage over the majors. Higher fuel prices hit the major airlines more heavily than the low-cost carriers. Not only did the low-cost carriers have newer, more fuel-efficient planes, but their stronger financial positions allowed them to make forward purchases to protect against escalating fuel prices.

The Quest for Differentiation

Under regulation, the inability to compete on price resulted in airline competition shifting to non-price dimensions – customer service and in-flight food and entertainment. Deregulation brutally exposed the myth of customer loyalty: most travelers could not distinguish major differences between the offerings of the different major airlines and were increasingly indifferent as to which airline they flew on a particular route. Increasing evidence that airline seats were fundamentally commodity products did not stop the airlines from attempting to differentiate their offerings and build customer loyalty.

For the most part, efforts to attract customers through enhanced services and facilities were directed towards business travelers. The high margins on first- and business-class tickets provided a strong incentive to attract these customers by means of spacious seats and intensive in-flight pampering. For leisure travelers it was unclear whether their choice of carrier was responsive to anything other than price, and the low margins on these tickets limited the willingness of the airlines to increase costs by providing additional services.

The most widespread and successful initiative to build customer loyalty was the introduction of frequent flyer schemes. American's frequent flyer program was introduced in 1981 and was soon followed by all the other major airlines. By offering free tickets and upgrades on the basis of number of miles flown, and building in different threshold levels for receiving benefits, the airlines encouraged customer loyalty and discouraged customers from switching airlines in response to small price differentials. By the end of 2006, airlines' unredeemed frequent flyer miles had surged to over 10 trillion miles. Through involving other companies as partners – car rental companies, hotel chains, credit card issuers – frequent flyer programs became an important source of additional revenue for the airlines, being worth over $10 billion annually.

TABLE 3.6 The US airline companies in 2006

Major airlines	ABX, Air Tran, Alaska, America West, American, American Eagle, ATA, Atlas Polar, Continental, Delta, ExpressJet, FedEx, Jet Blue, Mesa, Northwest, Skywest, Southwest, United, UPS, US Airways
National airlines	Air Transport International, Air Wisconsin, Aloha, Amerijet International, ASTAR, Atlantic Southeast, Champion, Comair, Continental Micronesia, Executive, Florida West, Frontier, Hawaiian, Horizon Air, Independence, Kalitta, Mesaba, Midwest, Pinnacle, PSA, Ryan Int'l, Spirit Air, Sun Country, Trans States, Transmeridian, USA 3000, USA Jet, World

Note: "Majors" have annual revenues exceeding $1 billion; "Nationals" have revenues between $100 million and $1 billion.

SOURCE: AIR TRANSPORT ASSOCIATION.

TABLE 3.7 Operating data for the larger airlines, 2003 and 2006

	Available seat miles (billions)		Load factor (%)		Operating revenue per available seat mile (cents)		Operating expense per available seat mile (cents)	
	2003	2006	2003	2006	2003	2006	2003	2006
American	165.2	175.9	72.8	82.0	8.7	12.48	10.2	12.47
United	136.6	139.8	76.5	82.1	9.4	13.13	10.5	13.08
Delta	134.4	133.5	73.4	77.8	9.9	12.98	10.5	13.57
Northwest	88.6	91.8	77.3	82.7	8.6	14.33	9.9	14.47
Continental	78.4	85.5	75.5	83.1	8.7	13.51	9.4	13.26
Southwest	71.8	85.2	66.8	73.0	8.3	9.52	7.6	8.45
US Airways	58.0	83.9	71.5	77.6	10.6	15.68	11.6	15.30
Air Tran	10.0	15.4	71.1	74.4	8.9	10.10	6.5	9.79
Jet Blue	13.6	23.8	84.5	82.5	7.3	7.55	6.0	7.48
Alaska	22.2	22.3	62.9	76.4	11.75	11.32	11.80	11.52

SOURCES: BUREAU OF TRANSPORTATION STATISTICS; COMPANY 10 K REPORTS.

The Industry in 2007

The Airlines

At the beginning of 2007, the US passenger airline industry comprised about 56 airline companies together with about 50 local carriers (see table 3.6). The industry was dominated by seven major passenger airlines – United, American, Delta, Northwestern, Continental, US Airways, and Southwest (see table 3.7). The importance of the leading group was enhanced by their networks of alliances with smaller airlines Given the perilous financial state of so many of the leading airlines, most observers expected that the trend towards consolidation in the industry would continue.

Market for Air Travel

At the beginning of the 21st century, airlines provided the dominant mode of long-distance travel in the US. For shorter journeys, cars provided the major alternative. Alternative forms of public transportation – bus and rail – accounted for a small proportion of journeys in excess of a hundred miles. Only on a few routes (e.g. between Washington, New York, and Boston) did trains provide a viable alternative to air.

Most forecasts pointed to continued growth in the demand for air travel – probably below the 5% annual trend rate of the previous two decades, but most likely faster than the rate of population growth. The chances of any significant shift of demand to alternative modes of transport seemed slight: there seemed little chance that the US would develop high-speed train services similar to those of Europe and Japan. Meanwhile, the communications revolution seemed to have done little to relieve business people of the need to meet face-to-face.

More important changes were occurring within the structure of market demand. Of particular concern to the airlines was evidence that the segmentation between business and leisure customers was breaking down. Conventional wisdom dictated that while the demand for air tickets among leisure travelers was fairly price elastic, that of business travelers was highly inelastic, allowing the airlines to subsidize leisure fares with high-margin business fares. Between 2001 and 2006, the price gap between leisure fares (restricted tickets typically requiring a Saturday night stay) and business fares (first-class tickets and flexible coach tickets without advance purchase requirements) continued to grow. The primary reason was falling leisure fares as low-cost carriers offered price competition over more and more routes. Moreover, widening differentials in air fares encouraged many companies to change their travel policies: more and more business travel was on restricted coach-class tickets.

Major changes were occurring within the distribution side of the industry. Historically, the primary channel of distribution of airline tickets was travel agencies – retailers that specialized in the sale of travel tickets, hotel reservations, and vacation packages. From 1996, airlines began pruning their commissions paid to travel agents with cuts from 10% to 8%, then to 5%. By 2003, all the major airlines had stopped paying commissions to independent travel agents. By 2006, commissions paid by the airline companies amounted to only 1.3% of operating expenses (see table 3.9 below), down from 6.2% in 1991.

Meanwhile the companies were developing their direct sales organizations using both telephone and web-based reservations systems. However, the airlines were slower than e-commerce startups in exploiting the opportunities of the internet. Despite the launch of Orbitz (the airlines' own online reservations service) in June 2001, Expedia and Travelocity lead online air ticket sales. As well as wielding greater bargaining power than traditional travel agencies, they also provided consumers with unparalleled transparency of prices, permitting the lowest price deals to be quickly spotted. The traditional travel agent sector was increasingly dominated by global leaders such as American Express and Thomas Cook.

Airline Cost Conditions

A little more than one-third of airline operating costs are accounted for by flying operations while servicing and maintenance account for another one-quarter (see table 3.8). In terms of individual cost items, labor and fuel costs are by far the biggest

TABLE 3.8 The cost structure of the US airline industry by activity, 2002 and 2005

	Percentage of total operating costs	
	2002	2005
Flying operations	30.1	36.5
Aircraft and traffic servicing	15.9	14.1
Maintenance	12.2	10.3
Promotion and sales	9.3	5.7
Transport related	10.0	16.7
Passenger services	8.3	6.2
Administrative	7.5	6.0
Depreciation and amortization	6.7	4.5
TOTAL	100.0	100.0

SOURCE: AIR TRANSPORT ASSOCIATION.

TABLE 3.9 Operating costs in the US airline industry, 2006

Cost item	Increase in cost 2000–6 (%)	Percentage of total operating expenses
Labor	12.8	23.8
Fuel	15.8	25.5
Aircraft ownership	(19.6)	6.9
Non-aircraft ownership	3.9	4.6
Professional services	7.9	7.8
Food and beverage	(43.2)	1.5
Landing fees	44.7	2.0
Maintenance material	(41.4)	1.4
Aircraft insurance	46.7	0.1
Non-aircraft insurance	140.5	0.5
Passenger commissions	(69.8)	1.3
Communication	(29.8)	0.9
Advertising and promotion	(36.2)	0.8
Utilities and office supplies	(21.4)	0.5
Transport-related expenses	337.9	14.7
Other operating expenses	(4.5)	7.6
Increase in total cost, 2000–6	**180.4**	**100.0**

SOURCE: BUREAU OF TRANSPORTATION STATISTICS.

(see table 3.9). A key feature of the industry's cost structure is the very high proportion of costs that are fixed. For example, because of union contracts, it was difficult to reduce employment and hours worked during downturns. The majors' need to maintain their route networks added to the inflexibility of costs – the desire to retain the integrity of the entire network made the airlines reluctant to shed unprofitable routes during downturns. An important implication of the industry's cost structure is that, at times of excess capacity, the marginal costs of filling empty seats on scheduled flights are extremely low.

Labor The industry's labor costs are boosted by the high level of employee remuneration – average pay in airlines was $52,732 in 2005; 40% higher than the average for all private industries. Labor costs were also boosted by low labor productivity that resulted from rigid working practices agreed with unions. Most airline workers belong to one of a dozen major unions, the Association of Flight Attendants, the Air Line Pilots Association, the International Association of Machinists and Aerospace Workers being the most important. These unions have a tradition of militancy and have been highly successful in negotiating pay increases far above the rate of inflation.

Between 2002 and 2006, the airlines forced major concessions from their employees. As a result, average compensation (including benefits) declined from $79,356 in 2003 to $73,055 in 2005. Industry employment fell from a peak of 679,967 in 2000 to 552,857 in 2005.

Fuel How much a carrier spends on fuel depends on the age of its aircraft and its average flight length. Newer planes and longer flights equate to higher fuel efficiency. Also, the fuel efficiency of different aircraft varies widely, primarily dependent on the number of engines. Fuel prices represent the most volatile and unpredictable cost item for the airlines due to fluctuations in the price of crude oil. Between January 2002 and July 2006, New York spot crude prices rose from $19 to $78 a barrel.

Equipment Aircraft were the biggest capital expenditure item for the airlines. At prices of up to $150 million apiece (the A380 will be over $200 million), the purchase of new planes represented a major source of financial strain for the airlines. While Boeing and Airbus competed fiercely for new business (especially when, as in 2002–4, they had spare capacity), aggressive discounts and generous financing terms for the purchase of new planes disguised the fact that a major source of profits for the aircraft manufacturers was aftermarket sales. Over the past 20 years the number of manufacturers of large jets declined from four to two. Lockheed ceased civilian jet manufacture in 1984; McDonnell Douglas was acquired by Boeing in 1997. The leading suppliers of regional jets were Bombardier of Canada and Embraer of Brazil. During 2005, Boeing had earned a net profit of $2.6 billion, representing a 23.3% return on equity.

Airport Facilities Airports play a critical role in the US aviation industry. They are hugely complex, expensive facilities and few in number. Only the largest cities are served by more than one airport. Despite the rapid, sustained growth in air transport over the 30 years since deregulation, only one major new airport has been built – Denver. Most airports are owned by municipalities and can generate substantial revenue flows for the cities. Landing fees are set by contracts between the airport and the airlines, and are typically based on aircraft weight. New York's La Guardia airport has the highest landing fees in the US, charging over $6,000 for a Boeing 747 to land. In 2005, the airlines paid over $2 billion to US airports in landing fees, and a further $2.6 billion in passenger facility charges.

Four US airports – JFK and La Guardia in New York, Chicago's O'Hare, and Washington's Reagan National – are officially "congested" and takeoff and landing slots are allocated to individual airlines where the airlines assume de facto ownership. Growth of air travel is likely to increase problems of congestion and increase the value of takeoff and landing slots. At London's Heathrow airport, slots have been traded between airlines at high prices: American and United paid more than $27 million each for PanAm's takeoff/landing slots; Qantas paid BA $30 million for two slots.

Cost Differences Between Airlines One of the arguments for deregulation had been that there were few major economies of scale in air transport; hence large and small airlines could coexist. Subsequently, little evidence has emerged of large airlines gaining systematic cost advantages over their smaller rivals. However, there are economies associated with network density – the greater the number of routes within a region, the easier it is for an airline to gain economies of utilization of aircraft, crews, and passenger and maintenance facilities. In practice, cost differences between airlines are due more to managerial, institutional, and historical factors rather than the influence of economies of scale, scope, or density. The industry's cost leader, Southwest, built its strategy and management systems around the goal of low costs. By offering services from minor airports, with limited customer service, a single type of airplane, job-sharing among employees, and salary levels substantially less than those paid by other major carriers, Southwest achieves one of the industry's lowest costs per available seat mile (CASM) despite flying relatively short routes. Conversely, US Airways has the highest operating costs of the majors. These are partly a result of external factors – short routes, smaller planes, and frequent adverse weather conditions in the north-east – but mainly the consequence of low productivity due to restrictive working arrangements agreed with unions.

A critical factor determining average costs is capacity utilization. Because most costs, at least in the short run, are fixed, profitable operation depends on achieving break-even levels of capacity operation. When airlines are operating below break-even capacity there are big incentives to cut prices in order to attract additional business. The industry's periodic price wars tended to occur during periods of slack demand and on routes where there were several competitors and considerable excess capacity.

Achieving high load factors while avoiding ruinously low prices is a major preoccupation for the airlines. All the major airlines have adopted yield management systems – highly sophisticated computer models that combine capacity and purchasing data and rigorous financial analysis to provide flexible price determination. The goal is to earn as much revenue on each flight as possible. Achieving this goal has meant a proliferation of pricing categories and a plethora of special deals.

Entry and Exit

Hopes by the deregulators that the US airline business would be a case study of competition in a contestable industry were thwarted by two factors: significant barriers to both entry and exit, and evidence that potential competition was no substitute for actual competition in lowering fares on individual routes. While the capital requirements of setting up an airline can be low (a single leased plane will suffice), offering an airline service requires setting up a whole system comprising gates, airline and aircraft certification, takeoff and landing slots, baggage handling services, and the marketing and distribution of tickets. At several airports, the dominance of gates and landing slots by a few major carriers made entry into particular routes difficult and forced start-up airlines to use secondary airports. Yet, despite the challenges of entry barriers and the dismal financial performance of the industry there seemed to be no shortage of willing entrepreneurs attracted to the apparent glamour of owning an airline. International airlines were also potential entrants into the US domestic market. There was the possibility that a new airline agreement between the US and the EU might lift US restriction on European airlines either acquiring US airlines or offering internal services within the US.

A key factor intensifying competition in the industry has been the barriers to exit that prevent the orderly exit of companies and capacity from the industry. The tendency for loss-making airlines to continue in the industry for long periods of time can be attributed to two key exit barriers: first, contracts (especially with employees) give rise to large closure costs; second, Chapter 11 of the bankruptcy code allows insolvent companies to seek protection from their creditors (and from their existing contracts) and continue operation under supervision of the courts. A critical problem for otherwise financially healthy airlines was meeting competition from bankrupt airlines, which had the benefit of artificially lowered costs.

Looking to the Future

The new-found optimism that pervaded the US airline industry at the beginning of 2007 had its basis in several factors. The revival in industry profitability could be attributed primarily to increasing industry load factors. Strong growth in demand together with the reluctance of the major airlines to add capacity (primarily because so many were mired in Chapter 11) resulted in an unprecedentedly high load factor for 2006. This did much to reduce their incentive to engage in price competition. Simultaneously, most of the major airlines had been able to offset the escalating price of fuel by reducing operating costs elsewhere. All the major airlines had achieved significant reductions in headcount while reducing levels of employee pay and benefits. If US Airways' bid for Delta marked the beginning of a new wave of industry consolidation, this could do much to create a more stable industry structure where the airlines would be much better able to avoid destructive price competition.

The key question was: Would the good times last? At the end of the 1990s, the industry had made similar progress in restoring profitability. Yet, September 11, 2001, a new wave of competition from budget airlines, and an escalation in fuel prices had brought the whole industry to the brink of financial ruin. The evidence of past revivals in the industry suggested that they came to an end either as a result of external events – a terrorist attack, a series of serious crashes, or an economic recession – or as a result of internal factors. These related primarily to the tendency for any emergence of prosperity to be undermined by the entry of new airlines and the expansion of capacity by established airlines.

The success of the major airlines in improving operational efficiency also raised some perplexing questions. The widespread assumptions had been that, if the major airlines could reduce their costs to the level of Southwest and the other low-cost carriers, they could enjoy profit levels similar to those experienced by Southwest. Yet despite the efforts of the majors, Southwest, Jet Blue and the other budget airlines still retained a substantial cost advantage over the legacy carriers. But even if the major airlines could continue to reduce costs, who would the beneficiaries be: the long-suffering shareholders of the companies or travelers as competition for business encouraged the airlines to pass on cost reductions to customers in the form of lower prices?

Ford and the World Automobile Industry in 2007

Ford in Crisis

By late November 2006, less than three months since arriving at Ford's Dearborn, Michigan, headquarters, CEO Alan Mulally was battling for the company's survival. The short-term challenge was financing Ford's cash drain – during the third quarter of 2006 the company had lost $5.2 billion. On November 27, Mulally and CFO Don Leclair had arranged an $18 billion debt financing package secured on Ford's North American assets. However, the bad news was unremitting. On the evening of November 30, Mulally received the November US sales figures. Ford had suffered a 10% fall in unit sales year-on-year with sharp declines in sales of pickup trucks and Jaguar cars. As a result, Ford slipped from no. 2 in market share behind General Motors (GM) to no. 4 behind DaimlerChrysler and Toyota.

Mulally was Ford's third CEO in four years. Jacques Nasser's attempt to transform Ford into a customer-focused, innovative, auto giant through a slew of acquisitions had ended in massive losses and a boardroom revolt. Chairman Bill Ford (great-grandson of founder Henry Ford) took over as CEO and reversed course. A "Revitalization Plan" involving the elimination of 35,000 jobs, annual cost reductions of $3 billion, and an accelerated program of new product launches was succeeded in January 2006 by a new turnaround plan: "The Way Forward." Despite job cuts, plant closures, and the reorganization of production, losses continued to grow throughout 2006. As confidence in Bill Ford's ability to execute a turnaround dissipated, the Board decided to appoint a CEO from outside the company.

With no prior experience of the auto industry (his prior career was with Boeing), Mulally was reluctant to chart a new strategic course for Ford. The company's most pressing problem, he surmised, was not lack of strategy, but was ineffective execution. Mulally perceived a lack of dialogue, inadequate cooperation, weak accountability, excessive complexity, turf battles, and debilitating cross-functional conflict – especially between finance and engineering. Ford would need to move faster and more purposefully in addressing entrenched problems of excess capacity, inflexible work practices, slow new product development, and erratic decision making.

But how long did Ford have? With a cash outflow forecast at $4 billion during the final quarter of 2006 and with automotive operations reckoned to generate a negative cash flow of $21 billion during 2007–9, Ford's financial situation would remain precarious. In these circumstances, Ford's ability to survive over the medium term would depend critically on the state of the world auto industry. As he reviewed the financial performance of other automakers, Mulally realized that Ford's problems were not wholly of its own making: the entire industry had been earning minimal profits for years. During 2005, the world's 34 largest automotive companies earned an average net margin of 2.1%; 2006 profitability was unlikely to be significantly higher. If the overall levels of competition and profitability in the world auto industry were to be much the same during the next five years as they had been during the past five, the challenge of turnaround would be considerable. However, what most worried Mulally was the potential for the industry to suffer a further deterioration in profitability. Given the likelihood of a slowdown in the world economy during 2007 and 2008, there seemed little chance that the industry's overhang of excess capacity would be resolved. In the meantime the industry was threatened by new pressures on profitability: new competitors from emerging market countries, the automakers' weakening control over their distribution systems, growing power of component suppliers, and increasing concern over the environmental impact of private motoring. Mulally quickly realized that automobiles were a very different industry from aerospace. In large passenger jets, Boeing faced just one competitor, Airbus. In autos, Ford was one of 12 major international players all battling for more market share.

The Market

Trends in Market Demand

During the 1880s, the first internal-combustion powered vehicles were produced in Europe – notably by Gottlieb Daimler and Karl Benz in Germany. By the turn of the century hundreds of small companies were producing automobiles both in Europe and in America. The subsequent 120 years saw the industry developing at different rates in different parts of the world. The US industry entered a period of rapid growth during 1910–28. Since the mid-1960s, the combined output of autos and trucks was broadly stable – despite cyclical fluctuations (see figure 4.1). In Europe and Japan too, total production has followed a fairly stable trend during the past two decades. The problem of market saturation was exacerbated by the tendency for cars to last longer (see table 4.1).

As a result, the automobile producers have looked increasingly to the newly industrializing countries for market opportunities. During the 1980s and 1990s countries such as Korea, Malaysia, Taiwan, Thailand, Turkey, Brazil, and Argentina offered the best growth prospects. As these markets became increasingly saturated, so China, India, and the former Soviet Union were seen as the "next wave" of attractive markets. With the opening of many of these countries to trade and direct investment, the world production of cars and trucks continued to grow (see figure 4.2).

FIGURE 4.1 US motor vehicle production, 1900–2005

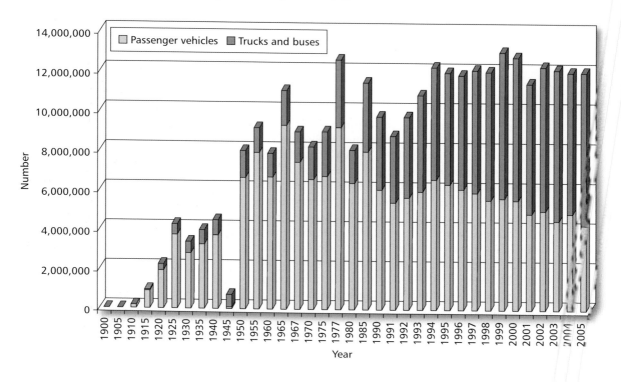

TABLE 4.1 Median age of passenger cars in the US (years)

Year	Median age	Year	Median age
1941	4.9	1990	6.5
1948	8.0	1992	7.0
1952	4.5	1994	7.4
1958	5.1	1996	7.4
1962	5.7	1998	8.1
1968	4.7	2000	8.3
1972	5.1	2002	8.4
1976	5.5	2003	8.6
1980	6.0	2004	8.9
1984	6.7	2005	9.0
1988	6.8		

SOURCE: R. L. POLK & CO.

The Evolution of the Automobile

The early years of the industry were characterized by considerable uncertainty over the design and technology of the motorcar. Early "horseless carriages" were precisely that – they followed design features of existing horse-drawn carriages and buggies.

FIGURE 4.2 World motor vehicle production (cars and trucks), 1950–2005

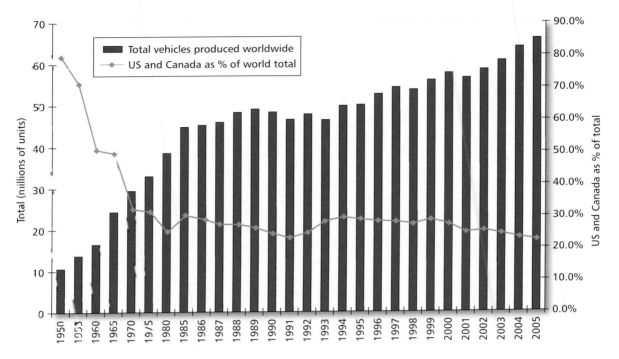

Early motorcars demonstrated a bewildering variety of technologies. During the early years, the internal-combustion engine vied with the steam engine. Among internal-combustion engines there was a wide variety of cylinder configurations. Transmission systems, steering systems, and brakes all displayed a remarkable variety of technologies and designs.

Over the years technologies and designs tended to converge as competition relegated many once-promising designs to the scrapheap of history. The Ford Model T represented the first "dominant design" in automobiles – the technologies and design features of the Model T set a standard for other manufacturers to imitate. Convergence of technologies and designs was the dominant trend of the next 90 years. During the 1920s, all manufacturers adopted enclosed, all-steel bodies. During the last few decades of the 20th century most models with distinctively different designs disappeared: the VW Beetle with its rear, air-cooled engine, the Citroen 2-CV and its idiosyncratic braking and suspension system, Daf with its "Variomatic" transmission, and the distinctive models made by Eastern European manufacturers. Engines became more similar: typically 4 cylinders arranged in-line, with V-6 and V-8 configurations for larger cars. Front-wheel drive and anti-lock disk brakes became standard on smaller cars; suspension and steering systems became more similar; body shapes became increasingly alike. Although the automobile continued to evolve, technological progress was incremental: innovations primarily involved new applications of electronics and new safety features. A 1950 Mercedes had about 10 meters of wiring. A 1995 SL 500 with full options had 3,000 meters of wiring and 48 different microcomputers. In terms of automotive engineering the main advances were multi-valve cylinders, traction control systems, all-wheel drive, electronic fuel injection, variable suspensions, and intercooled turbos. The quest for fuel economy resulted in the substitution of lighter materials (aluminum, plastics, ceramics, and composites) for iron and steel. Continuing advances in the application of electronics include satellite navigation systems, communications technology (telematics), emergency signaling, collision-avoidance radar, and intelligent monitoring systems.

While designs and technologies have converged, the range of vehicle types has increased. New vehicle types include passenger vans ("people carriers"), sport utility vehicles (SUVs), micro cars, and a variety of cars that combine features of different product segments ("crossovers" such as luxury SUVs and "mini-SUVs" built on automobile platforms). However, within individual product segments, different manufacturers' vehicles have tended to become more similar.

Convergence also occurred across countries. The same market segments tended to emerge in different countries. The major differences between countries were in the *sizes* of the various segments. Thus, in the US, the "mid-size" family sedan was the largest segment, with the Honda Accord and Toyota Camry the leading models. In Europe and Asia, small family cars ("subcompacts") formed the largest market segment. Yet for all the emphasis by manufacturers on global models, national markets are characterized more by their differences than by their similarities. For example, in 2006 in the US, light trucks (pickups and SUVs) outsold passenger cars. In Japan, minicars, such as the Suzuki Cervo, have grabbed 35% of the total car market.

The Evolution of Manufacturing Technology

At the beginning of the 20th century, car manufacture, like carriage-making, was a craft industry. Cars were built to order according to individual customers' preferences and specifications. In Europe and North America there were hundreds of companies producing cars, few with annual production exceeding 1,000 vehicles. When Henry Ford began production in 1903, he used a similar approach. Even with fairly long runs of a single model (the first version of the Model T, for example), each car was individually built. The development of more precise machine tools permitted interchangeable parts, which ushered in mass production: batch or continuous production of components which were then assembled on moving assembly lines by semi-skilled workers. The productivity gains were enormous. In 1912 it took 23 man-hours to assemble a Model T; just 14 months later it took only four. The resulting fall in the price of cars opened up a new era of popular motoring.

If "Fordism" was the first major revolution in process technology, then Toyota's "lean production" was the second. The system was developed by Toyota in post-war Japan at a time when shortages of key materials encouraged extreme parsimony and avoidance of inventories and waste. Key elements of the system were statistical process control, just-in-time scheduling, quality circles, teamwork, and flexible production (more than one model manufactured on a single production line). Central to the new manufacturing was the transition from static concepts of efficiency optimization towards continuous improvement to which every employee contributed. During the 1980s and 1990s all the world's car manufacturers redesigned their manufacturing processes to incorporate aspects of Toyota's lean production.

New manufacturing methods required heavy investments by the companies in both capital equipment and training. However, the essence of the Toyota system was not new manufacturing "hardware" in the form of robotics and computer-integrated manufacturing systems. The critical elements were the "software" – new employee skills, new methods of shop-floor organization, redefined roles for managers, and new relationships with suppliers.

Flexible manufacturing technology together with modular designs reduced the extent of scale economies in assembly since different models could be manufactured within the same plant. It was once believed that efficiency required giant assembly plants with outputs of at least 400,000 units a year. During the past decade, most new plants had output capacities of between 150,000 and 300,000 units. Scale economies in components and subassemblies were much more important. Minimum efficient scale for an engine plant is around 1 million units annually.

New Product Development

The critical scale economy in automaking is the ability to amortize the huge costs of new product development over a large enough number of vehicles.

The cost of developing new models has risen steeply as a result of increasing design complexity, the application of electronics, and new safety and environmental standards. By the late 1980s the cost of creating an entirely new, mass-production passenger car from drawing board to production line was about $1.25 billion. By the early 1990s, costs had escalated substantially above this level (see table 4.2).

Smaller manufacturers could survive only by avoiding these massive product development costs. One way was to avoid new model changes. Prior to its acquisition by Ford, Jaguar's two models, the XJ6 and XJS, were almost two decades old. The tiny Morgan car company has made the same model since the late 1930s. The alternative was to license designs from larger manufacturers. Thus, Tofas of Turkey built Fiat-designed cars, Proton of Malaysia built Mitsubishi-designed cars, and Maruti of India produced Suzuki-designed cars.

The cost of new product development has been the major reason for the wave of mergers and acquisitions in the industry. Economies from sharing development costs also encouraged increased collaboration and joint ventures: Renault and Peugeot established joint engine manufacturing; GM established collaborations with Suzuki, Daewoo, Toyota, and Fiat to build cars and share platforms and components. In China and India most new auto plants were joint ventures between local and overseas companies.

During the 1990s, new product development emerged as the critical organizational capability differentiating car manufacturers. Designing, developing, and putting into

TABLE 4.2 New car development costs during the 1990s and 2000s

Ford Mondeo/Contour (1994)	$6 billion
GM Saturn (1990)	$5 billion
Ford Taurus (1996 model)	$2.8 billion
Ford Escort (1997 model)	$2 billion
Chrysler Neon	$1.3 billion
Renault Clio (1999 model)	$1.3 billion
Honda Accord (1997 model)	$0.6 billion
BMW Mini (2001)	$0.5 billion
Rolls Royce Phantom (2003 model)	$0.3 billion

production a completely new automobile was a hugely complex process involving every function of the firm, up to 3,000 engineers, close collaboration with several hundred suppliers, and up to five years from drawing board to market launch. To reduce product development time, most automakers modeled their new product development process on those of Toyota and Honda, which had pioneered the use of cross-functional development teams. Attempts to lower product development costs focused around modular designs and "virtual prototyping" – the use of 3D computer graphics to design and test prototypes. However, pressure for increased fuel efficiency and more environmentally friendly vehicles seemed likely to put increasing upward pressure on product development budgets.

The Industry

The Manufacturers

The major automobile manufacturers are shown in table 4.3. The ranks of the leading producers were dominated by US, Japanese, and European companies: outside of

TABLE 4.3 The world's leading auto manufacturers

		Production ('000s of autos and commercial vehicles)					
		1992	1996	2000	2002	2004	2005
GM	US	6,764	8,176	8,114	8,326	9,221	9,200*
Toyota	Japan	4,249	4,794	5,897	6,626	7,674	7,974*
Ford	US	5,742	6,611	7,206	6,729	6,721	6,818*
Volkswagen	Germany	3,286	3,977	5,106	5,017	4,785	5,243*
DaimlerChrysler	Germany	2,782	4,082	4,666	4,456	4,551	4,829*
Nissan	Japan	2,963	2,712	2,698	2,719	3,226	3,569*
Honda	Japan	1,762	2,021	2,469	2,988	3,141	3,391
Peugeot	France	2,437	1,975	2,879	3,262	3,078	3,375
Hyundai	S. Korea	874	1,402	2,488	2,642	2,283	2,534*
Renault	France	1,929	1,755	2,515	2,329	2,490	2,533*
Suzuki	Japan	888	1,387	1,434	1,704	2,018	2,200
Fiat	Italy	1,800	2,545	2,639	2,191	1,776	1,703*
Mitsubishi	Japan	1,599	1,452	1,613	1,821	1,334	1,381
BMW	Germany	598	641	835	1,091	1,255	1,328*
Mazda	Japan	1,248	984	972	1,044	1,104	1,149*
Daihatsu	Japan	610	691	n.a.	n.a.	870	909
AutoVAZ	Russia	674	562	756	703	727	732
Fuji (Subaru)	Japan	648	525	581	542	555	571
Isuzu	Japan	473	462	572	437	578	542
Koc	Turkey	n.a.	n.a.	n.a.	n.a.	337	442
Maruti	India	n.a.	n.a.	n.a.	n.a.	384	430

n.a. = not available.

* Sales data.

SOURCES: WARD'S AUTOMOTIVE YEARBOOK; COMPANY ANNUAL REPORTS.

TABLE 4.4 Mergers and acquisitions among automobile manufacturers, 1986–2005

Year	Acquirer	Target	Notes
2005	Nanjing Automobile	Rover (UK)	
2005	Toyota	Fuji Heavy Industries	Acquired 8.7% stake from GM
2002	GM (US)	Daewoo (S. Korea)	42% of equity acquired
2000	Renault (France)	Samsung Motors (S. Korea)	70% of equity acquired
2000	GM (US)	Fiat (Italy)	20% of equity acquired
2000	DaimlerChrysler (Germ.)	Hyundai (S. Korea)	10% of equity acquired
2000	DaimlerChrysler (Germ.)	Mitsubishi Motors (Japan)	34% of equity acquired
1999	Renault (France)	Nissan (Japan)	38.6% of equity acquired
1999	Ford (US)	Volvo (Sweden)	Car business acquired from Volvo
1999	Ford (US)	Land Rover (UK)	Acquired from BMW
1998	Daimler Benz (Germany)	Chrysler (US)	
1998	VW (Germany)	Rolls Royce Motors (UK)	
1998	Hyundai (S. Korea)	Kia (S. Korea)	
1998	Daewoo (S. Korea)	Ssangyong Motor (S. Korea)	
1998	Daewoo (S. Korea)	Samsung Motor (S. Korea)	
1997	Proton (Malaysia)	Lotus (UK)	
1997	BMW (Germany)	Rover (UK)	
1996	Daewoo (S. Korea)	FSO (Poland)	
1996	Daewoo (S. Korea)	FS Lublin (Poland)	
1995	Fiat (Italy)	FSM (Poland)	
1995	Ford (US)	Mazda (Japan)	
1994	Daewoo (S. Korea)	Oltcit/Rodae (Romania)	
1991	VW (Germany)	Skoda (Czech Republic)	
1990	GM (US)	Saab-Scandia (Sweden)	50% of equity acquired
1990	Ford (US)	Jaguar (UK)	
1987	Ford (US)	Aston Martin (UK)	
1987	Chrysler (US)	Lamborghini (Italy)	
1986	VW (Germany)	Seat (Spain)	

these countries only Hyundai of Korea was among the leading manufacturers. All the major manufacturers are multinational: both GM and Ford produce more cars outside the US than within it; Honda produces more Accords in the US than in Japan. As a result some countries – notably Canada, Spain, and the UK – are significant auto producing countries without having any significant domestic auto companies. Over the past two decades the industry has consolidated through mergers and acquisitions (see table 4.4). The financial problems of Japanese and Korean auto companies during the late 1990s accelerated this process. As a result, US and European carmakers acquired significant proportions of the Japanese and Korean auto industries. At the same time, a number of small producers continued to survive, especially in protected markets. Trade liberalization represented a threat to these companies. China's accession to the

World Trade Organization meant that several Chinese automakers were attempting to build an international presence.

Outsourcing and the Role of Suppliers

Henry Ford's system of mass production was supported by heavy backward integration. In Ford's giant River Rouge plant, iron ore entered at one end, Model Ts emerged at the other. Ford even owned rubber plantations in the Amazon basin. The trend of the past 20 years has been towards increasing outsourcing of materials, components, and subassemblies. This has been led primarily by the desire for lower costs and increased flexibility. Again, leadership came from the Japanese: Toyota and Nissan have traditionally been much more reliant on their supplier networks than their US or European counterparts. At the end of the 1990s GM and Ford both spun off their component manufacturing businesses as separate companies: Delphi and Visteon, respectively.

Relationships with suppliers also changed. In contrast to the US model of arm's-length relationships and written contracts, the Japanese manufacturers developed close, collaborative long-run relationships with their "first-tier" suppliers. During the 1990s, the Japanese model of close collaboration and extensive technical interchange with a smaller number of leading suppliers became the model for the entire global auto industry – all the world's manufacturers outsourced more manufacturing and technology development while greatly reducing the number of their suppliers.

As the leading component suppliers have gained increasing responsibility for technological development – especially in sophisticated subassemblies such as transmissions, braking systems, and electrical and electronic equipment – they have also grown in size and global reach. Bosch, Johnson Controls, Denso, and Delphi were almost as big as some of the larger automobile companies (see table 4.5).

TABLE 4.5 Revenues and profitability of the biggest automotive component suppliers

	Revenues ($ billion)			ROE (%)
	1994	2000	2005	2005
Robert Bosch (Germany)	19.6	29.1	49.1	12.0
Denso Corp. (Japan)	11	18.2	29.0	9.4
Johnson Controls (US)	7.1	17.2	27.5	14.4
Delphi Automotive (US)*	–	29.1	26.9	–38.4
Magna International (Canada)	–	10.5	22.8	9.9
Lear Corp (US)	3.1	14.1	17.1	5.3
Aisin Seiki (Japan)	7.3	8.9	17	8.5
Visteon (US)	–	19.5	17	–**
Valeo SA (France)	3.8	8.9	11.8	8.1
Eaton (US)	4.4	8.3	11.1	21.9
Dana (US)*	5.5	12.7	8.6	–294.5

* Currently operating under Chapter 11 of US Bankruptcy Code.

** Not meaningful: company has negative shareholders' equity.

SOURCES: COMPANIES' FINANCIAL STATEMENTS.

The Quest for Cost Reduction

Increasing competition in the industry has intensified the quest for cost reduction among automobile manufacturers. Cost-reduction measures have included:

- *Worldwide outsourcing.* The tendency for increased outsourcing of components has been noted above. In addition, auto firms have developed original equipment manufacturer (OEM) supply arrangements amongst themselves: Daewoo supplies several of GM's models; GM supplies components to Fiat; Mitsubishi and Chrysler supply engines for the BMW Mini.
- *Just-in-time scheduling,* which has radically reduced levels of inventory and work-in-progress.
- *Shifting manufacturing to lower-cost locations*: VW's North American production is based in Mexico and it moved production from Germany to the Czech Republic, Spain, and Hungary; Japanese companies have moved more and more production to lower-cost locations in Southeast Asia; Mercedes and BMW developed greenfield plants in the deep south of the US.
- *Automation.* In high-cost locations (North America, Western Europe, and Japan), increased automation has reduced labor input.

Different companies have faced different cost issues. While European manufacturers were constrained by rigid working conditions, restrictions on layoffs, and generous benefits, US companies were hit by increased provisions for pensions and healthcare.

The quest for economies of scale and scope in relation to product development meant that companies sought to spread rising development costs over larger production and sales volumes. This resulted in the standardization of designs and components across the different models of each manufacturer. In 2003, Ford launched a global manufacturing program aimed at: ". . . realizing efficiencies in manufacturing, engineering and product costs for new vehicles by sharing vehicle platforms and components among various models and the re-use of those platforms and components from one generation of a vehicle model to the next."

For example, Ford's C1 platform is used for the Ford Focus, the Mazda 3, the Ford C-max, and the Volvo S40 and G50. In engines, Ford moved to three engine families: V-8 V-10, V-8, and I-4 (four in-line cylinders). The I-4 engine has over 100 variations, an annual volume of 1.5 million, and is built at three different plants – one in North America, one in Europe, and one in Japan. *Automotive News* explained: "The idea is to share systems in areas that customers can't see and feel, and differentiate the brands in areas they can."

Excess Capacity

A major problem for the industry was the tendency for the growth of production capacity to outstrip the growth in the demand for cars. During the 1980s and early 1990s, Japanese companies were major investors in new capacity with a number of greenfield "transplants" in North America and Europe. During the 1990s all the world's major car companies responded to the quest for globalization with new plants (many of them joint ventures) in the growth markets of Southeast Asia, China, India, South America, and Eastern Europe. During 1992–7, the Korean car companies were especially aggressive investors in new capacity. It was particularly worrying that, even in the markets where demand was growing fastest (such as China, where sales grew annually by almost 50% between 2002 and 2006), growth of production capacity outstripped growth in demand. The resulting overhang of excess capacity was a key factor exacerbating intense competition in the industry. During 2006, capacity utilization in the US auto and light truck industry was 70.4%. The average during 1972–2005 was 78.0%.

Looking ahead, it appeared as though capacity reductions by Ford, GM and a few other companies would be more than offset by the new plants that would begin production during 2007–9. These included three new Toyota plants (one in India, two in China), two new Honda plants in North America, Hyundai plants in the Czech Republic and US, PSA in Slovakia, and at least a dozen other new plants in China and India.

Internationalization

The driving force behind capacity expansion was internationalization. Although multinational growth extends back to the 1920s (when Ford and General Motors established their European subsidiaries), until the 1970s the world auto industry was made up of fairly separate national markets. Each of the larger national markets was supplied primarily by domestic production, and indigenous manufacturers tended to be market leaders. For example, in 1970 the Big Three (GM, Ford, and Chrysler) held close to 85% of the US market, VW and Daimler Benz dominated the market in Germany, as did Fiat in Italy, British Leyland (later Rover) in the UK, Seat in Spain, and Renault, Peugeot, and Citroen in France. Internationalization meant that all the world's leading manufacturers were competing in most of the countries of the world. As a result, the market dominance of local firms was undermined (see table 4.6).

Internationalization required establishing distributors and dealership networks in overseas countries; it also entailed building manufacturing plants – especially where import restrictions made it difficult to serve the overseas market from the home base. US and European quotas on Japanese automobile imports encouraged the Japanese automakers to build plants in these regions. Table 4.7 shows some of the North American auto plants established by overseas (mainly Japanese) companies. Similarly, to serve the booming Chinese market, all the leading Western and Japanese automakers established local production (mostly joint ventures).

Different companies pursued different internationalization strategies:

- Toyota and Honda had expanded throughout the world by establishing wholly owned greenfield plants.
- Ford, which had initially internationalized by creating wholly owned subsidiaries throughout the world, extended its global reach during 1987–99 by acquiring Mazda, Jaguar, Aston Martin, Land Rover, and Volvo.
- GM established a network of alliances and minority equity stakes: notably with Fiat, Suzuki, Saab, and Daewoo.
- DaimlerChrysler was created through a transatlantic merger in 1998, and established a position in Asia by acquiring equity in Mitsubishi Motors and Hyundai.

TABLE 4.6 Automobile market shares in individual countries (%)

	1988	1994	2000	2005
Japan				
Toyota	43.9	33.7	28.5	40.4
Nissan	23.2	18.0	11.8	15.0
Honda	10.8	8.5	16.2	12.3
Suzuki	n.a.	n.a.	10.0	12.1
Korea*				
Hyundai	55.9	46.5	50.3	50.0
Kia	25.0	26.5	19.7	23.3
Daewoo	19.1	16.0	24.8	10.0
Australia				
Toyota	15.3	19.0	16.8	21.9
GM-Holden	20.9	21.3	22.0	17.8
Ford	28.1	24.4	15.9	13.8
France				
Renault	29.1	30.0	28.2	25.8
Peugeot	34.2	31.1	30.9	30.6
VW	9.2	8.0	11.2	11.0
Ford	7.1	8.1	6.2	6.0
Italy				
Fiat	59.9	46.0	35.5	30.1
VW	11.7	10.4	11.8	10.3
Ford	3.7	9.6	8.8	8.8
Peugeot	n.a.	n.a.	7.6	9.7
Renault	7.1	7.0	7.0	6.4
UK				
Ford	26.3	22.2	20.7	19.5
GM	13.7	16.9	14.2	14.7
Peugeot	8.7	12.1	12.3	10.0
VW	n.a.	n.a.	11.1	12.7
BMW/Rover	15.0	12.8	7.7	6.6
Germany				
VW/Audi	28.3	20.9	27.8	29.8
GM	16.1	16.5	12.5	10.7
Ford	10.1	9.9	7.6	8.6
Mercedes	9.2	8.2	12.8	13.3
Japanese	15.2	12.5	10.8	11.0
US				
GM	36.3	34.3	28.6	25.5
Ford	21.7	22.6	19.1	17.7
DaimlerChrysler	11.3	9.8	10.5	12.6
Toyota	6.9	8.5	11.0	13.4
Honda	6.2	8.5	10.0	8.7

SOURCES: JAPAN AUTOMOBILE MANUFACTURERS ASSOCIATION; KOREAN AUTOMOBILE MANUFACTURERS ASSOCIATION; *WARD'S AUTOMOTIVE YEARBOOK.*

n.a. = not available.

* Domestic producers only (excludes imports).

TABLE 4.7 Japanese and European "transplants" in North America

Company	Parent(s)	Location	Production of cars and lt. trucks 2005
Honda of America	Honda	E. Liberty and Marysville, OH	939,868
Toyota USA	Toyota	Georgetown, KY	879,097
NUMMI	Toyota and GM	Fremont, CA	417,369
CAMI Automotive	Suzuki and GM	Ontario	189,997
Toyota Canada	Toyota	Ontario	305,996
Honda of Canada	Honda	Ontario	385,491
Diamond-Star Motors	Mitsubishi/Chrysler	Normal, IL	87,594
Subaru-Isuzu Auto	Fuji and Isuzu	Lafayette, IN	118,991
Nissan Motor USA	Nissan	Sryrna, TN and Canton, MS	836,011
BMW	BMW	Spartanburg, NC	124,816
AutoAlliance International	Mazda/Ford	Flat Rock, MI	272,632
Hyundai Motor America	Hyundai	Montgomery, AL	122,000
Volkswagen	Volkswagen	Puebla, Mexico	301,390

SOURCE: WARD'S AUTOMOTIVE YEARBOOK

- Volkswagen made a series of acquisitions in Europe (Seat, Skoda, and Rolls Royce) and had focused heavily on investing in manufacturing capacity outside the advanced industrial countries, notably in Eastern Europe, Latin America, and China.

Nevertheless, not all companies built global presence. Renault had effectively merged with Nissan and Samsung Motors, but lacked any presence in North America, while Fiat and Peugeot were essentially European manufacturers.

Industry Location

The shift in demand to the emerging market countries and the automakers' quest for lower production costs has resulted in the geographical distribution of production in recent decades. The major growth areas of the past decade have been Asia (notably Korea, China, and India) and central and eastern Europe. Nevertheless, compared with other manufacturing industries (textiles, consumer electronics) the shifts have been moderate. The three major manufacturing regions – western Europe, North America, and Japan – still account for close to three-quarters of world production. Tables 4.8 and 4.9 show production by different regions and countries in recent years.

While the newer locations have the advantages of lower labor costs, which were often a fraction of those in the older industrialized countries (see table 4.10), with the exception of Korea, none of the new auto-manufacturing countries has emerged as a major world center for motor vehicle production. The ability of the established auto-manufacturing countries to sustain their leadership points to the importance of local agglomeration factors driving competitiveness in the auto industry.

TABLE 4.8 World motor vehicle production by countries and regions (% of world total)

	1960	1989	1994	2000	2005
United States	52.0	23.8	24.5	22.2	20.0
Western Europe	38.0	31.7	31.2	29.9	28.4
Central and E. Europe	2.0	4.8	4.3	4.6	5.4
Japan	1.0	18.2	21.2	17.7	17.0
Korea	–	1.8	4.6	5.0	5.3
Other	7.0	19.7	14.4	20.6	24.0
Total units (millions)	12.8	49.5	50.0	57.4	60.5

Products for E. Europe and USSR included in "Other" for 1991 and 1992.

SOURCES: AAMA, AUTOMOTIVE NEWS

TABLE 4.9 Automobile production by country (thousands; excludes trucks)

	1987	1990	1995	2000	2005
US	7,099	6,077	6,338	5,542	4,321
Canada	810	1,072	1,339	1,551	1,356
Mexico	266	346	710	1,130	846
Total N. America	*8,175*	*7,495*	*8,387*	*8,223*	*6,523*
Germany	4,604	4,805	4,360	5,132	5,350
France	3,052	3,295	3,051	2,883	3,113
Italy	1,701	1,874	1,422	1,442	726
UK	1,143	1,296	1,532	1,641	1,596
Spain	1,403	1,679	1,959	2,445	2,098
Sweden	432	336	390	260	289
Total W. Europe	*13,471*	*13,672*	*14,350*	*14,853*	*14,550*
Japan	7,891	9,948	7,664	8,363	9,017
Korea	793	987	1,893	1,881	2,195
Australia	225	361	284	324	320
China	n.a.	n.a.	356	620	3,118
India	n.a.	n.a.	n.a.	541	999
Taiwan	175	277	271	265	324
Former USSR	1,329	1,260	834	967	2,554
Poland	301	256	260	533	527
Brazil	789	663	1,312	1,348	2,009

SOURCES: JAPAN AUTOMOBILE MANUFACTURERS ASSOCIATION; KOREAN AUTOMOBILE MANUFACTURERS ASSOCIATION; WARD'S AUTOMOTIVE YEARBOOK.

Market Segments and Market Positioning

As already noted, despite the globalization of the leading automakers, the world market by 2004 was still composed of many national markets due to differences in national regulations and customer preferences, differences in affluence and infrastructure, trade restrictions, and the need for each manufacturer to build a dealership

TABLE 4.10 Hourly compensation for motor vehicle workers (US$ per hour, including benefits)

	1975	1984	1994	1998	2002	2004
US	9.55	19.02	27.00	27.21	32.35	33.95
Mexico	2.94	2.55	2.99	2.21	3.68	3.50
Japan	3.56	7.90	25.91	22.55	24.22	27.38
Korea	0.45	1.74	7.81	7.31	12.22	15.82
Taiwan	0.64	2.09	6.93	6.87	7.05	7.50
France	5.10	8.20	18.81	18.50	18.73	26.34
Germany	7.89	11.92	34.74	34.65	32.20	44.05
Italy	5.16	8.00	16.29	16.44	15.67	21.74
Spain	–	5.35	15.37	15.34	15.11	21.55
UK	4.12	7.44	15.99	20.07	21.11	29.40

SOURCE: US DEPARTMENT OF LABOR, BUREAU OF LABOR STATISTICS.

network in each market it served. The world market was also segmented by types of product. At the top end of the market were "luxury cars" distinguished primarily by their price. There were also specific types of vehicle: sports cars, sport utility vehicles (SUVs), small passenger vans ("minivans"), and pickup trucks. Although industry statistics distinguish between automobiles and trucks – the latter being for commercial use – in practice, the distinction was less clear. In the US small pickup trucks were a popular alternative to automobiles; SUVs were also classed as trucks.

Margins varied considerably between product segments. The profitability of the US automakers during 1995–2004 was primarily the result of strong domestic demand for SUVs and pickup trucks – segments where they met limited competition. The luxury car segment, too, was traditionally associated with high margins. By contrast, small and medium-sized family cars have typically lost money. However, mobility barriers between segments tend to be low. Modular product designs and common platforms and components have facilitated the entry of the major manufacturers into specialty segments. As the pressure of competition has increased across all market segments, manufacturers have sought differentiation advantage through introducing models that combine design features from different segments ("crossover" vehicles).

Vertical segmentation was also an issue for the industry. Profitability varied across the different stages of the auto industry's value chain. The prevailing wisdom was that downstream activities offered better profit potential than manufacturing activities – certainly financial services (mainly customer and dealer credit) were far more profitable than vehicle manufacturing. It was this logic that had encouraged the auto companies to outsource and spin off most of their production of components.

The Outlook

As Alan Mulally reviewed projections by his corporate economics and strategy team for worldwide auto sales over the next three years, he wondered if favorable demand growth would provide much support for the industry's profit levels. Most of the growth would come from emerging market countries. Here the world's leading manufacturers were racing to set up new plants. In the mature markets of North America, Europe, and Japan, fuel costs and environmental factors complicated the picture. Despite concerns over the imminent "death of the automobile," Ford's projections suggested that high gasoline prices and concern over emissions were more likely to boost demand as motorists switched to hybrid, diesel, and more fuel-efficient autos. Mulally's main concern was the possibility that buyers would "trade down" to smaller, more economical cars in preference to the SUVs and luxury cars that had long supported Ford's profits.

Similar uncertainties clouded the likely evolution of industry structure. During the 1990s, most observers had assumed that scale economies would cause continuing consolidation of the industry to the point where only six major full-line car companies would survive. Certainly the industry had consolidated during the past decade: however, not only were some of the medium-sized carmakers stable and profitable (BMW, Renault, Peugeot), but several of the emerging-market newcomers were expanding internationally (e.g. Tata Motor and Maruti of India, Koc of Turkey, and Shanghai Auto).

Appendix
The World's Major Automobile Producers, Sales, and Profitability 1980–2005

TABLE 1.A1 Company sales ($ billion)

	1980–4*	1985–9*	1990–4*	1995–9*	2000	2001	2002	2003	2004	2005
GM	68	110	128	169	185	177	187	186	194	193
Ford	42	77	96	149	170	162	163	164	172	177
DaimlerChrysler	–	–	–	147	152	136	157	172	192	177
Chrysler	13	28	39	58	–	–	–	–	–	–
Daimler Benz	12	34	59	71	–	–	–	–	–	–
Toyota	18	42	82	107	121	106	107	129	164	173
VW	16	28	48	64	79	78	91	109	121	113
Honda	8	18	35	50	58	52	55	67	76	80
Fiat	18	27	42	50	53	58	55	61	67	55
Nissan	16	26	51	57	55	49	47	57	80	81
Peugeot	13	19	28	35	41	46	57	68	78	67
Renault	15	31	31	37	37	32	38	47	53	47
BMW	5	10	21	34	33	34	44	52	60	55
Mitsubishi	12	14	25	32	30	26	24	32	24	20
Hyundai Motor	n.a.	n.a.	n.a.	18	29	30	40	39	51	58
Mazda	n.a.	12	21	18	16	16	16	20	28	25

n.a. = not available.

* Annual average.

SOURCES: COMPANY FINANCIAL STATEMENTS.

TABLE 4.A2 Company profitability (return on equity, %)

	1980–4*	1985–9*	1990–4*	1995–9*	2000	2001	2002	2003	2004	2005
GM	11.4	11.8	3.2	27.5	14.8	3.0	25.6	15.1	13.1	n.a
Ford	0.4	21.8	5.9	35.4	18.6	−70.0	−17.5	4.2	26.3	18.8
DaimlerChrysler	–	–	–	15.9	18.3	−1.7	13.5	1.3	7.0	8.0
Chrysler	66.5	20.8	2.0	24.5	–	–	–	–	–	–
Daimler Benz	24.3	18.3	6.9	22.1	–	–	–	–	–	—
Toyota	12.6	10.6	6.1	6.8	7.5	9.5	7.7	10.5	15.2	13.8
VW	1.6	6.3	−0.4	11.1	12.1	10.5	–	4.4	3.0	4.7
Honda	18.1	11.8	5.3	15.1	11.8	10.6	14.0	16.1	13.5	14.9
Fiat	10.9	18.7	6.8	7.6	4.9	5.0	−3.7	−51.3	−75.9	3.5
Nissan	10.3	4.7	3.6	−0.1	39.2	36.4	23.0	27.2	20.8	17.2
Peugeot	−15.2	36.7	12.5	3.0	13.8	15.3	14.6	12.1	11.3	n.a.
Renault	−152.4	51.1	9.1	11.0	11.0	10.1	16.4	17.6	18.3	17.6
BMW	14.8	10.4	9.7	−4.0	20.6	17.3	14.5	11.8	12.7	13.2
Mitsubishi	10.0	7.9	4.8	−5.3	−123.2	n.a.	3.9	12.5	−470.0	−31.7
Hyundai Motor	n.a.	n.a.	n.a.	4.4	8.9	10.0	10.7	12.5	11.0	n.a.
Mazda	n.a.	4.8	5.0	6.3	−110.7	−93.2	4.9	12.0	15.8	17.1

n.a. = not available.

* Annual average.

SOURCE: COMPANY FINANCIAL STATEMENTS.

Wal-Mart Stores Inc., 2007

If you don't want to work weekends, you shouldn't be in retail.

SAM WALTON (EXPLAINING THE SATURDAY CORPORATE MEETING)

At the beginning of 2007, Wal-Mart's status as the world's biggest retailer was unassailable. It was more than three times the size of the world's no. 2 retailer (Carrefour). It earned about as much profit as the next five largest retailers combined. During the financial year ending on January 31, 2007, it appeared that Wal-Mart would achieve sales growth of 11% – above its average for the previous five years and a creditable performance during a year of unprecedented fuel costs.

Wal-Mart's transformation from a small chain of discount stores in Arkansas, Missouri, and Oklahoma in 1970 to the world's largest retailer was one of the most remarkable corporate success stories of the 20th century. Its founder, Sam Walton, had combined folksy charm and home-spun business wisdom with cutting-edge information technology and supply chain management to create the world's most efficient retail organization.

However, as Lee Scott prepared for his eighth year as CEO of this icon of American capitalism, he realized that sustaining Wal-Mart at the pinnacle of success would be increasingly challenging. Already the stock market was signaling doubts over Wal-Mart's ability to maintain its trend rate of profit growth. The stock price had peaked in March 2002; by the beginning of 2007 it was trading 32% off its peak. Maintaining sales growth meant that Wal-Mart was forced to explore new markets. By 2007, Wal-Mart was operating in 13 countries outside of the US. Within the US, Wal-Mart was continually seeking to broaden its range of offerings. During 2006, Wal-Mart moved heavily into prescriptions drugs (offering generic prescription drugs at a flat $4 price) and also expanded the range of financial services it offered.

Wal-Mart was facing stiffer competition everywhere. In its traditional area of discount retailing, Target was proving an increasingly formidable competitor, while several of the rivals that Wal-Mart had believed it had crushed – Kmart, Sears, and JC Penney – were being revitalized by new management. In warehouse clubs, its Sam's Clubs ran a poor second to Costco. While Wal-Mart could seldom be beaten on cost, it was continually facing competitors that sought to be more stylish (TJ Maxx), more quality-focused (Wholefoods), or more service oriented (Lowe's, Best Buy). As Wal-Mart reached a scale that was unprecedented in the history of retailing, adapting to new competition and changing customer requirements would be a continuing challenge.

Of particular concern to Scott was the need to compete on completely new and unfamiliar fronts. For years Wal-Mart had been a target for organized labor seeking to unionize Wal-Mart's million and a half employees. More recently, "The Beast of Bentonville" has attracted the ire of environmentalists, antiglobalization activists, women's and children's rights advocates, small-business representatives, and a growing number of legislators of varying political hues. The result was a series of senior appointments to new executive positions – a head of global ethics and a new executive vice president of government relations – plus more top management time spent in Washington and with the media.

Wal-Mart's success had been based on a strategy that emphasized a few key components: commitment to "everyday low prices," responsiveness to customer needs, matchless logistics supported by leading-edge IT, committed employees, and unremitting cost cutting founded on a culture of frugality. As Lee Scott looked ahead to the new financial year, two concerns filled his mind. First, could Wal-Mart sustain its leadership in costs, innovation, and flexibility? Second, would these traditional competitive advantages of Wal-Mart be sufficient for it to meet the new challenges that it would be facing in the coming years?

History

Sam Walton opened his first store – a franchised Ben Franklin variety store – in 1945. Over the next 15 years, Sam together with his brother, Bud, developed a chain of 15 Ben Franklin stores throughout rural Arkansas. During this period, Sam Walton became aware of the increasing price competition from discount retailers – large format stores that offered a broad range of products that included apparel, appliances, toiletries, household goods, and sometimes groceries as well. This new category of retailer emerged in the US following World War II. Discount stores were located within large towns – it was generally believed that a minimum population of 100,000 was necessary to support a discount store. Sam Walton believed that discount stores could be viable in smaller communities: if the prices were right, the stores would attract customers from a wide area: "Our strategy was to put good-sized stores into little one-horse towns that everyone else was ignoring."[1] Walton opened his first Wal-Mart in 1962 and within eight years had 30 discount stores in small and medium-sized towns in Arkansas, Oklahoma, and Missouri.

Distribution was a problem for Wal-Mart:

> Here we were in the boondocks, so we didn't have distributors falling over themselves to serve us like our competitors in larger towns. Our only alternative was to build our own distribution centers so that we could buy in volume at attractive prices and store the merchandise.[2]

In 1970, Walton built his first distribution center, and in the same year took the company public in order to finance the heavy investment involved. With this structure of large distribution hubs serving a group of 15 to 20 discount stores. Wal-Mart began its rapid expansion across the country. At the end of 1980, Wal-Mart had 330 stores in 11 states (Arkansas, Oklahoma, Missouri, Texas, Kansas, Kentucky, Tennessee, Mississippi, Louisiana, Alabama, and Illinois). By 1995, Wal-Mart had stores in all 50 states. Wal-Mart's geographical expansion was incremental. It moved into a new area, first, by building a few stores that were served by extending Wal-Mart's distribution lines from a nearby cluster; eventually, when a critical mass of stores had been established in the new area, Wal-Mart would build a distribution center to serve the new cluster. Expansion brought Wal-Mart into closer competition with other discount chains. In the small towns of the southwest and south, Wal-Mart faced few major competitors. As Wal-Mart became a national retail chain it entered more developed retailing areas, including larger cities. By 1993, 55% of Wal-Mart stores faced direct competition from Kmart and 23% from Target.[3]

Diversification

Wal-Mart has continuously experimented with alternative retail formats. Some, like Helen's Arts and Crafts and Dot Deep Discount Drugstores, were unsuccessful. Others – Sam's warehouse clubs and the Supercenters – grew rapidly to become important components of Wal-Mart's business.

Sam's Clubs imitated a distribution concept established by Price Club. The warehouse clubs were not retailers since they were not open to the public. They were clubs where access was through membership. They carried a small number of lines and most items were available in multipacks and catering-size packs. The clubs were literally warehouses with products available on pallets and minimal customer service. The rationale was to maximize economies in purchasing, minimize operating costs, and pass the savings on to members through very low prices. Competition among warehouse clubs was ferocious, resulting in rapid consolidation of the sector. Wal-Mart acquired The Wholesale Company in 1991 and Kmart's PACE clubs in 1993, while Costco Wholesale and PriceCo merged in 1993.

Supercenters were Wal-Mart stores with larger floor space (averaging 187,000 square feet, compared with 102,000 square feet for a Wal-Mart discount store and 129,000 square feet for a Sam's Club). Supercenters were modeled on the European concept of the "hypermarket" that had been pioneered by the French retailer Carrefour. A Supercenter combined a discount store with a grocery supermarket: in addition, a Supercenter incorporated a number of specialty units such as an eyeglass store, hair salon, dry cleaners, and photo lab. The Supercenters were open for 24 hours a day, seven days a week. The Supercenter stores and Sam's Clubs were supplied through a separate distribution network from the Wal-Mart discount stores. In 1990, Wal-Mart acquired McLane, a Texas-based wholesale distributor, that became the basis for Wal-Mart's distribution to Supercenters and Sam's Clubs throughout the US.

In 1998, Wal-Mart opened the first of its Neighborhood Markets. This chain of supermarkets had an average floorspace of 42,000 square feet.

International Expansion

By the end of the 1980s, Wal-Mart was concerned that it might be running out of new territory and began looking for opportunities abroad. In 1992, Wal-Mart

TABLE 5.1 Wal-Mart stores by country, November 2006

Country	Stores	Notes
USA	3,960	Included 2,176 Supercenters, 1,100 discount stores, 574 Sam's Clubs, and 110 Neighborhood Markets
Mexico	853	Entered 1991: JV with Cifra. Chains include Wal-Mart, Bodegas, Suburbia, Vips and Mercamas
Puerto Rico	54	Entered 1992
Canada	279	Entered 1994: acquired Woolco
Argentina	13	Entered 1995: greenfield venture
Brazil	299	Entered 1995: JV with Lojas Americana. Includes Todo Dias, Bompreço, and Sonae stores
China	67	Entered 1996: greenfield venture
UK	330	Entered 1999: acquired Asda. Operates Wal-Mart superstores and Asda supermarkets/discount stores
Japan	391	Entered 2002: acquired 38% of Seiyu. Mainly small stores but some superstores
Costa Rica	135	Entered 2005: 51% acquired from Royal Ahold*
El Salvador	59	Entered 2005: 51% acquired from Royal Ahold*
Guatemala	125	Entered 2005: 51% acquired from Royal Ahold*
Honduras	38	Entered 2005: 51% acquired from Royal Ahold*
Nicaragua	37	Entered 2005: 51% acquired from Royal Ahold*
Total	**6,640**	

* 30% stake in CARHCO acquired from Royal Ahold; this later increased to 51%.

SOURCE: WWW.WALMART.COM

established a joint venture with Mexico's largest retailer, Cifra S.A., and began opening Wal-Mart discount stores and Sam's Clubs in several Mexican cities. In 2000, the joint venture became a subsidiary of Wal-Mart when Wal-Mart acquired 51% of Cifra. By 2003, Wal-Mart Mexico was the country's biggest retailer.

In 1994, Wal-Mart entered the Canadian market by acquiring 120 Woolco stores from Woolworth and converting them to its own discount stores format. By 1999, Wal-Mart took 40% of total discount store sales, establishing itself as Canada's largest retailer.

In Europe, Wal-Mart established itself through acquisition: first in Germany, then in the UK. In Asia, Wal-Mart began with cautious scale entry into Korea and China. Table 5.1 shows Wal-Mart's international development.

Wal-Mart's performance in overseas markets was mixed. Its strongest performance was in adjacent countries – Mexico and Canada. Elsewhere Wal-Mart's performance has ranged from moderate to poor. Its biggest overseas presence is its Asda subsidiary in Britain. Since acquisition, Asda's market share has increased only modestly. In Hong Kong, Indonesia, South Korea and Germany, Wal-Mart's poor performance caused it to withdraw.

Sam Walton

Wal-Mart's strategy and management style was inseparable from the philosophy and values of its founder. Until his death in 1992, Sam Walton was the embodiment of Wal-Mart's unique approach to retailing. After his death, Sam Walton's beliefs and business principles continued to be the beacon that guided Wal-Mart's development. As Harry Cunningham, founder of Kmart Stores, observed: "Sam's establishment of the Walton culture throughout the company was the key to the whole thing. It's just incomparable. He is the greatest businessman of this century."[4]

For Sam Walton, thrift and value for money was a religion. Undercutting competitors' prices was an obsession, as was the never-ending quest for cost economies that would permit continuing price cutting. Walton established a culture in which every item of expenditure was questioned – was it necessary? Could it be done cheaper? He set an example that few of his senior colleagues could match: he walked rather than took taxis, shared rooms at budget motels while on business trips, and avoided any corporate trappings or manifestations of opulence or success. For Walton, wealth was a threat and an embarrassment rather than a reward and a privilege. His own lifestyle gave little indication that he was America's richest person (before being eclipsed by Bill Gates). He also felt uncomfortable about the wealth of his associates: "We've had lots of millionaires in our ranks. And it drives me crazy when they flaunt it. Every now and then somebody will do something especially showy, and I don't hesitate to rant and rave about it at the Saturday morning meeting. I don't think that big mansions and flashy cars is what the Wal-Mart culture is supposed to be about."[5]

His attention to detail was legendary. As chairman and chief executive, he was quite clear that his priorities lay with his employees ("associates"), customers, and the operational details through which the former created value for the latter. He shunned offices in favor of spending time in his stores. Most of his life was spent on the road (or in the air piloting his own plane), making impromptu visits to stores and distribution centers. He collected information on which products were selling well in Tuscaloosa; why margins were down in Santa Maria; how a new display system for children's clothing in Carbondale had boosted sales by 15%. His passion for detail extended to competitors' stores as well as his own: not only did he regularly visit competitors' stores, he was also known to count cars in their parking lots.

Central to his leadership role at Wal-Mart was his relationship with his employees – the Wal-Mart associates. In an industry known for low pay and hard working conditions, Walton created a unique spirit of motivation and involvement. He believed fervently in giving people responsibility, trusting them, but also continually monitoring their performance.

Since his death, Sam Walton's habits and utterances became hallowed principles guiding the values of the company and the behavior of its employees. For example, Wal-Mart's "10-foot attitude" pledge is based on Sam Walton's request to a store employee that: "I want you to promise that whenever you come within 10 feet of a customer, you will look him in the eye, greet him and ask if you can help him."[6] The "Sundown Rule" – that every request, no matter how big or small, gets same-day service – has become the basis for Wal-Mart's fast-response management system.

Sam Walton's ability to attract the affection and loyalty of both employees and customers owes much to his ability to generate excitement within the otherwise sterile world of discount retailing. Sam Walton brought a sense of unpredictability and fun to the business. He engendered a positive attitude among Wal-Mart employees and he reveled in his role as company cheerleader.

Sam Walton's contribution to the management systems and management style of Wal-Mart is reflected in Wal-Mart's website's description of "The Wal-Mart Culture" (see the Appendix).

Wal-Mart in 2004

The Businesses

Wal-Mart described its business activities as falling into four segments:

- *Wal-Mart stores*. Wal-Mart's core area of business was its US retail stores; these accounted for almost two-thirds of its total sales. Over time, Wal-Mart's traditional discount stores have increasingly been replaced by its Supercenters, much larger stores that combined a discount store with a supermarket. Superstores – based on the European "hypermarket" concept – allowed Wal-Mart to expand its range of product offerings. In groceries, Wal-Mart had established itself as US market leader, with a 20% share.

- *Sam's Clubs*. Wal-Mart's entry into warehouse clubs in the mid-1980s demonstrated its ability to transfer its retailing capabilities to a very different distribution format. These wholesale outlets offered a narrower range of products – typically around 4,000 stock-keeping units (SKUs) as compared with the 50,000 SKUs for most Wal-Mart discount stores – at prices significantly below those of discount stores. The development of Sam's Club also demonstrated Wal-Mart's capacity for continuous improvement and innovation. From the stark, austere warehouses of the 1980s, Wal-Mart had created a unique wholesale distribution experience. During 2002–6, Wal-Mart upgraded its Sam's Clubs to include more up-market products and services – principally in response to competition from Costco.

- *Wal-Mart's international operations*. These comprised a number of separate national subsidiaries, each attempting to interpret the basic Wal-Mart business principles and underlying approach to retailing within a distinctive economic structure and national culture. Wal-Mart's differentiated approach to different countries reflected the different retailing environments of these countries and the different entry opportunities that had presented themselves. Wal-Mart's joint ventures in Mexico and South America reflected its desire to access local knowledge and utilize the resources and capabilities of strong local players. Its acquisition of Asda in the UK was the result of the strong affinities that the two retailers felt for one another. In China and Argentina, Wal-Mart had entered in start-up mode, in the belief that these countries' retail markets were sufficiently underdeveloped to allow Wal-Mart to develop a market presence. In Japan, Wal-Mart acquired a minority stake in a struggling local retailer in order to explore the opportunities to transfer Wal-Mart's retail concepts to a very different retail environment. Wal-Mart's international expansion had been a process of learning and adaptation where senior executives openly acknowledged the difficulties. John Menzer, head of the international division, observed: "It wasn't such a good idea to stick so

TABLE 5.2 Wal-Mart: performance by segment

	2000	2001	2002	2003	2004	2005	2006
Sales ($ billion)							
Wal-Mart Stores	108.7	121.9	139.1	157.1	174.2	191.8	209.9
Sam's Clubs	24.8	26.8	29.4	31.7	34.5	37.1	39.8
International	22.7	32.1	35.5	40.8	47.6	56.3	62.7
Sales increase							
Wal-Mart Stores	14.0%	12.1%	14.1%	12.9%	10.9%	10.1%	9.4%
Sam's Clubs	8.4%	8.1%	9.7%	7.8%	8.8%	7.5%	7.3%
International	85.6%	41.4%	10.6%	14.9%	16.7%	18.3%	11.4%
Other	23.2%	19.3%	31.4%	0.0%	0.0%	0.0%	0.0%
Operating income ($ billion)							
Wal-Mart Stores	8.70	9.70	10.30	11.80	12.90	14.20	15.30
Sam's Clubs	0.85	0.94	1.03	1.02	1.13	1.30	1.40
International	0.82	1.11	1.46	2.00	2.40	3.00	3.30
Other	(0.26)	(0.29)	(0.71)	(1.57)	(1.39)	(1.30)	(1.50)
Operating income/sales							
Wal-Mart Stores	8.0%	8.0%	7.4%	7.5%	7.4%	7.4%	7.3%
Sam's Clubs	3.4%	3.5%	3.5%	3.2%	3.3%	3.5%	3.5%
International	3.6%	3.5%	4.1%	4.9%	5.0%	5.3%	5.3%
Other	−3.0%	−2.8%	−5.1%	0.0%	0.0%	0.0%	0.0%

SOURCE: WAL-MART STORES INC. 10-K REPORTS.

closely to the domestic Wal-Mart blueprint in Argentina or in some other international markets we have entered. In Mexico City we sold tennis balls that wouldn't bounce right in the high altitude. We built large parking lots at some of our Mexican stores only to realize that many of our customers there rode the bus to the store, then trudged across these large parking lots carrying bags of merchandise . . . We're now working smarter internationally to avoid cultural and regional problems on the front end."[7]

- *McLane Company Inc.* This company distributes to Sam's Clubs and Supercenters. It is the main component of the business segment denoted "other" in Wal-Mart's accounts (see table 5.2).

Table 5.2 shows sales and profits for the different business segments.

Performance

Table 5.3 summarizes some key financial data for Wal-Mart during the period 1994 to 2006. Table 5.4 shows Wal-Mart's recent performance compared with other discount retailers.

TABLE 5.3 Wal-Mart Stores Inc.: financial summary 1994–2006

	1994	1995	1996	1997	1998	1999	2000	2001	2002	2003	2004	2005	2006
Income ($ billion)													
Net sales	67.3	82.5	93.6	104.9	118.0	137.6	165.0	191.3	217.8	229.6	256.3	285.2	312.4
Net sales increase	21.0%	22.0%	13.0%	12.0%	12.0%	17.0%	20.0%	16.0%	4.0%	5.0%	12.0%	11.3%	9.5%
Same-store sales increase	6.0%	6.0%	4.0%	5.0%	6.0%	9.0%	8.0%	5.0%	6.0%	6.0%	4.0%	3.0%	3.0%
Other income – net	0.6	0.9	1.1	1.3	1.3	1.6	1.8	2.0	2.0	2.0	2.4	2.9	3.2
Cost of sales	53.4	65.6	74.5	83.5	93.4	108.7	129.7	150.3	171.6	178.3	198.7	219.8	240.4
SG&A expenses	10.3	12.9	15.0	16.9	19.4	22.4	27.0	31.6	36.2	40.0	44.9	51.2	56.7
Interest costs:													
Debt	0.3	0.5	0.7	0.6	0.6	0.5	0.8	1.1	1.1	0.8	0.7	0.9	1.2
Capital leases	0.2	0.2	0.2	0.2	0.2	0.3	0.3	0.3	0.3	0.3	0.3	0.3	0.2
Provision for income taxes	1.4	1.6	1.6	1.8	2.1	2.7	3.3	3.7	3.9	4.4	5.1	5.6	5.8
Minority interests	0.0	0.0	0.0	0.0	(0.1)	(0.2)	(0.2)	(0.1)	(0.2)	(0.2)	(0.2)	(0.2)	(0.3)
Net income	2.3	2.7	2.7	3.1	3.5	4.4	5.4	6.3	6.7	8.0	9.1	10.3	11.2
Financial position ($ billion)													
Current assets	12.1	15.3	17.3	18.0	19.4	21.1	24.4	26.6	28.2	30.7	34.5	38.9	43.8
Inventories (replacement cost)	11.5	14.4	16.3	16.2	16.8	17.5	20.2	21.6	22.7	24.4	26.6	29.8	32.2
Net PPE and capital leases	13.2	15.9	18.9	20.3	23.6	26.0	36.0	40.9	45.8	51.4	58.5	68.1	79.3
Total assets	26.4	32.8	37.5	39.6	45.4	50.0	70.3	78.1	83.5	94.8	104.9	120.2	138.2
Current liabilities	7.4	10.0	11.5	11.0	14.5	16.8	25.8	28.9	27.3	32.5	37.4	43.2	48.8
Long-term debt	6.2	7.9	8.5	7.7	7.2	6.9	13.7	12.5	15.7	16.6	17.1	20.1	26.4
Long-term lease obligations	1.8	1.8	2.1	2.3	2.5	2.7	3.0	3.2	3.0	3.0	3.0	3.2	3.7
Shareholders' equity	10.8	12.7	14.8	17.1	18.5	21.1	25.8	31.3	35.1	39.5	43.6	49.4	53.2
Financial ratios													
Current ratio	1.6	1.5	1.5	1.6	1.3	1.3	0.9	0.9	1	0.9	0.9	0.9	0.9
Return on assets*	9.9%	9.0%	7.8%	7.9%	8.5%	9.6%	9.5%	8.7%	8.5%	9.0%	9.0%	9.3%	8.9%
Return on equity**	23.9%	22.8%	19.9%	19.2%	19.8%	22.4%	22.9%	22.0%	20.1%	21.0%	21.0%	22.6%	22.5%
Other year-end data													
No. of US discount stores	1,950	1,985	1,995	1,960	1,921	1,869	1,801	1,736	1,647	1,568	1,478	1,353	1,209
No. of US Supercenters	72	147	239	344	441	564	721	888	1,066	1,258	1,471	1,713	1,980
No. of US Sam's Clubs	417	426	433	436	443	451	463	475	500	525	538	551	567
No. of US Neighborhood	–	–	–	–	–	4	7	19	31	49	64	85	100
Markets													
International units	24	226	276	314	601	715	1,004	1,071	1,170	1,272	1,355	1,587	2,285
Employees (thousands)	528	622	675	728	825	910	1,140	1,244	1,383	1,400	1,400	1,600	1,800

* (Net income before minority interest, equity in unconsolidated subsidiaries and cumulative effect of accounting change)/Average assets.

** Net income/Average shareholders' equity.

SOURCE: WAL-MART STORES INC. 10-K REPORTS.

TABLE 5.4 Wal-Mart and its competitors: performance comparisons ($ billions except where noted)

	Wal-Mart			Target			Dollar General			Costco		
	2004	2005	2006	2004	2005	2006	2004	2005	2006	2004	2005	2006
Income												
Sales revenue*	258.7	288.1	315.6	48.2	46.8	52.6	6.9	7.7	8.6	42.5	48.1	52.9
Gross profit	60.0	68.3	75.2	16.4	15.4	17.7	2.0	2.3	2.5	5.3	6.0	6.6
Gross margin (%)	23.2%	23.7%	23.8%	34.0%	32.9%	33.7%	29.0%	29.9%	29.1%	12.5%	12.5%	12.4%
SG&A expense	44.9	51.2	56.7	11.5	10.5	12.0	1.4	1.5	1.7	3.7	4.2	4.6
Depreciation and amortization	3.9	4.3	4.7	1.3	1.3	1.4	0.2	0.2	0.2	0.4	0.5	0.5
Operating margin (%)	4.3%	4.4%	4.4%	7.5%	7.7%	8.2%	6.5%	8.3%	7.1%	2.7%	2.9%	2.8%
Net income	9.1	10.3	11.2	1.8	1.9	2.4	0.3	0.3	0.4	0.7	0.9	1.1
Net margin (%)	3.5%	3.6%	3.5%	3.8%	4.1%	4.6%	4.4%	4.5%	4.1%	1.7%	1.8%	2.0%
Financial position												
Cash	5.2	5.5	6.4	0.7	2.2	1.6	0.4	0.3	0.2	1.5	3.1	3.5
Net receivables	1.3	1.7	2.7	5.8	5.1	5.7	0.0	0.0	0.0	0.6	0.3	0.6
Inventories	26.6	29.8	32.2	5.3	5.4	5.8	1.2	1.4	1.5	3.3	3.6	4.0
Total current assets	34.4	38.9	43.8	12.9	13.9	14.4	1.7	1.7	1.8	5.7	7.3	8.1
Total assets	104.9	120.2	138.2	31.4	32.3	35	2.7	2.8	3.0	13.2	15.1	16.5
Short-term debt	6.2	7.6	8.4	0.9	0.5	0.8	0.0	0.0	0.0	0.0	0.3	0.1
Total current liabilities	37.4	43.2	48.8	8.3	8.2	9.6	0.7	0.8	0.9	5.0	6.2	6.6
Long-term debt	17.1	20.1	26.4	10.2	9.0	9.1	0.3	0.3	0.3	1.3	1.0	0.7
Total liabilities	61.8	70.7	85	20.3	19.3	20.8	1.1	1.2	1.3	6.6	7.5	7.6
Shareholders' equity	43.6	49.4	53.2	11.1	13.0	14.2	1.6	1.7	1.7	6.6	7.6	8.9
Financial ratios												
Total asset turnover**	2.5	2.4	2.3	1.5	1.4	1.5	2.6	2.8	2.9	3.2	3.2	3.2
Receivables turnover***	199.0	169.5	116.9	8.3	9.2	9.2	227.0	309.2	722.7	76.5	143.6	94.7
Inventory turnover****	7.5	7.4	7.5	6.0	5.8	6.0	4.1	3.9	4.1	11.2	11.6	11.5
Debt/Equity	1.4	1.4	1.6	1.8	1.5	1.5	0.7	0.7	0.8	1.0	1.0	0.9
Return on assets	9.0%	9.3%	8.9%	5.9%	5.9%	6.9%	11.1%	12.3%	11.7%	5.5%	5.8%	6.4%
Return on equity	21.0%	22.6%	22.5%	14.5%	17.0%	18.0%	20.4%	20.4%	15.0%	11.6%	11.1%	11.0%

* For Wal-Mart, calculated as Net sales + Other income.

** Sales/Total assets.

*** Sales/Receivables.

**** COGS/Inventory.

SOURCES: HOOVERS.COM; VALUELINE.COM

Wal-Mart Stores' Operations and Activities[8]

Purchasing and Vendor Relationships

The size of Wal-Mart's purchases and its negotiating ability means that Wal-Mart is both desired and feared by manufacturers. Being accepted as a Wal-Mart vendor offers access to a huge share of the US retail market. At the same time, Wal-Mart buyers are well aware of their ability to take full advantage of economies of scale available to their suppliers and to squeeze their margins to razor-thin level. Purchasing is centralized. All dealing with US suppliers takes place at Wal-Mart's Bentonville headquarters. Would-be suppliers are escorted to one of 50 cubicles on "Vendor Row." Furnishings comprise just a table and folding chairs – sometimes no chairs. Suppliers regarded the experience of selling to Wal-Mart as intimidating and grueling: "Once you are ushered into one of the spartan little buyer's rooms, expect a steely eye across the table and be prepared to cut your price."[9] Another vendor commented: "All normal mating rituals are verboten. Their highest priority is making sure everybody at all times in all cases knows who's in charge . . . They talk softly, but they have piranha hearts, and if you aren't totally prepared when you go in there, you're in deep trouble."[10] The requirements that Wal-Mart imposes on its suppliers extends well beyond low prices. Increasingly Wal-Mart involves itself in its suppliers' employment policies, including workplace safety, working hours, and absence of child labor.

All negotiations are directly between manufacturers and Wal-Mart: Wal-Mart refuses to do business with manufacturers' representatives and agents. To avoid dependence on any one supplier, Wal-Mart limits the total purchases it obtains from any one supplier. The result is an asymmetry of bargaining power. Thus, Wal-Mart's biggest supplier, Procter & Gamble, accounts for about 3% of Wal-Mart's sales – but this represents 18% of P&G's sales.

International expansion has allowed Wal-Mart to increase its purchasing muscle through global procurement. By 2003, Asda was sourcing over 2,000 products from Wal-Mart's global network. This network included 23 procurement offices in 23 countries.[11]

During the past ten years, Wal-Mart established closer collaborative arrangement with its biggest suppliers. Wal-Mart's cooperation with Procter & Gamble provided a model for these relationships. The companies began electronic data interchange (EDI) at the beginning of the 1990s, and by 1993 there were 70 P&G employees working at Bentonville to manage sales and deliveries to Wal-Mart.

By the mid-1990s, Wal-Mart had extended EDI to cover about 70% of its vendors. Through Wal-Mart's "Retail Link" system of supply chain management, data interchange included point-of-sale data, levels of inventory, Wal-Mart's sales forecasts, vendors' production and delivery schedules, and electronic funds transfer.

Through collaboration with Cisco Systems, Retail Link was moved to the internet during the mid-1990s allowing suppliers to log on to the Wal-Mart database for real-time store-by-store information on sales and inventory for their products. This allows suppliers to work with Wal-Mart company's buyers to manage inventory in the stores – forecasting, planning, producing, and shipping products as needed. The result is faster replenishment, a product mix tuned to the needs of local customers, and lower inventory costs for Wal-Mart. A key benefit to suppliers is their ability to match production scheduling to Wal-Mart's sales.

Warehousing and Distribution

Wal-Mart was regarded as one of the world's leaders in logistics. It distributed a higher proportion of goods to its own stores than any other discount retailer. While most discount retailers relied heavily upon their suppliers to undertake distribution to individual stores, 81% of Wal-Mart's purchases were shipped to Wal-Mart's own distribution centers from where they were distributed in Wal-Mart trucks. The efficiency of the system rested on Wal-Mart's "hub and spoke" configuration. Distribution centers ("hubs") spanned over a million square feet, operated 24-hours, and served around 150 stores within a 200 mile radius. Deliveries into distribution centers were either in suppliers' trucks or Wal-Mart trucks, then deliveries were made to Wal-Mart stores. Grouping of Wal-Mart stores allowed trucks to deliver partial loads to several Wal-Mart stores on a single trip. On backhauls, Wal-Mart trucks would bring returned merchandise from stores and also pick up from local vendors. As a result, trucks were more than 60% full on backhauls. Unlike most retailers, which outsourced trucking, Wal-Mart owned some 3,500 trucks and some 14,000 trailers.

Wal-Mart was continually seeking ways to make its distribution system cheaper, faster, and more reliable. It was an early adopter of "cross-docking" – a system where goods arriving on inbound trucks were unloaded and reloaded on outbound trucks without entering warehouse inventory. In 2005, Wal-Mart introduced its "Remix" system designed to reduce inventories, speed deliveries to stores, and eliminate stock-outs. The new system created a new tier to Wal-Mart's distribution system. Third-party logistic companies were made responsible for making smaller, more frequent pickups from suppliers, establishing "consolidation centers" throughout the US, then making frequent deliveries to Wal-Mart's distribution centers. The new system would allow Wal-Mart to order from suppliers on a five-day rather than four-week basis and would lead to lower inventories in both distribution centers and retail stores.

In 2005, Wal-Mart extended its tightly controlled logistical system to embrace products from overseas suppliers. Its "direct import" initiative involved, first, purchasing directly from overseas suppliers rather than through importers and, second, taking control of import logistics. Covering 4 million square feet, its import distribution center in Baytown, Texas was America's largest distribution facility devoted to a single company's products. Not only did the new distribution center give Wal-Mart the opportunity to exert greater control over its supplies of imports, it allowed it to avoid the delays and congestion of west-coast ports such as Long Beach.[12]

In-Store Operations

Wal-Mart's management of its retail stores was based upon its objective of creating customer satisfaction by combining low prices, a wide range of quality products carefully tailored to customer needs, and a pleasing shopping experience. Wal-Mart's management of its retail stores was distinguished by the following characteristics:

- *Merchandising.* Wal-Mart stores offered a wide range of nationally branded products. Although Wal-Mart also sold its own brand – especially in clothing – it gave less emphasis to own-brand products than other retailers (e.g., Sears). Under its "Store of the Community" philosophy, Wal-Mart sought to tailor its selection of merchandise to the characteristics of the local market. Point-of-sale data for individual stores greatly assisted responsiveness to local needs (see below).

- *Decentralization of store management.* Individual store managers were given considerable decision-making authority in relation to product range, product positioning within stores, and pricing. This differed from most other discount chains where decisions over pricing and merchandising were made either at head office or at regional offices. Decentralized decision-making power was also apparent within stores, where the managers of individual departments (e.g., toys, health and beauty, consumer electronics) were expected to develop and implement their own ideas for increasing sales and reducing costs.

- *Customer service.* Discount stores were open 9 a.m. to 9 p.m. weekdays, with shorter hours on weekends. Supercenters were open continuously. Despite the fanatical emphasis on cost efficiency, Wal-Mart went to great lengths to engage with its customers at a personal level. Stores employed "greeters" – often retired individuals – who would welcome customers and hand out shopping baskets. Within the store, all employees were expected to look customers in the eye, smile at them, and offer a verbal greeting. To encourage customer loyalty, Wal-Mart maintained a "Satisfaction Guaranteed" program. This program assured customers that Wal-Mart would accept returned merchandise on a no-questions-asked basis.

Marketing

Wal-Mart had been founded on Sam Walton's belief that: "There is only one boss: the customer." For Wal-Mart, the essence of customer service was low prices. Hence, Wal-Mart's marketing strategy rested primarily upon its slogan "Everyday Low Prices" – the message that Wal-Mart's price cutting strategy was not restricted to particular products or to particular time periods, but was a basic principle of Wal-Mart's business.

As a result of its customer-focused, value-for-money approach, Wal-Mart was able to rely on word-of-mouth communication of its merits, and was able to spend comparatively little on advertising and promotion. Advertising spending was limited to one advertisement circular per month per store and some television advertising. During the early 1990s, Wal-Mart spent only 0.5% of every sales dollar on advertising, compared with 2.5% for Kmart and 3.5% for Sears. By 2006, Wal-Mart's advertising sales ratio was still 0.5%, one quarter that of Target.

In its attempt to identify itself with its local communities and build relationships with customers, Wal-Mart had always placed strong emphasis on patriotism and national causes. However, as it became a target for politicians and pressure groups, Wal-Mart was forced to put more effort into refining and projecting its image. In November 2005, CEO Lee Scott announced Wal-Mart's commitment to environmental sustainability and set ambitious targets for energy and waste reduction.[12]

Information Technology

Wal-Mart was a pioneer in applying information and communications technology to support decision making and promote efficiency and customer responsiveness. During the 1970s, Wal-Mart was among the first retailers to use computers for inventory control, to initiate electronic data interchange (EDI) with its vendors, and to introduce bar code scanning for point-of-sale and inventory control. To link stores and cash register sales with supply chain management and inventory control, Wal-

Mart invested $24 million in its own satellite in 1984. By 1990, Wal-Mart's satellite system was the largest two-way, fully integrated private satellite network in the world, providing two-way interactive voice and video capability, data transmission for inventory control, credit card authorization, and enhanced EDI.

During the 1990s Wal-Mart was pioneering the use of data-mining for retail merchandising:

> At Wal-Mart, information technology gives us that knowledge in the most direct way: by collecting and analyzing our own internal information on exactly what any given shopping cart contains. The popular term is "data-mining," and Wal-Mart has been doing it since about 1990. The result, by now, is an enormous database of purchasing information that enables us to place the right item in the right store at the right price. Our computer system receives 8.4 million updates every minute on the items that customers take home – and the relationship between the items in each basket.
>
> Data analysis allows Wal-Mart to forecast, replenish, and merchandise on a product-by-product, store-by-store level. For example, with years of sales data and information on weather, school schedules, and other pertinent variables, Wal-Mart can predict daily sales of Gatorade at a specific store and automatically adjust store deliveries accordingly.[14]

Point-of-sale data analysis also assisted in planning store layout:

> There are some obvious purchasing patterns among the register receipts of families with infants and small children. Well-thought-out product placement not only simplifies the shopping trip for these customers – with baby aisles that include infant clothes and children's medicine alongside diapers, baby food and formula – but at the same time places higher-margin products among the staples . . .
>
> Customers who buy suitcases are likely to be looking for other items they might need for traveling too – such as travel alarms and irons, which now, logically enough, can be found displayed alongside luggage at many Wal-Mart stores.
>
> The common thread is simple: We are here to serve the customer; and customers tend to buy from us when we make it easy for them. That sounds like a simple idea. But first you must understand the customer's needs. And that's where information comes in.[15]

Most important was the role of IT in linking and integrating the whole of Wal-Mart's value chain:

> Wal-Mart's web of information systems extends far beyond the walls of any one store. Starting from the basic information compiled at the checkout stand, at the shelves, and gathered by associates equipped with hand-held computer monitors, Wal-Mart works to manage its supplies and inventories not only in the stores, but all the way back to the original source. Wal-Mart has given suppliers access to some of our systems, which enables them to know exactly what is selling, and to plan their production accordingly. This not only helps us keep inventories under control, but also helps the supplier deliver the lowest-cost product to the customer. With sales and in-stock information transmitted between Wal-Mart and our supplier-partners in seconds over the internet, buyers and suppliers are privy to the same facts and negotiate based on a shared understanding – saving a significant amount of time and energy over more traditional, low-tech systems.

Our buyer benefits from the supplier's product knowledge, while the supplier benefits from Wal-Mart's experience in the market. Combine these information systems with our logistics – our hub-and-spoke system in which distribution centers are placed within a day's truck run of the stores – and all the pieces fall into place for the ability to respond to the needs of our customers, before they are even in the store. In today's retailing world, speed is a crucial competitive advantage. And when it comes to turning information into improved merchandising and service to the customer, Wal-Mart is out in front and gaining speed. In the words of Randy Mott, Senior Vice President and Chief Information Officer, "The surest way to predict the future is to invent it." [16]

Early in 2004, Wal-Mart pioneered the use of radio-frequency identification (RFID) tags embodying electronic product codes for tracking pallets and cases of merchandise throughout its system. Trials showed that RFID allows sharp reductions in stockouts, faster replenishment, reduced inventory, and allows manual orders from stores to be replaced by automated ordering.

Human Resource Management

Wal-Mart's human resource policies are based closely on Sam Walton's ideas about relations between the company and its employees and between employees and customers. All employees – from executive-level personnel to checkout clerks – are known as "associates." Wal-Mart's relations with its associates are founded on respect, high expectations, close communication, and clear incentives.

Although Wal-Mart's employees receive relatively low pay (in common with most of the retail trade), Wal-Mart offered strong profit incentives for employees and encouraged them to share in its wealth creation through its stock ownership scheme. Numerous employees have retired as millionaires as a result of their participation in the plan. Most of these were managers; however, in 1989, the first millionaire hourly associate retired from the company.

Wal-Mart resisted the unionization of its employees in the belief that union membership created a barrier between the management and the employees in furthering the success of the company and its members. Despite strenuous efforts by unions to recruit Wal-Mart employees, union penetration remained low. Between 2000 and 2004, the United Food and Commercial Workers together with AFL-CIO fought a concerted campaign to recruit Wal-Mart workers, but to little effect. [17]

Associates enjoyed a high degree of autonomy and received continuous communication about their company's performance and about store operations. Every aspect of company operations and strategy was seen as depending on the close collaboration of managers and shop-floor employees. To control "shrinkage" (theft), the company instituted a system whereby a store's cost savings from reduced shrinkage were shared between the company and the store's employees. Wal-Mart's shrinkage was estimated to be just above 1%, versus an industry average of 2%.

Wal-Mart's approach to employee involvement made heavy use of orchestrated demonstration of enthusiasm and commitment. The central feature of Wal-Mart meetings from corporate to store level was the "Wal-Mart Cheer" – devised by Sam Walton after a visit to Korea. The call and response ritual ("Give me a W!" "Give me an A!" . . .) included the "Wal-Mart squiggly," which involved employees shaking their backsides in unison.

Fortune suggested that the Wal-Mart Cheer's mixture of homespun and corporate themes provided an apt metaphor for what it called "the Wal-Mart paradox":

> *The paradox is that Wal-Mart stands for both Main Street values and the efficiencies of the huge corporation, aw-shucks hokeyness and terabytes of minute-by-minute sales data, fried-chicken luncheons at the Waltons' Arkansas home and the demands of Wall Street.*
>
> *Critics of Wal-Mart call the homespun stuff a fraud, a calculated strategy to put a human face on a relentlessly profit-minded corporation. What is paradoxical and suspect to people outside Wal-Mart, however, is perfectly normal to the people who work there. It reflects a deal that Sam Walton, Wal-Mart's founder, made with the people who worked for him.*
>
> *The deal was a lot more than just a matter of the occasional visit from Mr. Sam. Wal-Mart demonstrated its concern for workers in many ways that were small but specific: time and a half for work on Sundays, an "open door" policy that let workers bring concerns to managers at any level, the real chance of promotion (about 70% of store managers started as hourly associates).*[18]

The paradox of Wal-Mart's human resource practices continues. The enthusiasm it generates among employees supports a level of involvement and empowerment that is unique among large retail organizations. At the same time, the intense pressure for cost reduction and sales growth frequently results in cases of employee abuse, from unpaid overtime, discrimination, and unfair dismissal.

Organization and Management Style

Wal-Mart's management structure and management style had been molded by Sam Walton's principles and values. As Wal-Mart grew in size and geographical scope, Walton was determined that corporate executives should keep closely in touch with customers and store operations. The result was a structure in which communication between individual stores and the Bentonville headquarters was both close and personal. Wal-Mart's regional vice presidents were each responsible for supervising between ten and fifteen district managers (who, in turn, were in charge of eight to twelve stores). The key to Wal-Mart's fast-response management system was the close linkage between the stores and headquarters. Former CEO, David Glass explained the system:

> *The idea is very simple. Nothing very constructive happens in the office. Everybody else had gone to regional offices – Sears, Kmart, everybody – but we decided to send everybody from Bentonville out to the stores Monday though Thursday. And bring them back Thursday night. On Friday morning we'd have our merchandising meetings. But on Saturday morning we'd have our sales for the week. And we'd have the other information from people who'd been out in the field. They're telling us what our competitors are doing, and we get reports from people in the regions who had been traveling though the week. So we decide then what corrective action we want to take. And before noon on Saturday the regional manager was required to be hooked up by phone to all his district managers, giving them direction as to what we were going to do or change. By noon on Saturday we had all our corrections in place. Our competitors, for the most part, got their sales results on Monday for the week prior. Now, they're already ten days behind, and we've already made the corrections.*[19]

The Saturday morning meeting is preceded by three other key corporate meetings. On Thursday afternoon is the operations meeting. This is attended by 70 senior executives and logistics, planning, and information managers. The meetings review non-merchandising matters – including inventory management, supply chain efficiencies, and new store development. The meetings are held standing to encourage brevity.

Fridays begin with the 7 a.m. management meeting, which involves Wal-Mart's 200 most senior managers. To attend these meetings Wal-Mart's 39 regional vice presidents need to return on Thursday evening from their territories to the Bentonville "home office." The meetings deal with strategic and critical operational matters. At lunchtime, in the same auditorium, the merchandising meeting takes place. Here, buyers and corporate executives meet. The purpose of the meeting is, first, to give buyers direct insights into what is selling and what is not; second, to give the regional VPs a means to get instant action to solve merchandising problems in their stores; third, to report on what the competition is doing. The meeting deals with stockouts, excess inventory, new product ideas, and a variety of merchandising errors. By the early afternoon the regional VPs and merchandisers will be emailed a "priority note" of specific actions that they should take action on by the end of the day.

It is the two-and-a-half-hour Saturday morning meeting, however, that is the week's high point and the clearest representation of Wal-Mart's unique management style:

> *The meeting is the soul of this behemoth . . . It is the template for other vital gatherings that have evolved throughout the company, ranging from the daily shift-change meetings at the stores to the weekly management, merchandising, and operations meetings at the home office to the five company-wide mega-meetings each year that draw more than 10,000 participants apiece. Not only do these assemblies reinforce and personalize Wal-Mart's almost evangelical culture among its 1.5 million "associates" worldwide, but they are also largely responsible for the retailing giant's amazing agility in the aisles. The meetings enable the company to continue to operate its entire business on a weekly and sometimes a daily basis, just as the founder managed his first five-and-dime, moving quickly to outflank competition and growing almost as a matter of routine.[20]*

The Saturday meetings are a remarkable mixture of information sharing, educational inputs, and motivation recharging. They begin with a review of the week's performance data, then involve question and answer sessions targeting examples of good and bad performance. There are also presentations that focus on merchandising best practices or new product lines, and guest appearances that might include CEOs such as Carlos Ghosn, Steve Jobs, or Jack Welch, or celebrity singers or sports stars. The meetings close with a talk from the CEO.

Management development is a critical aspect of the Wal-Mart management system. Wal-Mart emphasizes internal recruitment and developing managers through moving them between line and staff positions and across functions. Most of Wal-Mart's senior managers are company veterans who have spent most of their careers in retailing. A large number of them are from Wal-Mart's mid-west and southwest heartland (see table 5.5).

TABLE 5.5 Wal-Mart's executive team

Name	Position	Joined W-M	Education
Eduardo Castro-Wright	EVP, President and CEO, Wal-Mart Stores Division	2001	Texas A&M University
M. Susan Chambers	EVP, People Division	1999	William Jewell College, Missouri
Patricia A. Curran	EVP, Store Operations	1983	N/A
Leslie A. Dach	EVP, Corporate Affairs and Government Relations	2006	Yale; Harvard
Douglas J. Degn	EVP, Food Merchandising	1983	University of Kansas
Linda M. Dillman	EVP, Risk Management and Benefits Administration	1991	University of Indianapolis
Johnnie C. Dobbs	EVP, Logistics and Supply Chain	1990	East Texas State University
Michael T. Duke	Vice Chairman, International	1995	Georgia Tech
John J. Fitzsimmons	SVP and Treasurer	1994	Notre Dame; University of Chicago
Rollin L. Ford	EVP and Chief Information Officer	1983	Taylor University, Indiana
Mark D. Goodman	EVP, Marketing, Membership & E-Commerce, Sam's Club	N/A	College of Wooster, Ohio; Tufts
Craig R. Herkert	EVP, President and CEO, Americas region, International	2000	St. Francis College; Northern Illinois University
Charles M. Holley	SVP, Finance	1994	University of Texas (Austin); University of Houston
Thomas D. Hyde	EVP and Corporate Secretary	2001	University of Kansas: University of Missouri
Lawrence V. Jackson	EVP, President and CEO, Global Procurement	N/A	Harvard
Gregory L. Johnston	EVP, Club Operations, Sam's Club	1982	N/A
Thomas A. Mars	SVP and General Counsel	2002	University of Arkansas
C. Douglas McMillon	EVP, President and CEO, Sam's Club	1984	University of Arkansas; University of Tulsa
John B. Menzer	Vice Chairman, United States	1995	Loyola University, Chicago
Thomas M. Schoewe	EVP and Chief Financial Officer	2000	Loyola University, Chicago; University of Chicago
H. Lee Scott	President and CEO	1979	Pittsburgh State University
William S. Simon	EVP, Professional Services, Wal-Mart Stores	2006	University of Connecticut
Gregory E. Spragg	EVP, Merchandising and Replenishment, Sam's Club	1998	North Carolina State University
S. Robson Walton	Chairman of the Board	1969	University of Arkansas; Columbia University
Claire A. Watts	EVP, Product Development	1997	University of Cincinnati
Eric S. Zorn	EVP and President, Wal-Mart Realty	1993	Fairleigh Dickinson University, NJ

SOURCE: WAL-MART 10-K REPORT, 2006.

Appendix
The Wal-Mart Culture

As Wal-Mart continues to grow into new areas and new mediums, our success will always be attributed to our culture. Whether you walk into a Wal-Mart store in your hometown or one across the country while you're on vacation, you can always be assured you're getting low prices and that genuine customer service you've come to expect from us. You'll feel at home in any department of any store . . . that's our culture.

Sam Walton's Three Basic Beliefs

Sam Walton built Wal-Mart on the revolutionary philosophies of excellence in the workplace, customer service and always having the lowest prices. We have always stayed true to the Three Basic Beliefs Mr. Sam established in 1962:

Respect the Individual

" 'Our people make the difference' is not a meaningless slogan – it's a reality at Wal-Mart. We are a group of dedicated, hardworking, ordinary people who have teamed together to accomplish extraordinary things. We have very different backgrounds, different colors and different beliefs, but we do believe that every individual deserves to be treated with respect and dignity."
– Don Soderquist, Senior Vice Chairman, Wal-Mart Stores, Inc.

Service to Our Customers

We want our customers to trust in our pricing philosophy and to always be able to find the lowest prices with the best possible service. We're nothing without our customers.

"Wal-Mart's culture has always stressed the importance of Customer Service. Our Associate base across the country is as diverse as the communities in which we have Wal-Mart stores. This allows us to provide the Customer Service expected from each individual customer that walks into our stores." – Tom Coughlin, President and chief executive officer, Wal-Mart Stores division.

Strive for Excellence

New ideas and goals make us reach further than ever before. We try to find new and innovative ways to push our boundaries and constantly improve. "Sam was never satisfied that prices were as low as they needed to be or that our product's quality was as high as they deserved – he believed in the concept of striving for excellence before it became a fashionable concept." – Lee Scott, President and CEO.

Sam's Rules for Building a Business

People often ask, "What is Wal-Mart's secret to success?"

In response to this ever-present question, in his 1992 book *Made in America*, Sam Walton compiled a list of ten key factors that unlock the mystery. These factors are known as "Sam's Rules for Building a Business."

Rule 1. Commit to your business. Believe in it more than anybody else. I think I overcame every single one of my personal shortcomings by the sheer passion I brought to my work. I don't know if you're born with this kind of passion, or if you can learn it. But I do know you need it. If you love your work, you'll be out there every day trying to do it the best you possibly can, and pretty soon everybody around will catch the passion from you – like a fever.

Rule 2. Share your profits with all your Associates, and treat them as partners. In turn, they will treat you as a partner, and together you will all perform beyond your wildest expectations. Remain a corporation and retain control if you like, but behave as a servant leader in a partnership. Encourage your Associates to hold a stake in the company. Offer discounted stock, and grant them stock for their retirement. It's the single best thing we ever did.

Rule 3. Motivate your partners. Money and ownership alone aren't enough. Constantly, day-by-day, think of new and more interesting ways to motivate and challenge your partners. Set high goals, encourage competition, and then keep score. Make bets with outrageous payoffs. If things get stale, cross-pollinate; have managers switch jobs with one another to stay challenged. Keep everybody guessing as to what your next trick is going to be. Don't become too predictable.

Rule 4. Communicate everything you possibly can to your partners. The more they know, the more they'll understand. The more they understand, the more they'll care. Once they care, there's no stopping them. If you don't trust your Associates to know what's going on, they'll know you don't really consider them partners. Information is power, and the gain you get from empowering your Associates more than offsets the risk of informing your competitors.

Rule 5. Appreciate everything your Associates do for the business. A paycheck and a stock option will buy one kind of loyalty. But all of us like to be told how much somebody appreciates what we do for them. We like to hear it often, and especially when we have done something we're really proud of. Nothing else can quite substitute for a few well-chosen, well-timed, sincere words of praise. They're absolutely free – and worth a fortune.

Rule 6. Celebrate your successes. Find some humor in your failures. Don't take yourself so seriously. Loosen up, and everybody around you will loosen up. Have fun. Show enthusiasm – always. When all else fails, put on a costume and sing a silly song. Then make everybody else sing with you. Don't do a hula on Wall Street. It's been done. Think up your own stunt. All of this is more important, and more fun, than you think, and it really fools the competition. "Why should we take those cornballs at Wal-Mart seriously?"

Rule 7. Listen to everyone in your company. And figure out ways to get them talking. The folks on the front lines – the ones who actually talk to the customer – are the only ones who really know what's going on out there. You'd better find out what they know. This really is what total quality is all about. To push responsibility down in your organization, and to force good ideas to bubble up within it, you must listen to what your Associates are trying to tell you.

Rule 8. Exceed your customers' expectations. If you do, they'll come back over and over. Give them what they want – and a little more. Let them know you appreciate them. Make good on all your mistakes, and don't make excuses – apologize. Stand behind everything you do. The two most important words I ever wrote were on that first Wal-Mart sign, "Satisfaction Guaranteed." They're still up there, and they have made all the difference.

Rule 9. Control your expenses better than your competition. This is where you can always find the competitive advantage. For 25 years running – long before Wal-Mart was known as the nation's largest retailer – we ranked No. 1 in our industry for the lowest ratio of expenses to sales. You can make a lot of different mistakes and still recover if you run an efficient operation. Or you can be brilliant and still go out of business if you're too inefficient.

Rule 10. Swim upstream. Go the other way. Ignore the conventional wisdom. If everybody else is doing it one way, there's a good chance you can find your niche by going in exactly the opposite direction. But be prepared for a lot of folks to wave you down and tell you you're headed the wrong way. I guess in all my years, what I heard more often than anything was: a town of less than 50,000 population cannot support a discount store for very long.

Source: "The Wal-Mart Culture" from www.walmartstores.com (includes "Sam's Rules for Building a Business." from Sam Walton and John Huey, *Made in America*, Doubleday, 1992).

Notes

1 Sam Walton, *Sam Walton: Made in America*, New York: Bantam Books, 1992.

2 *Forbes*, August 16, 1982, p. 43.

3 G. C. Strachan, *The State of the Discount Store Industry*, Goldman Sachs, April 1994 (quoted in *Wal-Mart Stores, Inc.*, Harvard Business School Case No. 9-974-024, 1994).

4 From the Wal-Mart website: www.walmart.com.

5 Sam Walton, *Sam Walton: Made in America*, New York: Bantam Books, 1992.

6 http://www.walmart.com/cservice/aw_samsway.gsp.

7 Wal-Mart Stores, Inc. Annual Report, 2000.

8 This description of Wal-Mart's retailing operations refers primarily to its US discount stores.

9 Bill Saporito, 'A week aboard the Wal-Mart Express," *Fortune*, August 24, 1992, p. 79.

10 Ibid.

11 "At Wal-Mart, less is more," *Journal of Commerce*, November 2005.

12 "Inside the world's biggest store," *Time Europe*, January 20, 2003.

13 "The Green Machine," *Fortune*, July 31, 2006.

14 Wal-Mart Stores, Inc. Annual Report, 1999, p. 9.

15 Ibid., p. 9.

16 Ibid., p. 11.

17 "Unions vs. Wal-Mart: Up against the Wal-Mart," *Fortune*, May 17, 2004.

18 "Sam Walton made us a promise," *Fortune*, March 18, 2002.

19 "The most underrated CEO ever," *Fortune*, April 5, 2004, pp. 242–8.

20 "Wal-Mart's $288 billion meeting," *Fortune*, April 18, 2005.

Manchester United: The Glazer Takeover

On June 14, 2005, US businessman Malcolm Glazer announced he had acquired over 90% of the shares of Manchester United plc. This would allow him to delist Manchester United's shares from the London Stock Exchange and turn it into a private company. Glazer's offer of £3 per share was over 40 times the previous year's net income and was almost double the average market price of Man United's shares during the preceding three years. All told, the buyout cost was £812 million – mainly financed by borrowings of £540 million. For the first time in its history, the club would go into debt.

The takeover generated outrage among Man United's most loyal fans. The *Financial Times* reported:

> The level of anger among Manchester United fans was palpable as they gathered last night outside the Theatre of Dreams, the name the club gives to its Old Trafford ground. A big "Not For Sale" sign was quickly erected on the club's gates. Rob Adams, a lifelong fan, said: "It is the worst thing that could have happened . . . He [Mr. Glazer] is a businessman and all he wants to do is scoop as much money out of the club as possible." Another said: "He's just not interested in the game of football."
>
> Margaret Crhan, company secretary of Shareholders United, which has been leading the fight against the Glazer bid, said: "We are opposed to any single person owning the club. It is 126 years old and belongs to the community it serves. We are opposed to anyone who is going to take away the fans' voices. You are talking £800m – none of which is his money. Who is going to have to pay it back? The profit that this club produces is not going to even pay the interest on what he is going to borrow. It is our money; we are the ones that put bums on seats; we buy the shirts and all the rest."

This case was written by Robert M. Grant and Simon I. Peck, assisted by Aude Le Minor and Drew Hoffman

The takeover had come at a critical juncture in Man United's development. It was the most financially successful professional sports team in the world – certainly the biggest earning soccer club, generating £172 million in revenue and £58.3 million in operating profit. However, its performance on the field seemed to be waning. Under the leadership of veteran team manager Alex Ferguson, the club had dominated English football for most of the 1990s.[1] Since 2001, however, Man United had been eclipsed first by Arsenal and then by Chelsea.

The question in the minds of many observers was whether Glazer could do anything to enhance Man United's performance, either financially or on the field. Unlike Chelsea's acquisition by Russian billionaire Roman Abramovich, Glazer's takeover would almost certainly leave Man United less able to lavish money on new players and facilities (it had been rumored that Glazer wished to limit expenditure on new players to £25 million a year). The consensus among financial experts was that Glazer had made a bad investment. He had paid a massive premium for a company that, in financial terms, was performing at the top of its game. Underlying both these doubts was concern that Glazer brought little relevant expertise to the club. Not only did Glazer know little about the game of soccer, it was unclear as to whether his experience as owner of the US National Football League team Tampa Bay Buccaneers was in any way relevant to Man United – arguably one of the most effectively managed professional sports teams in the world, with a global fan base and licensing revenues to match. Glazer's suggestions for expanding Man United's franchise and seeking an independent deal over television rights failed to impress most observers. The London *Sunday Times* noted that Man United fans were already deluged by commercial offers from their club – and not just with "£45 replica shirts . . . but their own MUTV subscription television channel, Manchester United credit cards, broadband internet access, loans, car insurance, home insurance, ISAs. Even mortgages."[2]

The Competitive Environment

The English League

The top league in English professional football is the Premier League, comprising the top 20 English teams. Each team plays every other team twice, once at home and once away, with teams receiving three points for a win, one for a tie, and zero for a loss. At the end of every season, the three teams at the bottom of the Premier League are replaced by the top three in the league below. The Premier League team that accumulates the most points throughout the season wins the English League Championship.

The governing body for English football is the Football Association (FA). The FA Cup pits teams from all the English leagues in a single elimination tournament – allowing little-known teams from the lower divisions to compete (and sometimes win) against the top clubs. Table 6.1 shows the league champions and FA Cup winners in English football between 1970 and 2005.

The European League

The Champions League is composed of the 32 top teams in European football. Teams qualify by finishing at or near the top of their respective national leagues. In England

TABLE 6.1 The top performing clubs in English football, 1970–2005

	League champion	Second place	Third place	FA Cup winner
2005	Chelsea	Arsenal	Manchester United	Arsenal
2004	Arsenal	Chelsea	Manchester United	Manchester United
2003	Manchester United	Arsenal	Newcastle United	Arsenal
2002	Arsenal	Liverpool	Manchester United	Arsenal
2001	Manchester United	Arsenal	Liverpool	Liverpool
2000	Manchester United	Arsenal	Leeds United	Chelsea
1999	Manchester United	Arsenal	Chelsea	Manchester United
1998	Arsenal	Manchester United	Liverpool	Arsenal
1997	Manchester United	Newcastle United	Arsenal	Chelsea
1996	Manchester United	Newcastle United	Liverpool	Manchester United
1995	Blackburn Rovers	Manchester United	Nottingham Forest	Everton
1994	Manchester United	Blackburn Rovers	Newcastle United	Manchester United
1993	Manchester United	Aston Villa	Norwich City	Arsenal
1992	Leeds United	Manchester United	Sheffield Wednesday	Liverpool
1991	Arsenal	Liverpool	Crystal Palace	Tottenham Hotspur
1990	Liverpool	Aston Villa	Tottenham Hotspur	Manchester United
1989	Arsenal	Liverpool	Nottingham Forest	Liverpool
1988	Liverpool	Manchester United	Nottingham Forest	Milton Keynes Dons
1987	Everton	Liverpool	Tottenham Hotspur	Coventry City
1986	Liverpool	Everton	West Ham United	Liverpool
1985	Everton	Liverpool	Tottenham Hotspur	Manchester United
1984	Liverpool	Southampton	Nottingham Forest	Everton
1983	Liverpool	Watford	Manchester United	Manchester United
1982	Liverpool	Ipswich Town	Manchester United	Tottenham Hotspur
1981	Aston Villa	Ipswich Town	Arsenal	Tottenham Hotspur
1980	Liverpool	Manchester United	Ipswich Town	West Ham United
1979	Liverpool	Nottingham Forest	West Bromwich Albion	Arsenal
1978	Nottingham Forest	Liverpool	Everton	Ipswich Town
1977	Liverpool	Manchester City	Ipswich Town	Manchester United
1976	Liverpool	Queen's Park Rangers	Manchester United	Southampton
1975	Derby County	Liverpool	Ipswich Town	West Ham United
1974	Leeds United	Liverpool	Derby County	Liverpool
1973	Liverpool	Arsenal	Leeds United	Sunderland
1972	Derby County	Leeds United	Liverpool	Leeds United
1971	Arsenal	Leeds United	Tottenham Hotspur	Arsenal
1970	Everton	Leeds United	Chelsea	Chelsea

the top four teams qualify for the Champions League; in Scotland, the top two teams qualify. The latter phase of the Champions League season is a knockout competition that results in one team winning the European Cup. Winning this championship represents the highest accomplishment in European club football, both competitively and financially. The 2004/5 winners, Liverpool, were expected to earn almost £30 million from their victory.

TABLE 6.2 The top European football clubs: index of team performance 1997–2006

Club	Country	Points
Real Madrid	Spain	1,250
Bayern Munich	Germany	1,240
Barcelona	Spain	1,228
Manchester United	England	1,228
Juventus	Italy	1,139
Arsenal	England	1,135
Porto	Portugal	1,100
Internazionale (Milan)	Italy	1,081
PSV Eindhoven	Netherlands	1,057
AC Milan	Italy	1,039
Valencia	Spain	990
Olympiakos Piraeus	Greece	967
Chelsea	England	961
Lazio	Italy	938
Olympique Lyonnais	France	924
Ajax	Netherlands	913
Liverpool	England	912
Deportivo de La Coruña	Spain	909
Roma	Italy	869
Dynamo Kiev	Ukraine	867

Note: The rankings are based on performance in the following competitions:

● European Cup and Intertoto Cup. (Points for wins and draws, and bonus points dependent on the reached stage. Extra points dependent on the aggregate result and the strength of the opposing club.)

● National League. (Points dependent on final league position, weighted by strength of the national league.)

● National Cup. (Points dependent on the stage reached.)

SOURCE: WWW.EUROPEAN-FOOTBALL-STATISTICS.CO.UK

Table 6.2 shows the top teams in Europe based on performance in both national and European competitions.

The inauguration of the European Champions League in 1992 and the revenues and prestige that it conferred had a major impact on English league football. A widening financial gap appeared between the top performing teams and the rest as revenues from the European competition fueled the purchases of better players, reinforcing the tendency for the leading group of clubs to break away from the pack.[3]

Sources of Team Success

What factors determine team performance in professional soccer? Quality of players is the most obvious determinant of team quality. The world's leading players in 2005 are shown in table 6.3.

TABLE 6.3 FIFA world player rankings, 2005

	Player	Club	Country	Points
1	Ronaldinho	FC Barcelona	BRA	620
2	Frank Lampard	Chelsea	ENG	306
3	Samuel Eto'o	FC Barcelona	CAM	190
4	Thierry Henry	Arsenal	FRA	172
5	Adriano	Internazionale	BRA	170
6	Andrei Shevchenko	AC Milan	UKR	153
7	Steven Gerrard	Liverpool	ENG	131
8	Kakà	AC Milan	BRA	101
9	Paolo Maldini	AC Milan	ITA	76
10	Didier Drogba	Chelsea	IVO	65
11	Michael Ballack	Bayern Munich	GER	64
12	Ronaldo	Real Madrid	BRA	63
13	Zinedine Zidane	Real Madrid	FRA	55
14	Zlatan Ibrahimovic	Juventus	SWE	36
15	Deco	FC Barcelona	ESP	24
16	Juan Roman Riquelme	Villareal	ARG	20
17	Robinho	Real Madrid	BRA	19
18	David Beckham	Real Madrid	ENG	17
19	Wayne Rooney	Manchester United	ENG	17
20	Cristiano Ronaldo	Manchester United	POR	13
21	Ruud van Nistelrooy	Manchester United	NED	11
22	Michael Essien	Chelsea	GHA	11
23	Raúl	Real Madrid	ESP	8
24	Pavel Nedved	Juventus	CZE	8
25	Arjen Robben	Chelsea	NED	5
26	Cafu	AC Milan	BRA	3
27	Jay-Jay Okocha	Bolton	NIG	3
28	Alessandro Nesta	AC Milan	ITA	3
29	Roberto Carlos	Real Madrid	BRA	3
30	Gianluigi Buffon	Juventus	ITA	1

Note: Based on assessment by 157 managers and 145 captains of national teams.

Measured by the number and ranking of leading players, table 6.3 shows Europe's best teams were: (1) AC Milan, (2) Barcelona, (3) Real Madrid, (4) Chelsea, (5) Manchester United. Certainly, these were among the top performing teams shown in table 6.2. However, owning star players is not the only source of superior performance. Bayern Munich, PSV, Porto, Valencia, and Olympiakos Piraeus were among Europe's leading clubs despite an absence of superstar players. Conversely, other teams had spent heavily on acquiring top players while achieving little success on the field (e.g. Inter Milan during the 1990s and Chelsea prior to the arrival of current coach, Jose Morinho). If team performance was solely determined by quality of players, then Real Madrid might be expected to have dominated European football given its ownership of so many of the world's best players. Between the 1995/6 and 2004/5 seasons,

Real Madrid won the European Cup three times and the Primera Liga three times – a better record than any other club, but not by a large margin, and since 2003 Real have not won any major trophy.

If star players are essential to success, what determines a club's ability to acquire such players? Critical, of course, is money. Typically, the world's best players gravitate towards the clubs that have the financial resources to offer large transfer fees and pay attractive salaries. However, the market for players is hardly efficient. Not only are players tied to clubs through contracts (typically up to five years), but individual skills are multifaceted and difficult to access. A key role of the coach – or, in British parlance, the team manager – is to identify potential and to coax performance out of the player.

Indeed, the coach is the most important position in any club – he is the primary architect of the team and the single person most responsible for its success. The great football teams of the past were almost all associated with a single coach.[4] Yet, what determined a great coach was hard to judge. Coaches succeed with very different leadership styles. Ferguson's tough, aggressive style contrasted sharply with Sven Eriksson's (Lazio's former coach and national coach to the England team) calm, controlled demeanor, with Arsene Wenger's (Monaco and Arsenal) intellectual approach, or with Jose Mourinho's (successful at both Porto and Chelsea) obsessive, idiosyncratic style. Certain styles are appropriate to different teams and to different circumstances: coaches that achieve outstanding success with one team are often dismal failures with another.[5]

However, some common factors are apparent. An eye for talent appears to be critical. The ability to recognize outstanding football potential before it is fully developed is essential to nurturing that talent within a team context. Second, the ability to mix and balance individual players into effective team combinations is critical to team design and development. Finally, all great coaches are able to motivate their players and inspire respect and loyalty from them.

Among Europe's top teams in 2005, it was possible to observe a variety of strategies at work. Real Madrid's approach was simply to buy the world's best players. Real's president Florentino Perez explained: "It's the only possible economic and sporting model for this club . . . We have the best players and we have an important image in the world. Our strategy is for the best players to come and everyone knows who the best players are." AC Milan relied on mature talent. In their 2004/5 Champions League campaign, several of AC Milan's leading players were between the ages of 34 and 36; their youngest player was 25. Arsenal's Arsene Wenger ("The Professor") built the outstandingly successful team of 2002–4 on a strategy of worldwide sourcing of talented young players, meticulously rigorous training, and developing an interactive, highly flexible pattern of team play. Man United has concentrated on finding and developing young players, then blending young talent with highly experienced players.

Probably the greatest achievement for any coach is to build a great team out of unknown players with meager financial resources. Thus, Alex Ferguson's achievement at Aberdeen, Jose Mourinho's at Porto, Alf Ramsey's at Ipswich, and Jock Stein's at Glasgow Celtic were triumphs of capability building amidst humble resources.[6] Real Madrid and Chelsea's lavishing of vast sums of money to build star-studded teams is a strategy that can bring results – but it can also be viewed as a consequence of these clubs' inability to build teams through long-term internal development. Between 1985 and 2005 there were nine managers at Chelsea[7] and 19 at Real Madrid.[8]

TABLE 6.4 Revenues of the top five European national leagues, 2003/4

National league	Total revenue (euros, millions)	Matchday revenue	Broadcast revenue	Sponsorship and commercial revenue	Average annual revenue growth, 1995/6–2003/4
England	1,976	30%	45%	25%	+19%
Italy	1,153	16%	55%	29%	+12%
Germany	1,058	20%	28%	52%	+14%
Spain	953	29%	41%	30%	+14%
France	655	20%	52%	28%	+11%

SOURCE: DELOITTE & TOUCHE, *ANNUAL REVIEW OF FOOTBALL FINANCE*, JUNE 2005.

Football Finances

Revenues

The English football league was the most affluent of the European national leagues in terms of both total revenue and revenue growth. The English league accounted for nearly 2 billion of the 5.8 billion euros earned by the European top five national leagues in 2003/4 (see table 6.4).

The principal revenue sources were:

● *Matchday revenues.* Revenues from the sale of tickets were determined by the number of home games played, the average attendance, and average seat price. The English Premier League earned the highest matchday income based on its highest aggregate attendance and highest average seat price.[9] Increased matchday revenues were almost entirely due to increased prices. Across most of Europe, average match attendances were either static or declining. The exception was Germany where the development of new stadiums in anticipation of the 2006 World Cup competition had increased attendance.

In the English Premiership, average attendance per match was: 1999/00, 30,700; 2000/1, 32,800; 2001/2, 34,300; 2002/3, 35,400; 2003/4, 35,000; 2004/5, 33,900. In reality, most revenue from tickets comprised season ticket sales rather than sales on the day of the match. A growing source of income for the leading clubs was the sale of corporate boxes and VIP hospitality packages.[10]

● *Broadcasting revenues.* Football is the world's most popular televised sport (the US, Canada, and Japan are among a small group of countries where this is not the case). The world's most popular sporting event is the Football World Cup. The 2002 World Cup was televised in 213 countries during 41,000 hours of programming and attracted a cumulative audience of 28.8 billion viewers (aggregating the audiences for all the games broadcast). Club level games were broadcast on national TV and increasingly on overseas TV networks too. Broadcasting rights were negotiated between each of the national leagues and domestic TV and radio channels. In 2003/4 season, the English Premier League had contracts with BSkyB (a satellite broadcaster), ITV (a terrestrial broadcaster), and pay-per-view television. The total TV revenue (£427 million in 2003/4) was divided between clubs in the form of a "basic award" (identical for each Premier League club), a "facility fee" (according to the number of matches televised for each club), and "merit award" (determined by the final league position of the club).

TV rights for the Champions League were managed by the European governing body for football, UEFA. The international TV audience for Champions League games resulted in a massive revenue boost for those teams that qualified for the league. During 2003/4, UEFA distributed €414 million to the Champions League clubs, including €28.9 million to Chelsea, €28.4 million to Arsenal, €27.9 million to Man United, €26.3 million to Monaco, €19.7 million to Porto, and €19.5 million to Real Madrid.

- *Sponsorship and commercial revenues* comprised payments from companies for advertising rights at stadiums, on club communications and websites; sponsorship agreements (payments for a company's brand name appearing on the team's shirts and on other club materials); and licensing arrangements – payments to license a club's trademarks for the manufacture of official club merchandise (replica shirts, scarves, games, drinking mugs, toys, and various other products). Commercial and sponsorship revenues were highly concentrated on the leading clubs. Thus, in Spain Real Madrid and Barcelona accounted for 58% of the Primera Liga's total, while AC Milan and Juventus accounted for 38% of the Serie A's total.[11] Over time, the leading European clubs had become increasingly sophisticated in marketing, merchandising, and brand management. Real Madrid and Manchester United were viewed as the leaders in promoting and exploiting their brands. Most clubs had two major sponsors: a sports clothing company that supplied team kit (as well as replica kit for the mass market) and a sponsor whose name appeared prominently on the team's shirts. Real Madrid was sponsored by Adidas for kit and by Siemens Mobil (for 12 millions euros annually) to feature the Siemens brand on the shirts. Man United had a 13-year 460 million euro contract with Nike to outfit the club and a four-year 50.5 million euro contract with Vodafone to feature the brand on the Man United shirts.

A key thrust of the clubs' marketing strategies was to move beyond their local supporters to create national and international fan bases with associated brand awareness. Man United, with millions of fans outside the UK, was the leader in internationalization. International marketing efforts involved linking team tours to an overseas country with marketing initiatives and the closing of licensing deals.

The strength of a club's brand combined the brand equity of the club and those of its leading players. When French superstar Zidane signed for Real Madrid in 2001, 480,000 Real Madrid shirts featuring Zidane's name were sold in the following year. When David Beckham was transferred from Man United to Real Madrid in 2003, 350,000 Real Madrid shirts were sold in Britain in the space of less than a week. Signing foreign players can do much to extend a team's international reputation. Man United's commercial revenues from South Korea grew substantially after signing Ji-Sung Park to their team.

As a result of its massive fan base, strong team performance, and astute commercial management, Man United has consistently earned the highest revenues of any European football club (see table 6.5).

TABLE 6.5 European football clubs with greatest revenues

Team	Revenues 2003/4 (euros, millions)	Ranking by revenues 1996/7 to 2003/4
Manchester United	259	1
Real Madrid	236	2
AC Milan	222	5
Chelsea	217	7
Juventus	215	3
Arsenal	174	10
Barcelona	169	6
Inter Milan	167	8
Bayern Munich	166	4
Liverpool	140	9
Newcastle	137	11
Roma	109	13
Glasgow Celtic	104	19
Tottenham	100	16
Lazio	99	12
Manchester City	94	28
Schalke	91	21
Olympique Marseille	88	24
Glasgow Rangers	86	17
Aston Villa	84	25

SOURCE: DELOITTE & TOUCHE, ANNUAL REVIEW OF FOOTBALL FINANCE, JUNE 2005.

TABLE 6.6 Wages and salaries in the top five European national leagues, 2003/4

National league	Total wages and salaries (euros, millions)	Average annual growth of wages and salaries 1995/6–2003/4	Wages and salaries as a % of revenue		
			1995/6	2002/3	2003/4
England	1,209	22%	47%	61%	61%
Italy	845	16%	57%	76%	73%
Spain	608	17%	53%	72%	64%
Germany	492	14%	46%	45%	47%
France	450	14%	58%	68%	69%

SOURCE: DELOITTE & TOUCHE, ANNUAL REVIEW OF FOOTBALL FINANCE, JUNE 2005.

Costs

Wages and salaries – most of which are accounted for by players' salaries – are the major cost item for European clubs (see table 6.6). In all the main European leagues, wages and salaries increased at a faster rate than revenues.

Within the English Premier League there are some significant differences between clubs. The most profligate club was Chelsea, whose 2003/4 wage bill was £115 million – £38 million more than the second highest spender, Man United. Indeed, Man United's wage bill was relatively modest – as a percentage of revenue it was the lowest of the Premiership clubs. The average gross pay of a Premiership footballer was approximately £800,000 a year (about £15,000 a week). Among the leading premiership clubs, the wages/revenues ratios were: Chelsea 80%, Everton 75%, Liverpool 71%, Arsenal 61%, Tottenham Hotspur 52%, Newcastle United 50%, Manchester United 45%.[12]

Other major cost items for the English Premier League clubs were:

- *Player transfer fees*. Players are transferred between clubs both within the Premier League and internationally. Players are signed to clubs on contracts of up to five years. At the end of their contracts they become free agents. Total expenditure by the English league on players in 2003/4 was £414 million, of which Chelsea accounted for £175 million.

- *Stadiums*. Leading clubs had invested substantially in upgrading their facilities – in a few cases (such as Arsenal) building completely new stadiums. Average annual expenditure on stadiums and facilities by the Premier League was £154 million during the four years 2000/1 to 2003/4 – during 1992/3 to 1995/6 it was £67 million.

Profitability

Like most other professional sports, European professional football is a highly unprofitable business. Deloitte's estimates of operating profitability show that the English and German leagues have earned modest levels of operating profit, but the French and Italian leagues earned substantial (and growing) operating losses. However, in terms of net profit, even the English Premiership turns in significant losses (see table 6.7).

The dismal profitability record of European professional football can be directly attributed to the goals of the owners. While about 20 European clubs were listed public companies (including Man United, Juventus, Arsenal, Rangers, Roma, Lazio, and Newcastle United), most were privately owned. These private owners were typically businessmen who had made their fortunes in other areas of businesses. Thus, AC Milan was owned by media magnate and Italian prime minister, Silvio Berlusconi, Inter Milan by Massimo Moratti, Olympique Marseille by Robert Louis-Dreyfus (whose Louis-Dreyfus Group spans commodities, telecom, and food processing), and

TABLE 6.7 Overall profitability of the English league, 2002/3 and 2003/4 (£ millions)

	2003/4			2002/3		
	Revenue	Operating profit	Pre-tax profit	Revenue	Operating profit	Pre-tax profit
Premiership	1,326	149	(128)	1,246	124	(153)
Other leagues	440	(52)	(67)	412	(110)	(155)
Overall	1,766	97	(195)	1,658	14	(218)

SOURCE: DELOITTE & TOUCHE, *ANNUAL REVIEW OF FOOTBALL FINANCE, JUNE 2005.*

Fulham by Mohammed Al Fayed (owner of Harrod's luxury store).[13] Chelsea's takeover by Russian billionaire Roman Abramovich reveals most startlingly how a wealthy individual willing to pursue the fame and prestige of owning a leading football club can elevate performance by lavishing a fortune on acquiring star players (Abramovich spent over £250 million during his first two years at Chelsea).

The financial performance of the ten top-performing English Premiership clubs is summarized in table 6.8.

Manchester United's History

Manchester United was founded in 1878 and became a professional club seven years later in 1885. Old Trafford, Man United's stadium, saw its first game in 1910. During the 1950s and '60s, Man United rose to prominence under the leadership of its legendary team manager, Matt Busby. However, in 1958, on a return flight from a European game, a plane crash killed eight of the "Busby Babes." Busby's rebuilding of the team was rewarded in 1968 when Man United became the first English team to win the European Cup.

During the club's 127-year history, Man United has won two European Club Championships, 15 league titles, and 11 FA Cups. The club has featured some of the world's most recognizable and lauded players including Bobby Charlton, George Best, Denis Law, Mark Hughes, Roy Keane, and David Beckham. However, Man United's history is not one of unmitigated success. During the 18 years before the arrival of Alex Ferguson, the club did not win a single league championship and was runner up just once (1980).

The Ferguson Era

During his first six years at Man United, Ferguson systematically rebuilt the team. Ferguson culled the existing squad, keeping outstanding talent such as Bryan Robson, and jettisoning those who he judged lacked the necessary talent or commitment, or who simply didn't fit. New signings included Mark Hughes, Paul Ince, Eric Cantona, and Roy Keane. In 1990, Ferguson achieved his first major success: the FA Cup, followed in 1991 by the European Cup Winners' Cup. By 1993, Ferguson had achieved his primary objective: the English Premier League Championship.

While reconfiguring and augmenting Man United's first team, Ferguson was also developing a stable of talented youth players. Between 1994 and 1996, these home-grown young players – Ryan Giggs, David Beckham, Nicky Butt, Gary and Phil Neville, and Paul Scholes – starred in the Man United team that was to dominate English football for the remainder of the 1990s. This golden era culminated in 1998/9 when Man United achieved a triumph unprecedented in English football history. During May and June 1999, Man United won the English league title, the FA Cup, and the European Cup. In November 1999, Man United were crowned world champions when they beat the South American champions, Palmeiras, in the Intercontinental Cup played in Tokyo.

The 1999 season was to prove the peak of Man United's success. In the years that followed, Man United remained among the top four English clubs, along with Arsenal, Chelsea, and Liverpool, but the winning streak was no longer so consistent. Man United won the premiership title in 2000, 2001, and 2003, but was unable to

TABLE 6.8 Financial information for top performing English Premiership clubs

Football clubs ranked by team performance[a]	Turnover 2003/4	Aggregate turnover, past 5 years[b]	Wages/ salaries 2003/4	Aggregate wages/ salaries, past 5 years[b]	Operating profit 2003/4[c]	Aggregate operating profit, past 5 years[c]	Net transfer fees paid 2003/4	Pre-tax profit 2004	Aggregate net transfer fees, past 5 years[b]	Net assets 2004
Manchester U.	171,500	742,182	76,874	321,996	51,749	194,788	28,804	27,907	109,907	173,354
Arsenal	114,562	435,279	69,889	266,532	20,109	61,978	12,188	10,577	40,595	84,363
Chelsea	143,615	473,461	114,784	322,304	(24,657)	(12,206)	131,049	(87,829)	187,170	67,134
Liverpool	92,349	424,756	65,635	265,084	10,607	47,464	3,324	(21,903)	59,035	35,606
Newcastle U.	90,468	358,061	44,880	177,685	21,175	69,047	7,773	4,220	48,621	32,336
Aston Villa	55,859	223,296	33,767	13,380	7,265	21,612	2,815	(10,652)	28,187	37,744
Everton	44,302	190,306	33,171	140,824	(2,658)	25	6,196	(15,376)	17,795	(23,075)
Tottenham	66,324	294,233	34,556	160,652	9,735	46,903	15,056	(2,464)	47,471	42,264
Charlton	42,606	148,451	29,913	103,025	3,686	6,838	(10,805)[d]	11,118	7,946	14,516
Middlesbrough	43,047	176,359	28,796	145,590	2,382	(12,892)	12,026	(21,793)	61,736	(51,468)

Notes: figures are in £'000s.

[a] Clubs are ranked by average finishing position in the Premier League, 2000/1 to 2004/5.

[b] Total for years 1999/2000 to 2003/4.

[c] Before player trading activity.

[d] Receipts from players transferred exceeded expenditure on transfers.

replicate its European triumph of 1999. The most recent two seasons of 2003/4 and 2004/5 were particularly disappointing. Man United exited the Champions League in the first round of the knockout stage in 2003/4 (its earliest exit since 1994/5) and lost again in that same round in 2004/5. In the English Premier League, Man United finished in third place in both seasons, 15 points behind champions Arsenal in 2003/4 and 18 points behind champions Chelsea in 2004/5. During this period Ferguson also set himself the challenge of rebuilding the team. The sale of David Beckham to Real Madrid in 2003 marked the breakup of Man United's world-beating team of the late 1990s and the beginning of a quest to recreate United's winning ways.

Malcolm Glazer

Man United's new owner, Malcolm Glazer, was born in 1928 in Rochester, New York. His business interests began with watch parts and expanded into real estate, healthcare, and broadcasting. First Allied Corporation was the holding company for the Glazer family's business operations. Glazer's net worth was estimated at around $1 billion.

Glazer was best known for his ownership of the Tampa Bay Buccaneers, an NFL franchise. Through First Allied, Glazer bought the Buccaneers for $192 million in 1995. At the time of the sale, the franchise had the worst overall record in NFL history, a very small fan base, and almost no merchandising revenues. Under Glazer's ownership, the Buccaneers acquired a new $168 million stadium (paid for entirely by the city through a hike in sales tax) and a new coach, Jon Gruden, bought from the Oakland Raiders for $8 million plus rights to four round draft picks. In 2003, the Buccaneers won the Super Bowl and by 2005 the value of the franchise was estimated at $800 million. Glazer was regarded as one of the most astute and successful owners of a professional sports team in the US. Referring to the Man United acquisition, Salvatore Galatioto, president of a New York sports investment firm, said: "The Glazers are extremely innovative and very bright people. If they're doing this, they have a plan that has a high likelihood of success."

Alex Ferguson

Alex Ferguson was born into a working class family in Govan, a tough, shipbuilding community close to Glasgow – a city famous for the passion and loyalty of its football fans. Ferguson's life was built around soccer. After a playing career that included the Scottish clubs St. Johnston, Glasgow Rangers, and Aidrie, Ferguson took to coaching. He began with bottom-of-the-league East Stirlingshire, moved to St. Mirren, then to Aberdeen. There, Ferguson broke the dominance of Scottish football by the Glasgow teams Rangers and Celtic, leading Aberdeen to the Scottish League Championship, Scottish Cup, and European Cup Winners' Cup.

His appointment as manager of Man United in 1986 was not followed by immediate success – indeed, 1986–9 were difficult years for both Ferguson and Man United. It was not until 1990, when Man United won the FA Cup, that Ferguson was able to point to any tangible success. Yet, all the while Ferguson was building the foundations for success:

> My aim in management has always been to lay foundations that will make a club successful for years, or even decades . . . When I joined United on 6 November 1986, they had gone 19 years without a title. No one had to tell me that if I did

not end that drought I would be a failure. Putting them in a position to challenge consistently would, I knew, be a long haul. I would have to build from the bottom up, rectifying the flaws I had recognized and spreading my influence and self-belief through every layer of the organization. I wanted to form a personal link with everyone around the place – not just the players, the coaches and the backroom staff but the office workers, the cooks and servers in the canteen and the laundry ladies. All had to believe that they were part of the club and that a resurgence was coming.[14]

The starting point was training and team discipline. Ferguson declared war on alcohol – a problem endemic to British professional soccer and an indulgence that Ferguson viewed as incompatible with professional sport. A new, more rigorous training regime was installed, backed by Ferguson's high expectations regarding attendance, punctuality, and effort. His training sessions built individual and team skills through continuous repetition: "refining technique to the point where difficult skills become a matter of habit."

In terms of long-term team building, Ferguson focused heavily on identifying and developing new talent:

From the moment I became manager of United, I was committed to the creation of a youth policy that would be the envy of every other club in Britain. The first imperative was to find the raw talent . . .[15]

Ferguson expanded the scouting staff from five to over 20 and instructed them to seek only the most outstanding talent. Manchester United's Youth Academy was built into what Ferguson declared was the finest youth coaching program in the country. During the 1990s, Man United's investment in youth began to pay dividends. In 1992, Man United's youth team won the FA Youth Cup. The team included Ryan Giggs, David Beckham, Nicky Butt, the Neville brothers, and Paul Scholes – players that would quickly graduate to the first team.

Yet, while the youth team was in development, Ferguson had to rely on the players he had inherited, plus what he could purchase with the club's modest transfer budget. The acquisitions of Paul Ince, Eric Cantona, and Roy Keane provided the catalysts for the team with which Ferguson won the League Championship in 1993 and 1994.

However, if Bryan Robson, Mark Hughes, Brian McClair, Paul Ince, Eric Cantona, and Roy Keane formed the core of Ferguson's first successful Man United team, by 1994–5 he was already dismantling that team to make way for his young players from the youth team. The period 1996–2001 was the most successful in United's history – winning the English league in five seasons out of six. The climax was winning "The Treble" in 1999.[16]

To Ferguson, team building was much more than acquiring and developing talented players, developing their skills, and building coordination between them:

The best teams stand out because they are teams, because the individual members have been so truly integrated that the team functions with a single spirit. There is a constant flow of mutual support among the players, enabling them to feed off strengths and compensate for weaknesses. They depend on one another, trust in one another. A manager should engender that sense of unity. He should create a bond among his players and between him and them that raises performance to heights that were unimaginable when they started out as disparate individuals.[17]

Ferguson's approach to motivating his players involved loyal support and withering criticism and anger. His ability to induce exquisite performances from the brilliant but volatile Frenchman, Eric Cantona, owed much to Ferguson's unflinching support during conflicts with authority.[18] At the same time, Ferguson was renowned for his temper and the ferociousness of the verbal lashings he dispensed to players whom he suspected of lack of effort. These verbal tirades were delivered to players at such close range that they became known as "Ferguson's hairdryer." One confrontation between Ferguson and David Beckham left the football superstar with a cut above his eye – the result of Ferguson kicking a football boot at him. Ferguson is particularly renowned for the effectiveness of his half-time talks to his team. During half-time at the European Cup Final in 1999, Man United was losing 1–0. He told his team:

At the end of this game, the European Cup will be only six feet away from you and you'll not even be able to touch it if we lose. And for many of you that will be the closest you will ever get. Don't you dare come back in here without giving your all.

In terms of team strategy and match tactics, Ferguson was committed to control over the midfield. This required "controlled, sustained possession that calls for players adept at holding the ball and spreading calculated and accurate passes . . . A high standard of passing in central midfield was the core of United's football."[19] Ferguson had long admired the ability of the top Italian teams to vary the pace of their game – to slow the game with a period of low-energy, possession football, followed by a sudden, lightning attack. Ferguson's team design was characterized as a closely coordinated midfield group built around players such as Keane, Scholes, Beckham, and Butt with creative attackers such as Cantona, Giggs, Sheringham, Cole, and Van Nistelrooy.

Ferguson's systematic approach to training was matched by his meticulous planning for major games. For Man United's European Cup final against Bayern Munich in June 1999, Ferguson commented:

We left nothing to chance, even flying our chef from Old Trafford and our nutritionist. On the medical side we had our doctor, Mike Stone, two of our main physios, David Fever and Robert Swire, and Jimmy Curran for massages. There were two kit men, Albert Morgan and Alec Wylie, and two stalwarts from the Club's administrative office. Club secretary Ken Merrett handled the organizational side and made sure that Steve McClaren, Jimmy Ryan, and I were never distracted from our work with the squad.[20]

As Ferguson prepared for the 2005/6 season, he was already developing his third team. As before, Ferguson maintained an interest in developing talent through Man United's Youth Academy. In 2002, Man United announced investment of £8 million in the Academy.[21] The difference was that Ferguson was looking further afield, bringing in Gerard Pique from Barcelona, Giuseppe Rossi from Parma, Jonathan Spector from the Chicago Sockers, and even courting DC United's sensational 16-year-old, Freddy Adu. An indication of Ferguson's commitment to developing young players is the fact that, during the 2002/3 season, out of a first-team squad of 23 players, nine had progressed from the youth team. The average age of the squad was 25 – comparatively low for both the English Premier League and the European Champions League. Yet, despite continued emphasis on youth, Ferguson increasingly recognized the need to acquire top talent if the club was to maintain its role in the top echelon of European football. Between July 2001 and August 2005, Man United spent an

TABLE 6.9 Manchester United major signings under Alex Ferguson (1986–2005)

Year	Player	Acquired from	Transfer fee (£m)	Age at time of transfer
1987	Brian McClair	Celtic	0.9	23
1988	Mark Hughes	Barcelona	1.8	25
1989	Neil Webb	Nottingham Forest	1.5	21
1989	Danny Wallace	Southampton	1.3	21
1989	Gary Pallister	Middlesbrough	2.3	24
1989	Paul Ince	West Ham	2.4	22
1991	Paul Parker	QPR	1.7	25
1992	Eric Cantona	Leeds	1.2	26
1992	Dion Dublin	Cambridge	1.0	23
1993	Roy Keane	Nottingham Forest	3.8	22
1994	David May	Blackburn	1.2	24
1995	Andy Cole	Newcastle	6.3	24
1996	Ole Gunnar Solskjaer	Molde	1.5	23
1997	Teddy Sheringham	Tottenham	3.5	31
1997	Karel Poborsky	Slavia Prague	3.5	25
1997	Henning Berg	Blackburn	5.0	27
1998	Jaap Stam	PSV Eindhoven	10.6	25
1998	Dwight Yorke	Aston Villa	12.6	26
1999	Mikael Silvestre	Inter Milan	4.3	22
1999	Quinton Fortune	Athletic Madrid	1.6	22
2001	Ruud Van Nistelrooy	PSV Eindhoven	19.0	25
2001	Juan Sebastián Veron	Lazio	28.1	25
2002	Rio Ferdinand	Leeds United	31.1	23
2003	David Bellion	Sunderland	2.8	20
2003	Eric Djemba Djemba	Nantes	3.5	22
2003	Tim Howard	NJ Metrostars	2.3	23
2003	Kleberson	Atletico Paranese	5.8	23
2003	Ronaldo	Sporting Lisbon	11.9	18
2004	Alan Smith	Leeds United	7.0	22
2004	Louis Saha	Fulham	12.0	25
2004	Gabriel Heinze	Paris St Germain	6.9	26
2004	Park Ji-Sung	PSV Eindhoven	4.0	23
2005	Edwin Van Der Sar	Fulham	1.0	35
2005	Wayne Rooney	Everton	25.6	19

unprecedented £280 million on transfers, the most expensive signings being Rio Ferdinand, Wayne Rooney, Ruud Van Nistelrooy, Louis Saha, and Cristiano Ronaldo (see table 6.9). However, Man United's net expenditure on players was much smaller. During financial years 2003/4 and 2004/5, proceeds from the sale of players – including Beckham (to Real Madrid), Stam (to Lazio), Butt (to Newcastle) and Veron (to Chelsea) – amounted to £280 million.

Manchester United's Commercial and Financial Performance

Man United was widely regarded as the most commercially focused club in the Premier League. It had been one of the first of the English clubs to go public and the most successful in establishing effective corporate governance and taking its responsibilities to shareholders seriously. In building its fan base then converting that support into revenues for the club, it was a model for clubs throughout Europe.

Customer Base

Mark Goodfellow, Man United's campaign and marketing manager, estimated the club had 75 million fans worldwide – 23 million in Europe, 4.6 million in the Americas, 40.7 million in Asia, and 5.9 million in southern Africa. There were more than 200 officially recognized branches of the Manchester United Supporters Club (MUSC), in 24 different countries.[22] The club's CRM (customer relationship management) database held 2.5 million fan records in July 2004, and over 3 million in mid-2005. The primary tool for identifying supporters and acquiring information on them was the Manutd.com website. The CRM system analyzed the data on these fans. One of Man United's objectives was to identify and enrol as customers 6.7 million of its fans across the world by 2007.

Brand management

"We're not just a sports club, we are an international brand . . . and building that brand is very important," observed commercial director Andy Anson. In addition to the overall Manchester United brand, the club had developed several sub-brands: "Fred the Red" was designed to appeal to children; the "MUFC" brand was targeted at teenagers, while "Red Devil" products were directed mainly towards adults.[23] Other brands were associated with specific licensing deals – notably "Red Cafes" and "Theatre of Dreams" restaurants. A subsidiary, Manchester United International, was created in 1998 for the purpose of developing Man United's business opportunities outside the UK – in North America and Asia especially. The primary emphasis of Man United's brand management was exploiting the brand through new commercial opportunities – developing Man United was achieved primarily by the team through its performances on the pitch.

Commercial initiatives in recent years included:

- Major sponsorship deals with Nike and Vodafone. The Nike relationship involved annual releases of redesigned team kit (new "home" and "away" outfits were released in alternate years). This drove sales of Nike-made replica kit to Man United's worldwide fan base.

- A "platinum sponsorship plan" allowing a range of other companies to become associated with Man United. The brands involved included: Budweiser ("official team beer"), Pepsi Cola, Ladbrokes, Dimension Data (provider of web services), Lycos (web services for Man United's Chinese website), Wilkinson Sword (shaving products), Fuji, and Audi cars.

- Brand licensing involving a wide range of merchandise. In addition to the traditional products – Man United shirts, scarves, jackets, footballs, watches, and toys – the club pioneered the growth of branded services. MU Finance offered a wide range of financial services, ranging from credit cards to retirement planning products; MU Mobile was a short-text messaging service offered to Man United fans by Vodafone; ManUtdpics.com supplied team photos through Fuji Film; the "Red Cinema" in Salford screened Man United video footage; Man United Soccer Schools were attractions at Disneyland in Paris and Hong Kong.

- Deriving revenues from its own MU.tv subscription service, which aired reruns of Man United matches, in addition to Man United's TV revenues through television contracts negotiated by the Premier League and the Champions League. There was also an MU radio service broadcast by Century Radio.

- Expanding revenues from Man United's stadium, which involved developing additional entertainment and leisure uses for the Old Trafford stadium. During the 2003/4 season, the stadium hosted 755 events, including conferences, corporate meetings, and weddings. The Manchester United Museum and Tour attracted 235,000 visitors in the same year. The 18,000 square-foot Megastore adjacent to the stadium supplied a wide variety of souvenirs and team-branded merchandise.

Appendix 1 shows financial information for Manchester United plc. Appendix 2 reprints extracts of the chairman's statement to shareholders in 2004.

Future Development

By the start of the 2005/6 football season – Manchester United's first fixture was against Everton on August 13 – the new leadership was well installed. Manchester United plc had become Manchester United Ltd and the new board of directors was dominated by the Glazer family. Of the nine-member board, six were Malcolm Glazer's children: Avram, Kevin, Bryan, Joel, Darcie, and Edward. Malcolm himself had no formal position at United. Otherwise, most of Man United's previous organization and management remained in place. David Gill remained Chief Executive, Nick Humby continued as Finance Director, as did Andy Anson as Commercial Director.

Early indications were that, among the Glazer family, fourth son, Joel, would be the most actively involved in the club's affairs. A long-time Man United fan, Joel positioned himself as family spokesman and primary liaison between the family and the club. Joel was particularly concerned to calm Man United fans and build trust between the family and the club's management. In particular, Joel moved quickly to quash rumors of a £25 million annual limit on transfers. "When I read about caps and hands being tied it is very frustrating," Joel told United's in-house TV station, MUTV. "It is absolutely not true. We are there to provide the manager with what he needs to win at the highest level."

However, the Glazer family also recognized that stabilizing Man United after the traumas of the takeover battle would not be enough to ensure the club's long-term success or to safeguard their £790 million investment. Revenue expansion was essential, and to grow revenues, a revival in team performance – both in the English league and in Europe – was essential.

Appendix 1
Manchester United Six-Year
Financial Summary, 2000–2005

	2005[a]	2004[b]	2003[b]	2002[b]	2001[b]	2000[b]
Turnover	157,171	169,080	173,001	146,062	129,569	116,005
Group operating profit before depreciation and amortization of intangible fixed assets	46,131	58,340	57,269	41,402	38,194	35,125
Depreciation	(6,054)	(6,591)	(7,283)	(6,923)	(6,514)	(5,052)
Amortization of players	(24,159)	(21,839)	(21,018)	(17,647)	(10,173)	(13,092)
Exceptional costs	(7,286)	–	(2,197)	(1,414)	(2,073)	(1,300)
Group operating profit	8,632	29,910	26,771	15,418	19,434	15,681
Share of results of joint venture and associate undertakings	(4)	(158)	(454)	(504)	(602)	(982)
Total operating profit (including profit from joint venture and associate undertakings)	8,628	29,752	26,317	14,914	18,832	14,699
Profit on disposal of associate	215	173	409	–	–	–
(Loss)/profit on disposal of players	(556)	(3084)	12,935	17,406	2,219	1,633
Net interest receivable/(payable)	2,477	1,066	(316)	27	727	456
Profit on ordinary activities before taxation	10,764	27,907	39,345	32,347	21,778	16,788
Taxation	(4,224)	(8,486)	(9,564)	(7,308)	(7,399)	(4,838)
Profit for the period	6,540	19,421	29,781	25,039	14,379	11,950
Dividends	(3,439)	(6,974)	(10,391)	(8,053)	(5,195)	(4,936)
Retained profit for the year	3,101	12,447	19,390	16,986	9,184	7,014
Equity shareholders' funds	180,846	173,354	156,418	137,443	120,457	114,950

Note: figures are in £'000s.

[a] 1 months to June 30.

[b] 12 months to July 31.

Appendix 2
Extracts from Chairman's Statement
(from Manchester United Annual Report, 2004)

The results for the 12 months to 21 July 2004 illustrate Manchester United's unique strength as both a business and a football club. We have demonstrated our ability to deal with new challenges whilst continuing to strive to be the best both on and off the pitch. These strengths helped us win the FA Cup for a record 11th time and, shortly after the year end, secure the services of the most exciting young English player of the last decade, Wayne Rooney . . .

Corporate Governance – Player Transactions

During the year the Board reviewed its processes surrounding transfers and wage negotiations. The Board set the parameters for player trading and contract negotiation, monitors closely the progression of negotiations, and approves all major transfers and contracts. All detailed negotiations are carried out by the Chief Executive, David Gill, who consults with the Team Manager, Sir Alex Ferguson and the Board. Sir Alex is responsible for identifying and recommending squad changes.

Our target of managing total staff costs to turnover ratio to around 50 per cent helps the Company in managing the balance between the squad composition and the long-term financial viability of the Club. The Board monitors the average age of the first team squad to prevent the need for wholesale changes in the future since the balance between stability and evolution is essential for a successful club. The annual net expenditure budget for player registration acquisitions is set in advance of each financial year, taking into consideration the overall market conditions, the expected financial performance of the Company, and the Manager's view of the current profile of the squad. The Company's success to date has been built on working within the cash generation capabilities of the business, without the use of long-term debt, to evolve the composition of the squad . . .

Medium-Term Strategic Plans

In order to grow revenue streams under our control, the Board has agreed five key strategies for the Company.

1 Maintaining Playing Success The first of these, which underpins all our plans, is the need to sustain the playing success of the last 12 years. Like our fans, we were disappointed by our performance in the Premiership and Champions League, but our success in winning the FA Cup for the first time since our treble winning season in 1999 came as a welcome reward at the end of a season that had originally promised so much. Going forward, we will continue to invest in our squad and play our sport in the proper spirit and style for which the Club has become famous. At the same time, we will work to preserve the financial strength of the Club by seeking to structure players' pay such that it is increasingly dependent on European Champions League qualification, appearances and team success. No individual player can generate the success to which we aspire, but a strong squad is required to secure European qualification and show progress in each season's Champions League.

2 Treating Fans as Customers Our second key strategy is to ensure we treat our fans as customers, offering them a good matchday experience, and a range of additional products and services which meets their interests, while enabling them to demonstrate their affinity with the Club. By working with partners who can promote our membership scheme, our financial services and other products and services, we see good opportunities to grow our relationship with the millions of fans worldwide. During the year our membership scheme, One United, reached 193,000 members (2003 151,000 members).

3 Leveraging the Global Brand Thirdly, we continue to work to develop our partnership with our sponsors. Nike, for example, has shown its commitment to building our relationship with fans through its subsidiary, Manchester United Merchandising Limited (MUML). They have generated profits in excess of the minimum guarantee over the first two years of our thirteen-year deal, staged the worldwide Under-15 Premier Cup, and launched the Disneyland Paris Soccer School. Vodafone has demonstrated the mutual benefits of our associate by the renewal of its four-year relationship with the Club for 36 million pounds. Together we will build our MU Mobile business by offering new services to mobile phone users who want to stay in tune with the latest news and events at the Club.

4 Developing Media Rights Fourthly, we must use our media rights more effectively, and so are planning to consolidate the management of our delayed video rights, with our matchday media, publications and use of the internet. The unique content that the Club can generate provides an excellent opportunity to build our relationship with our fans around the world by delivering news and images to them wherever, whenever, and however they want.

5 Maximising the Use of Old Trafford Finally, the venue of Old Trafford provides unique opportunities to develop new revenues, not just by the planned stadium expansion, but also by continuing to improve the matchday experience for our customers. The installation of electronic point of sale equipment in our kiosks and suites, together with new recruitment and training initiatives, should ensure our customers receive a faster, more satisfying service. In addition, the stadium offers a perfect venue for many conferences and events on non-matchdays. Proactive marketing and servicing of those organisations will grow our venue revenues.

It is inevitable that there is some volatility in our results given that a significant portion of our revenue in any year is a function of both the previous and current season's performance. However, this five-pronged strategy is designed to drive consistency and growth in revenues not directly related to team performance. This in turn will allow us to continue investing in players and challenging for trophies.

Running a Football Club as a Business

Manchester United has built a sound business on the heritage of a great football club and its unique record of success under Sir Alex Ferguson. This year, once again, our committed and loyal staff have worked tirelessly to deliver on the high expectations of our fans and partners. This, combined with our proven financial discipline and prudent management of the cash generated by the business, should continue to provide long-term growth for shareholders and further playing success for our fans.

Sir Roy Gardner, Chairman
27 September 2004

Notes

1   In British professional football, the head coach is referred to as the "manager." The manager is responsible for coaching and training, team selection, player discipline, team strategy and game tactics, and makes recommendations to the board about the purchase and sale of players.

2   "Profile: Malcolm Glazer: Putting one through the legs of the Man U mob," *Sunday Times*, London, May 15, 2005.

3   Jonathan Michie and Christine Oughton show that the English Premier League has become more "competitively imbalanced over the past decade, to the extent that the

top four clubs are accounting for a growing percentage of points earned" (*Competitive Balance in Football: Trends and Effects*, Football Governance Research Centre, Birkbeck College, 2004).

4   In British football, these included Man United under Matt Busby, Liverpool under Bill Shankly, Celtic under Jock Stein, Leeds under Don Revie, Nottingham Forest under Brian Clough, and Ipswich under Alf Ramsey.

5   Claudio Ranieri was highly successful at Fiorentina and Valencia, but much less so at Chelsea, Athletico Madrid, and in his second stint at Valencia; Brian Clough was unable to replicate his remarkable performance at Derby and then Nottingham Forest at either Brighton or Leeds; Bobby Robson's 37-year coaching career included outstanding success at Ipswich, Porto, and Barcelona and poorer team performance at Eindhoven, Sporting Lisbon, and Newcastle.

6   Celtic was the first British club to win the European Cup. Ten members of Stein's cup winning team were born within 10 miles of the Celtic ground; the eleventh was born some 30 miles away.

7   John Hollins, 1985–8; Bobby Campbell, 1988–91; Ian Porterfield, June 1991–3; David Webb, 1993; Glenn Hoddle, July 1993–June 1996; Ruud Gullit, June 1996–February 1998; Gianluca Vialli, February 1998–September 2000; Claudio Ranieri, September 2000–May 2004; Jose Mourinho June 2004–.

8   Leo Beenhakker, 1986–9; John Benjamin Toshack 1989–90; Alfredo Di Stéfano – José Antonio Camacho, 1990–1; Radomir Antic, 1991–2; Leo Beenhakker, 1992; Benito Floro, 1992–4; Vicente del Bosque, 1994; Jorge Valdano, 1994–6; Arsenio Iglesias, 1996; Fabio Capello, 1996–7; Jupp Heynckes, 1997–8; José Antonio Camacho, 1998; Guus Hiddink, 1998–9; John Benjamin Toshack, 1999; Vicente del Bosque, 1999–2003; Carlos Queiroz, 2003–4; José Antonio Camacho 2004; Mariano García Remón, 2004; Wanderlei Luxemburgo, 2004.

9   Deloitte's *Annual Review of Football Finance, June 2005*, p. 17 shows the following:

	Total attendance, 2003/4 (millions)	Average income per match (euros '000s)	Average revenue per attendee (euros)
England	13.30	1,550	44
Spain	10.95	720	25
Italy	7.85	610	24
Germany	10.73	680	19
France	7.66	320	16

10   These typically comprised seats, parking, pre-match champagne lunch, and other services.

11   See Deloitte's *Annual Review*, p. 16.

12   Deloitte's *Annual Review*, p. 38.

13   Some teams are owned by companies – for example, Bayern Munich is owned by Adidas-Salomon. The leading Spanish clubs were mainly not-for-profit companies owned by their members, who held season tickets and elected the club president.

14   Alex Ferguson, *Managing My Life* (London: Hodder & Stoughton, 1999), p. 242.

15   Ibid., p. 274.

16   The Premier League Championship, the FA Cup, and the European Champions League (the European Cup).

17   Alex Ferguson, *Managing My Life*, op. cit., p. 274.

18   The most serious incident was a kung-fu kick on a rival fan that resulted in Cantona being arrested for criminal assault and suspended from football for eight months.

19   Alex Ferguson, *Managing My Life*, op. cit., p. 437.

20   Ibid.

21   Manchester United PLC Annual Report, 2002, p. 9.

22   Under the "One United" membership scheme, supporters can choose to become Match Members allowing them to apply for match tickets, or Non-ticket Members. For younger supporters, One United offers Junior Match Memberships or Non-ticket Junior Membership. In addition to these membership plans, supporters can register as E-members – allowing access to communications and services provided through the Man United website.

23   *Real Madrid Club de Futbal*, Harvard Business School Case No. 9-504-063, 2004.

Eastman Kodak: Meeting the Digital Challenge

January 2004 marked the beginning of Dan Carp's fifth year as Eastman Kodak Inc.'s chief executive officer. By late February, it was looking as though 2004 would also be his most challenging.

The year had begun with Kodak's dissident shareholders becoming louder and bolder. The critical issue was Kodak's digital imaging strategy that Carp had presented to investors in September 2003. The strategy called for a rapid acceleration in Kodak's technological and market development of its digital imaging business – involving some $3 billion in new investment. This would be financed in part by slashing Kodak's dividend. Of particular concern to Carp was Carl Icahn, who had acquired 7% of Kodak's stock. Icahn was not known for his patience or long-term horizons – he was famous for leading shareholder revolts and leveraged buyouts. His opposition to Carp's strategy was based on skepticism over whether the massive investments in digital imaging would ever generate returns to shareholders. He viewed Kodak's traditional photography business as a potential cash cow. If Kodak could radically cut costs, a sizable profit stream would be available to shareholders. The release of Kodak's full-year results on January 22 2004 lent weight to Carp's critics: top-line growth was anemic while, on the bottom line, net income was down by almost two-thirds. Press commentary was mostly skeptical over Kodak's future prospects. The *Financial Times*' Lex column observed:

> . . . *Two key problems remain. The first is that, as Kodak extends its imaging technology into consumer electronics, it will encounter severe competition from existing camera makers and the brutal profit margins of a business where prices seem in perpetual freefall. If prices continue to plummet, it may still all be too little too late. Though few would question Kodak's technological expertise, its relative lack of experience in hardware was shown*

by its pride in attending the Las Vegas consumer electronics show for the first time this year. It has also been hit by a failure to develop new models fast enough and has tended to focus on the ultra-competitive entry-level market. . . .

The other potential problem stems from predicting that descent curve for film. Much hope has been placed on growing demand for old-fashioned film cameras in emerging markets like China, India and Russia. So far, sales in the rest of the world as a whole have been declining at the same speed as the US . . .[1]

Carp resolutely believed that to deviate from Kodak's goal of establishing leadership in the field of digital imaging would betray Kodak's heritage and mission and would condemn the company to a lingering death. The challenge, he believed, was to sharpen the focus of Kodak's digital strategy, to articulate that strategy more persuasively, and to ensure that the strategy was implemented with greater speed and effectiveness.

As a first stage, Kodak needed to emphasize the distinct strategies for Kodak's "traditional businesses" and its "digital businesses." The traditional businesses would be "managed for cash to maximize value." This meant revenue contraction of around 7% per year together with aggressive cost cutting. During 2004–6, between 12,000 and 15,000 jobs would be axed and one-third of traditional factory space would close.

For digital businesses, Kodak's options were broader, but the uncertainties were more daunting. The transition from traditional to digital imaging over the next few years was a certainty. With digital revenues projected to grow at 26% annually, the balance of Kodak's business would shift: in 2002 "traditional" had accounted for 70% of Kodak's revenues; by 2006 this would be down to 40%. But how technologies, products, and customer usage would develop remained unclear. The greatest uncertainties related to Kodak's potential for competitive advantage in digital imaging. Kodak's traditional strengths were its brand, its global distribution network, and its chemical imaging capabilities. Digital imaging was a very different market. Not only were the technologies very different, but also Kodak faced a different array of competitors. In hardware Hewlett-Packard, Canon, and Sony were leaders. In software, the key players were Microsoft and Adobe – not to mention the online services companies such as AOL, Google, and Yahoo! For Kodak to succeed in digital imaging required that it establish a view of how the market would evolve, evaluate its strengths and weaknesses in relation to this emerging future, articulate a clear strategy of where and how it would compete, and develop the resources and capabilities needed to realize this strategy.

Kodak's History, 1880–1993

George Eastman transformed photography from an activity undertaken by professional photographers working in studios into an everyday consumer hobby. Between 1880 and 1888 Eastman developed a new type of dry photographic plate, silver halide roll film, and then the first fully portable camera. In 1901 he established the Eastman Kodak Company whose strategy was to provide a fully integrated photographic service supplying the camera and film through to processing and printing. Its first advertising slogan was "You push the button, we do the rest." The business principles established by Eastman were:

- Mass production at low cost
- International distribution
- Extensive advertising
- A focus on the customer
- Fostering growth and development through continuing research
- Treating employees in a fair, self-respecting way
- Reinvesting profits to build and extend the business

By the time George Eastman died in 1932, he had created a vast new market that Eastman Kodak dominated.

By the end of the 1970s, Kodak was facing its first competitive challenges. In cameras, Kodak's leadership was undermined by the rise of the Japanese camera industry, with its sophisticated yet easy-to-use 35 mm cameras. In film, Fuji Photo Film Company embarked on a strategy of aggressive international expansion. Fuji's sponsorship of the 1984 Los Angeles Olympic Games proclaimed its presence in Kodak's backyard. New imaging technologies were also making their mark. In instant photography, Polaroid was the dominant player. In copying, Xerox had established itself as the leader in the new field of electrostatic plain-paper copying (Kodak had turned down the opportunity to acquire the original patents on xerography), while the personal computer was ushering in a new array of printing technologies.

Diversification 1983–1993

Under the new management team of Colby Chandler and Kay Whitmore, Kodak launched a series of diversification initiatives in two main areas – imaging and life sciences – with several new imaging ventures:

- Eikonix Corp., acquired in 1985, gave Kodak a leading position in commercial imaging systems that scanned, edited, and prepared images for printing.
- Kodak developed the world's first megapixel electronic image sensor with 1 4 million pixels (1986). This was followed by a number of new products for electronic publishing, scanning, and editing for the printing and publishing industry, including Imagelink for document imaging and Optistar for micrographic digital image capture (1989).
- Kodak became a leader in image storage and retrieval systems. Its KAR4000 Information System provided computer-assisted storage and retrieval of microfilm images (1983). The Ektaprint Electronic Publishing System and Kodak Image Management System offered integrated systems to edit, store, retrieve, and print text and graphics (1985).
- Kodak became involved in a range of data storage products including floppy disks (Verbatim was acquired in 1985), a 14-inch optical disk capable of storing 6.8 billion bytes of information (1986), and magnetic recording heads for disk drives (through the 1985 acquisition of Garlic Corp.).
- Through a joint venture with Matsushita, Kodak began supplying alkaline batteries and videocassettes.
- Kodak acquired IBM's copier services business.

- As a result of its collaboration with Philips, Kodak announced its Photo CD system in 1990. Photo CDs allowed digitized photographic images to be stored on a compact disk, which could then be viewed and manipulated on a personal computer.

The second area of development built on Kodak's capabilities in chemical technology. Eastman Chemicals had been established in the 1920s to supply photographic chemicals both to Kodak's film and processing division and to third-party customers. By the 1980s, Eastman was a major international supplier of photographic chemicals, fibers, plastics (especially for soft-drink packaging), printing inks, and nutrition supplements.

Building on its capabilities in chemicals and its existing healthcare activities (e.g., nutritional supplements and diagnostic equipment), Kodak established its Life Sciences Division in 1984. In 1986 Kodak established Eastman Pharmaceuticals and in 1988 acquired Sterling Drug.

Creating a Digital Strategy: George Fisher, 1993–2000

By the early 1990s, it was clear that Kodak was extended over too many initiatives with too little commitment to any area outside of its traditional imaging business. In 1993, the Kodak board ousted Whitmore and replaced him with George Fisher, then CEO of Motorola. Fisher was a leader of America's resurgence in high technology and was on every headhunter's list – he had already turned down the opportunity to become IBM's CEO (IBM's board subsequently turned to Lou Gerstner). Moreover, with a doctorate in applied mathematics and ten years of R&D experience at Bell Labs, he had a scientist's grasp of electronic technology.

From the outset, Fisher's strategic vision for Kodak was as an imaging company: "We are not in the photographic film business or in the electronics business, we are in the picture business."[2] To focus Kodak's efforts and lower debt, Fisher approved the spin-off of Eastman Chemical Company and the sale of most healthcare businesses (other than medical imaging), including the Sterling Winthrop pharmaceutical company.

Fisher's digital strategy was to create greater coherence among Kodak's many digital imaging projects, in part through creating a single digital projects division headed by newly hired Carl Gustin (previously with Apple Computer and DEC). In developing a digital strategy, he emphasized three key themes.

An Incremental Approach

"The future is not some harebrained scheme of the digital information highway or something. It is a step-by-step progression of enhancing photography using digital technology," declared Fisher.[3] This recognition that digital imaging was an evolutionary rather than a revolutionary change would be the key to Kodak's ability to build a strong position in digital technology. If photography was to switch rapidly from the traditional chemical-based technology to a wholly digital technology where customers took digital pictures, downloaded them onto their computers, edited them, and transmitted them through the internet to be viewed electronically, then Kodak would face an extremely difficult time. Apart from Kodak's positions in digital cameras and picture-editing software, most of this digital chain was in the hands of computer hardware and software companies. However, fortunately for Kodak, during the 1990s digital technology would make only selective incursions into traditional photographic imaging. For example, by 2000 digital cameras had achieved limited market penetration; the vast majority of photographic images were still captured on traditional film.

Hence, central to Kodak's strategy was a hybrid approach where Kodak introduced those aspects of digital imaging that could offer truly enhanced functionality for users. Thus, in the consumer market, Kodak recognized that image capture would continue to be dominated by traditional film for some time (digital cameras offered inferior resolution compared with conventional photography). However, digital imaging offered immediate potential for image manipulation and transmission.

This hybrid approach involved Kodak in providing facilities in retail outlets for digitizing and editing images from conventional photographs, then storing, transmitting and printing these digital images. Kodak's first walk-up, self-service systems were its CopyPrint Station and Digital Enhancement Station. In 1994, Kodak launched its Picture Maker, which allowed digital prints to be made from either conventional photo prints or from a variety of digital inputs. Picture Maker allowed customers to edit their images (zoom, crop, eliminate red-eye, and add text), and print them in a variety of formats. By the end of 2000, some 30,000 retail locations worldwide offered Picture Maker facilities.

Kodak also used digital technology to enhance the services offered by photofinishers. Thus, the Kodak I.Lab system offered a digital infrastructure to photofinishers that digitized every film negative and offered better pictures by fixing common problems in consumer photographs.

Kodak's hybrid approach was also evident in introducing digital enhancement of conventional film. In 1996, Kodak launched its Advantix advanced photo system that allowed both chemical film images and electronic data to be stored on a single film. The new standard failed to make much impact on the market.

Despite the inferior resolution of digital cameras, Fisher recognized their potential and pushed Kodak to establish itself in this highly competitive market. Kodak's digital cameras addressed both the top end and the bottom end of the market. In January 1994, Kodak launched a Professional Digital Camera (the camera alone costing $8,500) and the Apple Quicktake computer camera (manufactured by Kodak, marketed by Apple Computer), which, at $75, was the cheapest digital camera available at the time. In March 1995, Kodak introduced the first full-featured digital camera priced at under $1,000. During the subsequent six years, Kodak continued to bring out new, more sophisticated digital cameras, including professional cameras developed in conjunction with Canon. By 2000, Kodak offered a wide range of digital cameras. At the top end was its DC4800 camera with 3.1 megapixel resolution; at the other a PalmPix camera that allowed a Palm personal digital assistant to be used as a digital camera.

For digital camera users, Kodak was quick to recognize the potential of the internet for allowing consumers to transmit and store their photographs and order prints. Picture Vision's PhotoNet system replaced Kodak's own Picture Network (first introduced in 1997). This allowed consumers to drop off film at retail locations and view their digitized images on Kodak's PhotoNet website from which prints could be ordered. In addition, Kodak partnered with AOL to offer *You've Got Pictures*, which allowed AOL members to send photographic images to one another.

Distinct Strategies for Consumer and Commercial Markets

Fisher advocated different approaches to consumer and commercial markets. Kodak's incremental strategy – providing a pathway for customers from traditional to digital photography – was most evident in the consumer market, where Kodak could exploit its brand and distribution strengths.

> *Four years ago, when we talked about the possibilities of digital photography, people laughed. Today, the high-tech world is stampeding to get a piece of the action, calling digital imaging perhaps the greatest growth opportunity in the computer world. And it may be. We surely see it as the greatest future enabler for people to truly "Take Pictures. Further."*
>
> *We start at retail, our distribution stronghold. Here consumers are at the peak moment of satisfaction, when they open their photofinishing envelopes. We believe the widespread photo-retailing infrastructure will continue to be the principal avenue by which people obtain their pictures. Our strategy is to build on and extend this existing market strength which is available to us, and at the same time be prepared to serve the rapidly growing, but relatively small, pure digital market that is developing. Kodak will network its rapidly expanding installed base of* Image Magic *stations and kiosks, essentially turning these into nodes on a massive, global network. The company will allow retailers to use these workstations to bring digital capability to the average snapshooter, extending the value of these images for the consumers and retailers alike, while creating a lucrative consumable business for Kodak.*[4]

It was in the commercial and professional markets where Kodak launched its major innovations in digital imaging. The sophisticated needs of the government in satellite imaging, planning military campaigns, weather forecasting, and surveillance activities favored digital technologies for transforming, transmitting, and storing images; medical imaging (especially CT, MRI, and ultrasound) required digital technologies for 3D imaging, diagnosis, and image storage; publishers and printers needed digital imaging to complement the new generation of computerized publishing and printing systems for newspapers and magazines. For commercial applications ranging from journalism to highway safety to real estate, digital imaging provided the linkage to the internet and sophisticated IT management systems. In professional photography, the huge price premium of professional over consumer products encouraged Kodak to focus R&D on these leading-edge users in the anticipation of trickle-down to the consumer market. Most manufacturers – including Kodak – maintained clearly differentiated product ranges for each segment, which was reflected in clear price differentials. During 1999, price multiples between professional and consumer models were as much as 150 times for cameras ($30,000 vs. $200), 100 times for scanners ($10,000 vs. $100), and 15 times for color laser printers ($30,000 vs. $2,000).

In addition to the sophisticated digital cameras that Kodak released first to the professional market, Kodak sought leadership in digital systems for medical diagnostic imaging, commercial printing, and document management systems for large organizations. For example:

● In the medical field, Kodak's Ektascan Imagelink system – which enabled medical images to be converted into digital images that could be transmitted via phone between hospitals – was launched in 1995 followed by its Ektascan medical laser printer in 1996. This leadership was extended with the acquisition of Imation's Dry View laser imaging business in 1998. By the end of the 1990s, Kodak had built a powerful position in digital health imaging based on both laser imaging and digital radiography.

- In the US space program, Kodak cameras and imaging equipment accompanied a number of missions, including the Mars probe and the IKONOS Earth-orbiting satellite.

- Elsewhere in the public sector, Kodak's digital scanning and document management systems were used in national censuses in the US, UK, France, Australia, and Brazil. At the German post office, a Kodak team achieved a world record, creating digitized copies of 1.7 million documents in 24 hours.

- In commercial printing and publishing, Kodak held a strong position in high-quality, high-speed digital printing systems. Kodak's involvement in this market was increasingly through NexPress, a joint venture between Kodak and Heidelberg, which developed and supplied a range of high-end color and black-and-white printing machines.

- In moving pictures, Kodak offered services for digitizing conventional movie films, digital formats for cinema and TV film, and systems for generating visual effects.

Alliances

In its traditional photographic business, Kodak's strategy was one of vertical integration: it had sought to dominate the photographic value chain from image capture through to the processing of customers' photographic film. In digital imaging such dominance was inconceivable: the digital imaging field was already heavily populated – with some firms holding dominant positions. In digital cameras, Kodak was just one among more than 20 suppliers. In computers and printers, there was Dell, Compaq, Toshiba, HP, and Canon. In software, Microsoft dominated operating systems and browsers while Adobe Systems dominated image formatting software. Willy Shih, head of Kodak's digital imaging products from 1997 to 2003, observed: "We have to pick where we add value and commoditize where we can't."[5] The difficult decision was identifying the activities and product areas where it could add value, and those that were best left to other companies.

Fisher recognized that for Kodak to become a key player in digital imaging, it would need to partner with companies that were already leaders in digital technologies and hardware and software products. Under Fisher's leadership, Kodak forged a web of joint ventures and strategic alliances. In addition to the already mentioned alliances with Canon, AOL, and Heidelberg, Kodak's alliances included:

- Intel Corporation: development and co-marketing of Picture CD; development of digital image storage media; and development of an ASP system for archiving and downloading medical images on a pay-per-use basis

- Hewlett-Packard: a primary source of inkjet technology for Kodak, Phogenix Imaging was a joint venture between Kodak and HP to develop high-quality inkjet solutions for micro and mini photo-finishing labs utilizing Kodak's DLS software.[6]

- Microsoft: cooperation to establish standards for Windows-based Picture Transfer Protocols and cooperation in the development of Photo-CDs and development of FlashPix image storage for digital cameras (also with HP).
- Olympus: sharing digital camera technology; developing common standards for web-based storage and printing of photographs (each company had over one thousand patents relating to digital cameras and digital photographic systems).
- Sanyo Electric Co.: joint development of color, active matrix organic electroluminescent (OLED) displays.

The Digital Transfomation Gathers Pace: Dan Carp, 2000–2004

Daniel A. Carp succeeded George Fisher as CEO on January 1, 2000. Unlike Fisher, Carp was a Kodak veteran – he started at Kodak in 1970 as a statistical analyst. As chief executive, his approach was to develop and refine the strategic direction established by Fisher. His key priority was to provide greater focus for Kodak's efforts in terms of specifying areas of business together with products and services where Kodak would build market leadership. To this end he articulated the following vision for Kodak:

Kodak will be the brand and market share leader for:

- *Consumers who take, share, album and print their life experiences in pictures;*
- *Commercial customers who use integrated imaging systems to communicate and educate;*
- *Healthcare professionals who manage, diagnose, and treat patients using image-centric technologies.*[7]

Carp's emphasis on developing products and services for specific customer groups was reflected in Kodak's organizational structure (see figure 7.1).

The Consumer Market

In the consumer market, Carp believed that Kodak should establish a market position in digital imaging that was similar to its positioning within traditional imaging: Kodak should be the mass-market leader providing security and reliability for customers bewildered by the pace of technological change. This required Kodak to maintain its strategy of providing a transition path for customers seeking to migrate from traditional to digital imaging. Thus, Kodak would offer an array of services that would allow consumers to digitize conventional photographs, edit digitized images, and obtain printed photographs in a variety of formats.

Mass-market leadership also required that Kodak provided the fully integrated set of products and services needed for digital photography. The essential characteristic of the Kodak system would be ease of use. "For Kodak, digital photography is all about ease of use and helping people get prints – in other words, getting the same experience they're used to from their film cameras," said Martin Coyne, head of Kodak's Photographic Group, at the 2002 Kodak Media Forum. He supported his argument with data showing that while 90% of consumers were satisfied with the

FIGURE 7.1 Kodak's organizational structure, February 2004

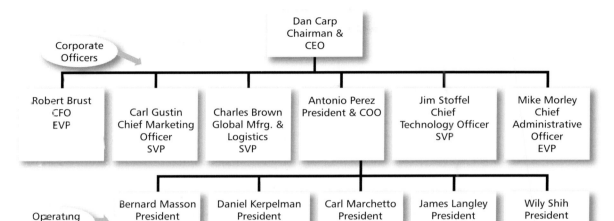

pictures obtained from traditional photography, for digital photography the numbers were only between 50 and 70%.[8] A systems approach rather than a product approach was based on the recognition that most consumers had neither the time nor the patience for reading instructions and integrating different devices and software. Kodak believed that its integrated system approach would have particular appeal to women – who comprised the major part of the consumer market.

The result was Kodak's EasyShare system, launched in 2001. According to Willy Shih, head of digital and applied imaging, EasyShare's intention was to:

> ... provide consumers with the first easy-to-use digital photography experience.... Digital photography is more than just about digital cameras. This is just the first step.... People need to get their pictures to their PCs and then want to share by printing or e-mail. So we developed a system that made the full experience as easy as possible.[9]

The result would be a digital system within which consumers could take digital pictures (or have conventional photographs digitized) and could print their digital images at home, at kiosks, at retail outlets, or through an online processing service (see figure 7.2).

By 2003, most of the main elements of the EasyShare system were in place.

- Kodak had a broad range of EasyShare digital cameras.
- EasyShare camera docks allowed the transfer of digital images from camera to PC at the touch of a button.
- EasyShare software allowed the downloading, organization, editing, and emailing of images, as well as ordering online prints. EasyShare software was bundled with Kodak's cameras as well as being available for downloading for free from Kodak's website.
- EasyShare printer docks enabled photographic prints to be made direct from the camera without the need for downloading to a PC.

FIGURE 7.2 Kodak's EasyShare Network: "Enabling the picture experience anytime, anywhere: at home, at retail, or on the road"

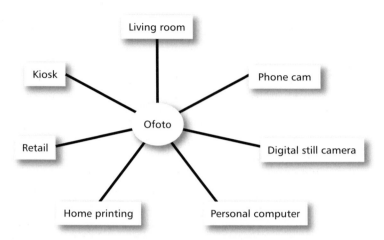

SOURCE: BASED ON EASTMAN KODAK COMPANY, 4TH QUARTER 2003 REPORT AND 2004 *DII/LOOK,* JANUARY ?? 2004.

The EasyShare initiative combined Kodak's offerings in four product areas, only one of which (photographic paper) was a traditional strength of Kodak's:

● *Digital cameras.* Casio had been the early leader, with over half the world market during the early 1990s. By 1998, 45 companies were offering digital cameras. Suppliers including long-established camera manufacturers (Canon, Kodak, Fuji, Olympus), electronics companies (Casio, HP), and – most recently – manufacturers of wireless handsets (Nokia, Motorola, Samsung, and others). When Kodak entered the digital camera business, it was already weak in conventional cameras and lacked the electronic imaging capabilities of Canon, Sony, and HP. Its EasyShare range resulted in substantial market share gains – by the fourth quarter of 2003, it was among the top three market leaders in the US, western Europe, and China. (See table 7.1 for market share data.)

TABLE 7.1 Brand shares of the world market for digital still cameras (by units)

Brand	2003	2002	2001	2000
Sony	18%	20%	25%	26%
Canon	16%	14%	10%	9%
Olympus	13%	16%	11%	18%
Kodak	12%	10%	14%	1?%
Hewlett-Packard	n.a.	3%	8%	?%
Fuji Film	10%	15%	14%	12%
Total units sold	48m	28m	17m	n.a.

SOURCE: COMPILED FROM DIFFERENT NEWSPAPER ARTICLES.

- *Printers*. Like digital cameras, printers were a brutally competitive market where, in 2000, Kodak had a strong position in commercial and medical printers (using thermal, inkjet, and laser technologies) but almost no presence in the consumer market. The appointment of Antonio Perez as President and COO in 2003 reinforced Kodak's push into printers: Perez was formerly the head of HP's Consumer Business. He argued: "If a company wants to be a leader in digital imaging, it necessarily has to participate in digital output."[10] In the consumer market Kodak focused on special purpose printers for producing photographic images. Initially, Kodak sourced inkjet printers from Lexmark. The 2003 EasyShare dock printer represented a major step forward for Kodak: a combined printer and camera dock that offered "one touch simple" thermal-dye printing either with a PC or direct from the camera. In 2002, Kodak acquired Scitex, a leader in continuous-flow inkjet printing, to augment its capabilities in variable data digital printing.

- *Software*. Software for digital imaging comprised editing software for manipulating images, color control software, file format and storage software, and software for transferring image files between computers through the internet. Editing software ranged from programs to fulfill basic image manipulation, such as Microsoft's Picture It, to more comprehensive picture editing and formatting software, where Adobe's Photoshop dominated the market. Kodak's main strengths were in its color management software and its DLS System Management and Enhanced Services Software for managing retail processing and printing operations. In 2003 – despite Adobe Systems' domination of the market for image display, formatting, and editing with its Photoshop and Acrobat products – Kodak released its EasyShare software. Adobe quickly followed with Photoshop Album – a $49 derivative of its Photoshop software.

- *Photographic paper*. To complete its home printing system, Kodak offered a number of technical advances in inkjet printing paper designed to place it ahead of the competition. Most significant was its Colorlast technology designed to preserve the fidelity and vibrancy of photographic prints for a hundred years or more.

Kodak's EasyShare system provided an integrated digital photography home-based solution for the consumer market. However, the key market advantage over rival systems would come from Kodak's linking of its hardware and software products to the capabilities offered by its retail network and online presence. Under Carp and Perez, Kodak invested heavily in both of these networks:

- *Kodak's retail-based processing*. By the beginning of 2004, Kodak was the clear leader in self-service digital printing kiosks, with 24,000 installed Kodak Picture Makers in the US and over 55,000 worldwide. The kiosks offered consumers a number of scanning, editing, and printing services, with particular emphasis on the scanning of conventional photographic images. During 2004, Kodak began installing its G3 Picture Maker kiosk, which had the ability to print pictures in as little as five seconds.

- *Kodak's online digital imaging services*. The internet was central to Kodak's strategy for the consumer market. According to Willy Shih: "the next killer app . . . is when photography meets the network effect. Or, in other words, when the internet is coupled with digital photography." In 2001, Kodak increased its presence in online photographic processing by acquiring Ofoto, the leading online photographic company. In addition to offering online processing, whereby consumers emailed their digital images and received their photographic prints by mail, Ofoto allowed members to build online albums through which family and friends could view and order prints for themselves. Kodak's press release stated: "Ofoto will serve as a critical connection between Kodak's film scanning and uploading services and Kodak's output capabilities through labs operated by its Qualex Inc. subsidiary. These capabilities will give customers and consumers unlimited flexibility in storing, sharing, enhancing and printing pictures." In 2002, several online providers of photographic services exited the market – leaving Shutterfly, Snapfish, Wal-Mart, and Fuji as Kodak's main rivals. Kodak also sought a leading position in "mobile photography" – the use of cellphone cameras to capture and transmit images. Kodak partnered with Cingular, Nokia, and AT&T to launch its Kodak Mobile Service, which allowed users to store and organize pictures and phone-captured video in one location and order prints.

The Commercial Sector

In the commercial sector, Carp's approach was to focus on a few markets that were both attractive and where Kodak's distinctive capabilities gave it a competitive edge. By 2004, Kodak's commercial business was organized around three divisions:

- *Health Imaging*. This was viewed as an especially attractive segment by Carp on the basis of the margins available and Kodak's potential to carve out a strong niche in medical imaging products using both chemical and digital technologies. In 2000 alone, 45 new health imaging products were introduced, including digital radiography systems and a new dental radiography film. It also acquired Lumisys, a provider of desktop radiography systems, and PracticeWorks, a producer of dental practice management software.

- *Commercial Imaging*. Kodak's strength in commercial imaging has been built around its leadership in certain types of hardware (notably, high-speed scanners), its ability to supply integrated document management systems (allowing images of paper-based documents to be created, archived, referenced, and retrieved), and its relationships with customers (both commercial and public sector).

- *Commercial Printing*. Under Dan Carp, Kodak had built up a strong presence in several parts of the commercial printing business – chiefly through joint ventures and acquisitions. These included: (a) Polychrome Graphics (a JV with Sun Chemical), which produces offset printing plates and proofing equipment; (b) NexPress (a JV with Heidelberg[11]), which makes high-end digital printers; (c) the production of inkjet printers by Encad (a producer of wide-format inkjet printers) and Versamark (previously Scitex Digital Printing), which makes high-speed, narrow-format inkjet printers. Commercial printing products were focused on specific market segments, notably short-run "on-demand" printing and "transactional printing" (e.g. bills, statements, checks, and invoices). Government sales were an important component of commercial printing revenues. Commercial printing was seen as an important market opportunity for Kodak: the shift to digital printing was creating serious disruption and Kodak was able to offer a comprehensive range of hardware, consumables, and customer support.

In both consumer and commercial segments, a key element of Kodak's strategy was the use of acquisitions to reinforce Kodak's position in certain markets, extend its range of products and services into new markets, and build Kodak's technical capabilities. Table 7.2 shows Kodak's major acquisitions under CEOs Fisher and Carp.

TABLE 7.2 Kodak's major acquisitions, 1994–2004

1994	Qualex, Inc.	Provider of photo-finishing services. Became key link in Kodak's online photofinishing service
1997	Wang Laboratories	Acquisition of Wang's software unit
1998	PictureVision, Inc.	Provider of PhotoNet online digital imaging services and retail solutions; this service integrated within Kodak's Picture Network business
	Shantou Era Photo Material, Xiamen Fuda Photographic Materials	Kodak strengthens its position in the photographic film market in China
1999	Imation	Kodak acquires Imation's medical imaging business
2000	Lumisys, Inc.	Leading provider of desktop computed radiography systems and x-ray film digitizers
2001	Bell & Howell	Imaging businesses only acquired
	Ofoto, Inc.	Leading online photography service
	Encad, Inc.	Wide-format commercial inkjet printers
2003	Practiceworks	Digital dental imaging and dental practice management software
	Lucky Film Co., Ltd.	20% of the largest maker of photo film headquartered in China
	Laser-Pacific Media Corporation	A provider of post-production services for filmmakers
	Algotec Systems Ltd.	Developer of picture archiving and communications
	Applied Science Fiction	Digital PIC rapid film processing technology
2004	NexPress	Acquired Heidelberg's half-share of this joint venture which supplied high-end, on-demand color printing systems and black-and-white variable-data printing systems
	Scitex Digital Printing	A leader in high-speed variable data inkjet printing (renamed Kodak Versamark, Inc.)
	Chinon Industries	Kodak purchases outstanding shares
	National Semiconductor	Kodak acquires National's imaging sensor business

SOURCE: EASTMAN KODAK 10-K REPORTS.

Kodak's Resources and Capabilities

Building a competitive advantage in digital imaging, Carp realized, would require, first, that Kodak's strategy was firmly based on its existing resource and capability strengths and, second, that Kodak quickly put in place the resources and capabilities necessary to success that it did not already possess. The central problem was that the resources and capabilities that were the foundation of Kodak's dominance of traditional photography were very different from those required by digital imaging. In digital imaging, Kodak was but one of many companies that had been drawn to the emerging sector as a result of the convergence of imaging and electronics. Kodak, like Fuji, had entered digital imaging to protect itself against the threat that digital technologies presented to photographic film. Canon, Olympus, and Minolta had entered from their positions in cameras. Casio, Ricoh, and Hewlett-Packard entered from office electronics and printing, while Sony came out of consumer electronics. All these companies possessed different sets of resources and capabilities, with strengths and weaknesses in different areas. In reviewing Kodak's competitive position, Carp focused on the following resources and capabilities.

Brand and Distribution

Foremost among Kodak's resource strengths were its brand equity and distribution presence. After almost a century of global leadership in the photographic industry, Kodak possessed brand recognition and worldwide distribution reach that was unrivaled in the photographic industry. Kodak could bring new products to consumers' attention and support these products with one of the world's best-known and most widely respected brand names, giving the company a huge advantage in a market where technological change created uncertainty for consumers. Kodak's brand reputation was supported by its massive, worldwide distribution presence – primarily through retail photography stores, film processors, and professional photographers. This retail presence was critical to Kodak's entire digital strategy, which was built around providing consumers with a pathway to digital imaging using services offered through retail stores and photo-finishers.

To what extent would Kodak's distribution and brand strengths continue to be a source of competitive advantage in digital imaging? Kodak's retail network was a depreciating asset as consumers' own home-based computer, email, and print capabilities increased. The brand, according to Chief Marketing Officer Carl Gustin, would continue to be Kodak's most valuable asset: "I have always said our brand is almost bulletproof when it comes to images, to memories, to trust, reliability, family values, and more." In studies of digital imaging products, Kodak's brand had ranked either No. 1 or No. 2 in recent years. However, the huge changes in the market might necessitate changes in Kodak's brand strategy. As Gustin remarked: "Does the Kodak name go everywhere, or is a variance of the Kodak name required? Does the name need some tagline? Multiple taglines? Does it mean the same in the commercial and services sector as it does in the consumer sector? That's all being investigated."[12] Nor was it clear that the Kodak brand would carry the same weight in digital as in traditional photography – especially when it was competing against brands such as Canon, Hewlett-Packard, and Sony. In relation to professional, commercial, medical, and government markets, Dan Carp believed that Kodak's market presence might be more secure. The long-established relationship between Kodak and its corporate and institutional customers and the range of support services that Kodak was able to supply provided a greater barrier to consumer electronics companies and high-tech upstarts.

Technology

In technology, Kodak came to digital imaging with some well-established strengths. Its huge R&D investments in digital imaging since the early 1980s had created proprietary technologies across a broad front. Despite R&D cutbacks during the late 1990s, Kodak maintained one of the world's biggest research efforts in imaging. At its research labs in the US, UK, France, Japan, China, and Australia, Kodak employed more than 5,000 engineers and scientists, including more than 600 PhDs. In 2003, Kodak filed more than 900 patent applications and received 748 US patents, an increase of 11% over 2002. Table 7.3 identifies some of Kodak's principal areas of technological strength.

Moreover, its century of innovation and development of photographic images gave Kodak insight and intuition that transcended specific imaging technologies. Central to Kodak's imaging capability was its color management capability. As *Business Week* observed more than a decade earlier when Fisher joined Kodak: "The basic know-how of combining electronic image capture and color management has been Kodak's for years. Kodak is a world-beater in electronic sensors, devices that see and capture an image, and has a raft of patents in color thermal printing. It also has the best understanding of color management software, which matches the colors you see on the screen with what's on the printed page."[13] Kodak used the term "color science" to refer to the production, control, measurement, specification, and visual perception of color; this included "colorimetry" – the measurement of color characteristics.

Kodak's technological capabilities meant that it was positioned at each of the principal stages in the digital imaging value chain – even though, at most of these stages, it was not a clear market leader (see figure 7.3).

At the image-output level, Kodak believed that consumers would continue to demand printed photographs. In print media, particularly specialty coated papers, Kodak was world leader. During 2000–3, Kodak introduced a number of new inkjet papers embodying new technologies.

New Product Development

Despite Kodak's strengths in basic and applied research and its long history of successful new product launches, Carp was acutely aware of the criticisms that had been leveled at Kodak for its weaknesses in bringing new products to market: Kodak was too slow and its marketers had little understanding of the digital world.

Kodak's product development process still reflected the company's origins in chemistry. Product development traditionally began with basic research where innovations were exploited through a long and meticulous product development process before being rolled out onto the world market. One of George Fisher's major initiatives as Kodak Chairman and CEO had been to streamline and speed Kodak's cumbersome product development process. In place of Kodak's sequential "phases and gates" development process, Fisher transferred approaches that had worked well at Motorola – greater decentralization of new product development and the use of cross-functional

TABLE 7.3 Kodak's technical capabilities

Area of technology	Kodak capabilities
Color science	Kodak is a leader in the production, control, measurement, specification, and visual perception of color. Essential to predicting the performance of image-capture devices and imaging systems. Kodak has pioneered colorimetry – measuring and quantifying visual response to a stimulus of light
Image processing	Includes technologies to control image sharpness, noise, and color reproduction. It is used to maximize the information content of images and to compress data for economical storage and rapid transmission. Kodak is a leader in image processing algorithms for automatic color balancing, object and text recognition, and image enhancement and manipulation. These are especially important in digital photo-finishing for image enhancement, including adjustments for scene reflectance, lighting conditions, sharpness, and a host of other conditions
Systems analysis	Provides techniques to measure the characteristics of imaging systems and components. Predictive system modeling is especially important in Kodak's new product development, where it can predict the impact of individual components on the performance of the entire system
Sensors	Kodak is a world leader in image sensor technology, with 30 years' experience in the design and manufacture of electronic image sensors, including both CCD and CMOS image sensors that serve both high-volume and specialty imaging markets, ranging from satellite and medical imaging to digital cameras, camera phones, and machine vision products
Printing technologies	
Ink technology	Kodak leads in technical understanding of dyes and pigments. It has pioneered *micro-milling technology* (that it originally invented for drug delivery systems). It has advanced knowledge of *humectants* (which keep printhead nozzles from clogging) and *surface tension and viscosity modifiers* (which control ink flows)
Microfluidics	Microfluidics – the study of miniature devices that handle very small quantities of liquids – is relevant to film coating, fluid mixing, chemical sensing, and liquid inkjet printing
Print media	Kodak has unrivaled know-how in applying polymer science and chemical engineering to the materials that receive ink: paper, glass, fabric. Key strengths include *specially constructed inkjet media* in which layers of organic and/or inorganic polymers are coated onto paper or clear film and *multi-layer coated structures* of hydrogels, inorganic oxides, and similar substances
Electronic display technology	Kodak pioneered *organic light-emitting diode* (OLED) technology, which allows flat panel displays to be self-luminous
Software	Kodak supplies software for image manipulation and printer control. It has particular strengths in control software and printing algorithms that can overcome many of the technical limitations of inkjet printing and optimize color and tone reproduction (e.g. the Kodak One Touch Printing System)

SOURCE: WWW.KODAK.COM

FIGURE 7.3 Kodak's technological position within the digital imaging chain

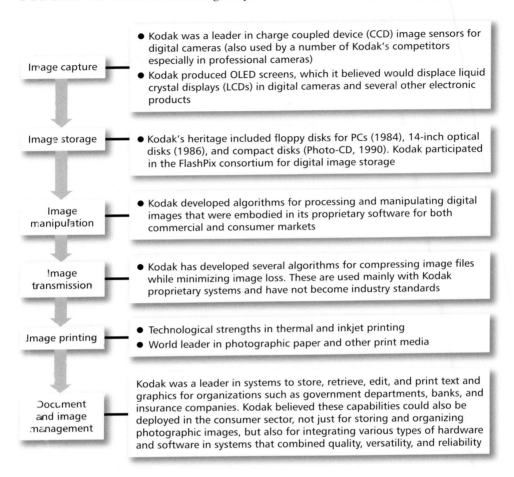

development teams to accelerate cycle times. Speed also required collaboration to access the technologies and capabilities of outside companies. Kodak had no problem in establishing collaborative agreements with other companies – its size, brand name, and technological strength were sufficient to make it a highly attractive partner for small, technology-intensive firms in digital imaging. The real challenge was for Kodak to overcome a long history of insularity and hierarchical control in order to make its new-found alliances fruitful. Kodak's track record of alliances and joint ventures was mixed. Its Phoenix joint venture with HP to develop digital minilabs for film and image processes was dissolved in May 2003 after three years.[14]

Under Dan Carp, Kodak has greatly increased the flow of new digital imaging products to the markets. To enhance Kodak's ability to develop successful new products, Carp continued Fisher's strategy of hiring senior executives from leading-edge IT companies. Table 7.4 shows the backgrounds of Kodak's senior executives. In addition, Carp increased the pace of Kodak's acquisitions of companies that could fill key gaps in its own know-how. Despite these positive developments, there were lingering

TABLE 7.4 Eastman Kodak's senior management team, March 2004

Name	Position	Joined Kodak	Prior company experience
Corporate Officers			
Daniel Carp	Chairman & CEO	1970	Kodak veteran
Antonio Perez	President & COO	2003	CEO, HP Inkjet Imaging
Robert Brust	Chief Financial Officer	2000	Unisys, General Electric
Michael Morley	Chief Admin. Officer	1964	Kodak veteran
Gary Graafeiland	General Counsel	1979	Kodak veteran
Charles Brown	Director, Global Manufacturing & Logistics	1973	Kodak veteran
Carl Gustin, Jr.	Chief Marketing Officer	1994	DEC, Apple Computer
Henri Petit	Director, International	1975	Kodak veteran
James Stoffel	Chief Technology Officer	1997	Xerox
William Lloyd	Director, Inkjet Systems	2003	Inwit, Gemplus, HP
Daniel Meek	Director, Operating System	1973	Kodak veteran
Kim VanGelder	Chief Information Officer	1984	Kodak veteran
Divisional Presidents			
Bernard Masson	Digital & Film Imaging	2002	Lexmark
Daniel Kerpelman	Health Imaging	2002	GE Medical Systems
Carl Marchetto	Commercial Imaging	1996	Lockheed Martin
James Langley	Commercial Printing	2003	HP
Willy Shih	Display & Components	1997	Silicon Graphics

SOURCES: EASTMAN KODAK ANNUAL REPORT, 2003; WWW.KODAK.COM

doubts as to whether a former monopolist of the photographic industry, with its activities heavily concentrated on Rochester, New York, could ever adapt to the fast-cycle product development practices of Silicon Valley.

Finances

One of Kodak's key advantages in withstanding the uncertainties and rapid technological changes of the market for digital imaging was its size and financial security. In contrast to the many start-up companies that sought to establish themselves in the sector, Kodak was independent of venture capitalists and the vagaries of the IPO market. In contrast even to some of its large and well-established rivals, Kodak had the security of cash flows from its traditional photographic business.

By the beginning of 2004, Eastman Kodak remained a financially strong company, but it was no longer the financial powerhouse of yesteryear. Since the late 1990s, debt had risen considerably, and retiree healthcare benefits represented a substantial long-term liability. Meanwhile, profitability declined substantially between 2000 and 2003 – both because of the deterioration of the core photography business and because of the restructuring charges that were becoming a regular feature of Kodak's income statement. As a result, some analysts doubted Kodak's ability to finance its "digital growth strategy," which involved investing some $3 billion in capital expenditures and acquisitions during 2004–6. Tables 7.5 and 7.6 summarize Kodak's recent financial results.

TABLE 7.5 Eastman Kodak: selected financial data, 1997–2003 ($ million)

	1997	1998	1999	2000	2001	2002	2003
From income statement							
Sales	14,713	13,406	14,089	13,994	13,234	12,835	13,317
Costs:							
Cost of goods sold	7,979	7,293	7,987	8,019	8,670	8,225	9,033
Selling, general, and admin.	3,912	3,303	3,295	2,977	2,627	2,530	2,648
R&D costs	1,044	922	817	784	779	762	781
Operating earnings	1,778	1,888	1,990	2,214	345	793	238
Interest expense	98	110	142	178	219	173	148
Other income (charges)	(1,441)	328	261	96	(18)	101	51
Restructuring and other costs	1,441	–	350	(44)	659	98	484
Provision for income taxes	48	716	717	725	32	153	(66)
Net earnings	5	1,390	1,392	1,407	76	770	265
From balance sheet							
Total current assets	5,475	–	5,373	5,491	4,683	4,534	5,455
Including:							
Cash and cash equivalents	728	–	20	246	448	569	1,250
Receivables	2,271	–	2,537	2,653	2,337	2,234	2,389
Inventories	1,252	–	1,519	1,718	1,137	1,062	1,075
Property, plant, and equipment	5,509	–	6,189	5,919	5,659	5,420	5,094
Other noncurrent assets	1,231	–	1,801	1,767	2,072	3,540	4,269
Total assets	13,145	–	14,370	14,212	13,362	13,494	14,818
Total current liabilities	5,177	–	3,832	3,275	5,354	5,502	5,307
Including:							
Payables	3,832	–	1,163	3,403	3,276	3,351	3,707
Short-term borrowings	611	–	612	2,058	1,378	1,442	946
Other liabilities:							
Long-term borrowings	585	–	936	1,166	1,666	1,164	2,302
Post-employment liabilities	3,075	–	2,776	2,610	2,728	3,412	3,344
Other long-term liabilities	1,019	–	859	671	720	639	601
Total liabilities	9,984	–	10,458	10,784	10,468	10,717	11,554
Shareholders' equity	3,161	–	3,912	3,428	2,894	2,777	3,264
Total liabilities (& equity)	13,145	–	14,370	14,212	13,362	13,494	14,818
From cash flow statement							
Cash flows from operating activities:							
Earnings from continuing operations	5	1,390	1,392	1,407	76	770	265
Adjustments for non-cash items	2,075	93	541	(425)	1,989	1,448	1,361
Net cash provided by operating activities	2,080	1,483	1,933	982	2,065	2,204	1,645
Cash flows from investing activities:							
Additions to properties	(1,485)	(1,108)	(1,127)	(945)	(743)	(577)	(506)
Proceeds from sale of businesses/assets	(85)	238	422	277	0	27	26
Acquisitions net of cash acquired	(341)	(949)	(3)	(130)	(306)	(72)	(679)
Net cash used in investing activities	(1,896)	(1,839)	(685)	(783)	(1,074)	(758)	(1,267)
Net cash flows from financing activities	(1,198)	77	(1,327)	(314)	(804)	(1,331)	270
Number of employees (thousands)	97.5	86.5	80.7	78.1	75.1	70.0	63.9

TABLE 7.6 Eastman Kodak: results by business segments, 1999–2003 ($ millions)

	1999	2000	2001	2002	2003
Net sales:					
Photography	10,265	10,231	9,403	9,002	9,232
Health Imaging	2,159	2,220	2,262	2,274	2,431
Commercial Imaging	1,479	1,417	1,454	1,456	1,559
All other	186	126	110	103	95
Consolidated total	14,089	13,994	13,229	12,835	13,317
Earnings from operations:					
Photography	1,709	1,430	787	771	418
Health Imaging	483	518	323	431	481
Commercial Imaging	257	233	172	192	166
All other	(109)	(11)	(60)	(28)	(78)
Total of segments	2,340	2,170	1,222	1,366	987
Net earnings:					
Photography	1,261	1,034	535	550	347
Health Imaging	324	356	221	313	382
Commercial Imaging	178	90	84	83	99
All other	(61)	(2)	(38)	(23)	(73)
Total of segments	1,702	1,478	802	923	755
Total assets:*					
Photography	6,875	7,100	9,225	8,798	8,905
Health Imaging	1,229	1,491	2,038	2,011	2,600
Commercial Imaging	963	1,045	1,438	1,405	1,396
All other	(123)	(92)	(16)	66	10
Total of segments	8,944	9,544	12,685	12,280	12,911

*Net operating assets for 1999 and 2000.

Looking Forward

As he reviewed Kodak's results for 2003 and plans for 2004, Dan Carp felt that after ten years of struggle, Kodak's digital strategy was coming together and beginning to yield fruit.

In the medical and commercial sectors, the company had strong, profitable positions in several markets where Kodak possessed particular technical strengths and strong customer relationships. However, it was in the consumer photographic sector that Carp felt that Kodak had made particularly significant progress under his leadership. Kodak was finally a full-system supplier – it was positioned at every stage in the digital imaging chain and under its EasyShare brand was communicating its system capabilities to consumers. Particularly important was Kodak's ability to serve the needs of several types of customer. Through its retail network it provided digital scanning, enhancement, and storage facilities to consumers who took pictures with conventional film. For consumers with digital cameras, it offered editing and printing services both through retail kiosks and on-line. And, with its EasyShare printers, it allowed customers the independence to pursue digital photography without using any of Kodak's retail services. In addition, Kodak had established strongholds in a number of key technologies, from sensors and flat screens to inks and specialty papers and – most impressive – Kodak had established itself as a leading supplier of digital cameras.

Despite this progress, the financial outlook remained troubling. Carp realized that the 2004–6 period would be critical for Kodak – especially in the consumer sector. Carp's excitement at gaining US market leadership in digital cameras was tempered by the realization that Kodak lost money on every one. The situation was much the same throughout the consumer market for digital photography: competition was brutal and margins either thin or non-existent. Kodak's most direct competitor was Fuji Film. While Kodak had experienced stagnant revenues for the past four years, Fuji had grown rapidly and had achieved much higher operating earnings than Kodak.[15] Fuji was strongly positioned across a broad range of the technologies relevant to the new world of digital imaging: digital image-processing software, nano-technology, pigmentation technology, CCD technology, lenses, and lasers. Its "Vision 75" strategy (culminating in Fuji's 75th anniversary in 2007) planned for heavy investment and rapid sales growth. Many of the targeted markets were precisely the same as those where Kodak was also focusing: digital cameras, flat panel displays, print-on-demand digital commercial printing, digital minilabs, and the Chinese market.

Apart from Fuji, a number of other competitors – well established in the electronics industry – were growing their presence in digital imaging: Hewlett-Packard, Sony, and Canon, to mention a few. Given the tendency for most of the standards in the industry to be open rather than proprietary, it seemed likely that competition would continue to be aggressive, with no one company building a dominant position.

Meanwhile, the strategy of supporting investments in digital imaging with the cash flow from Kodak's traditional film business was threatened by the accelerating decline in sales of photographic film. Of particular concern was the likelihood that emerging markets where the demand for home photography was expected to grow rapidly – China in particular – might move directly to digital photography, missing out on film-based photography almost entirely.

Given this outlook, what were Kodak's prospects for gaining a satisfactory rate of return on its investments in digital imaging? This depended on whether Kodak's present digital strategy – especially its strategy of integrated digital solutions for the consumer market – was sound. Even if it was, would Kodak win against so many powerful competitors? And, if it gained market leadership, would the profit returns justify the investments required? Given the pressure from activist shareholders, an alternative strategy might be for Kodak to abandon its ambitious attempt to position itself as a broad-line supplier of digital imaging solutions, and to focus on those products and markets where it had already established a strong market position and where margins were strong: the commercial and medical imaging markets and the supply of photo-finishing services and consumables such as paper and ink.

Notes

1 Lex, "Kodak focuses on digital future," *Financial Times*, January 23, 2004.
2 Address to the Academy of Management, Boston, August 1997.
3 "Kodak's new focus," *Business Week*, January 30, 1995, pp. 62–8.
4 Eastman Kodak Company, "Kodak leaders outline road ahead to get Kodak 'back on track'," Press Release, November 11, 1997.
5 "Why Kodak still isn't fixed," *Fortune*, May 11, 1998.
6 Eastman Kodak Company, "Kodak and HP joint venture to be named Phogenix Imaging," Press Release, August 1, 2000.
7 Kodak Strategy Review, September 2003.
8 Eastman Kodak Company, "The Big Picture: Kodak and Digital Photography," www.Kodak.com/US/en/corp/presscenter/presentations/020520mediaforum3.shtml
9 Ibid.
10 Interview with Antonio Perez, President and COO, Kodak, www.photomarketing.com/0204_PEREZ.htm

11 In March 2004, Kodak agreed to purchase Heidelberg's 50% share of NexPress, together with Heidelberg's digital black and white printing systems (see Annual Report for 2003, p. 17).
12 Interview with Carl Gustin, Chief Marketing Officer, Kodak, www.photomarketing.com/0204_Gustin.htm
13 "Kodak's new focus," op. cit.
14 Jeff Macher and Barak Richman ("Organizational responses to discontinuous innovation: A case study approach," *International Journal of Innovation Management*, Vol. 8, 2004, pp. 87–114) describe Kodak's joint project with Intel to develop the Picture CD: "Meetings scheduled to discuss the new product suffered from logistical constraints and unsolicited and unnecessary input from neighboring divisions . . . [T]he project's slow start highlighted that the firm's current routines and practices were not capable of developing a new technology for an uncertain, albeit rapidly emerging, market."
15 Fuji's ratio of operating income to sales was 11.0% in 2000, 10.8% in 2001, 7.0% in 2002, and 7.3% in 2003.

Organizational Restructuring within the Royal Dutch Shell Group

At the beginning of 2000, the Royal Dutch Shell Group of Companies (Shell) was emerging from one of the most ambitious and far-reaching organizational restructurings of its 93-year history. The restructuring had involved the shift from a geographically based to a business sector-based structure, the elimination of over 1,000 corporate positions, the sale of much of its London headquarters, and the redesign of its systems of coordination and control. The restructuring had been precipitated by the realization that Shell would need to change the way it did business if it was to retain its position as the world's largest petroleum company and offer an adequate return to shareholders in an increasingly turbulent industry environment.

By the end of 1999, it was clear that the changes were bearing fruit. Head office costs had been reduced and the increased coordination and control that the new sector-based organization permitted were helping Shell to control costs, focus capital expenditure, and prune the business portfolio. Return on capital employed (ROCE) and return on equity (ROE) for 1999 were their highest for ten years. However, much of the improvement in bottom-line performance was the result of the recovery in oil prices during the year. Once the benefits of higher oil prices were stripped out, Shell's improvements in financial performance looked much more modest.

At the same time, Shell's competitors were not standing still. BP, once government-owned and highly bureaucratized, had become one of the world's most dynamic, profitable, and widely admired oil majors. Its merger with Amoco quickly followed by its acquisition of Atlantic Richfield had created an international giant of almost identical size to Shell. In the meantime, Shell's longtime archrival, Exxon, was merging with Mobil. Shell was no longer the world's biggest energy company – its sales revenues lagged some way behind those of Exxon Mobil. Other oil and gas majors were also getting caught up in the wave of mergers and restructurings. In particular, Shell's once-sluggish European rivals were undergoing extensive revitalization. The merger of Total, Fina, and Elf Aquitaine in September 1999 had created the world's fourth "super-major" (after Exxon Mobil, Shell, and BP). Also asserting itself on the world stage was Italy's recently privatized Eni SpA.

The reorganization that had begun in 1994 under chairman of the Committee of Managing Directors, Cor Herkstroter, and continued under his successor, Mark Moody-Stuart, had transformed the organizational structure of Shell. From a decentralized confederation of over 200 operating companies spread throughout the world, a divisionalized group with clear lines of authority and more effective executive leadership had been created. Yet, Shell remained a highly complex organization that was a prisoner of its own illustrious history and where corporate authority remained divided between The Hague, London, and Houston. Had enough been done to turn a sprawling multinational empire into an enterprise capable of deploying its huge resources with the speed and decisiveness necessary to cope with an ever more volatile international environment?

History of the Royal Dutch Shell Group

The Royal Dutch Shell Group is unique among the world's oil majors. It was formed from the 1907 merger of the assets and operations of the Netherlands-based Royal Dutch Petroleum Company and the British-based Shell Transport and Trading Company. However, the two parents remained legally separate corporations. It is the world's biggest and oldest joint venture. Both parent companies trace their origins to the Far East in the 1890s.

Marcus Samuel inherited a half share in his father's seashell trading business. His business visits to the Far East made him aware of the potential for supplying kerosene from the newly developing Russian oilfields around Baku to the large markets in China and the Far East for oil suitable for lighting and cooking. Seeing the opportunity for exporting kerosene from the Black Sea coast through the recently opened Suez Canal to the Far East, Samuel invested in a new tanker, the *Murex*. In 1892, the *Murex* delivered 4,000 tons of Russian kerosene to Bangkok and Singapore. In 1897, Samuel formed the Shell Transport and Trading Company, with a pecten shell as its trademark, to take over his growing oil business.

At the same time, August Kessler was leading a Dutch company to develop an oilfield in Sumatra in the Dutch East Indies. In 1896, Henri Deterding joined Kessler and the two began building storage and transportation facilities and a distribution network to bring their oil to market.

The expansion of both companies was supported by the growing demand for oil resulting from the introduction of the automobile and oil-fueled ships. In 1901 Shell Transport and Trading began purchasing Texas crude, and soon both companies were engaged in fierce competition with John D. Rockefeller's Standard Oil. Faced with the might of Standard Oil, Samuel and Deterding (who had succeeded Kessler as chairman of Royal Dutch) began cooperating, and in 1907 the business interests of the two companies were combined into a single group, with Royal Dutch owning a 60% share and Shell Transport and Trading a 40% share (a ratio that has remained constant to this day).

The group grew rapidly, expanding East Indies production and acquiring producing interests in Romania (1906), Russia (1910), Egypt (1911), the US (1912),

Venezuela (1913), and Trinidad (1914). In 1929 Shell entered the chemicals business, and in 1933 Shell's interests in the US were consolidated into the Shell Union Oil Corporation. By 1938, Shell crude oil production stood at almost 580,000 barrels per day out of a world total of 5,720,000.

The post-war period began with rebuilding the war-devastated refineries and tanker fleet, and continued with the development of new oilfields in Venezuela, Iraq, the Sahara, Canada, Colombia, Nigeria, Gabon, Brunei, and Oman. In 1959, a joint Shell/Exxon venture discovered one of the world's largest natural gas fields at Groningen in the Netherlands. This was followed by a series of major North Sea oil and gas finds between 1971 and 1976.

During the 1970s, Shell, like the other majors, began diversifying outside of petroleum:

- In 1970 it acquired Billiton, an international metals mining company, for $123 million.
- In 1973 it formed a joint venture with Gulf to build nuclear reactors.
- In 1976–7 it acquired US and Canadian coal companies.
- In 1977 it acquired Witco Chemical's polybutylene division.

By the beginning of the 1980s, Shell had built global metals and coal businesses and established several smaller ventures including forestry in Chile and New Zealand, flower growing in the Netherlands, and biotechnology in Europe and the US.

The 1980s saw a reversal of Shell's diversification strategy, with several divestments of "non-core businesses" and a concentration on oil and gas – especially upstream. One of Shell's major thrusts was to increase its presence within the US. After acquiring Belridge Oil of California, it made its biggest investment of the period when it acquired the minority interests in its US subsidiary Shell Oil for $5.4 billion.

Shell's Organization Structure Prior to 1995

Shell's uniqueness stems from its structure as a joint venture and from its internationality – it has been described as one of the world's three most international organizations, the other two being the Roman Catholic Church and the United Nations. However, its organizational structure is more complex than either of the other two organizations. The structure of the Group may be looked at in terms of the different companies that comprise Royal Dutch Shell and their links of ownership and control, which Shell refers to as *governance responsibilities*. The Group's structure may also be viewed from a management perspective – how is Royal Dutch Shell actually managed? The day-to-day management activities of the Group, which Shell refers to as *executive responsibilities*, are complex, and the structure through which the Group is actually managed does not correspond very closely to the formal structure.

The Formal Structure

From an ownership and legal perspective, the Royal Dutch Shell Group of Companies comprised four types of company:

- *The parent companies.* Royal Dutch Petroleum Company N.V. of the Netherlands and the Shell Transport and Trading Company plc of the UK owned the shares of the group holding companies (from which they received dividends) in the proportions 60% and 40%. Each company had its shares separately listed on the stock exchanges of Europe and the US, and each had a separate Board of Directors.

- *The group holding companies.* Shell Petroleum N.V. of the Netherlands and The Shell Petroleum Company Ltd of the UK held shares in both the service companies and the operating companies of the Group. In addition, Shell Petroleum N.V. also owned the shares of Shell Petroleum Inc. of the US – the parent of the US operating company, Shell Oil Company.

- *The service companies.* During the early 1990s, there were nine service companies located either in London or The Hague. They were:
  - Shell Internationale Petroleum Maatschappij B.V.
  - Shell Internationale Chemie Maatschappij B.V.
  - Shell International Petroleum Company Limited
  - Shell International Chemical Company Limited
  - Billiton International Metals B.V.
  - Shell International Marine Limited
  - Shell Internationale Research Maatschappij B.V.
  - Shell International Gas Limited
  - Shell Coal International Limited.

The service companies provided advice and services to the operating companies but were not responsible for operations.

- *The operating companies* (or "opcos") comprised more than 200 companies in over 100 countries (the 1993 annual report listed 244 companies in which Shell held 50% or more ownership). They varied in size from Shell Oil Company, one of the largest petroleum companies in the US in its own right, to small marketing companies such as Shell Bahamas and Shell Cambodia. Almost all of the operating companies operated within a single country. Some had activities within a single sector (exploration and production (E&P), refining, marketing, coal, or gas); others (such as Shell UK, Shell Canada, and Norske Shell) operated across multiple sectors. Figure 8.1 shows the formal structure of the Group.

Coordination and Control

Managerial control of the Group was vested in the Committee of Managing Directors (CMD), which forms the Group's top management team. The Committee comprised five Managing Directors. These were the three-member Management Board of Royal Dutch Petroleum and the Chairman and Vice Chairman of Shell Transport and Trading. The chairmanship of the CMD rotated between the President of Royal Dutch Petroleum and the Managing Director of Shell Transport and Trading. Thus, in 1993, Cor Herkstroter (President of Royal Dutch) took over from J. S. Jennings (Managing Director of Shell Transport and Trading) as Chairman of the CMD, and Jennings became Vice Chairman of CMD. Because executive power was vested in a committee rather than a single chief executive, Shell lacked the strong individual leadership that characterized other majors (e.g., Lee Raymond at Exxon and John Browne at BP).

FIGURE 8.1 The formal structure of the Royal Dutch Shell Group

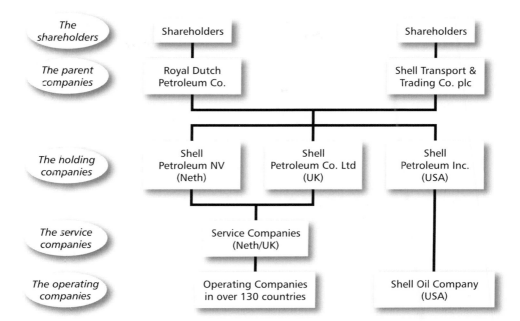

The CMD provided the primary linkage between the formal (or *governance*) structure and the management (or *executive*) structure of the Group. The CMD also linked together the two parent companies and the group holding companies.

The combination of diffused executive power at the top together with operating authority and financial responsibility dispersed through 244 operating companies meant that, compared with every other oil major, Shell was highly decentralized. However, the technical and economic realities of the oil business limited the autonomy of each operating company – interdependence resulted from linkages between upstream and downstream, between refining and chemicals, and from common financial and technological needs. It was the job of the service companies to provide the necessary coordination. During the early 1960s, Shell created, with the help of McKinsey & Company, a matrix structure within its service companies to manage its operating companies. This structure was viewed as a critical ingredient of Shell's ability to reconcile the independence of its operating companies with effective coordination of business, regional, and functional commonalities. This matrix organization continued into the 1990s (see figure 8.2).

The three dimensions of this matrix were represented by the principal executives of the service companies, who were designated "coordinators." Thus, the senior management team at the beginning of 1995 included the following:

Committee of Managing Directors

● Chairman
● Vice Chairman
● three other Managing Directors

FIGURE 8.2 The Shell Matrix (pre-1996)

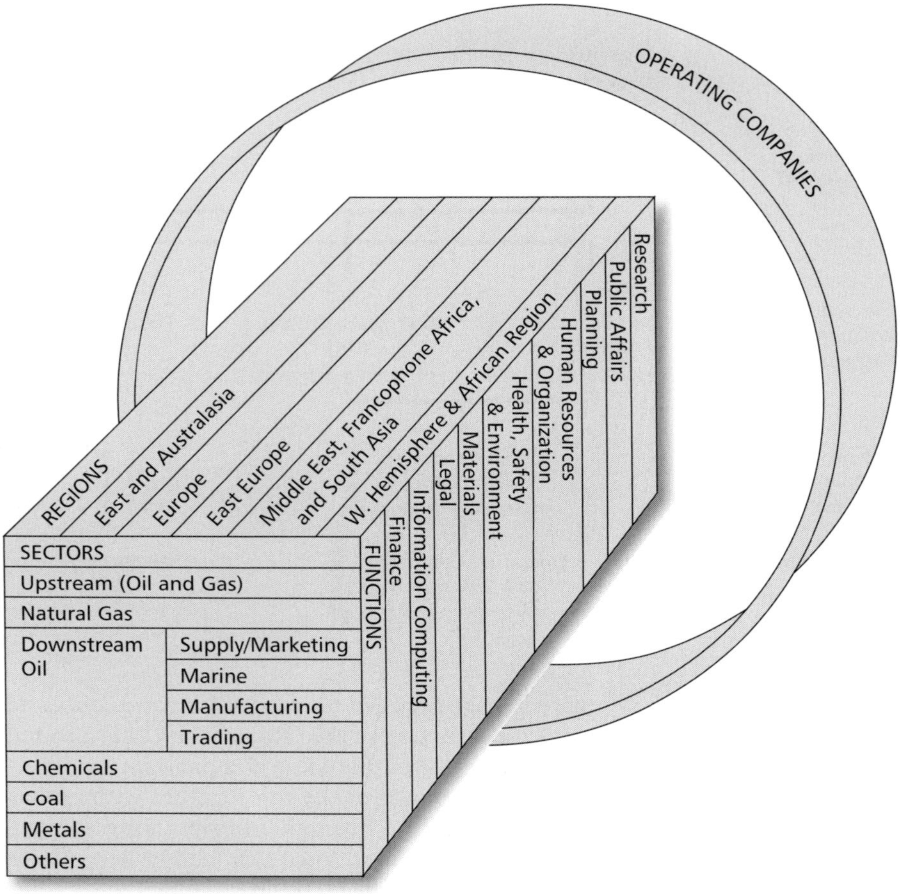

Principal executives of the service companies

- Regional coordinators:
  - Europe
  - Western Hemisphere and Africa
  - Middle East, Francophone Africa, and South Asia
  - East and Australasia
- Sector coordinators:
  - E&P Coordinator
  - Chemicals Coordinator
  - Coal/Natural Gas Coordinator
  - Metals Coordinator
  - President – Shell International Trading
  - Marine Coordinator
  - Supply and Marketing Coordinator

- Functional coordinators:
  - Director of Finance
  - Group Treasurer
  - Group Planning Coordinator
  - Manufacturing Coordinator
  - Group HR and Organization Coordinator
  - Legal Coordinator
  - Group Public Affairs Coordinator
  - Group Research Coordinator
  - Director of The Hague Office
  - Director of the London Office

Strategic Planning at Shell

Within this three-way matrix, the geographical dimension was traditionally the most important. The fact that the operating companies were national subsidiaries provided the basis for the geographical emphasis of operational and financial decision making. This was reinforced through the strategic planning process, which put its main emphasis on planning at the national and regional levels.

Shell's planning system lay at the heart of its management system. It was viewed as one of the most sophisticated and effective of any large multinational. It was much discussed and widely imitated. Its main features were the following:

- A strong emphasis on long-term strategic thinking. Shell's planning horizon extended 20 years into the future – much further than the four- or five-year planning that most companies engage in. Unlike most other companies, the basis for these strategic plans was not *forecasts* but *scenarios* – alternative views of the future that allowed managers to consider strategic responses to the different ways in which the future might unfold.

- A breadth of vision, and emphasis on the generation and application of ideas rather than a narrow focus on financial performance. Shell's planning department was receptive to concepts and ideas drawn from economics, psychology, biochemistry, biology, mathematics, anthropology, and ecology. As a consequence, Shell pioneered many new management techniques, including multiple scenario analysis, business portfolio planning, cognitive mapping, and the application of organizational learning concepts to planning processes.

- More generally, Shell was in the vanguard of the transition from the role of the strategy function as *planning* towards one where the primary roles of strategy were encouraging *thinking about the future*, developing the capacity for *organizational learning*, promoting *organizational dialogue*, and facilitating organizational *adaptation* to a changing world.

Planning at Shell was primarily bottom–up. The CMD identified key issues, set strategic direction, and approved major projects, and the planning department formulated the scenarios. However, most strategic decisions and initiatives originated among the operating companies. The role of the planning staff and the regional and sector coordinators was to coordinate the operating company strategic plans.

Forces for Change

Between the early 1970s and the early 1990s, the world petroleum industry was transformed by a number of fundamental changes.[1] The growing power of the producer countries was seen not just in the sharp rise in crude oil prices during the first oil shock of 1974, but even more fundamentally in the nationalization of the oil reserves of the international majors. By the 1990s, the list of the world's top 20 oil and gas producers was dominated by state-owned companies such as Saudi Aramco, Petroleos de Venezuela, Kuwait Oil, Iran National Oil Company, Pemex (Mexico), and Russia's Gasprom and Lukoil. In addition, the old-established majors faced competition from other sources. The "new majors," integrated oil companies such as Elf Aquitaine (France), Total (France), Eni (Italy), Nippon Oil (Japan), Neste (Finland), and Respol (Spain), were expanding rapidly, while in North America and the North Sea independent E&P companies such as Enterprise Oil, Triton, and Apache were becoming significant global players. Between 1970 and 1990, the share of world oil production of the "Seven Sisters" fell from 31% to 7%.[2] The loss of control over their sources of crude oil was a devastating blow for the majors – their whole strategy of vertical integration had been based around the concept of controlling risk through owning the downstream facilities needed to provide secure outlets for their crude oil. As market transactions for crude oil and refinery outputs became increasingly important, so prices became much more volatile. Between 1981 and 1986, crude prices fell from $42 a barrel to $9 before briefly recovering to $38 in the wake of the Iraqi invasion of Kuwait, and then resuming their downward direction.

Between 1985 and 1993, almost all the world's oil majors underwent far-reaching restructuring. Restructuring involved radical simultaneous changes in strategy and organizational structure in a compressed time-frame. Key features of restructuring by the oil majors were:

- Reorienting their goals around shareholder value maximization.
- Greater selectivity in their strategies, involving the divestment of unprofitable businesses, refocusing around core petroleum and gas businesses, withdrawing from countries where investments were not justified by the returns being earned, and outsourcing those activities that could be performed more efficiently by outside suppliers.
- Cutting back on staff, especially at the corporate level. (Table 8.1 shows changes in numbers of employees among the majors.)
- Reducing excess capacity through closures of refineries and filling stations.
- Decentralization of decision making from corporate to divisional levels and from divisional to business unit levels at the same time as giving divisions and business units full profit and loss responsibility.
- Shifting the basis of organizational structure from geographical organization around countries and regions to worldwide product divisions (many of the majors formed worldwide divisions for upstream activities, downstream activities, and chemicals).
- "Delayering" through eliminating administrative layers within hierarchical structures. For example, Amoco broke up its three major divisions (upstream, downstream, and chemicals) and had 17 business groups reporting direct to

TABLE 8.1 Employment among the oil majors ('000)

	1985	1990	1993	1996	1999
Shell	142	136	117	101	99
Elf Aquitaine[c]	78	92	94	85	81
EN.	125	128	106	83	79
Exxon[a]	147	101	91	79	79
Total[c]	41	43	50	57	57
BP[b]	132	118	73	53	99
Mobil[a]	72	68	62	43	–
Amoco[b]	48	53	46	42	–
Chevron	62	50	48	41	39
Texaco	57	40	33	29	25
Arco[b]	31	28	25	23	17

[a] Exxon merged with Mobil in 1998.
[b] Amoco merged with BP in 1997. BP acquired Arco in 1999.
[c] Total merged with Fina in 1998 and with Elf Aquitaine in 1999.

SOURCE: FORTUNE GLOBAL FIVE 1000, 1994, 1991, AND 1996.

the corporate center. Mobil also broke up its divisional structure, and created 13 business groups. (The Appendix shows the organizational structure of several of the majors.)

Shell in the Early 1990s

Shell was the only major oil company that did not undergo radical restructuring between 1985 and 1993. The absence of restructuring at Shell appeared to reflect two factors:

- Shell's flexibility had meant that Shell had been able to adjust to a changing oil industry environment without the need for discontinuous change. For example, Shell had been a leader in rationalizing excess capacity in refining and shipping, in upgrading its refineries with catalytic crackers, in establishing arm's-length relationships between its production units and its refineries, in moving into natural gas, and in taking advantage of opportunities for deep-water exploration.
- Because of Shell's management structure, in particular the absence of a CEO with autocratic powers, Shell was much less able to initiate the kind of top–down restructuring driven by powerful CEOs such as Larry Rawl at Exxon, Jim Kinnear at Texaco, Serge Tchuruk at Total, or Franco Bernabè at Eni.

Nevertheless, during the early 1990s, a combination of forces was pushing the CMD towards more radical top–down change. The most influential of these pressures was dissatisfaction over financial performance. The early 1990s were difficult years for the industry. The fall in oil prices to the mid-teens meant that returns from the traditional fount of profit – upstream – were meager. At the same time, refining and

TABLE 8.2 Royal Dutch Shell Group: performance data, 1992–9

	1992	1993	1994	1995	1996	1997	1998	1999
Gross sales ($ bill.)	128.4	125.8	129.1	150.7	172.0	171.7	138.3	149.7
Operating profit ($ bill.)	9.2	8.9	9.6	12.5	17.1	15.3	3.1	15.2
Net income ($ bill.)	5.4	4.5	6.2	6.9	8.9	7.8	0.4	8.6
Cash flow from operations ($ bill.)				14.9	16.6	16.7	14.7	11.1
ROCE (%)	9.0	7.9	10.4	10.7	12.0	12.0	2.8	12.1
ROE (%)	9.7	8.7	11.5	11.8	15.1	12.8	0.7	15.4
Capital expenditure ($ bill.)	10.4	9.5	10.5	11.8	12.1	13.4	12.9	7.4
Employees ('000)	127	117	107	106	104	105	102	99

(The data are for continuing operations only. Hence, Shell's numbers of employees shown in table 8.1 differ from those here because of acquisitions and disposals.)

chemicals suffered from widespread excess capacity and price wars. Meanwhile, investors and the financial community were putting increased pressure on companies for improved return to shareholders. The CMD was forced to shift its attention from long-term development to short-term financial results. Against a variety of benchmarks, Shell's profit performance looked less than adequate:

● Cost of capital was the most fundamental of these – during the early 1990s Shell was earning a return on equity that barely covered the cost of equity.

● Long-term stability was a further goal. Top management asked, "What rate of return is needed to provide the cash flow needed to pay dividends and replace assets and reserves?" The returns of 1990–4 were somewhat below this figure.

● Shell's rates of return, margins, and productivity ratios were below those of several leading competitors.

Table 8.2 shows Shell's financial performance during the 1990s.

Evidence of the potential for performance improvement through restructuring was available from inside as well as from outside the Group. During the late 1980s and early 1990s, several Shell operating companies – notably those in Canada, the US, UK, South Africa, Germany, Malaysia, and France – showed the potential for organizational restructuring, process redesign, and outsourcing to yield substantial cost savings and productivity improvements.

The operating company executives that had been in the vanguard of cost cutting were increasingly resentful of the corporate structure. By 1994, Shell employed 6,800 people in its central organization (in London and The Hague) and in its corporate research and support functions. Even allowing for the differences in organizational structure between Shell and its competitors, this was bigger than the corporate and divisional administration of any other oil and gas major. As the operating companies struggled to reduce their own costs and improve their bottom-line performance, so they became antagonistic towards what they saw as a bloated corporate center whose support and services offered little discernible value. A major gripe was the failure of

Shell's elaborate matrix structure to provide effective coordination of the operating companies. Lack of coordination in Europe resulted in UK refineries selling into Spain and Portugal, the Marseilles refinery supplying Belgium, natural geographical units such as Scandinavia split between different operating companies, and difficulties in launching Europe-wide initiatives such as the Shell credit card.

As Chairman Cor Herkstroter noted:

> *Many Operating Companies are sending us clear signals that they feel constrained by the management processes of the Service Companies, that the support and guidance from them is ineffective or inefficient, and that the services are too costly. They do not see the eagerness for cost reductions in the Operating Companies sufficiently mirrored in the center.*[3]

The essential issue, however, was to prepare Shell for an increasingly difficult business environment:

> *While our current organization and practices have served us very well for many years, they were designed for a different era, for a different world. Over the years significant duplication and confusion of roles at various levels in the organization have developed. Many of you notice this on a day-to-day basis.*
>
> *We anticipate increasingly dynamic competition. We see the business conditions of today, with flat margins and low oil prices continuing into the future. In addition, there will be no let up on all players in the industry to strive for higher productivity, innovation quality and effectiveness.*
>
> *Our vision of the future is one of increasing competitive surprise and discontinuity, of increasing change and differentiation in skills required to succeed; and of increasing demands by our people at the front line for accountability within a framework of clear business objectives, and with access to a global source of specialist expertise.*[4]

The Change Process

Within Shell, proponents of organizational change, including the heads of several of the operating companies, the finance function, and Group Planning, had had little success in persuading the Committee of Managing Directors of the need for large-scale change. In May 1993, Cor Herkstroter took over as Chairman of the CMD. A Dutch accountant, who had spent his entire career at Shell, Herkstroter was an unlikely pioneer of change. Fellow executives described him as a private, Old World personality without much charisma, and with a preference for written communication. Nevertheless, Herkstroter was widely respected for his intelligence and courage. "He's Shell's Gorbachev," said Philip Mirvis, a consultant working with Noel Tichy at Shell.[5]

Faced with growing evidence of suboptimal financial performance and an over-complex, inward-looking organizational structure, Herkstroter called a meeting of Shell's 50 top managers at Hartwell House, an English country manor, in May 1994. The meeting was a shock for the CMD. The request for frank discussions of the reasons for Shell's lagging return on capital provided a series of barbed attacks on top management and sharp criticism of the service company organization. The corporate center was castigated for taking months to approve operating company budgets and for the general laxness of financial controls. E&P coordinator Robert Sprague tossed a blank transparency onto the overhead projector and commented, "I don't know what to report, this issue is really a mess." The meeting had a powerful impact on the CMD: "We were bureaucratic, inward looking, complacent, self-satisfied, arrogant," observed then Vice Chairman John Jennings. "We tolerated our own underperformance. We were technocratic and insufficiently entrepreneurial."[6] The outcome was the appointment of a high-level team to study Shell's internal organization and come up with options for redesign.

The team, set up in July 1994, was headed by Ernst van Mourik-Broekman, the head of HR, together with Basil South from Group Planning, Group Treasurer Stephen Hodge, an executive from Shell France, and the head of Shell's gas business in the Netherlands. The internal team was joined by three senior consultants from McKinsey & Company: two from the Amsterdam office and one from the London office.

The starting point for the internal team was a program of interviews with 40–50 managers at different levels within the company. This provided a basis both for assessing the existing structure and for generating ideas for change. The role of the McKinsey consultants was to provide perspective, to challenge the ideas of the Shell team, to introduce the experiences of other large multinationals (ABB for instance), to provide the backup research needed to refine and test out ideas and concepts, and to organize the program of work and consultation.

By October 1994, the group had prepared a diagnosis of the existing Shell structure together with a suite of options for reorganization. During October and November, a series of workshops was conducted, mainly in London, to explore in greater detail the specific dimensions of change and to clarify and evaluate the available options. Each workshop team provided input on a specific area of change. The results of this exercise were written up towards the end of November, and a report was submitted to the CMD. It identified the areas for change and the options.

During December 1994, the team spent two "away days" with the CMD to identify the objects of change and how the different options related to these. The result was a blueprint which the team wrote up mid-December. After six or seven drafts, the report was approved by the CMD during the weekend of Christmas. At the beginning of January, the report was circulated to the chief executives of the main opcos and the coordinators within the service companies with a request for reactions by the end of January. In the meantime, Chairman Herkstroter gave a speech, directed to all company employees, to prepare them for change, but without any specifics as to the organizational initiatives that were likely to occur.

The driving force behind the redesign was the desire to have a simpler structure with clearer reporting relationships, thereby allowing the corporate center to exert more effective influence and control over the operating companies. A simpler structure would help eliminate some of the cost and inertia of the head office bureaucracies that had built up around Shell's elaborate committee system. There was also a need to improve coordination between the operating companies. This coordination, it was felt, should be based on the business sectors rather than geographical regions. Globalization of the world economy and the breakdown of vertical integration within the oil majors had meant that most of the majors had reorganized around worldwide business divisions. As was noted above, most of the majors formed upstream, downstream, and chemicals divisions with worldwide responsibility. For Shell, achieving integration between the different businesses within a country or within a region was less important than achieving integration within a business across different countries and regions. For example, in exploration and production, critical issues related to the development and application of new technologies and sharing of best practices. In downstream, the critical issues related to the rationalization of capacity, the pursuit of operational efficiency, and the promotion of the Shell brand.

By the end of January, a broad endorsement had been received. In February a two-day meeting was held with the same group of Shell's 50 senior managers that had initiated the whole process some ten months earlier. The result was a high level of support and surprisingly little dissent. The final approval came from the two parent company Boards. On March 29, 1995, Cor Herkstroter, Chairman of the Committee of Managing Directors, gave a speech to Shell employees worldwide outlining the principal aspects of a radical reorganization of the Group, which were to be implemented at the beginning of 1996.

In the meantime, two totally unexpected events only increased the internal momentum for change. While Shell faulted itself on its ability to produce a return on capital to meet the levels of its most efficient competitors, in managing health, safety, and the environment and in responding to the broader expectations of society it considered itself the leader of the pack. Then came the Brent Spar incident. A carefully evaluated plan to dispose of a giant North Sea oil platform in the depths of the Atlantic produced outcry from environmental groups, including Greenpeace. Consumer boycotts of Shell products resulted in massive sales losses, especially in Germany. Within a few months, Shell was forced into an embarrassing reversal of its decision.

A few months later the Nigerian military regime executed Ken Saro-Wiwa, a prominent Nigerian author who had protested Shell's poor environmental record in his country. Again, Shell was found to be flat-footed and inept at managing its public relations over the incident. The handling of the Brent Spar and Nigerian incidents convinced many that Shell's top management was both unresponsive and out of touch. "We had to take a good look at ourselves and say, 'Have we got it right?'" said Mark Moody-Stuart, then a Managing Director. "Previously if you went to your golf club or church and said, 'I work for Shell,' you'd get a warm glow. In some parts of the world that changed a bit."[7]

The New Shell Structure

The central feature of the reorganization plan of 1995 was the dismantling of the three-way matrix through which the operating companies had been coordinated since the 1960s. In its place, four business organizations were created to achieve closer integration within each business sector across all countries. It was intended that the new structure would allow more effective planning and control within each of the businesses, remove much of the top-heavy bureaucracy that had imposed a costly burden on the Group, and eliminate the power of the regional fiefdoms. The new structure would strengthen the executive authority of the Committee of Managing Directors by providing a clearer line of command to the business organizations and subsequently to the operating companies, and by splitting central staff functions into a Corporate Center and a Professional Services Organization. The former would support the executive role of the CMD; the latter would provide professional services to companies within the Group. Figure 8.3 shows the new structure.

At the same time, the underlying principles of Shell's organizational structure were reaffirmed:

FIGURE 8.3 Shell's management structure, 1996

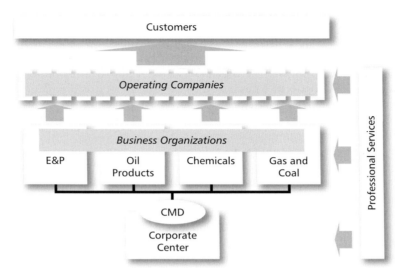

- The decentralized structure based on the autonomy of the Shell operating companies vis-à-vis the Group was to be maintained.
- The new structure continued the distinction between *governance* and *executive responsibility* which was described above. Thus, the formal structure of parent companies, holding companies, operating companies, and service companies was continued without significant changes. The Boards of these companies discharged the governance functions of the Group, including exercise of shareholder rights, the fulfillment of the legal obligations of the companies, and the appointment and supervision of the managers who fulfil executive responsibilities. It was the management structure where the major changes occurred, especially within the service companies.

The Formal Structure

As noted, the formal corporate structure shown in figure 8.1 was little changed. The principal changes in the formal structure were changes involving the identities and roles of the service companies to create a closer alignment with the new management structure. Thus, the new Corporate Center and Professional Services Organization were housed within Shell International Ltd (in London) and Shell International B.V. (in The Hague). Other service companies housed the new Business Organizations. Figure 8.4 shows the relationship between the new management structure and Shell's formal legal structure.

The Management Structure

The new organizational structure can be described in terms of the four new organizational elements – the Business Organizations, the Corporate Center, Professional

FIGURE 8.4 The service companies in 1996: links between the formal structure and the management structure

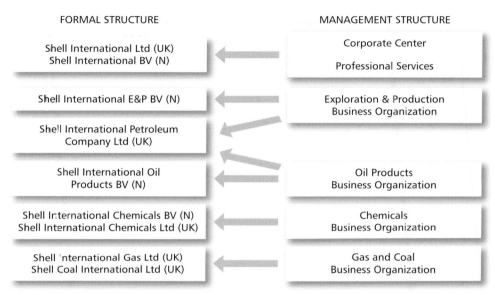

N = Netherlands

Services, and the Operating Units – together with the two organizational units that continued from the previous structure, the operating companies and the Committee of Managing Directors.

The Business Organizations The central features of the new organization structure were the new Business Organizations. The CMD was supported by four Business Organizations: E&P ("upstream"), oil products ("downstream"), chemicals, and gas and coal. The Business Organizations were headed by Business Committees made up of a number of Business Directors appointed by the CMD. These Business Directors included:

- Business Directors with responsibility for particular business segments. For example, among the members of the E&P Business Committee in 1998 were J. Colligan, Regional E&P Business Director for Asia-Pacific and South America, H. Roels, Regional E&P Business Director for Middle East and Africa, and R. Sprague, Regional E&P Business Director for Europe.

- Certain of the operating companies were so important that their Chief Executives were also Business Directors. For example, in 1998, the E&P Business Committee included A. Parsley, Managing Director of Shell E&P International Venture B.V., while the Oil Products Business Committee included M. Warwick, President of Shell International Trading and Shipping Co. Ltd, and P. Turberville, President of Shell Europe Oil Products B.V.

- A Business Director for Research and Technical Services.

- A Business Director for Strategy and Business Services.

The Business Committees were accountable to the CMD for:

- the strategy of their business area;
- endorsing the capital expenditure and financial plans of the operating companies and business segments within their business area;
- appraising operating company and business segment performance; and
- the availability of technical, functional, and business services to the operating companies within their business sector.

Chairing each of the Business Committees was a member of the CMD. Thus, in early 1998, E&P reported to Managing Director P. B. Watts, Oil Products to Managing Director S. L. Miller, Chemicals to Vice Chairman M. Moody-Stuart, and Gas and Coal to Managing Director M. van den Bergh.

The Corporate Center This supported the CMD in its role in:

- setting the direction and strategy of the Group;
- growing and shaping the Group's portfolio of investments and resources;
- enhancing the performance of Group assets;
- acting as custodian of the Group's reputation, policies, and processes; and
- providing internal and external communication.

Apart from supporting the work of the CMD, the Corporate Center assisted the parent companies and the Group holding companies in managing their financial, tax, and corporate affairs. The Corporate Center represented the other two dimensions of Shell's former matrix organization. For example, the Director for Planning, Environment and External Affairs chaired the meetings of Shell's Technology Council and Health, Safety and Environment Council. Also, the Corporate Advice Director undertook ad hoc country reviews.

The Corporate Center comprised six directorates:

- Planning, Environment and External Affairs
- Corporate Advice (supporting each of the Managing Directors in their regional roles as well as responsibility for IT, security, contracting and procurement)
- Group Treasurer
- Group Controller
- Human Resources
- Legal

In addition to these directorates, the Corporate Center also included the Head of Group Taxation, the Chief Information Officer, the Head of Intellectual Property, the Head of Contracting and Procurement, the Head of Group Security, the Head of Learning, and the Secretary to the CMD.

Professional Services These new units provided functional support for the operating companies and service companies within the Group. They offered their services on an arm's-length basis and competed with external service providers for the business of the operating companies. They were also able to provide services to third-party customers outside the Group. The services provided included:

- Finance (e.g., treasury services, accounting, tax advice)
- HR (e.g., recruitment, training)
- Legal
- Intellectual property (intellectual property protection, licensing)
- Contracting and procurement
- Group Security (security advice)
- Shell Aircraft Ltd (corporate jets)
- Office services (e.g., accommodation, personnel services)
- Health (medical services, environmental and occupational health advice)

Each Professional Services unit was headed by the relevant director from the Corporate Center. For example, HR was headed by the HR Director; legal and intellectual property services were headed by the Legal Director.

The Operating Companies In the new organizational structure, the operating companies retained their role as the primary business entities within Shell. Each operating company was managed by a Board of Directors and a Chief Executive. The Chief Executive of an operating company was responsible to his/her Board and to his/her Business Director for the effective management of the operating company. The Chief Executive's responsibilities included the following:

- setting the company's strategic aims against the backdrop of any guidelines established by the Business Committee;
- providing leadership to put the strategic aims into effect and instill an entrepreneurial company culture;
- setting internal financial and operating targets and overseeing their achievement;
- supervising the management of the business and setting priorities;
- effective reporting on the company's activities and results to the Group.[8]

Operating Units The superimposition of the Business Organizations on top of the operating companies created a problem for Shell because the operating companies were defined by country rather than by business sector and included activities which crossed business sectors. Hence, to achieve alignment between the new Business Organizations and the operational activities of the Group, Operating Units were created:

> In the context of the Group organizational structure, Operating Unit refers to the activities in one of the Group Businesses which are operated as a single economic entity. An Operating Unit can coincide with an Operating Company, be a part of an Operating Company or straddle part or all of several Operating Companies.[9]

Thus, where an operating company was in one business only, the operating company was the relevant Operating Unit. However, multibusiness operating companies, such as Shell UK and Shell Australia, which included upstream, downstream, chemical, and gas businesses, were divided into separate Operating Units to align operating activities with the new Business Organizations. Each of these Operating Units was headed by a manager with executive responsibilities who reported to the relevant Business Director. Where several Operating Units operated in a country under different Chief

Executives, the Managing Director with responsibilities for that particular region appointed one of them as a "country chairman" to fulfill country-level responsibilities (with regard to matters of taxation, conformity with national legislation, national government relations, and the like).

In addition, some Operating Units spanned several operating countries. To achieve more effective integration across countries and to save on administrative and operating costs, the trend was to form Operating Units that combined businesses in several countries. Thus, in Europe there was a desire to run chemicals and oil products as single business entities.

Changing Culture and Behavior

Changes to the formal organizational structure were only one dimension of the organizational changes of this period. If Shell was to improve its operational and financial performance and improve its responsiveness to the multitude of external forces that impacted its many businesses, then change needed to go beyond formal structures. The criticisms leveled at Shell for being bureaucratic, inward looking, slow, and unresponsive were not about organizational structure, they were about behavior and attitudes. In any organizational change, a new structure may provide the right context, but ultimately it is the effects on individual and group behavior that are critical.

During 1996 and 1997, the Shell management development function moved into a higher gear. Organizational development and change consultants included Noel Tichy from Michigan Business School, Larry Selden from Columbia, McKinsey & Company, Boston Consulting Group, and Coopers & Lybrand. These were in addition to Shell's internal change management team, known as LEAP (Leadership and Performance Operations). The result was a substantial increase in Shell's management development and organizational development activities. *Fortune* magazine reported:

> *This army has been putting Shell managers through a slew of workshops. In early February, teams from the gasoline retailing business in Thailand, China, Scandinavia and France spent six hours in a bitter Dutch downpour building rope bridges, dragging one another through spider webs of rope, and helping one another climb over 20-foot walls.*
>
> *The Shell managers especially liked Larry Selden. He teaches people to track their time and figure out whether what they're doing contributes directly to growth of both returns and gross margins. Selden calls this "dot movement," a phrase he has trademarked and which means moving the dot on a graph of growth and returns to the north-east. "The model is very powerful," says Luc Minguet, Shell's retail manager in France. "It's the first time I've seen such a link between the conceptual and the practical. And I realized I was using my time very poorly."*
>
> *In a particularly revealing exercise, the top 100 Shell executives in May took the Myers–Briggs personality test, a widely-used management tool that classifies people according to 16 psychological types. Interestingly, of its top 100 managers, 86% are "thinkers," people who make decisions based on logic and objective analysis. Of the six-man CMD, 60% are on the opposite scale. They are "feelers" who make decisions based on values and subjective evaluation. No wonder all those "thinkers" had such a hard time understanding the emotion behind Nigeria and Brent Spar. And no wonder the CMD gets frustrated with the inability of the lower ranks to grasp the need for change.[10]*

Further Developments, 1996–1999

Cost Cutting and Restructuring

The most evident short-term impact of the reorganization was a substantial reduction in Service Company staffs. Towards the end of 1995, Shell began shrinking its head offices in London and The Hague in anticipation of the introduction of the new organizational structure at the beginning of 1996. During 1996, the downsizing of central services and administrative functions within the Service Companies accelerated. Also in 1996, one of the two towers at the London Shell Centre was sold and was converted into residential apartments.

The quest for cost reductions did not stop at the Service Companies but extended to the operating companies as well. Between 1995 and 1997, unit costs were reduced by 17% in real terms, and between 1994 and 1997, savings in procurement costs amounted to $600 million each year. A priority for the Group was rationalization of capacity and reductions in operating costs in its downstream business. To facilitate this, Shell embarked on three major joint ventures:

- the amalgamation of Shell Oil's downstream assets in the western US with those of Texaco;
- the amalgamation of Shell's European downstream businesses with those of Texaco; and
- the merging of Shell's Australian downstream business with that of Mobil.

Restructuring in Shell's other businesses included a swap of oil and gas properties with Occidental and the creation of a single global chemicals business. The chemicals business demonstrated clearly the benefits of global integration. In addition to cost savings of around 7% each year, investment decisions became better coordinated. "The Center's full control over chemicals, for instance, led Shell to put a new polymer plant closer to customers in Geismar, Louisiana, instead of near the existing plant in Britain. Two years ago that plant automatically would have been added to the UK fiefdom."[11]

Further Organizational Changes under Moody-Stuart

In June 1998, Mark Moody-Stuart succeeded Cor Herkstroter as Chairman of the CMD against a background of declining oil and gas prices and weakening margins in refining and chemicals. With Shell's operating profit and ROCE falling well below the projections for 1998, it was clear that further organizational change and cost reduction would be essential. In September he announced a series of restructuring measures aimed at reducing Shell's cost base while reaffirming Shell's commitment to the target of 15% ROACE (return on average capital employed) by 2001. Refinery cutbacks included the closure of Shellhaven refinery and partial closure of Berre refinery in France. The national head offices in the UK, Netherlands, Germany, and France would be closed.[12]

A key element of the organizational changes pushed by Moody-Stuart was the desire to replace Shell's traditional consensus-based decision making with greater individual leadership and individual accountability. To this end, the Business Committees that had been set up to manage the new business sectors were replaced by Chief Executives:

From today we have CEO's and executive committees running each of our businesses. We have entered a new period where executive decisions have to be made rapidly and business accountability must be absolutely clear. So we have changed our structures.

The major change we announced is establishing executive structures, with CEO's, in Oil Products and Exploration and Production. CEO's already run our other businesses: Gas and Coal, Chemicals and Renewables, as well as Shell Services International. Now we are structured to make rapid progress to our objective in each of our businesses.

Business Committees served us in good stead in a period of transition but as from today they are a thing of the past. We will still have discussion, but we will make business decisions rapidly.[13]

The trend towards executive power and personal accountability was also apparent in the Committee of Managing Directors. In place of the traditional "committee of equals," Moody-Stuart recast the CMD more as an executive group where individual members had clearly defined executive responsibilities.

Moody-Stuart also accelerated the integration of Shell's US subsidiary, Shell Oil Inc., into its global structure. By the end of 1998, the chemicals sector was a truly global division and by early 1999 upstream operations in the US had been integrated into the global exploration and production sector. During 1999, the historically separate Shell Oil corporate office in Houston became integrated within Shell's Corporate Center and Professional Services organization. Thus, Shell Oil's Human Resource function staff became part of a new global Shell People Services organization, while Finance, Tax, Legal, and Corporate Affairs also integrated with their counterparts in London. The President and CEO of Shell Oil, Inc. became a de facto member of the CMD.

Figure 8.5 shows Shell's management structure under Mark Moody-Stuart's leadership.

Towards a Second Century

As Royal Dutch Shell approached the second century of its corporate life, there was a clear consensus within the company that the organizational changes made during 1995–9 had created a structure that was much better able to respond to the uncertainties and discontinuous changes that affected the oil industry. Outside the company, Shell-watchers both in the investment community and in other oil companies had little doubt that the 1996 reorganization had contributed substantially to the efficient and effective management of the Group. The stripping away of much of the administrative structure in the Group head offices in London and The Hague, the elimination of the regional coordinating staffs, and the closure of some of Shell's biggest national headquarters not only reduced cost, but seemed to be moving Shell towards a swifter, more direct style of management. The restructuring of chemicals and downstream businesses revealed both a tough-mindedness and a decisiveness that few had associated with the Shell of old.

The former vice chairman of the CMD outlined the way in which the changes in organization had impacted Shell's business portfolio and its strategic management:

FIGURE 8.5 Shell's management structure, 2000

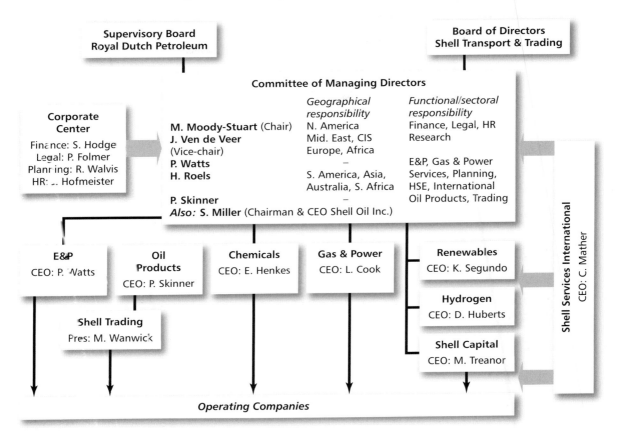

We used to have a complex regional matrix system – with multiple reporting lines. In compensation relatively modest annual raises were awarded – and more often than not expected – without being strictly tied to performance. Our businesses were tightly linked to national markets and then to regions. Accountability was, through the matrix system, diffuse. It wasn't a bad system. When it was launched – in 1958 – it was an excellent system. But, by the early '90s, it had definitely reached its "use by" date. Hurdle rates were used – good guides – but they allowed unbridled investment growth, which tended to exacerbate portfolio weaknesses. Jobs were for life in the old Shell and virtually all recruitment was internal.

By the early '90s we had a problem. There was no crisis – which in some ways was part of the problem. But ROACE was not good enough and it was obvious that something needed to be done. In the middle of the '90s we instituted something we called "transformation." As you can see here there were results, things were improving, but not really as quickly as they should have been. Then, in 1999 we had a particularly difficult environment, which galvanized us to *rapidly complete the transformation process. Tough decisions were made, write-downs taken, and the whole process accelerated.*

As a consequence, today we have global businesses, headed by personally accountable CEOs. Reporting lines are direct, uncomplicated. Incentive pay and stock options are the norm. Every project has to compete globally for capital. Everyone in the organization can compete for any job – and we also actively hire from outside.

This has resulted in a significantly improved profile. Earnings are up on basically stable net revenues. Oil production is up, as are gas, chemical and oil product sales. The number of employees required has declined.

Capital has moved away from the poor performers and declining areas to new opportunities.[14]

The new organization had permitted far-reaching restructuring of Shell's downstream and chemicals businesses:

In the early 1990s we operated refineries in all parts of the world and our refining cover was over 80%. We have been closing or selling refineries . . . Our goal in this effort is twofold – one is to reduce our refinery cover to a range of 65%–70% by 2001. The other is to achieve a return on average capital employed of 15% by 2001 . . .

At the beginning of the '90s we had [chemical] plants scattered across the globe with 30 plants in Europe, 7 in Asia Pacific, and 17 in America. The plants produced products that were sold through some 22 different product groups, each having profit and loss responsibility. Today we are concentrating on a few, world-scale plants and a much more limited product line. We will have 7 plants in Europe, 6 in Asia Pacific and 4 in America and products will be sold through 12 product groups.[15]

The question in most people's minds was whether Shell was moving ahead of the pack or playing catch up. For all Shell's pride in being a pioneer of modern management ideas – from scenario analysis to organization learning – Shell had created by year 2000 a business-sector-based organization of a kind that most other diversified multinationals had been using for decades. Moreover, some of Shell's leading competitors were moving away from such structures. BP – hailed by many to be the most dynamic and responsive of any of the petroleum majors – had abandoned its traditional divisional structure in favor of a flatter structure in which individual business units reported directly to the corporate center.

In addition, Shell still retained some relics of the old structure that could compromise the new philosophy of responsiveness and single-point accountability. For example, Shell was still a joint venture rather than a single corporation. Its Committee of Managing Directors was still composed of board members from its dual parent companies. The principle of rotating leadership between the two parents with fixed single terms of office for the CMD Chairman was still intact. While Shell had been consumed with its internal restructuring, other companies had been transforming themselves through mergers and acquisitions. Had Shell missed out on the Great Oil Patch M&A Boom? Probably, but if Royal Dutch Shell was to get serious about mergers, its first priority should be to merge with itself, noted the *Financial Times'* Lex column.

Appendix
The Organizational Structures of Other Oil Majors

FIGURE 8.A1 Exxon Mobil

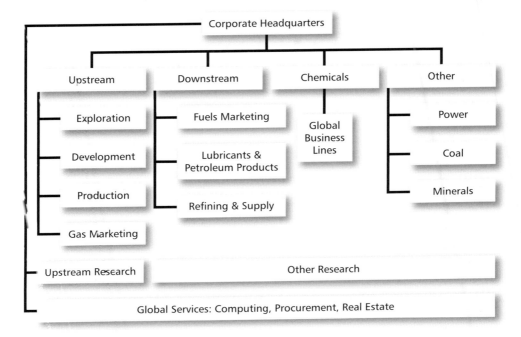

FIGURE 8.A2 Mobil (prior to merger with Exxon)

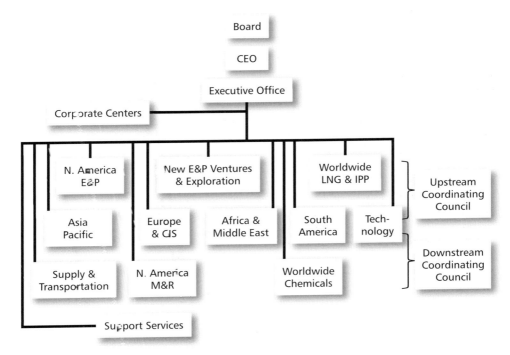

FIGURE 8.A3 BP

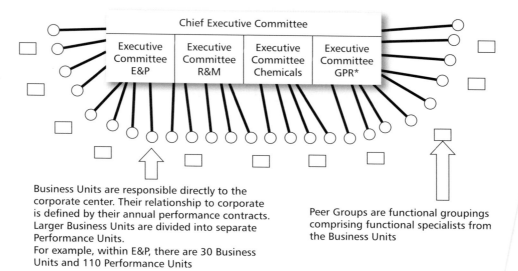

Business Units are responsible directly to the corporate center. Their relationship to corporate is defined by their annual performance contracts. Larger Business Units are divided into separate Performance Units.
For example, within E&P, there are 30 Business Units and 110 Performance Units

Peer Groups are functional groupings comprising functional specialists from the Business Units

* Gas, Power, and Renewables.

FIGURE 8.A4 Elf Aquitaine (prior to merger with Total-Fina)

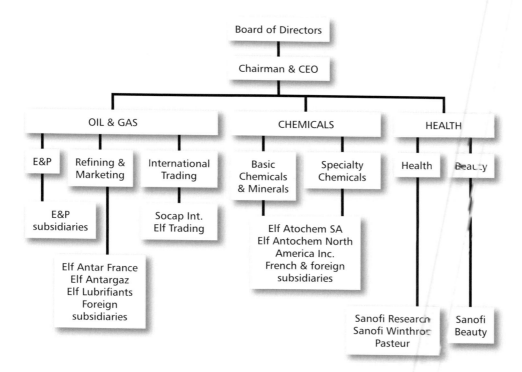

Notes

1 This section draws from R. Cibin and R. M. Grant, "Restructuring among the world's largest oil majors," *British Journal of Management*, December 1996.

2 The "Seven Sisters" were the original international oil majors: Shell, Exxon, Mobil, BP, Chevron, Texaco, and Gulf. (Gulf was acquired by Chevron in 1984.)

3 C. A. J. Herkstroter, "Right for the times and right for Shell," speech delivered in London, March 29, 1995.

4 Ibid.

5 "Why is the world's most profitable company turning itself inside out?" *Fortune*, August 4, 1997, pp. 121–5.

6 Ibid.

7 Ibid.

8 *Reference Guide to Group Organizational Structure*, Shell International Ltd, August 1996.

9 Ibid., p. 17.

10 "Why is the world's most profitable company turning itself inside out?" *Fortune*, August 4, 1997, pp. 121–5.

11 Ibid.

12 "Shell shapes up for future," speech by M. Moody-Stuart, San Francisco, September 18, 1998 (www.shell.com).

13 M. Moody-Stuart, Changes in Shell's organization: comments to the Shell Global Leadership Conference, London, December 10, 1998.

14 Marten van den Bergh, "Strengthening the Portfolio," Shell Press Release, April 3, 2000.

15 Ibid.

Harley-Davidson, Inc., January 2007

You've shown us how to be the best. You've been leaders in new technology. You've stuck by the basic American values of hard work and fair play . . . Most of all, you've worked smarter, you've worked better, and you've worked together . . . as you've shown again, America is someplace special. We're on the road to unprecedented prosperity . . . and we'll get there on a Harley.

PRESIDENT RONALD REAGAN, HARLEY-DAVIDSON PLANT, YORK, PENNSYLVANIA, MAY 6, 1987

The recovery of this company since the 1980s has been truly remarkable. When you were down in the dumps, people were saying American industry was finished, that we couldn't compete in the global economy, that the next century would belong to other countries and other places. Today, you're not just surviving – you're flourishing, with record sales and earnings; and one of the best-managed companies in America.

PRESIDENT BILL CLINTON, HARLEY-DAVIDSON PLANT, YORK, PENNSYLVANIA, NOVEMBER 10, 1999

I want to thank the folks here at the Harley plant for their wonderful hospitality. I've been impressed by Harley-Davidsons. It's one of America's finest products. And today I add to my impressions about the product the impressions of the workforce . . . I'm impressed by the esprit de corps, I'm impressed by the fact that these people really enjoy what they're doing, I'm impressed by the fact that they're impressed by the product they make.

PRESIDENT GEORGE W. BUSH, HARLEY-DAVIDSON PLANT, YORK, PENNSYLVANIA, AUGUST 16, 2006

At the beginning of 2007, Harley-Davidson could claim to be America's most successful manufacturing company. Unlike America's struggling automobile producers 300 miles away in Detroit, Harley had beaten back Japanese competitors and established itself as market leader in heavyweight motorcycles and the world's most profitable motorcycle company. On January 18, CEO James Ziemer announced record annual sales and profits for the company for the 20th consecutive year. The 103-year-old company had never been in such robust health either financially or operationally.

Yet, Ziemer also knew that the next few years would be the most challenging of his 37-year career with Harley-Davidson. Wall Street's expectations of Harley-Davidson's profit performance had been fueled by past performance and by the company's own ambitious targets: Ziemer had committed to earnings-per-share growth of between 11 and 17% during each of the next three years. Ultimately, profit growth depended on Harley's ability to keep expanding the sales of its high-priced, heavyweight motorcycles. For 20 years, most of Harley's sales growth had been accounted for by expanding domestic sales. Yet the health of domestic demand was far from assured. Combined federal and trade deficits, record levels of consumer debt, and falling house prices posed a threat to any company selling leisure products priced between $6,600 and $22,000. Harley's potential for growing market share also seemed limited – for the past eight years, Harley's share of the US heavyweight market had hit a ceiling at just under 50%. Indeed, Harley's own market might be vulnerable to competition. While no other company could replicate the emotional attachment of riders to the "Harley Experience," there was always the risk that motorcycle riders might seek a different type of experience and become more attracted to the highly engineered sports models produced by European and Japanese manufacturers. Such concerns were fueled by demographic trends. Harley's core market was the baby-boomer generation – and this cohort was moving more towards retirement homes than outdoor sports.

TABLE 9.1 Annual shipments of motorcycles by Harley-Davidson (selected years)

Year	Production	Year	Production
1901	3	1994	95,811
1903	150	1995	105,104
1913	12,904	1996	118,771
1920	28,189	1997	132,285
1933	3,700	1998	150,818
1936	9,812	1999	177,187
1948	31,163	2000	204,592
1953	14,050	2001	234,500
1966	36,310	2002	263,700
1975	75,403	2003	291,147
1981	41,586	2004	317,289
1986	36,700	2005	329,017
1990	62,500	2006	349,196
1992	76,500		

SOURCE: WWW.HARLEY-DAVIDSON.COM

The History of Harley-Davidson

1903–1981: From Birth to Maturity

Harley-Davidson, Inc. was founded in 1903 by William Harley and brothers William Davidson, Arthur Davidson, and Walter Davidson. Harley's 1903 model was made in the Davidson family shed and had a three-horsepower engine. In 1909 Harley introduced its first two-cylinder, V-twin engine, featuring the deep, rumbling sound for which Harley motorcycles are renowned. In 1953, the closure of Indian meant that Harley-Davidson was the sole survivor of the 150 US motorcycle producers that had existed in 1910.

The post-war era saw new challenges for Harley-Davidson. Growing affluence and the rise of youth culture created a growing demand for motorcycles. However, this was satisfied primarily by imports: first the British (by 1959, BSA, Triumph, and Norton took 49% of the US market), then the Japanese. While Harley initially benefitted from the Japanese-led expansion of motorcycling among Americans, soon Harley was facing direct competition. In 1969 Honda introduced its four-cylinder CB750, a huge technical advance on anything produced by Harley or the British. In the same year, Harley-Davidson was acquired by AMF, which proceeded to expand production capacity to 75,000 units a year – with disastrous consequences for product quality. By the end of the 1970s, Honda had replaced Harley as market leader in heavyweight motorcycles in the US.

1981–2006: Rebirth

In 1981, Harley's senior managers, led by Vaughn Beals, organized a leveraged buyout of AMF's Harley-Davidson subsidiary. Harley emerged as an independent, privately owned company, heavily laden with debt. The buyout coincided with a severe recession and soaring interest rates. Harley's 1982 unit sales were down by more than a third from 1979. During 1981 and 1982, Harley-Davidson lost a total of $60 million. Struggling for survival, the new management dismissed 30% of office staff and drastically reduced hourly workers too.

At the same time, the management team also devoted itself to rebuilding production methods and working practices in order to cut costs and improve quality. Managers visited several Japanese automobile plants and carefully studied Toyota's just-in-time (JIT) system. Less than four months after the buyout, Harley management began a pilot JIT inventory and production-scheduling program called "MAN" (Materials As Needed) in its Milwaukee engine plant. The objective was to reduce inventories and costs and improve quality control. Within a year, all Harley's manufacturing operations were being converted to JIT: components and sub-assemblies were "pulled" through the production system in response to final demand.

The revolution in production methods and new spirit of cooperation between workers and management – plus help from the US government in the form of a temporary 49% tariff on imports of Japanese heavyweight motorcycles – soon fed through into both the top line and bottom line of Harley's income statement. To fuel its continuing development, Harley-Davidson went public in 1986. Between 1986 and 1990, Harley's share of the heavyweight market expanded steadily from about 30% to over 60%, with demand outstripping production. During this time, management improved the quality and reliability of its product, and began to explore growth opportunities in retail clothing and international sales.

The 1990s saw year-on-year uninterrupted growth in the heavyweight motorcycle market and a continued increase in Harley's market share. The company's biggest challenge continued to be balancing production capacity with surging demand for its products. To overcome this constraint, in 1996, the company announced the ambitious Plan 2003. Plan 2003 was a vision to dramatically increase production capacity over the eight years preceding the company's 100th anniversary. New production plants in Kansas City and York, Pennsylvania, the launching of several new models, and international expansion resulted in sales approaching 350,000 in 2006 – ten times the 1983 total.

The Heavyweight Motorcycle Market

The heavyweight segment (over 650 cc) was the most rapidly growing part of the world motorcycle market between 1990 and 2006, with the US accounting for a major part of this growth. Sales of heavyweight motorcycles in the major markets of the world almost trebled between 1990 and 2006. North America was the largest market for big bikes, representing 56% of the sales in the major world markets.

In North America, Harley consolidated its market leadership, accounting for almost half of big bike sales. Overseas, however, Harley was unable to replicate this market dominance despite strong sales in a few markets – Harley achieved the remarkable feat of becoming heavyweight market leader in Japan, pushing Honda into second place. In Europe, on the other hand, Harley lagged behind its Japanese competitors and BMW (see tables 9.2 and 9.3).

TABLE 9.2 Retail sales of heavyweight motorcycles (651+ cc), 1997–2006 (in thousands of units)

	1997	1998	1999	2000	2001	2002	2003	2004	2005	2006
North America (total)	206	246	298	365	423	475	495	531	554	579
Harley-Davidson[a]	99	116	142	163	186	220	238	256	265	282
Market share (%)	48.1	47.2	47.7	44.6	43.9	46.4	48.1	48.2	47.8	48.6
Europe (total)	250	270	307	293	321	332	323	336	351	377
Harley-Davidson	16	17	20	22	23	24	26	25	30	34
Market share (%)	6.4	6.4	6.5	7.4	7.1	7.1	8.1	7.3	8.5	9.1
Japan/Australia (total)	59	69	63	63	64	64	59	n.a.	n.a.	n.a.
Harley-Davidson[b]	10	11	12	13	14	14	15	10	11	13
Market share (%)	17.2	15.6	19.6	20.5	21.9	21.2	25.8	n.a.	n.a.	n.a.

n.a. = not available.

[a] Excludes Buell.

[b] Years 2004–6 include Japan only.

TABLE 9.3 Market shares in heavyweight motorcycles (651+ cc), 2003–2005 (%)

	North America			Europe		
	2003	2004	2005	2003	2004	2005
Harley-Davidson	48.1	48.2	47.8	8.1	7.7	8.9
Honda	18.6	18.8	16.6	16.7	15.4	13.0
Kawasaki	7.1	6.9	6.9	10.0	13.7	12.6
Suzuki	10.3	10.5	12.6	15.5	12.6	13.3
Yamaha	9.1	9.3	9.3	16.0	17.3	15.8
BMW	2.8	2.3	3.3	15.3	15.5	17.7
Ducati	–	–	–	6.0	5.1	5.2
Triumph	–	–	–	3.7	4.0	5.0
Other	4.0	4.0	4.5	8.7	8.7	8.5

SOURCE: HARLEY-DAVIDSON ANNUAL REPORT, 2003, 2005.

The heavyweight motorcycle market comprised three segments:

- *Cruiser motorcycles:* These were "big, noisy, low riding, unapologetically macho cycles,"[1] typically with V-twin, large displacement engines and an upright riding position. Their design reflected the dominance of styling over either comfort or speed. For the urban males (and some females) in Los Angeles, New York, Paris, and Tokyo, the cruiser motorcycle was practical transportation in congested metropolises, but was primarily a statement of style. The cruiser segment was practically created by Harley and was preeminent in the US, representing over half of the heavyweight market. Most of Harley's competitors in this segment had imitated the main features of traditional Harley design.

- *Touring bikes:* These included cruisers specially equipped for longer distance riding and bikes specially designed for comfort over long distances (including the Honda Goldwing and the bigger BMWs). These tourers featured luxuries such as audio systems, two-way intercoms, and heaters. While Harley led this segment on the basis of style and image, Honda and BMW had engineered their motorcycles for greater smoothness and comfort over long distances through the use of multi-cylinder, shaft-drive engines, and advanced suspension systems.

- *Performance models:* These were based on racing bikes, with high-technology, high-revving engines, an emphasis on speed, acceleration, and race-track styling; minimal concessions were provided to rider comfort. The segment was the most important in the European and the Asian/Pacific markets, representing 62% and 66% of total heavyweight bike sales, respectively. The segment was dominated by Japanese motorcycle companies, with a significant representation of European specialists such as Ducati and Triumph. Harley entered the performance segment in 1993 through Buell Motorcycles, which it fully acquired in 1998.

It is worth noting that the conventional segmentation into lightweight, middle-weight, and heavyweight did not clearly define Harley-Davidson's market. Harley's strength lay in just one part of the heavyweight market: the super-heavyweight segment, comprising bikes with cylinder displacement of more than 850 cc.

Harley-Davidson in 2007

The Brand

The Harley-Davidson image and the loyalty it engendered among its customers were its greatest assets. Harley-Davidson was one of the archetypes of American style. The famed spread eagle signified not just the brand of one of the world's oldest motorcycle companies, but an entire lifestyle with which it was associated. Harley has been described as "the ultimate biker status symbol . . . a quasi religion, an institution, a way of life."[2] Together with a few other companies – Walt Disney and Levi Strauss – Harley had a unique relationship with American culture. The values that Harley represented – individuality, freedom, and adventure – could be traced back to the cowboy and frontiersman of yesteryear, and before that to the motives that brought people to America in the first place. As the sole surviving American motorcycle company from the pioneering days of the industry, Harley-Davidson represented a tradition of US engineering and manufacturing.

This appeal of the Harley brand was central not just to the company's marketing, but also to its strategy as a whole. The central thrust of the strategy was reinforcing and extending the relationship between the company and its consumers. Harley-Davidson had long recognized that it was not selling motorcycles, it was selling the Harley Experience. Prominent in annual reports of recent years were pictures and prose depicting this experience:

> *A chill sweeps through your body, created by a spontaneous outburst of pure, unadulterated joy. You are surrounded by people from all walks of life and every corner of the globe. They are complete strangers, but you know them like your own family. They were drawn to this place by the same passion – the same dream. And they came here on the same machine. This is one place you can truly be yourself. Because you don't just fit in. You belong.*[3]

If the appeal of the Harley motorcycle was the image it conveyed and the lifestyle it represented, then the company had to ensure that the experience matched the image. To increase Harley's involvement in its consumers' riding experience it formed the Harley Owners' Group in 1983. Through HOG, the company became involved in organizing social and charity events. Employees, from the CEO down, were encouraged to take an active role in HOG activities. During 2005, senior managers attended over 150 different shows, rallies, and rides. The bond between the company and its customers is captured in Willie G. Davidson's phrase: "We ride with you." HOG provided the organizational link for this sense of community: "the feeling of being out there on a Harley-Davidson motorcycle links us like no other experience can. It's made HOG like no other organization in the world . . . The atmosphere is more family reunion than organized meeting."[4] The loyalty of Harley owners was reflected in their repurchase and upgrading of Harley products. During 1999–2005, more than one half of all sales were to customers who had owned a Harley previously, while about 20% were first-time motorcycle buyers.

From the 1980s to the 2000s, the demographic and socioeconomic profile of Harley customers had shifted substantially. Traditionally, Harley owners were blue-collar men in their 20s and 30s. By 2005, the median income of a Harley owner was over $80,600, up from $38,400 in 1987. The average age grew to 46, up from 35 in 1987. Also, women accounted for about 10% of sales – up from 2% in 1987.

The Products

Broadening Harley's market appeal had major implications for product policy and design. Ever since its disastrous foray into small bikes during the AMF years, Harley had recognized that its competitive advantage lay with super-heavyweight bikes. Here it stuck resolutely to the classic styling that had characterized Harleys since the company's early years. At the heart of the Harley motorcycle was the air-cooled V-twin engine that had been Harley's distinctive feature since 1909. Harley's frames, handlebars, fuel tanks, and seats also reflected traditional designs.

Harley's commitment to traditional design features may be seen as making a virtue out of necessity. Its smaller corporate size and inability to share research expenditure across cars and bikes (unlike Honda and BMW) limited its ability to invest in technology and new products. As a result, Harley lagged far behind its competitors in the application of automotive technologies: its motorcycles not only looked old-style, much of the technology was old-style. When Harley introduced its new Twin Cam 88 engine in 1998, *Motorcycle* magazine reported:

> *Honda comes out with an average of two new (or reworked) motors every year. The other Japanese manufacturers are good for about one. Count on Ducati and BMW to do something every few years. That leaves only Moto Guzzi and Harley. So it goes to say that when either of these two old farts gets off the pot, they really raise a stink, so to speak.*
>
> *The Twin Cam 88 is Harley's first new engine since the Evolution Sportster motor of 1986, and their first new Big Twin motor since the original Evolution, released in 1984. Fifteen years between engines is not really that long a span for Harley. The Evo's predecessor, the Shovelhead lasted 19 years (with a revision after five), and the Panhead lasted nearly as long.*[5]

Harley's engines were most representative of its technological backwardness. Long after Honda had moved to multiple valves per cylinder, overhead camshafts, liquid cooling, and electronic ignition, Harley continued to rely on air-cooled push-rod engines. In suspension systems, braking systems, and transmissions too, Harley lagged far behind Honda, Yamaha, and BMW. Nevertheless, Harley was engaged in constant upgrading – principally incremental refinements to its engines, frames, and gearboxes aimed at improving power delivery and reliability, increasing braking power, and reducing vibration. Harley also accessed automotive technology through alliances with other companies, including Porsche AG, Ford, and Gemini Racing Technologies.

Despite being a technological laggard, Harley was very active in new product development and the launching of new models. By 2006, Harley offered 36 models, of which seven had been added in that year. Harley's product development efforts were assisted by doubling the size of its Product Development Center in 2004 and the creation of a Prototyping Lab. Most of Harley's product development efforts involved style changes, new paint designs, and engineering improvements.

Between 2000 and 2006, Harley accelerated technological progress and new product development. Its V-Rod model introduced in October 2001 featured innovative styling and an all-new liquid-cooled engine. The Buell range also offered Harley engineers an opportunity to be more innovative. The 2002 Buell Firebolt featured a new engine, an all-aluminum frame, and the "naked" styling pioneered by Ducati, while the 2006 Ulysses was Harley-Davidson's first ever "adventure sportbike." In 2006, Harley introduced another new engine, the Twin Cam 96, which featured electronic ignition and was teamed with a new six-speed gearbox.

Central to Harley's product strategy was the idea that every Harley rider would own a unique, personalized motorcycle. This implied not just offering a wide model range, but providing a wide range of customization opportunities. New bikes allowed multiple options for seats, bars, pegs, controls, and paint jobs, with the potential for augmentation through a range of 7,000 accessories, and special services such as "Chrome Consulting."

Reconciling product differentiation with scale economies was a continuing challenge for Harley. The solution was to offer a wide range of customization options while standardizing on key components. For example, among the 36 different Harley models there were three engine types (Evolution XL, Twin Cam 88, and Revolution), four basic frames, four styles of gas tank, and so on.

The Harley product line also covered a wide price range. The Sportster model was positioned as an entry-level bike and priced at $6,595, less than one-third of the price of the Ultra Classic Electra Glide, with two-tone paint, at $21,135 (see table 9.4).

Buell

Harley's involvement with Buell was to broaden its customer base – especially overseas. Harley's market research found that many potential riders were put off by motorcycles being "hard to learn," with Harley models viewed as "intimidating" or "something an old guy would ride." Founded by ex-Harley engineer Erik Buell, Buell Motor Company developed bikes that synthesized the comfort and style of a Harley cruiser with the performance attributes of a sports bike. Harley acquired complete ownership of Buell in 1998. Buell bikes used Harley engines and other components, but mounted them on a lighter, stiffer frame. The lighter weight and superior handling and acceleration of Buell models were seen as appealing to younger motorcyclists and also to the European market, where customers put greater emphasis on sporty performance and a cheaper price tag. In the US, the age of the typical Buell customer was seven years younger than that of Harley buyers, and the price was about $10,000 compared with an average Harley price of $17,000. Through the Buell Riders Adventure Group (BRAG), Buell attempted to foster the close relations with customers that characterized the Harley-Davidson brand. With the Buell Blast, an entirely new model with a 490 cc single cylinder engine and a price tag of $4,595, Harley entered the middleweight motorcycle market for the first time since the 1970s. With the Buell Firebolt, Lightning, and Ulysses models, Buell positioned itself in direct competition with Japanese and European producers of high-performance sports bikes. Yet, despite heavy investments in developing and launching new models, there was little overall growth in Buell's unit sales between 2001 and 2006 (table 9.5).

Distribution

Upgrading Harley's distribution network was a key aspect of its development strategy during the 1980s and 1990s. Many of Harley's 620 US dealerships were poorly

TABLE 9.4 Heavyweight motorcycles: price comparisons, 2007

Manufacturer and model	Engine	Recommended retail price ($)
Harley-Davidson		
XL 883 Sportster	V-twin, air-cooled, 883 cc	6,595
Fat Boy FLSTF	V-twin, air-cooled, 1,540 cc	17,095
V-Rod VRSCX	V-twin, liquid-cooled, 1,131 cc	19,995
Heritage Softail Classic	V-twin, air-cooled, 1,450 cc	17,820
H-D Ultra Classic Electra Glide	V-twin 1,450 cc, injection (two tone)	21,135
Honda		
Shadow VLX	V-twin, liquid-cooled, OHC, 745 cc	5,499
VTX1300C	V-twin, liquid-cooled, OHC, 1,312 cc	9,599
VTX1800R	V-twin, liquid-cooled, OHC, 1,800 cc	13,399
Suzuki		
Boulevard S50	V-twin, liquid-cooled, OHC, 850 cc	6,499
Boulevard C90	V-twin, air-cooled, OHC, 1,475 cc	10,499
Boulevard M109R	V-twin, liquid-cooled, 1,783 cc	12,599
Kawasaki		
Vulcan 900 Classic	V-twin, 8-valve, OHC	7,349
Vulcan 1600 Mean Streak	V-twin, air-cooled, 1,600 cc	11,039
Yamaha		
V-Star Custom	V-twin, OHC, air-cooled, push-rod, 649 cc	5,799
Road Star	V-twin, OHC, air-cooled, push-rod, 1,670 cc	11,399
BMW		
R1200 Sports Tourer	1,170 cc, horizontal twin, air-cooled	14,990
K1200R	1,200 cc, 4-cylinder, liquid-cooled	14,350
Polaris		
Victory Kingpin	V-twin, 4-valve per cylinder, 1,634 cc	15,999

SOURCE: WEBSITES OF DIFFERENT MOTORCYCLE MANUFACTURERS

managed shops, operated by enthusiasts, with erratic opening hours, a poor stock of bikes and spares, and indifferent customer service. If Harley was in the business of selling a lifestyle and an experience, then dealers were the primary point of contact between the company and its customers. Moreover, if Harley's future lay with customers who possessed the disposable income to lay out $18,000 on a motorcycle for occasional leisure rides, then the retail environment had to be appropriate to the needs of this group.

Harley's dealer development program increased support for dealers while imposing higher standards of pre- and after-sales service, and requiring better dealer facilities. The dealers were obliged to carry a full line of Harley replacement parts and accessories, and to perform service on Harley bikes. Training programs helped dealers to meet the higher service requirements, and encouraged them to recognize and meet the needs of the professional, middle-class clientele that Harley was now courting. Harley pioneered the introduction of new services to customers. These included test ride facilities, rider instruction classes, motorcycle rental, assistance for owners in

TABLE 9.5 Harley-Davidson shipments 1997–2006

	1997	1998	1999	2000	2001	2002	2003	2004	2005	2006
H-D motorcycle shipments										
United States ('000s)	96.3	110.9	135.6	158.9	186.9	212.8	237.7	260.6	266.5	273.2
Export ('000s)	36.1	39.9	41.6	45.8	47.5	50.8	53.5	56.7	62.5	76.0
Motorcycle product mix (%)										
Sportster	23.8	22.5	23.6	22.6	21.7	19.4	19.7	22.0	21.3	18.5
Custom[a]	53.5	51.3	49.6	49.3	50.5	53.7	52.0	48.6	45.2	46.2
Touring	22.8	26.2	26.8	28.1	27.9	26.8	28.4	29.4	33.5	35.4
Buell motorcycle shipments										
Worldwide ('000s)	3.1	5.5	6.8	6.9	9.9	10.9	10.0	9.9	11.2	12.5
Company total ('000s)	135.5	156.3	184.0	211.6	244.3	274.5	301.2	327.2	340.2	361.6

[a] Includes VRSC models.

customizing their bikes through dealer-based design centers and chrome consultants, and insurance services. Close to 85% of Harley dealerships in the US were exclusive – far more than for any other motorcycle manufacturer.

Given the central role of dealers in the relationship between Harley-Davidson and its customers, dealer relations continued to be a strategic priority for Harley. Its Retail Environments Group liaised closely with dealers with a goal of bringing the same retail experience to customers everywhere in the world. Harley-Davidson University was established to "enhance dealer competencies in every area, from customer satisfaction to inventory management, service proficiency, and front-line sales." Dealer relationships were critical to Harley's goal of growing sales of financial services, parts and accessories, and general merchandise. Harley believed that the quality and effectiveness of its dealer network was a key determinant of the strong demand for its products. Despite a fivefold increase in production capacity since 1990, demand for Harley motorcycles continued to outstrip supply, with the result that used bikes frequently sold at higher prices than new bikes. More generally, the rate of price depreciation of Harleys was lower than for any other manufacturer.

Other Products

Sales of parts, accessories, and "general merchandise" (clothing and collectibles) represented 20% of total revenue in 2000 – much higher than for any other motorcycle company (see table 9.6). Clothing sales included not just traditional riding apparel, but a wide range of men's, women's, and children's leisure apparel.

Only a small proportion of the clothing, collectibles, and other products bearing the Harley-Davidson trademark were sold through the Harley dealership network. Most of the "general merchandising" business represented licensing of the Harley name and trademarks to third-party manufacturers. For example, Nice Man Merchandising supplied Harley-Davidson children's clothes; a giftware company supplied Harley holiday bulb ornaments, music boxes, and a Road King pewter motorcycle

TABLE 9.6 Harley-Davidson's revenues from parts and accessories, general merchandise, and financial services, 1992–2006 ($ million)

	1992	1993	1994	1995	1996	1997	1998	1999	2000	2001	2002	2003	2004	2005	2006
Parts and accessories	103.6	127.8	162.0	192.1	210.2	241.9	297.1	362.6	447.9	509.6	629.2	712.8	781.6	815.7	862.3
General merchandise	52.1	71.2	94.3	100.2	90.7	95.1	114.5	132.7	151.4	163.9	231.5	211.4	223.7	247.9	277.5
Financial services	–	–	–	–	–	–	102.9	132.7	140.1	181.5	211.5	279.5	305.3	331.6	384.9

SOURCE: HARLEY-DAVIDSON 10-K REPORTS.

replica; L'Oréal offered a line of Harley-Davidson cologne; Harley-Davidson Cafés operated in Manhattan and Las Vegas.

Harley-Davidson Financial Services was established to supply credit, insurance, and extended warranties to Harley dealers and customers. Between 2000 and 2003 it was Harley's most rapidly growing source of profits, accounting for 15% of total operating income in 2003.

International Expansion

A key part of Harley-Davidson's growth strategy was expanding sales outside of the US. A critical issue was the extent to which Harley needed to adapt its products, image, and customer approach to conditions in overseas markets. Harley's image was rooted in American culture – to what extent was Harley's appeal to European and Asian customers rooted in its status as an American icon? "The US and Harley are tied together," observed Hugo Wilson of Britain's *Bike* magazine, "the guy who's into Harleys here is also the guy who owns cowboy boots. You get a Harley and you're buying into the US mystique."[6] At the same time, the composition of demand and the customer profiles were different in overseas markets.

Europe was the focal point of Harley's overseas ambitions, simply because it was the second largest heavyweight motorcycle market in the world. Europe was also a huge challenge for Harley. Unlike in the US, Harley had never had a major position in Europe – it needed to fight to take market share from the established leaders in the heavy bike segment: BMW, Honda, Kawasaki, and Yamaha. The European motor-cycle market differed significantly from the American market in that 70% of the heavy-weight motorcycle market was for performance bikes, while touring and cruiser bikes accounted for just 30%. European buyers were knowledgeable and style conscious, but their style preferences were different from those of US riders. Also, European roads and riding styles were different from the US. As a result, Harley modified some of its models for the European market. The US Sportster, for example, had a straight handle-bar instead of curled buckhorns and a new suspension system to improve cornering. The name was also changed to the "Custom 53." The Harley Softail also received a new look, becoming the "Night Train." As in the US, HOG played a critical role in building brand image and customer loyalty. Harley's anniversary celebration in Barcelona on June 2003 attracted some 150,000 people, including Harley owners from all over Europe. Central to Harley's international strategy was building its dealer network. Between 2000 and 2006, Harley expanded its overseas dealership network and built a new European headquarters in Oxford, England. In 2006, Harley's dealer network comprised 667 in the US, 75 in Canada, 359 in Europe (including the Middle East and Africa), 118 in Asia/Pacific, and 31 in Latin America.

TABLE 9.7 Harley-Davidson's main facilities, 2005

Location	Function	Square feet
Wisconsin		
Milwaukee	Corporate headquarters	515,000
Wauwatosa	Product development center	409,000
Wauwatosa	Engine manufacturing	422,000
Menomonee Falls	Engine and transmission production	479,000
Franklin	Parts/accessories distribution center	250,000
Tomahawk	Fiberglass parts production/painting	211,000
Pennsylvania		
York	Final assembly plant, parts and painting	1,321,000
Missouri		
Kansas City	Manufacturing, painting	450,000
Brazil		
Manaus	Assembly	35,000

SOURCE: HARLEY-DAVIDSON 10-K REPORT, 2005

Operations

Since emerging as an independent company in 1981, Harley-Davidson had continuously upgraded its manufacturing operations. This involved continuous investment in plant and equipment, both to introduce advanced process technologies and to expand capacity. Even more important was the development of manufacturing capabilities through total quality management, just-in-time scheduling, CAD/CAM, and the devolution of responsibility and decision making to the shopfloor. Table 9.7 shows Harley's main manufacturing and development facilities.

Despite constant development of its manufacturing facilities and operational capabilities, Harley's low production volumes relative to Honda and the other Japanese manufacturers imposed significant cost disadvantages. A key cost disadvantage was in the purchasing components. Bought-in, customized components accounted for a large proportion of manufacturing costs and Harley lacked the buying power of Honda or even BMW. To compensate for lack of bargaining clout, Harley fostered close relations with its key suppliers and placed purchasing managers at senior levels within its management structure. Its supplier advisory council (SAC) promoted collaboration and best practice sharing within the Harley network.[7] Harley's director of purchasing, Garry Berryman, commented: "Through the SAC, we're able to take some of the entrepreneurial aspects of our smaller, privately held suppliers and inject that enthusiasm, spirit, and energy into those that may be larger, publicly held companies. In this way, the SAC serves not only to improve purchasing efficiency, but also provides a forum to share information, ideas, and strategy."[8]

People and Management

Central to Harley-Davidson's renaissance was the creation of a new relationship between management and employees. Following the management buyout in 1981, Harley's new management team systematically rethought management–employee relationships, employee responsibilities, and organizational structure. The result was a transformation in employee commitment and job satisfaction. Harley's employee relations focused on involvement, self-management, open communication, and the provision of generous health and leave benefits. Harley's Kansas City assembly plant, opened in 1998, featured a management structure and working methods designed to promote employee commitment and involvement. The plant manager and other administrators worked in a "bullpen area" on the production floor rather than in separate offices, and the whole plant was organized around three types of work teams:

- *Natural work groups* – every worker belonged to a work group, with 8–15 people per group.

- *Process operating groups* – comprised representatives from each work group. There were four process operating groups, one for each of the plant's four operating divisions: paint, assembly, fabrication, and engine production.

- *Plant leadership groups* – a 14-member committee, responsible for governing the facility. They comprised the plant manager, the presidents of both unions representing the plant workforce, four elected representatives from the process groups, an elected representative from maintenance, and six administrators.[9]

Harley's belief in the effectiveness of non-hierarchical, team-based structures in fostering motivation and accelerating innovation and learning was evident throughout the company. The Harley-Davidson Operating System was a philosophy and a methodology for continuous improvement involving team-based efforts to identify wasted steps, pare costs, and enhance quality throughout manufacturing.

The movement toward a flatter, more team-based organizational structure extended to Harley's corporate headquarters. "In our new organization," explained Clyde Fessler, VP for Business Development, "the Harley-Davidson Motor Company has been divided into three broad, functional areas called Circles. They are: the Create Demand Circle (CDC), the Produce Product Circle (PPC), and the Provide Support Circle (PSC). Each Circle is composed of the leaders representing the functions within it. The flexibility of the organization extends even to the decision of which functional areas are identified within a given circle. It is quite possible that Circle definitions may shift from time to time, depending on the demands of the business."[10] Each Circle operated as a team with leadership moving from person to person, depending on the issue being addressed. Overall coordination was provided by the Strategic Leadership Council (SLC), comprising individuals nominated by each of the three Circles.

Competition

Despite Harley's insistence that it was supplying a unique Harley experience rather than competing with other motorcycle manufacturers, the more it took market share from other manufacturers and expanded its product range and geographical scope, the more it came into direct competition with other producers. The clearest indication of direct competition was imitation: Honda, Suzuki, Yamaha, and Kawasaki had long been offering V-twin cruisers styled closely along the lines of the classic Harleys, but at lower prices and with more advanced technologies. In competing against Harley, the Japanese manufacturers' key advantage was their sales volume – Honda produced over five million bikes per year.

In addition, Harley lacked the diversification of its rivals. Honda, BMW, and Suzuki were important producers of automobiles and more than one-third of Yamaha's turnover came from boats and snowmobiles. These companies could benefit from sharing technology, engineering capabilities, and marketing and distribution know-how across their different vehicle divisions. In addition, sheer size conferred greater bargaining power with suppliers.

Imitators also included several specialist companies producing retro-styled cruiser bikes. In recent years Excelsior, Polaris (Victory), and a resuscitated Indian had all entered the US super-heavyweight market.

Figure 9.1 shows competitive product offerings while table 9.4 shows price comparisons. Appendix 2 gives profiles of several leading competitors.

FIGURE 9.1 Cruiser motorcycles, 2007 models

Harley-Davidson Fat Boy

Honda Shadow Spirit 750

Yamaha Roadstar

Suzuki Boulevard C50

Kawasaki Vulcan 900

Polaris Victory Kingpin

Meeting the Challenges of Tomorrow

CEO Jim Ziemer recognized that the target of 11 to 17% earnings per share growth over each of the next three years was ambitious. However, with growing sales of parts, accessories, and financial services and continued productivity increases from improved business processes, Ziemer considered this target well within Harley's grasp. Ultimately, maintaining Harley's remarkable record of profit growth would require selling more bikes and reducing costs in order to grow margins. In both areas, progress would be increasingly difficult. Over past years, Harley had benefitted from several favourable trends: growth of the overall market plus the quest of the baby boomer generation for leisure and the appeal of Harley's values of rugged individualism. Even Harley's recent overseas success could be linked to the advantages of a depreciating US dollar.

In considering the potholes that might throw Harley-Davidson off course, Ziemer grappled with some of the implications of a strategy that emphasized selling an experience rather than selling a product. The problem of selling experiences was that they were dependent upon the social and psychological identity and aspirations of the customer. Were the values embodied in the "Harley Experience" universal and enduring or were they the result of cultural, social demographic phenomena that were particular to the United States during the past two decades? Harley's ability to maintain its market share would depend increasingly on its ability to recruit new and younger customers and expand sales overseas. In both areas, Harley had achieved only modest success.

In terms of Harley's ability to grow its margins, a key factor would be the changing balance of supply and demand as a result of Harley's substantial expansion of production capacity. The changing market dynamics were evident in the weakening prices for used Harleys and the increasing rarity of waiting lists for new Harleys.

Appendix 1
Harley-Davidson: Summary of Financial Statements, 1994–2006

TABLE 9.A1 Harley-Davidson: selected items from financial statements, 1994–2006 ($ million)

	1994	1995	1996	1997	1998	1999	2000	2001	2002	2003	2004	2005	2006
Net sales	1,159	1,350	1,531	1,762	2,064	2,453	2,906	3,407	4,091	4,624	5,015	5,342	5,801
Gross profit	358	411	490	586	691	836	991	1,153	1,418	1,666	1,900	2,040	2,233
R&D	28	30	37	53	59	70	76	130	140	150	171	179	n.a.
Selling, admin., engineering	204	234	269	329	377	448	513	552	639	684	727	762	n.a.
Operating income	154	181	228	270	334	416	515	663	883	1,149	1,361	1,470	1,603
Of which:													
Financial services	–	4	8	12	20	28	37	61	104	168	189	192	211
Interest income	2	0	3	8	4	8	18	17	17	23	23	23	27
Other income/(expense)	1	(5)	(4)	(2)	(1)	(3)	16	(7)	(13)	(6)	(5)	(5)	(5)
Income before taxes	156	176	228	276	336	421	549	673	886	1,166	1,379	1,488	1,624
Provision for income taxes	60	65	84	102	123	154	n.a.	236	306	405	490	528	581
Net income	104	112	166	174	213	267	348	438	580	761	890	960	1,043
Balance sheet													
Assets													
Cash	59	31	142	147	165	183	419	439	281	329	275	141	238
Finance receivables, net	–	170	184	249	319	355	581	921	1,139	1,391	1,656	1,943	2,101
Accounts receivable, net	143	134	141	103	113	102	98	119	109	112	121	122	143
Inventories	173	84	101	118	156	169	192	181	218	208	227	221	288
Total current assets	406	337	613	704	845	949	1,297	1,665	2,067	2,729	3,683	3,145	3,551
Property, plant, equipment	263	285	409	529	628	682	754	892	1,033	1,046	1,025	1,012	1,024
Total assets	739	1,001	1,230	1,599	1,920	2,112	2,436	3,118	3,861	4,923	5,483	5,255	5,532
Liabilities													
Current liabilities													
Current portion of debt	18	3	9	91	147	181	89	217	383	324	495	205	832
Accounts payable	64	103	101	106	123	138	170	195	227	224	244	271	763
Total current liabilities	216	233	251	362	468	518	498	716	990	956	1,173	873	1,596
Non-current liabilities													
Debt	0	164	258	280	280	280	355	380	380	670	800	1,000	870
Other long-term liabilities	90	109	70	62	67	65	97	158	123	86	91	82	109
Post-retirement benefits	n.a.	n.a.	66	68	72	76	81	90	105	127	150	61	201
Stockholders' equity	433	495	663	827	1,030	1,161	1,406	1,756	2,233	2,958	3,218	3,084	2,757
Total liabilities and equity	739	1,001	1,230	1,599	1,920	2,112	2,436	3,118	3,861	4,923	5,483	5,255	5,532
Cash flows													
Operating activities	81	169	228	310	318	416	565	757	546	597	832	961	762
Capital expenditures	(95)	(113)	(179)	(186)	(183)	(166)	(204)	(290)	(324)	(227)	(214)	(198)	(220)
Total investing activities	(97)	(188)	(214)	(406)	(340)	(300)	(171)	(772)	(720)	(540)	(570)	177	(35)
Financing activities	(3)	(10)	96	102	40	(98)	(158)	34	80	81	(316)	(1,272)	(637)
Net increase in cash	(18)	(26)	(111)	5	(18)	18	236	20	(95)	137	(54)	(134)	97

n.a. = not available.

Appendix 2
Harley-Davidson's Competitors

TABLE 9.A2 Comparative financial data for Harley-Davidson, Honda, Yamaha, and BMW ($ million, unless otherwise indicated)

	Honda Motor		Yamaha Motor		BMW		Harley-Davidson	
	2004	2005	2004	2005	2004	2005	2004	2005
Revenue	75,912	80,446	9,711	11,648	60,473	55,255	5,015	5,342
Gross profit margin	31.30%	30.20%	27.35%	27.12%	23.20%	22.90%	37.89%	38.19%
SGA expense	16,175	16,324	1,983	2,284	8,902	8,137	727	762
Operating income	5,581	5,868	673	875	5,108	4,492	1,361	1,470
Net income after tax	3,619	3,628	366	542	3,031	2,652	890	960
Net margin	5.70%	5.60%	3.77%	4.65%	5.00%	4.80%	17.75%	17.97%
Operating income/total assets	7.21%	6.77%	9.14%	10.78%	5.55%	5.09%	24.82%	27.97%
Inventory turnover	7.33	7.42	4.10	4.40	4.75	5.15	14.86	15.36
Return on equity	13.54%	11.86%	14.00%	18.90%	12.69%	13.19%	27.60%	31.10%
Operating cash flow	6,630	6,944	416	562	12,700	12,661	832	961
Cash flow from investing activities	(8,997)	(7,513)	(425)	(610)	(16,309)	(14,168)	(570)	177
R&D expenditure	4,248	4,356	493	607	n.a.	2,918	171	179
Advertising expenditure (all products)	2,038	1,932	n.a.	n.a.	n.a.	n.a.	49	67
Motorcycles shipped (thousands of units)	10,482	10,271	3,171	3,849	92	97	327	340
Employees	131,600	137,827	36,668	39,381	105,972	105,798	9,580	9,700

n.a. = not applicable.

SOURCES: COMPANY FINANCIAL STATEMENTS.

Notes

1 Gary Strauss, "Born to be bikers," *USA Today*, November 5, 1997.
2 Marc Ballon, "Born to be wild," *Inc*, November 1997, p. 42.
3 Harley-Davidson, Inc. Annual Report, 2000.
4 www.harley-davidson.com/experience/family/hog
5 *Motorcycle* magazine, February 1998.
6 Marco R. della Cava, "Motorcycle maker caters to the continent," *USA Today*, April 22, 1998.
7 Kevin R. Fitzgerald, "Harley's supplier council helps deliver full value," *Purchasing*, September 5, 1995.
8 Ann Millen Porter, "One focus, one supply base," *Purchasing*, June 5, 1997.
9 Stephen Roth, "Harley's goal: unify union and management," *Kansas City Business Journal*, May 16, 1997.
10 Clyde Fessler, "Rotating leadership at Harley-Davidson: from hierarchy to interdependence," *Strategy & Leadership*, July 17, 1997.

Raisio Group and the Benecol Launch*

Case [A]: The Situation in January 1997

During 1996, Raisio Group, a 57-year-old grain-milling company based in Raisio in the south-west of Finland, emerged from obscurity to become the second most valuable public company in Finland (after Nokia) and the focus of worldwide attention. The launch of Benecol, its cholesterol-lowering margarine, at the end of 1995 had attracted the interest of food processors and supermarket groups throughout the world and fueled a surge of investor interest. Demand for the product had outstripped Raisio's capability to produce the active ingredient in Benecol, stanol ester. On the Helsinki stock market, foreign demand pushed Raisio's share price from FIM61 at the beginning of the year to FIM288 at the end (after touching FIM322 during the summer).[1] CEO Matti Salminen commented:

> 1996 will go down in the Raisio Group's history as the "Benecol year" – such was the role of this new cholesterol-reducing margarine in increasing the Group's visibility and raising its profile in all our sectors of operations. Although we have not been able to meet even the domestic demand for Benecol margarine so far, the product is already known worldwide and great expectations are attached to it. The Benecol phenomenon quintupled the value of our shares, increasing the Group's capitalization by billions of Finnish marks.[2]

It was the international prospects for Benecol margarine (and potentially other food products incorporating stanol ester) that had drawn a bevy of stock analysts

* This case draws upon an earlier case by Michael H. Moffett and Stacey Wolff Howard, *Benecol: Raisio's Global Nutriceutical*, Thunderbird, The American Graduate School of International Management. Case No. A06-99-0004, 1999. I am grateful to Ayan Bhattacharya for assistance in preparing this case.

and portfolio managers to Raisio's headquarters. Not only was the potential market for Benecol considered huge – the US alone was seen as having a multi-billion market potential – but the profit opportunities also appeared excellent. In Finland, Benecol was selling at about six times the price of regular margarine. In addition to being first to market, Raisio had the ability to sustain its market leadership through its patents relating to the production and use of the active ingredient, stanol ester, and recognition of its Benecol brand name.

However, within Raisio, a vigorous debate had broken out as to the best strategy for exploiting the vast commercial potential that Benecol offered. Raisio was a significant margarine manufacturer in Finland and the domestic launch of Benecol was the result of its own independent efforts. Outside of Finland, Raisio had few facilities and limited experience. A number of multinational food companies and leading food retailers had approached Raisio expressing interest in licensing agreements, joint ventures, and supply agreements – for Benecol margarine, for the active ingredient stanol ester, or for both.

History

The Raisio Group began life in 1939 as Vehnä Oy, a grain-milling company located in the town of Raisio. In 1950, a vegetable oil factory called Oy Kasviöljy-Växtolje Ab was founded next to the milling plant. The two companies cooperated in introducing rapeseed cultivation to Finland. They eventually merged in 1987 to form Raisio Tehtaat Oy Ab.[3] From cereals and vegetable oil, the company expanded into animal feeds, malt production, potato starch, and margarine. In the 1960s, production of starch provided the basis for the supply of a number of chemical products, mainly to the paper industry.

During this period Raisio developed a substantial export business. This began with malt exports to Sweden, followed by exports of margarine, pasta, and other food products to the Soviet Union and subsequently to Poland. In the St. Petersburg area of Russia and in Estonia, Raisio's Melia-branded products were market leaders in flour, pasta, and muesli. Finland's accession to the European Union in 1995 allowed Raisio to expand its sales in other European countries. By 1996, 39% of Raisio's sales were outside of Finland. Raisio's increased international presence included margarine plants in Sweden and Poland, and joint-venture plants supplying starch and other products for the paper industry in Sweden, the US, France, Germany, and Indonesia.

From its earliest days, Raisio had shown considerable entrepreneurial initiative and technical ingenuity. Its first oil-milling plant was constructed by its own employees using spare parts, scrap metal, and innovative improvisation. Raisio's first margarine plant was built partly to stimulate demand for its own production of rapeseed oil, which was not widely used in margarine production at that time. Raisio also maintained an active program of R&D. Benecol was the result of Raisio's research into plant sterols. Raisio's annual report tells the story:

The cholesterol-reducing effects of plant sterols were known as early as the 1950s and ever since that time, scientists all over the world have been studying plant sterols and their properties.

In 1972, a project led by Professor Pekka Puska was launched in North Karelia. The purpose of the project, which enjoyed international prestige, was to reduce the high cardiovascular rates in the region.

In 1988, the Department of Pharmacy at the University of Helsinki started cooperation with the Helsinki and Turku Central Hospitals and the Raisio Group aimed at studying the effect of rapeseed oil on blood cholesterol levels. Professor Tatu Miettinen, who had already done extensive research on fat metabolism, suggested research on plant sterols to the Raisio Group.

The following year, R&D Manager Ingmar Wester (of Raisio's Margarine Sub-division) and his research team found a way of turning plant sterol into fat-soluble stanol ester suitable for food production. A patent application was filed in 1991. This started a period of intense research aimed at producing indisputable evidence of the cholesterol-reducing effect of stanol ester. In 1993, the North Karelia project launched a long-range stanol ester study as part of its other clinical research.

The digestive tract receives cholesterol from two sources, i.e. food and the human body itself. Normally, some 50% of the cholesterol that enters the digestive tract is disposed of and the rest is absorbed by the body. Fat-soluble plant stanol was shown as efficiently preventing the absorption of cholesterol. In a diet containing stanol ester, 80% of the cholesterol entering the digestive tract is disposed of and only 20% is absorbed by the body. The plant stanol itself is not absorbed, but disposed of naturally.

The findings of the North Karelia study were published in the New England Journal of Medicine *in November 1995. (The article reported that, after a 14-month trial, a daily intake of 25 grams reduces total cholesterol in the bloodstream by 10% and the level of more harmful LDL cholesterol by 14%.) At the same time the first patents were issued for the production and use of stanol ester.*

The first stanol ester product, Benecol margarine, was introduced on the Finnish market. The interest it aroused soon exceeded all expectations both in Finland and internationally. The registered name, Benecol, has since been confirmed as the common name for all products containing stanol ester.

Production of stanol ester began with experimental equipment, which limited the supply. The availability of plant sterol, the raw material, was another limiting factor. All plants contain small amounts of plant sterol, but it can be recovered economically only from plants processed in very large quantities. Since there had been no demand for plant sterols, no investments had been made in separation facilities.[4]

Exhibit 10.1 describes the cholesterol reducing properties of sterols and stanols. The appendix gives information on Raisio's main patents relating to stanol ester.

Raisio in 1997

At the beginning of 1997, the Raisio Group had annual sales of $866 million and 2,594 employees. The Group comprised three divisions:

- Foodstuffs (47% of total sales), including the subdivisions: margarine (39% of sales), Melia Ltd. (flour, pasta, breakfast cereal, muesli), oil milling, potato processing (mainly frozen French fries), malting, and Foodie Oy (rye products, pea soup, frozen pastry dough, salad dressings).
- Chemicals (34% of sales).
- Animal feeds (19% of sales).

EXHIBIT 10.1
Sterols and Stanols

Sterols play a critical role in maintaining cell membranes in both plants and animals. Plant sterols (phytosterols) can reduce the low-density lipoprotein (LDL) in human blood, therefore reducing the risk of coronary heart disease. In plants, more than 40 sterols have been identified, of which sitosterol, stigmasterol, and campesterol are the most abundant.

Plant stanols (phytostanols) are similar to sterols and are also found naturally in plants – though in much smaller quantities than sterols.

The effect of plant sterols in lowering human cholesterol levels has been known since the 1950s. Sitosterol has been used as a supplement and as a drug (Cytellin, marketed by Eli Lilly) to lower serum cholesterol levels. However, the use of plant sterols was limited by problems of poor solubility.

A important breakthrough was made by Finnish chemist Ingvar Wester, who hydrogenated plant sterols (derived from tall oil, a byproduct of pine wood pulp) to produce stanol, then esterified the stanol to produce stanol ester which is fat-soluble. Unlike sterol ester, stanol ester is not absorbed by the body. Clinical trials in Finland showed stanol ester reduced total blood serum cholesterol in humans by up to 15%.

Plant sterols can also be produced as a byproduct of vegetable oil processing. One of the final stages of processing of vegetable oil is deodorization – high-temperature distillation that removes free fatty acids. From the resulting distillate sterols can be recovered.

Plant sterols themselves have a waxy consistency and a high melting point, creating solubility issues for the food processor. While they are oil-dispersible to some extent in their raw form, the amount required to produce an efficacious effect in a finished product can cause granulation. The answer to this problem is esterification to make stanols and sterols fat-soluble. During 1996, Unilever was working on the esterification of plant sterols. Meanwhile, Archer Daniels Midland was believed to be developing processes that would allow the introduction of sterols into nonfat systems, thus creating entirely new product lines (e.g. adding sterols to beverages).

Outside of Finland, Raisio had subsidiaries in Sweden, Estonia, Latvia, UK, France, Spain, Germany, Belgium, Poland, Canada, USA, and Indonesia. Raisio also had joint ventures in Mexico (49% ownership) and Chile (50%). Figure 10.1 shows Raisio's share price. Table 10.1 shows Raisio's financial performance.

The Benecol Launch

Raisio launched Benecol margarine with a retail price of around FIM25 ($4.50) for a 250 gram tub – this compared with FIM4 for regular margarine. Despite the high price, the product flew off the shelves as quickly as it appeared and Raisio was forced to institute a system of rationing supplies to distributors. During 1996, Raisio estimated that it was only able to satisfy about two-thirds of domestic demand.

TABLE 10.1 Raisio's financial performance, 1987–1996

	1987	1988	1989	1990	1991	1992	1993	1994	1995	1996
Sales (FIM m)	2,011	2,184	2,487	2,557	2,315	3,070	3,549	3,518	3,224	3,928
change, %	+9	+9	+14	+3	−9	+33	+16	−1	−8	+22
Exports from Finland (FIM m)	126	106	110	136	172	241	389	358	519	735
International sales (FIM m)	288	16	189	217	279	405	561	568	886	1,541
Operating margin (FIM m)	214	247	232	213	316	431	492	428	383	420
% of turnover	10.6	11.3	9.3	8.3	13.6	14.0	13.9	12.2	11.9	10.7
Profit after depreciation (FIM m)	147	167	120	90	185	252	294	230	183	196
% of turnover	7.3	7.6	4.8	3.5	8.0	8.2	8.3	6.5	5.7	5.0
Pre-tax profit[a] (FIM m)	97	98	91	64	63	114	185	35	140	162
% of turnover	4.8	4.5	3.7	2.5	2.7	3.7	5.2	1.0	4.3	4.1
Return on equity (%)	15.5	15.3	5.4	0.1	6.9	10.3	10.3	9.4	6.8	5.8
Return on investment (%)	12.6	13.1	9.0	5.8	10.7	13.7	12.4	10.3	8.5	8.5
Shareholders' equity (FIM m)	670	994	1,123	1,224	1,246	1,426	1,517	1,564	1,648	1,973
Balance sheet total (FIM m)	1,831	2,257	2,493	2,872	2,702	3,268	3,302	3,071	3,175	3,678
Equity ratio (%)	36	44.3	46.0	43.7	47.3	44.3	46.5	51.4	52.1	54.0
Quick ratio	0.8	1.0	0.8	0.8	0.9	0.8	1.0	1.1	0.9	1.1
Current ratio	1.6	1.7	1.6	1.5	1.6	1.5	1.6	1.6	1.6	1.8
Gross investments (FIM m)	101	329	269	462	197	293	174	188	380	387
% of turnover	5.0	15.1	10.8	18.1	8.5	9.5	4.9	5.3	11.8	9.9
R&D expenditure (FIM m)	16	28	31	52	31	35	40	54	54	87
% of turnover	0.8	1.3	1.2	2.0	1.3	1.1	1.1	1.5	1.7	2.2
Direct taxes (FIM m)	5	10	27	25	20	20	47	21	32	64
No. of employees	1,538	1,581	1,877	1,987	803	1,985	2,106	1,958	2,054	2,365

[a] Before appropriations, taxes, and minority interest.

SOURCE: RAISIO GROUP ANNUAL REPORTS.

FIGURE 10.1 Raisio's share price (unrestricted shares, Helsinki Stock Exchange)

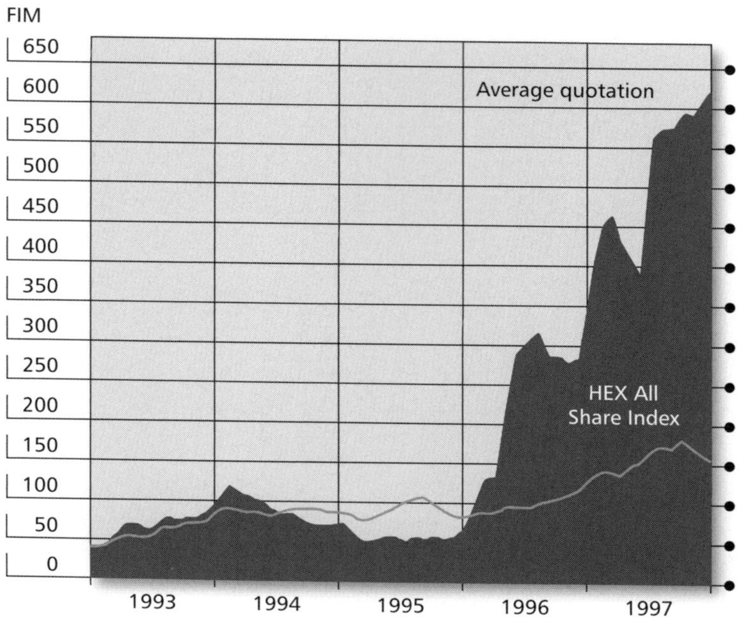

To facilitate the speedy development of the Benecol business, in March 1996 Benecol margarine was transferred from the Margarine Subdivision to a separate Benecol Unit. The unit was headed by Jukka Kaitaranta, who reported to deputy chief executive and head of the Food Division, Jukka Maki. It was intended that, during 1997, Benecol would become a separate division within Raisio. The Benecol Unit was responsible for developing all aspects of the business. It was responsible for acquiring plant sterol, producing stanol ester, managing international publicity of the project, and conducting research.

The key problem was limited supplies of the active ingredient, stanol ester. While plant sterols – the raw material from which stanol ester is produced – are a common by-product of industries that mass-process vegetable matter, almost no one had the systems in place to collect them. Raisio's primary source of supply of plant stanols was UPM-Kymmene, Europe's biggest pulp and paper company. During 1996, it negotiated increased supplies from UPM-Kymmene and also sought access to sterols from vegetable oil processors. Also in 1996, the Group built its first stanol ester plant, which was located in Raisio, and announced plans for a second plant to bring total stanol ester capacity up to 2,000 tonnes a year by January 1998. Mr. Kari Jokinen, chief executive of Raisio's Margarine Division, estimated that this production of stanol ester would allow the production of 25 million kilos of margarine, which could supply a total market of 60 million people.[5] The Benecol Unit also began work on a new 1,500 square meter R&D laboratory at Raisio's main industrial site.

During 1996, Raisio began planning for the international launch of Benecol. Its first overseas market was to be Sweden. The Swedish launch would be facilitated by Raisio's acquisition of a 77.5% stake in Carlshamm Mejeri AB, one of Sweden's main margarine producers, for $44.4 million. However, Raisio's horizons were not limited to Scandinavia – nor even to Europe. Benecol margarine was seen as having a huge international potential. Sales to the US market could be massive, given that Americans spent some $33 billion a year on health foods and slimming products. Some estimates suggested that sales of Benecol margarine could reach $3 billion.

By January 1997, Raisio was being bombarded with requests and proposals from all over the world. Sainsbury, at the time Britain's leading supermarket chain, requested an own-label version of Benecol margarine.[6] Other food processing companies were interested in purchasing licenses either for Benecol margarine or for Raisio's stanol ester technology, or for both.

Raisio's senior executives recognized that product formulation, marketing strategy, and distribution policies would need to be adapted to the requirements of different national markets. Moreover, there were complex national regulations relating to the marketing of food products – especially those that included additives claiming to have health benefits. The Raisio executives were especially interested in an approach from McNeil Consumer Products, a division of the US-based pharmaceutical and consumer products company Johnson & Johnson. McNeil was the world's biggest supplier of over-the-counter medicines, and was known by its leading brand-name products such as Tylenol, Imodium, and Motrin. McNeil was headquartered in Fort Washington, Pennsylvania and was able to field a range of relevant resources – not least Johnson & Johnson's worldwide marketing and distribution system.

Competition

In formulating a strategy for the global exploitation of Benecol, Raisio faced a number of uncertainties. One issue that especially concerned Raisio executives was the potential for Benecol to encounter competition. In 1991, Raisio had filed its first patent relating to its process for the production of stanol ester from plant sterols and for its use in reducing cholesterol as an additive to human foods. In 1996, its first US patent relating to stanol ester was issued. In the same year, Raisio filed a broader patent relating to the processing and use of stanol ester (see the appendix). However, a number of competing products were available for reducing cholesterol. In particular, the cholesterol-reducing properties of naturally available plant sterols were well known. While Raisio believed it owned the only effective means for converting plant sterols into a fat-soluble form, it thought it likely that other processes might offer alternative approaches to the use of plant sterols as a food additive. Tor Bergman, head of chemicals (and soon to be appointed head of the Benecol Division as well) reckoned that Raisio had an 18- to 24-month lead over competitors.

Apart from plant sterols and stanols, a growing array of cholesterol-reducing drugs was available on the market. The major category was statins, which included Lovastatin (brand name Mevacor), Simvastatin (brand name Zocor), Pravastatin (brand name Pravachol), Fluvastatin (brand name Lescol), and Atorvastatin (brand name Lipitor). Statins worked through slowing down the production of cholesterol by the body and by increasing the liver's ability to remove the LDL-cholesterol already in the blood.

In addition there are a number of natural food products that have the effect of reducing cholesterol within the blood. These include fish oil, garlic, flax seed, dietary fiber, policosanol (fatty alcohols derived from waxes of sugar cane), and guggulipid (an ancient herb from India).

Regulation

Benecol margarine falls into a wide category of products generally referred to as "nutraceuticals" or "functional foods." These are food products or supplements that may have a functional or physiological effect that is beneficial. Nutraceuticals have traditionally included food supplements such as vitamin pills, herbal products, and more recently food products with additives that offer particular nutritional benefits – energy enhancing drinks, vitamin-enriched cereals, and the like. Nutraceuticals occupy a middle ground between food and medicines. The regulations relating to them also fall between food regulations and drug regulations. They also vary greatly between countries. Thus, Japan was one of the few countries that recognized functional foods as a distinct category and, since 1991, has had a well-developed administrative system for vetting and approving health claims relating to food. Canada, on the other hand, made no distinction between functional foods and drugs in relation to health claims – inevitably, this resulted in a highly restrictive regulatory climate for functional foods. Typically, regulations required that claims regarding the beneficial effects of food products could only be *health* claims (i.e. improved health) and not *medicinal* claims (i.e. claims relating to the prevention or cure of a disease). The most important markets for Benecol would be the US and European Union. Here the regulations were far from clear-cut (see exhibit 10.2).

EXHIBIT 10.2

Country Regulations Relating to "Functional Foods"

USA

Under the 1990 *Nutrition Labeling and Education Act* (NLEA), the US Food and Drug Administration allowed health claims in the case of certain well-documented relationships, e.g. between calcium and osteoporosis and sodium and hypertension.

The 1997 *Food and Drug Administration Modernization Act* (FDAMA) allowed for two types of health claim:

1 Authoritative statement health claims (e.g. relating to whole grain foods and risk of heart disease and certain cancers, and potassium and risk of high blood pressure and stroke).

2 Qualified claims restricted to dietary supplements – typically in the form of pills, capsules, tablets or liquids, labeled as dietary supplements and not represented or marketed for consumption as a conventional food or sole item of a meal. Such claims could be based on a preponderance of scientific evidence.

In practice this meant three possible paths for gaining approval of a food product offering stated heath benefits:

1 As a dietary supplement. This was the simplest path. The applicant had to file notification to the FDA 60 days prior to commercial rollout together with supporting evidence.

2 As a food additive. This was a more time-consuming process involving much stronger evidence and a determination by an independent panel of experts assembled by the applicant and reporting to the FDA.

3 As a pharmaceutical. Finally, a new food product could be approved as a drug. This process typically required several years.

Canada

The Canadian Food and Drug Act stipulated that all products represented for the cure, treatment, mitigation, prevention, risk reduction, and correction or modification of body structure and function are regulated as a "drug" regardless of the available scientific evidence.

European Union

During the 1990s, the EU was in the process of harmonizing legislation among its individual member countries regarding health claims for food products. Regulation No. 258/97 concerning novel foods and novel food ingredients applied to new foods or ingredients that were primary molecular structures, micro-organisms, or were isolated from plants or isolated from animals (but was not applicable to food additives). Such novel foods were to be assessed by the government of a member state, which would make an initial assessment to determine whether the product met EU standards of safety and accurate labeling and whether an additional assessment was needed. "If neither the Commission nor the Member States raise an objection, and if no additional assessment is required, the Member State informs the applicant that he may place the product on the market . . . Any decision or provision concerning a novel food or food ingredient which is likely to have an effect on public health must be referred to the Scientific Committee for Food."

Fast-track approval was possible for products that were essentially similar to products already on the market, but entirely new products required a full assessment by the Scientific Committee for Food. It would appear that Benecol was a new food product (given its first-time use of stanol ester). However, the fact that it had already been marketed in Finland before the EU's regulation had taken effect might provide it with a loophole to avoid full-assessment approval.

Japan

In 1991, Japan became the first global jurisdiction to implement a regulatory system for functional foods. Under the Japanese system, Foods for Specific Health Use (FOSHU) had a specific regulatory approval process separate from foods fortified with vitamins and minerals, and dietary supplements not carrying FOSHU claims. FOSHU are defined as "foods in the case of which specified effects contributing to maintain health can be expected based on the available data concerning the relationship between the foods'/ food's contents and health, as well as foods with permitted labeling which indicates the consumer can expect certain health effects upon intake of these particular foods." Approved FOSHU bear a seal of approval from the Japanese Ministry of Health, Labor and Welfare (MHLW) identifying their role in disease prevention and health promotion. To achieve FOSHU status and an approved health claim, companies submit a scientific dossier to MHLW, which includes scientific documentation demonstrating the medical and nutritional basis for the health claim, including the recommended dose of the functional ingredient. MHLW has established a detailed approval process, which typically takes about one year to complete. Japan was estimated to have the world's second largest functional food market behind the US.

Sources: Michael H. Moffett and Stacey Wolff Howard, *Benecol: Raisio's Global Nutraceutical*, Thunderbird, The American Graduate School of International Management, 1999. Jean A. MacDonald, "A Comparative Analysis of the Regulatory Framework Affecting Functional Food and Functional Food Ingredient Development and Commercialization in Canada, the United States (US), the European Union (EU), Japan and Australia New Zealand," *Agriculture and Agri-Food Canada*, August, 2001.

The Emerging Strategy

Until the beginning of 1997, Raisio had pursued a largely self-sufficient strategy for the exploitation of its stanol ester technology. It had fabricated stanol ester itself in its own plant using its own technology. Rather than selling the stanol ester to other food manufacturers for incorporation into their own products, it had followed a strategy of vertical integration. Its stanol ester was used only in its own branded margarine, Benecol, which was produced in its own factories and marketed and distributed through its own sales and distribution system.

If it was to exploit the full potential of its innovation, Raisio would need to draw upon the resources of other companies. Clearly the market for cholesterol-reducing foods was worldwide. Also, the potential for using stanol ester in foods was not restricted to margarine. Raisio envisaged its use in a variety of health food products, including salad dressings, dairy products, and snack bars. If Raisio's stanol ester technology was to be exploited effectively throughout the EU, in North America, the Far East, and Australasia, then this would require food processing facilities, market knowledge, regulatory know-how, and distribution facilities that were quite beyond Raisio's ability to provide. A critical issue was time. Raisio patents related to its own process of producing stanol ester and incorporating it within food products. While Raisio's technology and the patent protection it had received bought it a few years' lead-time, it was unlikely that other companies would not find alternative approaches to use plant sterols as a cholesterol-reducing food additive.

In Johnson & Johnson, Raisio had a potential partner that had the capabilities needed to introduce Benecol margarine – and other Benecol products – to the world market. Not only did J&J possess global manufacturing, marketing, and distribution capabilities, it also possessed extensive experience in the food and drug approval procedures of the US, Europe, and most other countries. J&J was widely considered to be one of the most effective health product marketing companies in the world, with an outstanding reputation for quality and social responsibility, a global sales and distribution reach, and vast experience in guiding products through government regulations relating to foods and drugs. It viewed nutraceuticals as an important strand of its growth strategy. Its first neutraceutical was Lactaid for people unable to digest lactose. Lactaid was sold in caplets and as lactose-reduced milk and lactose-free foods. It also supplied sucralose, a low-calorie sweetener that had been approved by the US Food and Drug Administration and was sold in nearly 30 countries.

At the same time, there were voices within Raisio that saw risks in an exclusive relationship with Johnson & Johnson. If stanol ester was a potential additive to a wide range of products, did it make sense for Raisio to become identified with a single product – margarine – and was it desirable for Raisio to link its fortunes with a single partner? An alternative approach for Raisio would be to focus on the supply of its key ingredient, stanol ester. At one meeting of Raisio's executive committee, the case of Monsanto and NutraSweet was discussed. It was noted that following the development of NutraSweet (the branded name for aspartame), Monsanto did not forward integrate into the production of diet foods and beverages, but became a supplier of NutraSweet to a wide range of different beverage suppliers and food processors.

In relation to the production and supply of stanol ester, Raisio also faced some critical strategic choices. The crucial problem in 1996 appeared to be limited capacity for producing stanol ester. Even with a new plant planned for 1997, Raisio would still be unable to supply the potential market for Benecol margarine in Finland and nearby markets. If, as anticipated, the demand for Benecol products was to be world-wide, it would need to produce stanol ester in all regions where Benecol products were manufactured and marketed. Thus, even if Raisio agreed a licensing agreement with Johnson & Johnson to produce and market Benecol products, Raisio would need to specify the terms under which stanol ester would be supplied. All Raisio's sterol requirements were supplied by the pulp and paper group, UPM-Kymmene. Raisio had cooperated closely with UPM-Kymmene in developing the technology for separating plant sterols during wood pulp processing. To ensure access to adequate supplies of plant sterols for its stanol ester production, Raisio would need to collaborate closely with the processors of forest and agricultural products. Raisio was considering forming a joint venture with UPM-Kymmene specifically for the extraction and supply of plant sterols. Irrespective of whether the global licensing deal with J&J for the production and distribution of Benecol products went ahead, Raisio faced critical decisions with regard to the production of stanol ester and the supply of plant sterols. Should it keep its production of stanol ester in-house, or should it license this technology also?

Case [B]: Developments 1997–2000

The Agreement With Johnson & Johnson

During 1997, negotiations between Raisio Group and Johnson & Johnson's McNeil subsidiary progressed to the point where an agreement was signed between the two companies. Raisio's 1997 Annual Report outlined the deal:

> *In July 1997, the Raisio Group signed a cooperation agreement with the American McNeil Consumer Products Company, which is part of the Johnson & Johnson Group. The contract gives McNeil the sole right to use the Benecol trademark and patents on the US, Canadian, and Mexican markets. The Raisio Group retains the right to supply the stanol ester required for the products. McNeil aims to introduce the first products during 1998. Raisio received a lump payment for assignment of these license rights and will receive remunerations related to operative development and royalties for the sales of Benecol products and for deliveries of stanol ester.*
>
> *Johnson & Johnson is the world's biggest and most versatile producer of health-related products. Its turnover totaled USD21.6 billion in 1996 and it has 170 operative companies in 50 countries.*
>
> *In November a new letter of intent was signed, which will extend cooperation with Johnson & Johnson to global dimensions. Europe and Japan will take their places by the side of the United States as the chief Benecol markets. The agreement also includes a plan to strengthen the position of the Benecol brand by cooperating with other companies producing strong brands that fit in with the Benecol product family. The letter of intent leads to a final agreement on March 2, 1998.*
>
> *These agreements confirm the principle that the Raisio Group will keep the entire production of stanol ester in its own hands and will develop Benecol production and marketing in Finland and neighboring areas. Global marketing will be carried out with a strong and skilled cooperation partner.*[7]

Expectations for Benecol were high. Raisio's consultants estimated total world-wide sales of nutraceuticals at $35 billion a year, excluding supplements (such as vitamins and minerals). Of these, functional foods comprised about one-third ($10–12 billion) with an annual growth of 25–35%. If consumer reaction to Benecol in other industrialized nations was anything like that in Finland, Benecol promised to be a blockbuster. By the beginning of 1998, Raisio's share price exceeded EUR12 – up 1,200% over three years.

The agreement would involve close cooperation between Raisio and Johnson & Johnson. Not only would Raisio be supplying J&J with stanol ester, the agreement also provided for the two companies to coordinate medical and clinical research and marketing, and cooperate in product development on a project-by-project basis.

Putting together the partnership with J&J was the dominant priority of Raisio's top management during the first half of 1997. As a result, several other initiatives were put on hold. Raisio's 1997 annual report noted that: "The introduction of Benecol products was delayed on the Finnish market because of the extensive license negotiations at group level and the need to adopt a common approach on all markets."[8]

Stanol Ester Production

Given the optimism for worldwide sales of Benecol and Raisio's current inability to meet home demand because of a shortage of stanol ester, the worldwide launch of Benecol margarine depended critically on expanding the production of stanol ester.

The first priority was increasing Raisio's purchases of plant sterol. Raisio's 1997 Annual Report described the quest:

> The plant sterol needed to produce stanol ester has from the very beginning been supplied by Kaukus Oy, part of the UPM-Kymmene Group. Kaukas separates the sterol during the pulp cooking process and is a pioneer in sterol separation techniques.
>
> In April 1997, Raisio and UPM-Kymmene set up a joint venture called Sterol Technologies Ltd. Raisio's holding is 65%. The company develops sterol separation methods and markets them to the forest industry. In October 1997, Sterol Technologies began to build an experimental sterol recovery unit at the Kaukas mill, which is scheduled for completion in March 1998.
>
> An agreement has been made with the French company Les Derives Raisiniques et Terpeniques to achieve a major increase in its sterol production. The new plant covered by the agreement should go on stream in 1999. The entire additional capacity has been reserved for Raisio Benecol.
>
> In August, a letter of intent was signed with the American Westvaco Corporation on cooperation in studying ways of producing plant sterol in America. The aim is to build a sterol production plant in South Carolina to go on stream in 2000.
>
> In November, an agreement was signed with the Chilean company Harting S.A. on establishing a joint venture called Detsa S.A. in Chile. Raisio's holding is 49%. Detsa will build a sterol plant and Sterol Technologies will be responsible for the technology.
>
> When the Detsa plant is completed in 1999, Raisio Benecol will have close to 400 tonnes of raw sterol a year at its disposal. Refined into stanol ester, this amount will satisfy the daily needs of 4 million people. If the percentage of

population accounted for by users of Benecol settles at the same level as in
Finland, this amount will be sufficient to supply markets comprising close on
200 million consumers.[9]

Raisio had been operating a prototype stanol ester plant at its headquarters since
1996. It had planned to build an adjoining unit to expand stanol ester production.
However, following the J&J deal Raisio decided that the priority was to begin stanol
ester production in America. Hence, in June 1997, Raisio began construction of a
stanol ester plant at Charleston, South Carolina.

The International Launch

United States   During 1998, J&J planned for the launch of Benecol margarine both
in the US and Europe. After considerable analysis and discussion, J&J decided that,
for the purposes of meeting the FDA regulations, it would introduce Benecol spreads
to the US market as a dietary supplement. As exhibit 10.2 explains, this would involve the least delay and would allow J&J to promote Benecol's cholesterol-reducing
benefits.

However, in October 1998, a letter from the FDA torpedoed the US launch:

The purpose of this letter is to inform you that marketing the product with the
prototype label . . . would be illegal under the Federal Food, Drug and Cosmetic
Act . . . The label for the Benecol spread, through the statement that the product
replaces butter or margarine, vignettes picturing the product in common butter or
margarine uses, statements promoting the texture and flavor of the product, and
statements such as ". . . helps you manage your cholesterol naturally through the
food you eat," represents this product for use as a conventional food. Therefore,
the product is not a dietary supplement.

As a food with an additive that had not been approved as safe, Benecol margarine
was subject to FDA regulation and J&J would have to embark on the protracted process of submitting evidence of stanol ester's safety and efficacy.

J&J halted the US launch of Benecol and decided that it would introduce the product as a food product without any explicit health claims. By early 1999 Benecol received "Generally Recognized As Safe" (GRAS) status from a panel of independent
experts that allowed Benecol to be launched in May 1999.

Europe   In Europe, J&J avoided the regulatory tussles that had delayed the US
launch of Benecol, principally because the 1995 introduction into Finland had pre-
dated the new EU regulations. Nevertheless, the European launch still needed to take
account of different national regulations and Benecol's formulation also needed to be
adapted to different national preferences. In March 1999, Benecol was launched in
the UK and in Belgium, the Netherlands, and Luxemburg in September. The European
launch comprised four products: regular and low-fat Benecol spread (margarine) and
a natural and a herb cheese spread. In the fall of 2000, Benecol products were
launched in Sweden and Denmark.

Competition

Unilever   The delays to Benecol's international launch eliminated Raisio's first-
mover advantage in cholesterol-reducing margarine. Almost simultaneous with

Benecol's US debut, Unilever launched its rival product, Take Control, which contained sterol esters derived from vegetable oil. Because Take Control's sterol esters were simpler and less expensive to prepare than Raisio's stanol ester (it did not require a complex hydrogenation process), the Unilever product could be sold at a lower price. Initially, Raisio and J&J were not overly concerned at the price differential, in the belief that stanol ester was more effective than sterol ester in cholesterol reduction. However, some new research suggested that the differential was probably very small.

In September 2000, Raisio and J&J received some rare good news from the FDA. After a careful review of the evidence, the FDA had determined that J&J could issue explicit health claims for the effects of stanol ester within Benecol margarine in reducing coronary heart disease. The only downside was that the ruling gave equal rights to Unilever for its sterol ester ingredient.

Despite overcoming the regulatory hurdles, the market reaction to Benecol was disappointing. J&J spent $49 million on advertising Benecol within the US, but US retail sales for Benecol between May and December 1999 reached just $17 million. Another estimate put US sales between May 1999 and August 2000 at $42 million.

Unilever's initial launch met similar results. During 1999 it was estimated that Take Control was supported by $15 million in advertising only to generate $13 million in sales. By January 2000, Take Control had gained 1.6% of the US margarine market, with Benecol holding 1.2%. In response to this poor consumer response, J&J shifted the emphasis of its marketing strategy from consumer advertising to providing information to US doctors on the health benefits of Benecol.

In Europe, J&J was able to enter the market for cholesterol-reducing margarine before Unilever in most countries. Unilever launched its sterol ester margarine as "Pro-activ" – an extension to its existing Flora and Becel ranges of low saturated fat margarines. In the UK, Unilever's Flora Pro-activ was launched early in 2000 – nine months after Benecol. Yet, Unilever's superior sales and distribution for grocery products and its lower price (Benecol retailed at £2.49 per 250 g pack compared with Flora Pro-activ at £1.99) meant that Unilever soon had twice the market share of Benecol.[10] Market observers also noted that Unilever's marketing was more effective than J&J's:

> The brand is backed by the Flora Project, a nutrition marketing effort that educates people about heart disease prevention including diet, smoking cessation, lifestyle habits and exercise. Flora sponsors the London marathon, as well as other sporting events. Before Pro-activ came onto the market, tubs of regular Flora already bore the words, "as part of a healthy diet helps lower cholesterol," a statement scientifically backed by Unilever. Moreover, the Flora name had a massive "share of mind" – from the 1980s until the mid-1990s, the Flora brand accounted for 60 per cent of media spending in the spreads category. Because Flora was associated in consumers' minds for 30 years with heart health – and with good taste – it was logical to leverage the Flora brand assets.
>
> The London Flora marathon seamlessly became the London Flora Pro-activ marathon. There is little company communication about the ingredient – the words "plant sterols" are mentioned only on about page six of the information leaflet. But that is as it should be – Unilever is selling the benefits of Flora, a known and trusted food brand; it is not selling plant sterols, specifically.
>
> In contrast, rival Johnson & Johnson's McNeil Consumer Products group had no pre-existing supermarket brand to extend when it launched the

cholesterol-lowering spread, Benecol, in Finland in late 1995 (then owned by Raisio). Benecol, therefore, started out with zero brand equity in the UK. By the time Pro-activ joined it on the market, Benecol had garnered £30 million in sales – no small achievement for an entirely new brand – and it held a 0.5 per cent volume share and 2.5 per cent value share.

As the brand creator, Benecol had to set the price point, which it did at seven times the price of regular spreads. In response, Unilever added to Pro-activ's competitive advantage by bringing it to market 25 per cent cheaper than Benecol.

Add to these factors the massive brand equity of the Flora name, and it is no surprise that Flora Pro-activ is now outselling Benecol in the UK by a factor of almost three-to-one.[11]

Other competitors Unilever was not the only company interested in the market for stanol and sterol esters. By 2000, some of Raisio's worst fears were being realized. Several companies had either entered the market for cholesterol-reducing nutraceuticals, or had announced their intention to enter:

- *Forbes Medi-Tech and Novartis.* In April 1999, the Swiss pharmaceutical company Novartis signed a five-year agreement with Canadian biotechnology company Forbes Medi-Tech to license Phytrol – a plant sterol-based ingredient with similar cholesterol-reducing properties to stanol ester. Novartis would become responsible for clinical trials, regulatory submissions, and commercialization of end products. Phytrol (marketed also as Reducol) received FDA "Generally Recognized As Safe" approval in May 2000.[12] In 2000, Novartis announced a joint venture with Quaker Oats to form Altus Foods, which would manufacture healthy foods containing Phytrol. Novartis launched a number of products including breakfast cereals and cereal bars under the Aviva brand name. However, market response was, at best, tepid. In the UK, the Aviva range was withdrawn six months after the launch.

- *Paulig.* In July 1999, Finland's Paulig (a company known for its coffee and spice operations) announced its own plant sterol ingredient, Teriaka, derived from maize, soy, and pine trees. Because its manufacture utilizes normal processing technology and does not require chemical synthesis or high temperatures/pressures, it was believed that it could gain quick approval under the EU's Novel Foods Regulations.

- *Procter & Gamble* introduced a line of cooking oils containing sterol esters under the brand name CookSmart.

- *Archer Daniels Midland* developed a patent-pending sterol ingredient that is dispersible in liquids, allowing sterols to be added to beverages, milk products, and other water-based and non-fat products.

- *Monsanto* in 2000 received a patent on a "phytosterol protein complex" composed of sterols, proteins, and edible oil. The product claimed to enhance the cholesterol-reducing effects of sterols.

Mounting Crisis

During 2000, Raisio was incurring rapidly increasing losses from its Benecol Division. During the first half of 2000, it reported losses of €44.0 million, mostly resulting from a non-recurring charge of €38.0 million. This compared with a profit

TABLE 10.2 Raisio Group financial indicators, 1996–2000

	1996	1997	1998	1999	2000
Sales and operations					
Turnover (€m)	661	858	833	763	800
change, %	+22	+30	−3	−8	+5
Exports from Finland (€m)	124	135	178	145	131
Total international turnover (€m)	259	423	421	374	399
% of turnover	39.2	49.3	50.5	49.0	49.9
Gross investments (€m)	65	73	75	61	49
R&D expenditure (€m)	15	17	18	16	18
% of turnover	2.2	1.9	2.1	2.1	2.3
Average personnel	2,365	2,817	2,904	2,897	2,775
Profitability					
Operating result (€m)	33	41	52	16	−32
% of turnover	5.0	4.8	6.3	2.1	−4.0
Result before extraordinary items (€m)	28	35	42	6	−47
Result before taxes and minority interest (€m)	27	20	39	−2	−47
% of turnover	4.1	2.3	4.7	−0.3	−5.8
Return on equity (ROE), %	4.5	7.8	9.2	0.4	−14.9
Return on investment (ROI), %	9.2	10.1	11.1	4.0	−4.2
Financial and economical position					
Shareholders' equity (€m)	291	298	317	304	260
Net interest-bearing liabilities (€m)	119	143	174	233	251
Balance sheet total (€m)	619	643	690	744	750
Equity ratio, %	47.3	46.6	46.0	41.0	34.7
Quick ratio	1.1	0.8	0.7	0.6	0.7
Current ratio	1.8	1.5	1.2	1.2	1.2
Cash flow from business operations	43	60	47	6	16

SOURCE: RAISIO GROUP 2000 ANNUAL REPORT

that totaled €11.2 million during the corresponding period in 1999 (although this resulted entirely from a one-time payment under the agreement with J&J). Between the first half of 1999 and first half of 2000, revenues for the first six months of Raisio's Benecol Division were down from €47 million to €16 million, reflecting the end of payments from J&J and sharply reduced sales of stanol ester to J&J. Tables 10.2 and 10.3 show Raisio's financial performance between 1996 and 2000.

The company's report for the first half of 2000 analyzed the problems:

The development of the Group's Benecol business derives from a vision dating back to 1996–97 which predicted a rapid and impressive rise in Benecol products containing stanol ester into global functional foods. This vision was based on Raisio and McNeil's joint assessment and on market and need analyses by leading international consultants.

Raisio then made safeguarding long-term availability of the main raw material in Benecol products – sterol – its strategic goal. Action aimed at large-scale

TABLE 10.3 Raisio Group divisional performance, 1997–2000 (millions of euros)

		1997	1998	1999	2000
Benecol	Turnover	16	48	52	23
	Operating profit	n.a.	n.a.	7.5	−45.6
Margarine	Turnover	282	235	200	204
	Operating profit	n.a.	n.a.	79.5	78.0
Grain	Turnover	287	274	235	244
	Operating profit	n.a.	n.a.	0.8	0.7
Chemicals	Turnover	278	277	299	347
	Operating profit	n.a.	n.a.	20.3	11.9

n.a. = not available.

SOURCE: RAISIO GROUP ANNUAL REPORTS 1998–2000.

procurement of sterol was therefore taken immediately on both the plant and the wood sterol markets. Plant sterols were acquired under long-term purchasing agreements, as world supply was limited and indeed inadequate for the targets then set for Benecol operations.

The limited nature of plant sterol production thus faced Raisio with a strategic challenge, in view of which several projects were launched aimed at developing more wood sterol separation. The biggest are a tall oil and sterol separation project in Chile (Detsa) and the Westerol project planned for North America. Supplies of wood sterol were also ensured through various contracting and financing arrangements.

Since the launch in Finland in 1995, however, Benecol products have actually reached the market only in the USA, UK, Ireland and the Benelux countries, and mainly only in the second half of 1999, and in Sweden and Denmark this autumn. Market penetration has thus been slower than expected, partly due to regulatory obstacles. Current experience suggests that the expectations concerning cholesterol-reducing foods on which Raisio's plans were based were overly optimistic. So far, less than 20 per cent of the targets have been achieved.

As a result of its high expectations and targets, Raisio has tied up substantial resources in both wood sterol projects and sterol and stanol stocks. In today's market situation, however, the company has had to review and re-assess its sterol strategy and the preconditions for completing ongoing projects, as well as the value of the sterols and stanols already procured.

To stem the losses, Raisio renegotiated several of its long-term sterol purchase agreements, withdrew from its sterol separation joint venture in Chile, and suspended its Sclexin plant sterol project in New Zealand. Other sterol separation projects were to be reviewed on a case-by-case basis. Inventories of sterol and stanol were re-valued at current market prices and several of the fixed assets involved written down.

The central problem, Raisio believed, lay with the agreement with J&J. J&J's world-wide license meant that Raisio was completely dependent on J&J's commitment to Benecol and the success of J&J's marketing strategy. Observing Unilever's ability to push Benecol into second place in the US and Europe, many at Raisio believed that the company had backed the wrong horse. Despite J&J's expertise with

FIGURE 10.2 Raisio Group plc, price of unrestricted shares (Helsinki Stock Exchange)

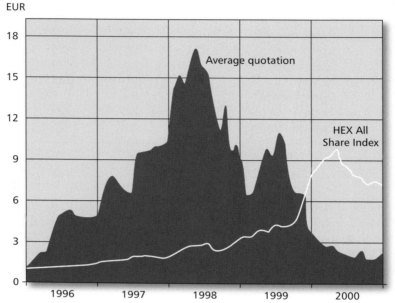

Note: Figures 10.1 and 10.2 are not directly comparable because of a 10:1 share split in June 1998. Figure 10.2 shows Raisio's share price adjusted for the share split.

FDA regulations and healthcare, and its massive R&D budget, in terms of marketing food products and selling to supermarkets, J&J like other big pharmaceutical companies had limited expertise and channel power in branded, packaged foods.

During 2000, Raisio's share price was in free-fall. By October 2000, Raisio's shares had lost 85% of their value compared with the peak in mid-1998 (see figure 10.2) CEO Tor Bergman, who, as head of Raisio's Chemical Division and head of the Benecol Division, had been the primary architect of the Benecol strategy, was the main casualty of the collapse. He left Raisio in August 2000 and was replaced as CEO by Lasse Kurkilahti. The new CEO's review of 2000 was in sharp contrast to the optimistic tone of previous communications to shareholders. After acknowledging 2000 to be "the worst in the past ten years," he went on to outline the challenge of Raisio competing internationally:

> *Earlier, Raisio competed with Finnish and Nordic companies; now, its competitors are European or global players . . . The diversified enterprises that formed during the '80s in a closed economy will not survive in today's open economy, where a business's only hope lies in being competitive. The Raisio Group has to focus its resources on the fewer fields.*[13]

Benecol would occupy a prominent position among these "fewer fields." However, to succeed, the Division needed a new strategy. The starting point was a new relationship with J&J. By December 2000, a new agreement was reached:

. . . This gives the Benecol Division the opportunity to implement a global strategy concentrating on functional food ingredients – that is, stanol and sterol ester – in certain clinical areas. The new agreement covers two main aspects of the Benecol stanol ester business. The companies agreed that McNeil would concentrate on markets in North America, the EU (excluding Finland, Sweden and Denmark), Japan and China. Raisio's market area, in turn, comprises Scandinavia, the Baltic region, the former East European countries, the Near East, Latin America, the Far East and Oceania. The two companies also agreed on a new market-driven delivery agreement for Benecol ingredients. Further, Raisio acquired global rights to sell and market sterol ester. Both companies may agree independently to involve third parties in their market areas in order to expand the product range. Since the agreement was signed, a number of promising openings have been made with prospective new partners . . .

During 2001 the Benecol Division will put its new global ingredient strategy into operation . . . The objective is to create a global network of business partners through which it can market stanol and sterol ester to consumers in various types of food. New cooperation agreements with Mastellone Hnos in Argentine (December, 2000), and Valio (December, 2000) and Atria (January, 2001) in Finland are the first examples of implementation of Raisio's new strategy. These agreements provide an excellent basis for further progress in 2001.[14]

Appendix
Raisio's Principal Patents Relating to Stanol Ester

US Patent No. 5,502,045 "Use of a stanol fatty acid ester for reducing serum cholesterol level"
Inventors: Tatu Miettinen, Hannu Vanhanen, Ingmar Wester.
Assignee: Raision Tehtaat Oy AB
Filed: November 22, 1993
Awarded: March 26, 1996

Abstract
The invention relates to a substance which lowers cholesterol levels in serum and which is a .beta.-sitostanol fatty acid ester or fatty acid ester mixture, and to a method for preparing the same. The substance can be used as such or added to a food.

Claims
We claim:

1 The method of reducing the absorption of cholesterol into the bloodstream comprising orally introducing into the body an effective amount of a substance containing a .beta.-sitostanol fatty acid ester prepared by the interesterification of .beta.-sitostanol with a fatty acid ester containing between 2 and 22 carbon atoms in the presence of an interesterification catalyst.

2 The method according to claim 1, wherein the interesterification of .beta.-sitostanol is carried out in a solvent free food grade process.

3 The method according to claim 2, wherein the interesterification occurs at a temperature of approximately 90 degree–120 degree C and a vacuum of approximately 5–15 mmHg.

4 The method according to claim 3, wherein the catalyst is sodium ethylate.

5 The method of claim 1, wherein the fatty acid ester comprises a mixture of fatty acid esters.

6 The method according to claim 1, wherein the .beta.-sitostanol is prepared by hydrogenation of a commercial .beta.-sitosterol mixture.

7 The method according to claim 1, wherein the interesterification is carried out in the presence of a stoichiometric excess of the fatty acid ester.

8 The method according to claim 1, wherein an effective amount of the substance is between about 0.2 and about 20 grams per day.

Extract from "Description" Section

. . . The present invention relates to the use of a sterol of an entirely different type for lowering the cholesterol level in serum. What is involved is fatty acid esters of alpha-saturated sterols, especially sitostanol fatty acid esters (sitostanol = 24-ethyl-5.alpha.-cholestane-3.beta.-ol), which have been observed to lower cholesterol levels in serum with particular efficacy. The said esters can be prepared or used as such, or they can be added to foods, especially to the fatty part of a food. The sitostanol fatty acid ester mixture is prepared by hardening a commercial .beta.-sitosterol mixture (sitosterol = 24-ethyl-5-cholestene-3.beta.-ol). .beta.-sitostanol can be prepared by a prior-known cholesterol hardening technique by hardening .beta.-sitosterol by means of a Pd/C catalyst in an organic solvent (43). This mixture has the approval of the FDA (Cytellin, Eli Lilly). A hardening degree of over 99% is achieved in the reaction. The catalyst used in the hardening is removed by means of a membrane filter, and the obtained sitostanol is crystallized, washed and dried. In accordance with the invention, the .beta.-sitostanol mixture, which contains campestanol approx. 6%, is esterified with different fatty acid ester mixtures by a commonly known chemical interesterification technique (44, 45, 46). A methyl ester mixture of the fatty acids of any vegetable oil can be used in the reaction. One example is a mixture of rapeseed oil and methyl ester, but any fatty acids which contain approx. 2 to 22 carbon atoms are usable. The method according to the invention for the preparation of stanol fatty acid esters deviates advantageously from the previously patented methods in that no substances other than free stanol, a fatty acid ester or a fatty acid ester mixture, and a catalyst are used in the esterification reaction. The catalyst used may be any known interesterification catalyst, such as Na-ethylate.

US Patent No. 5,958,913 "Substance for lowering high cholesterol level in serum and methods for preparing and using the same"

Inventors: Tatu Miettinen, Hannu Vanhanen, Ingmar Wester.
Assignee: Raisio Benecol Ltd.
Filed: November 5, 1996
Awarded: September 28, 1999

Abstract

The invention relates to a substance which lowers LDL cholesterol levels in serum and which is fat soluble .beta.-sitostanol fatty acid ester, and to a method for preparing and using the same. The substance can be taken orally as a food additive, food substitute or supplement. A daily consumption of the .beta.-sitostanol ester in an amount between about 0.2 and about 20 grams per day has been shown to reduce the absorption of biliary and endogenic cholesterol.

Claims

What is claimed is:

1 A food composition suitable for reducing blood serum cholesterol levels or reducing absorption of cholesterol from the intestines into the bloodstream, the food composition comprising a nutritional substance and a blood serum cholesterol level reducing or cholesterol absorption reducing effective amount of a sterol component comprising at least one 5.alpha.-saturated sterol fatty acid ester.

2 The food composition as claimed in claim 1, wherein the sterol component comprises .beta.-sitostanol fatty acid ester.

3 The food composition as claimed in claim 1, wherein the fatty acid contains about 2 to 22 carbon atoms.

4 The food composition as claimed in claim 2, wherein the fatty acid contains about 2 to 22 carbon atoms.

5 The food composition as claimed in claim 1, wherein the 5.alpha.-saturated sterol fatty acid ester is produced by esterifying the alpha-saturated sterol and a fatty acid ester in a solvent-free food grade process.

6 The food composition as claimed in claim 2, wherein the .beta.-sitostanol fatty acid ester is produced by esterifying .beta.-sitostanol and a fatty acid ester in a solvent-free food grade process.

7 The food composition as claimed in claim 5, wherein the esterifying step is conducted in the presence of an esterification catalyst.

8 The food composition as claimed in claim 6, wherein the esterifying step is conducted in the presence of an esterification catalyst.

9 The food composition as claimed in claim 7, wherein the esterification catalyst comprises sodium ethylate.

10 The food composition as claimed in claim 8, wherein the esterification catalyst comprises sodium ethylate.

11 The food composition as claimed in claim 5, wherein the esterifying step is conducted at a temperature of about 90–120 degree C under a vacuum of about 5–15 mmHg.

12 The food composition as claimed in claim 6, wherein the esterifying step is conducted at a temperature of about 90–120 degree C under a vacuum of about 5–15 mmHg.

13 The food composition as claimed in claim 5, wherein the esterifying step is conducted without the presence of additional interesterifiable lipids.

14 The food composition as claimed in claim 6, wherein the esterifying step is conducted without the presence of additional interesterifiable lipids.

15 The food composition as claimed in claim 1, wherein the nutritional substance comprises a member selected from the group consisting of cooking oil, margarine, butter, mayonnaise, salad dressing and shortening.

16 The food composition as claimed in claim 2, wherein the nutritional substance comprises a member selected from the group consisting of cooking oil, margarine, butter, mayonnaise, salad dressing and shortening.

17 A method for reducing the cholesterol level in blood serum of a subject in need thereof, comprising orally administering to the subject the food composition as claimed in claim 1, wherein the sterol component is present in a blood serum cholesterol level reducing effective amount.

18 A method for reducing the cholesterol level in blood serum of a subject in need thereof, comprising orally administering to the subject the food composition as claimed in claim 2, wherein the sterol component is present in a blood serum cholesterol level reducing effective amount.

19 The method as claimed in claim 17, wherein about 0.2 to 20 grams per day of the sterol component are orally administered.

20 The method as claimed in claim 18, wherein about 0.2 to 20 grams per day of the sterol component are orally administered.

21 A method for reducing the absorption of cholesterol from the intestines into the bloodstream of a subject in need thereof, comprising orally administering to the subject the food composition as claimed in claim 1, wherein the sterol component is present in a cholesterol absorption reducing effective amount.

22 A method for reducing the absorption of cholesterol from the intestines into the bloodstream of a subject in need thereof, comprising orally administering to the subject the food composition as claimed in claim 2, wherein the sterol component is present in a cholesterol absorption reducing effective amount.

23 The method as claimed in claim 21, wherein about 0.2 to 20 grams per day of the sterol component are orally administered.

24 The method as claimed in claim 22, wherein about 0.2 to 20 grams per day of the sterol component are orally administered.

Brief Description of the Invention

The present invention relates to a sterol of an entirely different type for lowering the cholesterol levels in blood serum. The substance comprises a fatty acid ester of alpha saturated sterols, especially sitostanol fatty acid esters, which have been observed to lower cholesterol levels in serum with particular efficacy.

The present invention includes a method of reducing the absorption of cholesterol into the bloodstream from the digestive tract by orally introducing into the body an effective amount of a fatty acid ester of a beta-sitostanol. More preferably, the invention further includes orally introducing between about 0.2 and about 20 grams per day of beta-sitostanol fatty acid ester into the body. The ester is introduced either as a food additive, a food substitute or a food supplement. When used as a food additive, the fatty acid ester of the beta-sitostanol may be added to food products such as cooking oils, margarines, butter, mayonnaise, salad dressings, shortenings, and other foods having an essential fat component.

Notes

1 FIM = Finnish marks. The average exchange rate during 1996 was US$1 = FIM4.54.
2 "Chief Executive's Review," Raisio Group Annual Report, 1996, p. 3.
3 The company was renamed Raisio Group plc in September 1997. Throughout this case we shall refer to the company as "Raisio Group."
4 Raisio Group 1997 Annual Report, p. 38.
5 "Market split over 'miracle' margarine," *Financial Times*, October 25, 1996, p. 26.
6 "Wonder spread from Finland," *The Grocer*, May 18, 1996, p. 9.
7 Raisio Group 1997 Annual Report, p. 39.
8 Ibid.
9 Ibid., p. 40.
10 www.nutraingredients.com/news/ng.asp?id=36575-the-benecol-story
11 Julian Mellentin, "Trusted brands sell healthy hearts," *Functional Foods and Nutraceuticals*, June 2002 (www.ffnmag.com/NH/ASP/strArticleID/105/strSite/FFN Site/articleDisplay.asp).
12 *Chemical Business Newsbase*, October 20, 2000.
13 Raisio Group 2000 Annual Report, p. 5.
14 Ibid., p. 19.

Rivalry in Video Games

At the beginning of 2007, the world video games industry was entering a new and unusual stage of its development. For 11 years the industry had been dominated by Sony, whose PlayStation had accounted for well over half of world console sales during the previous two product generations. However, in the new generation of video game consoles, an entirely new situation was emerging. As a result of its own missteps, Sony's iron grip on the industry had been broken and the seventh generation of video consoles was shaping up into a three-way battle between Sony, Microsoft, and Nintendo.

The stakes were high. With each new generation of consoles, the industry had surpassed its previous sales peak (see figure 11.1). Industry forecasts suggested that the seventh generation machines would be no exception – worldwide sales of video games hardware (consoles and handheld players) and software were estimated at around $24 billion in 2006, of which software accounted for around 60%. The market was expected to be bigger in 2007 – especially for hardware.

For the three main players in the industry, the key issue was how revenues and profits would be split among them. The evidence of the past was that the video game consoles tended to be a "winner-take-all" industry where customers gravitated towards the market leader. The result was that one company tended to establish a market share of over 60% of the market and scooped the major part of the industry profit pool (see table 11.1).

However, for all of the three leading players, there was more at stake than the lure of profits from the new generation of video game consoles. For Nintendo, the situation was relatively simple. Video games were Nintendo's sole business. Its Wii console launched in November 2006 was widely regarded as the last throw of the dice for Nintendo in the console market – with several billion dollars spent on development and marketing, Nintendo had to achieve market success to remain a viable player; otherwise it would need to retreat to the hand-held video game market, which it dominated. For Sony and Microsoft, the situation was

FIGURE 11.1 Worldwide unit sales of video game consoles by product generation

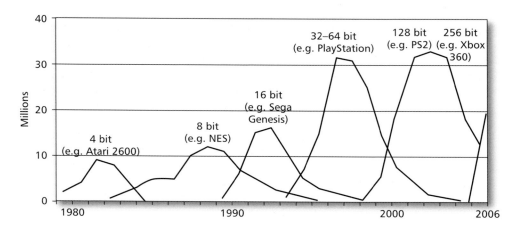

TABLE 11.1 Worldwide sales of video game consoles by platform

	Second generation	Third generation	Fourth generation	Fifth generation	Sixth generation	Seventh generation (to end 2006)
Nintendo	–	NES: 60m	Super NES: 49m	N-64: 32.9m	GameCube: 21.2m	Wii: 3.2m
Sega	–	Master System: 13m	MegaDrive/ Genesis: 29m	Saturn 9.3m	Dreamcast: 10.6m	–
Sony	–	–	–	PlayStation: 100m	PS2: 140m	PS3: 2.2m
Microsoft	–	–	–	–	Xbox: 24.0m	Xbox 360: 10.4m
Others	Atari 2600 Fairfield Channel F Magnavox Odyssey	Atari 7800: <0.3m	NEC TurboGrafx: 11m	3DO: 1.2m	–	–

SOURCE: WIKIPEDIA.

more complex. Both companies viewed video game consoles as important products in their own right, but also as critical components of their strategies for building strength within the fast-moving market for home entertainment. For Sony, the PS3 had a special significance. Not only was PlayStation Sony's most important product of the previous ten years, PS3 was Sony's standard-bearer in its battle with Toshiba over technical standards for the next generation of high-definition video disks. Its new PlayStation 3 (PS3) was its first product that embodied its Blu-Ray DVD system.

The coming 12 months would be critical for all three companies. For Sony, maintaining leadership in the worldwide market for video game consoles was the company's preeminent strategic goal. For Microsoft and Nintendo, 2007 offered the best opportunity over five years to overturn Sony's market leadership.

Development of the Video Game Industry, 1972–1995

Atari and the 4-bit Consoles: 1972–1985

The home video games market emerged during the late 1970s as an extension of arcade video games. The first generation of home video consoles were dedicated machines that embodied a single game. One of the first of these was *Pong*, created by Nolan Bushnell in 1972. He formed Atari to market this game player. The second generation of players began with Fairfield's release of Channel F – the first home video game system to accept interchangeable cartridges. Bushnell seized the opportunity and designed the Atari 2600 home video game console which retailed at $200 in the US. Atari's release of *Space Invaders* (1979) and *Pac-Man* (1981) unleashed a craze for video games. By 1982 Atari held almost 80% share of the video game market.

However, competition in both hardware and software intensified. Mattel, Coleco, and Activision all introduced rival consoles. During 1982, 20 new suppliers of Atari-compatible consoles entered the market and 350 new game titles were released in that year. Atari was unable to prevent independent software developers from marketing games for the Atari 2600, though Atari was able to collect a royalty. The market became oversupplied, forcing software manufacturers with slow-selling game titles to liquidate their inventories at closeout prices during 1983 and 1984: on some games, prices were slashed from $40 to $4. Slumping sales and excess inventories of video game cartridges resulted in Warner Communications reporting a $539 million loss on its consumer electronics business in 1983. Industry sales of video games collapsed from $3 billion in 1982 to $100 million in 1985.

Nintendo and the 8-bit Era: 1986–1991

During 1975, Nintendo – a Japanese toy company – entered the arcade video game business in Japan, and in 1980 the US. In 1981, Nintendo had a big arcade hit with *Donkey Kong*, created by its brilliant game developer Sigeru Miyamota. In 1983, Nintendo released its 8-bit Famicom home video system that used interchangeable cartridges.[1] The ¥24,000 ($100) machine sold 500,000 units in Japan during its first two months. The US launch of Famicom – renamed the Nintendo Entertainment System (NES) – in fall 1985 was a huge success, with over a million units sold during the first year. NES's sales were driven by a series of games developed by Miyamota: *Legend of Zelda* (the first video game to sell over a million copies) and, in 1986, *Super Mario Brothers* (which eventually sold 40 million copies worldwide). By 1988, Nintendo had an 80% market share of the $2.3 billion US video games industry.

The key to Nintendo's dominance of the market for third generation consoles (and its profitability) was its careful management of the relationship between hardware and software. Unlike Atari, Nintendo kept tight control of the supply of games, carefully managing their quality and their releases. Its dominant market share in consoles allowed it to dictate stringent terms to game developers. Developers were required to follow strict rules for the creation and release of games for the NES console. Nintendo ensured that only licensed developers could produce games for NES through designing its consoles such that only cartridges that incorporated a "security chip" would operate on Nintendo's consoles. Nintendo approved the content of every game, controlled all manufacturing of cartridges, and charged its independent games developers a 20% royalty and a manufacturing fee of $14 per cartridge (the manufacturing cost was $7). The minimum order was 10,000 cartridges for the Japanese market and 50,000 for the US market – paid in advance. Cartridges were delivered to licensees at the shipping dock at Kobe, Japan, and then distribution became the licensees' responsibility. Licensees were also limited to developing five NES games a year and could not release an NES game on a competing system for a period of two years. Retail distribution was tightly controlled. New games were released according to a carefully designed schedule and were quickly withdrawn once interest began to wane. Nintendo typically restricted shipments of its most popular games, and discouraged its retailers from carrying competitive products. By 1983, 70% of the NES cartridge sales were of games developed by licensed third-party developers.

Between 1984 and 1992, Nintendo's sales rose from $286 million to $4,417 million. By 1990, one-third of US and Japanese households owned an NES and in both countries its share of the home video console market exceeded 90%. Nintendo's return on equity over the period was 23.1%, while its stock market value exceeded that of both Sony and Nissan during most of 1990–1.

Sega and the 16-bit Era: 1992–1995

Sega Enterprises, Ltd (Sega) is a Japanese company founded by Americans. Like Atari and Nintendo, it began in arcade games machines and in 1986 introduced an 8-bit home video game console, the Master System. In October 1988, Sega launched the fourth generation of consoles with the Japanese release of its 16-bit Genesis home video system. Eleven months later, Genesis was launched in the US priced at $190, with games selling at between $40 and $70. Yet, despite superior graphics and sound to Nintendo's 8-bit system, sales of Genesis were initially sluggish until the introduction of *Sonic the Hedgehog* in June 1991.

With the advertising slogan "Genesis does what Nintendon't" Genesis positioned itself as the cool alternative to the Nintendo NES. It also recruited new games players by targeting a broader market than Nintendo, directing its appeal to adults as well as teenagers. Despite having licensing terms that were very similar to those of Nintendo (the main difference was no exclusivity clause), Sega was able to use Nintendo's un-popularity to recruit many independent developers. By September 1991 there were 130 software titles available for the Genesis.

Nintendo launched its 16-bit machine, the Nintendo Super-NES, in September 1991. In response to competition from Sega, it abandoned its exclusivity clause. Despite Nintendo's huge installed base, brand awareness, and distribution strength, Sega's bigger library of 16-bit titles (320, compared with 130 for Nintendo by January 1993) gave Sega a huge boost. During 1992–6, the two companies split the US market almost evenly. In Japan, Nintendo maintained its market dominance: the Super-NES outsold Genesis by about nine to one. Nintendo also maintained market leadership in Europe – but only just. Sega took the lead in several European countries and was a close follower in others.

Sony PlayStation and the 32-/64-bit Generation: 1995–1998

Established in Japan in May 1946, Sony Corporation emerged during the 1970s and 1980s as one of the world's most successful and innovative consumer electronics companies. In 1987, under the leadership of Ken Kutaragi, Sony began developing a video games console employing the new generation of 32-bit processors and compact disks for video games. Initially the new console was to be a collaborative venture with Nintendo and would be capable of playing both CD-ROM games and Nintendo Super-NES cartridges. However, disagreement between the two parties resulted in Kutaragi and his team developing an entirely new console. PlayStation was launched in Japan in December 1994, in the US in September 1995, and four weeks later in Europe.

Sony was not first to market with 32-bit CD-ROM consoles. Sega's Saturn was launched in Japan a month before PlayStation, and in the US three months before. However, it was Sony that quickly established market leadership – mainly because, prior to launch, it had built a large library of games titles. It had courted the top games developers, financed the development of games for the PlayStation, and, through its hardware and operating system design and provision of software development tools, facilitated game development. Its US launch was supported by games of almost all main genres.

Sony's reputation and brand presence was also influential in gaining the support of both developers and retailers. It possessed global distribution capability, brand awareness, and rich content from its movie libraries and ongoing production of movies and TV shows at its subsidiaries Columbia Pictures and Tri-Star Entertainment. Its launch of PlayStation was well-orchestrated and supported by a massive advertising budget – prelaunch promotion included a number of cryptic and ambiguous advertisements that were designed to capture the interest of the gamer community.

By contrast, Sega, despite its solid reputation among video game consumers and its well-known brand, suffered from the ill-coordinated product launch of its Saturn system. Only a handful of game titles were available at the launch, the supply of machines was limited by lack of manufacturing capacity, and distribution was haphazard. Sony's machine attracted such a huge early following that Sega could not recover. Sega's US sales were sluggish throughout 1996 and 1997. At the end of 1997, Saturn had an estimated total installed base of fewer than 2 million units. Almost no third-party licensees published titles exclusively on the Saturn, and very few planned to publish any new titles for the Saturn system. Saturn's market failure was attributed to its comparatively high launch price, its lack of blockbuster exclusive titles, and a development system that many developers felt was inferior to that of the PlayStation. To bolster the declining market share of its Saturn player, Sega instituted rebate and incentive programs. Sega stopped marketing the Saturn in the United States in the spring of 1997.

Meanwhile, Nintendo attempted to recapture market leadership by leapfrogging Sony in technology. The N-64 system – launched in Japan in June 1996, in the US in September 1996, and in Europe in the spring of 1997 – used a 64-bit processor. The introduction of the N-64 was very successful, with half a million units sold in the first day of the US launch. One of its launch games – *Super Mario 64* – was acclaimed as one of the best games ever developed, while *Legend of Zelda* and the James Bond game *GoldenEye 007* were major hits.

A key difference between the N-64 and PlayStation was Nintendo's use of cartridges rather than CD-ROMs. Cartridges permitted cheaper hardware – N-64 was introduced at $199 in the US compared with $299 for PlayStation. Also, cartridges had a quicker load time than CDs and were nearly impossible to pirate. However, CD-ROMs possessed several key advantages. They had greater storage capacity (important for complex, high-resolution games) and they were cheaper to manufacture. The average PlayStation title retailed for $45 or less; N-64 titles averaged close to $60. From a software publisher's point of view, the key advantage of CD-ROMs was that a game could be pressed and shipped to retailers much faster than Nintendo cartridges (manufactured in Japan). Furthermore, N-64 cartridges had to be paid for at the time of order placement. The longer lead times for getting N-64 cartridges on retailer shelves also meant greater inventory and sales risks for Nintendo game publishers. It was difficult to judge how quickly a title would sell, particularly in the case of newly introduced games. To keep from losing out on sales, publishers of Nintendo games were motivated to order larger quantities to avoid retailer stockouts of what might prove to be a best-selling title. In contrast, retailers could normally be resupplied with additional copies of hot-selling PlayStation titles within a matter of days (CD pressing was near-instantaneous, but packaging and booklets took longer). Developers were attracted by the lower break-even point for recovering development costs: for the N-64 this was estimated at 190,000 units, versus 172,000 units for the PlayStation.

The result was that Sony pursued a different software strategy from Nintendo. While Nintendo concentrated on a smaller number of big-selling games, Sony went for a much bigger library of games (over 300 titles at any point of time). The average N-64 title sold over 400,000 units in 1997 compared with 69,000 copies for the average PlayStation game. However, PlayStation users bought more games: the number of games sold per console (the "tie ratio") for the PlayStation was 5.82 in 1997 and 6.40 in 1998 compared with 2.55 for the N-64.

The combination of PlayStation's lead time, powerful marketing, and wide range of games titles propelled it to a significant market share advantage over both the Sega Saturn and the Nintendo 64. Over its product life, the Sony PlayStation sold about 100 million units compared with 33 million for the Nintendo 64 and a little over 8 million for the Sega Saturn. In response to PlayStation's lead and the perceived disadvantages of its cartridges, Nintendo began cutting the prices it charged third-party licensees for N-64 cartridges from over $30 to as low as $21. Both companies also cut their console prices – the outcome was rapid growth of consumer expenditure on video games hardware and software between 1996 and 1998 (see table 11.2).

The Battle for the 128-bit Generation: 1999–2005

The Sega Dreamcast

With the failure of Saturn, Sega sought to establish an early lead in the sixth generation of video game consoles. Dreamcast was launched in Japan in November 1998. It embodied a 128-bit machine and used PC-based technology, which facilitated game development and the porting of existing PC-based games. However, its most innovative feature was the ability to allow simultaneous, interactive games playing through the internet. The launch was seen as Sega's last chance: "This is the last roll of the dice for Sega. If it doesn't work, it will have to pull out of the sector," said Stuart Dinsey of trade magazine *MCV*. Nick Gibson of stockbroking and consulting firm Durlacher added: "Sega has to make this work; it has no contingency plans. It is heavily in debt to fund the marketing." The development and launch of Dreamcast strained Sega's financial resources to the limit. In the year to March 1999, Sega reported a net loss of ¥45bn ($490m), forcing massive cost cutting.

TABLE 11.2 US retail sales of video game hardware and software by console type, 1990–2007

	1990	1991	1992	1993	1994	1995	1996	1997	1998
Total hardware and software ($ m)	3,216	3,110	3,847	4,534	4,066	2,686	3,174	5,004	5,541
Sales composition									
Hardware	31%	37%	40%	37%	34%	34%	43%	43%	36%
Software	69%	63%	60%	63%	66%	66%	57%	57%	64%
	1999	2000	2001	2002	2003	2004	2005	2006	2007[e]
Total hardware and software ($ m)	5,999	4,942	6,445	8,967	8,359	8,106	7,401	9,800	10,600
Sales composition									
Hardware	22%	32%	46%	43%	41%	38%	41%	45%	44%
Software	78%	68%	54%	57%	59%	62%	59%	55%	56%

[e] = estimated.

SOURCES: IDC, GERARD KLAUER MATTISON & CO., MINTEL, AND CASE WRITER ESTIMATES.

Sega's president, Shoichiro Irimajiri, set a target for Dreamcast at half the global market. To undermine the Dreamcast launch, Sony provided advance publicity about its new version of PlayStation (PlayStation2) that was under development, emphasizing its incorporation of DVD technology and its backward compatibility with the original PlayStation.

Software remained a challenge for Sega: "The fact that there's a new machine with 128 bits is irrelevant to consumers to a large extent. Sega needs a killer application such as PlayStation's *Lara Croft* – and *Sonic* is not so sexy. It needs to woo developers to support the platform, something Sony has worked hard to do," said Jeremy Dale, commercial and marketing director at Nintendo. The failure of Saturn made many developers reluctant to invest in software for another Sega platform.

The initial launch was successful. In Japan, 900,000 units were sold during the first quarter – just short of Sega's target of a million. The fall 1999 launches in North America and Europe were also successful. In the US, Sega sold 1.5 million of its $199 Dreamcast machines and 4.5 million games in the last quarter of 1999, giving it 15% of console sales – up from 0.1% a year earlier. Nevertheless, Dreamcast failed to deliver a knockout blow to Sony's market leadership. The advantages of 128-bit over 64-bit technology were marginal and standard internet connections did not support fast-action interactive play. Most important, Sega failed to find a killer app for its Dreamcast – *Sonic Adventure* was its biggest selling game. Throughout 1999, PlayStation continued to outsell Dreamcast.

PlayStation2

PlayStation2 was the result of a massive product development initiative led by Ken Kutaragi. In the summer of 1996, Kutaragi had assembled a team of engineers from Sony and its manufacturing partner, Toshiba, and asked them to design a games machine with performance that exceeded any PC and with graphics processing power ten times that of the original PlayStation. To counter Sega's 15-month lead, Sony continually leaked information about the technical merits of its new console and engaged in massive prelaunch publicity for its PlayStation2. The March 4, 2000 Japanese launch was the most eagerly anticipated event in the history of the Japanese consumer electronics industry. During the first 48 hours, one million PlayStation2s were sold, ten times the number sold when the original PlayStation was made available.

At ¥39,800, PlayStation2 (PS2) was a 128-bit machine offering cinematic-style graphics, a DVD player capable of showing films, and the potential for internet connectivity. Nobuyuki Idei, Sony's president, aimed to make the PlayStation2 the main mechanism for consumers to access the internet, offering online games, e-commerce, e-mail, and the ability to download music, software, and video. As Kazuo Hirai, president of Sony US, enthused, "PlayStation 2 is not the future of video games entertainment, it is the future of entertainment, period." Yet, initially, PS2 did not include a modem; Idei argued that, with technology moving so fast, it was better to sell them as add-ons.

PS2 was a huge investment for Sony. In addition to product development costs, Sony invested $1 billion in two plants, one a joint venture with Toshiba to make the main central processing unit (the "Emotion Engine"), and another to manufacture the graphics synthesizer. Marketing expenses incurred in the global rollout of PS2 were even greater. "The great thing about the games console business is that products last for three years," said Mr. Idei. "In the world of the PC, a product is doing well if it lasts three months. With the PlayStation2 we have lots of time to recoup our investment." Idei anticipated three profit streams: one from sales of hardware, the second (and most important) from software (primarily royalties on software sold by third-party games developers and publishers), and the third from online usage.

The hoopla of the launch could not disguise two critical problems of the PS2's introduction. Shortages of key components – notably the graphics synthesizer (made by Sony) and the "Emotion Engine" central processor – resulted in a shortage of PS2s for the critical US Christmas shopping period. There was also a lack of software. The power and sophistication of PS2, together with its technical quirks, created complex problems for developers. At the time of its launch, most PS2 games were revisions of earlier titles.

Nintendo: the GameCube

The battle between Sega and Sony was bad news for Nintendo. In the fourth quarter of 1999, Nintendo sold 1.9 million of its N-64s, compared with 2.4 million in fourth quarter 1998. Between its launch in 1996 and April 2000, it had sold 29.6 million N-64s against 70 million PlayStations. Increasingly, the N-64, with its games cartridges, was viewed as technologically outdated. However, Nintendo still dominated the handheld market, and continued to be profitable. Like Sony, Nintendo tried to head-off declining sales by cutting console prices: its N-64 was reduced from $129 to $99 in the fall of 1999. It also accelerated development of its new 128-bit console.

GameCube went on sale in Japan on September 14, 2001; its US debut was on November 18. Despite massive publicity, a US marketing budget of $75 million for the fourth quarter of 2001, and a low retail price ($199 in the US), GameCube's initial sales were limited by two factors. First, only three entirely new games were available for GameCube at the time of its Japanese launch; second, GameCube's US debut occurred just three days after the launch of the Microsoft Xbox.

The Microsoft Xbox

The most talked about development in the competitive battle for the 128-bit genera-tion of games consoles was the entry of Microsoft. Throughout 2000 and most of 2001, Microsoft's development efforts were the subject of a frenzy of speculation. The software giant's entry was seen as symbolizing the potential of video games con-soles. Once viewed as children's toys, games consoles were emerging as the primary tool for electronic entertainment, with the ability to offer movies, music, and many of the communications functions currently performed by PCs.

The Xbox was designed to place Microsoft far ahead of any other games machine in terms of technological capabilities. The *Financial Times* described it as: "Arguably the most powerful games console ever made, developed after consultation with more than 5,000 gamers and games creators, it has a staggering array of features: an inter-nal hard disk with a 733MHz processor, 64MB of memory, a DVD player, Dolby Digital 5.1 Surround Sound and an Ethernet port that makes it the only game console that's internet-ready and broadband-enabled."[2]

Yet, for all its state-of-the-art technology, Xbox did not offer an obviously superior user experience: "Although the Xbox is very good, it doesn't offer a sufficiently dif-ferent gaming experience from existing consoles . . . The technological difference between generations of consoles is getting smaller all the time, and all three consoles now on the market in the US (Xbox, GameCube, PS2) have great graphics. It's hard for the average player to tell the difference."[3] As with all newcomers to the video games industry, software availability was Xbox's major weakness. When Xbox was launched in the US in November 2001, 19 games were available. Although this was substantially more than the GameCube, it paled in comparison to PS2's more than 200 titles. Moreover, Xbox also lacked the recognizable characters owned by its estab-lished rivals, such as Mario Brothers and Lara Croft. As Nick Gibson, games analyst at Durlacher, observed: "By the time Microsoft and Nintendo complete their global launches in 2002, Sony will have built up an installed base of over 25m units com-pared with 4m to 5m for the others at best. This momentum, combined with strong developer and publisher support, gives Sony an unassailable lead in this console cycle."[4] Xbox's US launch was successful, with 1.5 million sold in the six-week Christ-mas shopping period.

Xbox's biggest challenge was to establish itself in Japan. Microsoft's Japanese launch on February 22, 2002 featured the release of 12 new games and the presence of Bill Gates to sell the very first Xbox in Japan. Priced at ¥34,800 ($259.3), the Xbox cost 17% more than PS2 and 39% more than GameCube. However, Xbox's reception in Japan was a disappointment for Microsoft. In its first three days, 150,000 units were sold, of the 250,000 that were shipped (PS2 had sold 720,000 in its first three days). Soon after the launch, a number of consumers began making complaints that the Xbox was scratching their CDs and DVDs. Microsoft's hesitant response to these complaints alienated many Japanese consumers and retailers. Moreover, none of Xbox's initial games releases proved to be major hits with Japanese games players.

The Outcome

Despite Sega's early lead, the launch of PlayStation2, Xbox, and GameCube soon put pressure on sales of the Dreamcast. Although Sega sold 2 million Dreamcast consoles in Japan between its launch in November 1998 and the first quarter of 2000, Sony sold 1.8 million PS2s in just two months. During the first half of 2000, pessimism grew over Sega's prospects: its share price more than halved between February and June 2000. In August 2000, Sega began a last-ditch stand to grab market share: it offered the Dreamcast free of charge to customers who signed up to Sega's online service, SegaNet, for two years at $21.95 a month. Existing Dreamcast customers received a free keyboard and a $200 check if they subscribed. Sega was betting on the potential for its games console to become its users' primary device for email and web surfing. By the fall of 2000, mounting losses forced Sega to announce its withdrawal from video games hardware. Henceforth it would concentrate on games software.

Sega's withdrawal did little to moderate competition between the other three players. All three of them – Sony, Nintendo, and Microsoft – recognized the criticality of establishing market leadership, and all had the resources to finance a fierce battle for sales. For Sony the key was to utilize its incumbency advantages of massive installed base and huge library of titles to thwart its two rivals. In March 2002, Sony cut the US price of its PS2 from $299 to $199; Microsoft also cut the price of its Xbox from $299 to $199, and Nintendo reduced its GameCube from $199 to $149. Despite PS2's problematic launch, it was clearly established as market leader, with an installed base of 30 million worldwide as compared with about 4.5 million each for GameCube and Xbox.

Microsoft's ability to challenge Sony rested on two factors. Its ability to launch blockbuster games: *Halo* and *Halo2* provided this drawing power. Second was exploitation of Xbox's online capabilities. In November 2002, Microsoft launched its Xbox Live online gaming service, which allowed interactive, internet gaming and direct downloading of new game content to the Xbox's hard drive. By July 2005, Xbox Live had 2 million subscribers.

By 2004, it was clear that Sony had retained its market leadership in the 128-bit generation of games consoles. During the six years up to October 2006, Sony had sold around 111 million PS2s. The Xbox had built a strong no. 2 position in the US, but elsewhere its performance was less impressive. Sales of Xboxes totaled 24 million by December 2006; GameCube sold 21 million units over the same period; Dreamcast's sales were 10.6 million.

The Video Games Industry in January 2007

Competition for the new generation of video game consoles comprised the three survivors from the previous round: Sony, Microsoft, and Nintendo. The new round of competition was kicked off on November 25, 2005 with Microsoft's release of its Xbox 360. By January 2007, all three of the key players had launched their new generation consoles into a market where the stakes were bigger than ever. It was also a market that had become increasingly complex and where the competitive positions of the three leading players were shifting rapidly.

The Video Games Market

At the beginning of 2007, most forecasts indicated that the world video games market was on the threshold of its biggest ever expansion phase. Each generation of games consoles had surpassed its predecessor in terms of unit sales. The general expectation was that the new generation of consoles would lead a similar expansion. As a form of entertainment, video game playing was one of the biggest. In the US over 40% of households owned video game consoles and annual expenditures on consoles and games exceeded cinema box office receipts. Unlike most forms of electronic hardware, video games consoles had not suffered the same decline in prices that had afflicted computers.

Central to the expanding size of the video games market was a broadening of the consumer base: once the preserve of teenage boys, by 2005, the majority of the age group 18–44 was video games players. Even among the 55–64 age group, 21% played video games. Female participation had also increased strongly. While children who grew up playing video games continued to do so as adults, game preferences changed greatly with age. Adolescents were more concerned with what was "in" and "hot." The adult market was composed of numerous niches, each with an interest in a different type of game. Adults liked titles that fit in with their lifestyle and interests. Sports-based games were very popular among adult males. However, in terms of intensity of game playing, teenage boys remained clear leaders: US males between the ages of 12 and 17 with a video game console in their home devoted an average of 14 hours a week to game playing. Females in the same age bracket played an average of 4 hours a week.

The growth of video games playing had opened up an entirely new source of revenue for video games publishers: advertising. Product placement within video games generated advertising revenues of $56 million in 2005 in the US alone. Both Microsoft and Google acquired advertising agencies specializing in video game ad placement.

Software

Each of the video game console makers ("platform providers") licensed third-party software companies to develop and distribute games for its system. Two types of company were involved in video games software: video games publishers, who were responsible for financing, manufacturing, marketing, and distributing video games, and video game developers that developed the software. Video game publishing was increasingly dominated by a few large companies – the most prominent being Electronic Arts (see table 11.3). Typically, the software publisher submitted a proposal or a prototype to the console maker for evaluation and approval. The licensing agreement between the software company and the hardware provider gave the console maker the right to approve game content, control over release timing, and provided for a royalty payment from the software company. As the power of the publishers had grown and the costs of development had risen, so exclusivity ties had disappeared from most licensing contracts – most leading games titles were cross-platform. Game developers were paid a royalty, typically between 5 and 15%, based on the publishers' revenues from the game.

Escalating game development costs were a result of the demand for multifeatured, 3-D, cinematic-quality games made possible by increasingly powerful consoles. Atari's *Pac-Man* released in 1982 was created by a single developer and cost about $100,000. *Halo 2* released for the Xbox in 2004 involved 190 developers and cost $40 million. By late 2006, *Halo 2* had sold 8 million copies at $50 each. For the new generation of consoles, most games cost more than $10 million to develop. In terms of both costs and revenue patterns, video games closely resembled movies, with similar success rates

TABLE 11.3 Share of US video games market by publisher, 2005

Publisher	Market share by value (%)
Electronic Arts	24
Take-Two Interactive	9
Activision	7
Sony	7
Nintendo of America	6
Microsoft	5
THQ	5
Atari	4
Konami	3
Ubisoft	3

– a mere few became money-spinning blockbusters. Like movies, too, creating a brand franchise through a succession of sequels had become a key competitive strategy.

The development of video games required a blend of technology and creative talent. The development process included game development and design, prototyping, programming, art, computer graphic design, animation, sound engineering, technical writing, editorial review, and quality assurance. It took 18 to 36 months to complete a new title based on a new platform, and 6 to 14 months to make existing titles compatible with a different platform. Many games were based on characters and themes that were either owned by the game developer or licensed from third parties. The licensing fees paid by software publishers for exclusive rights to the intellectual property of media companies and sports organizations grew substantially between 1998 and 2002. Securing the license to produce a game based on a hit movie (e.g. *Harry Potter*) could cost several millions of dollars. In the sports market, licenses paid to sports leagues (NFL, NHL, MLB, NBA, FIFA) typically involved an up-front payment, plus a royalty of 5 to 15% of the wholesale price for each unit sold.

Not only did software sales exceed hardware sales, most of the profits received by the console manufacturers were derived from software. The console makers followed a "razors and blades" business model: the consoles were sold at a loss; profits were re-couped on software sales – both games developed internally and royalties received from third-party games publishers. Licensing fees paid by the games publisher to the console manufacturer were typically about $10 per copy. The result was strongly cyclical earnings of the hardware companies. The launch of a new console would result in massive cash outflows. It was not until a healthy installed base had been established that the manufacturer would begin to recoup the investment made. Table 11.4 shows leading titles in 2006.

The Competitive Situation, January 2007

Microsoft The introduction of Xbox 360 marked a significant shift of strategy for Microsoft. In contrast to the original Xbox, Microsoft was first to market in the new generation of consoles, with the prospect of using first-mover advantage to build market share. Xbox 360 was the first major console with a near simultaneous global launch as opposed to a phased rollout. The North American launch was on

TABLE 11.4 Top-selling console games in the US, 2005 (by units sold)

Title/platform	Publisher	Release date	Units sold ('000s)	Av. retail price ($)
Madden NFL 2006 (PS2)	Electronic Arts	Aug. '05	2,900	46
Gran Turismo 4 (PS2)	Sony Computers Ent.	Feb. '05	1,500	49
Madden NFL 2006 (Xbox)	Electronic Arts	Aug. '05	1,200	47
NCAA Football 2006 (PS2)	Electronic Arts	Jul. '05	1,100	48
Star Wars: Battlefront II (PS2)	LucasArts	Nov. '05	1,000	47
MVP Baseball 2005 (PS2)	Electronic Arts	Feb. '05	970	29
Star Wars Episode III: Revenge of the Sith (PS2)	LucasArts	May. '05	930	47
NBA Live 2006 (PS2)	Electronic Arts	Sep. '05	820	44
LEGO Star Wars (PS2)	Eidos	Mar. '05	800	37
Star Wars: Battlefront II (Xbox)	LucasArts	Nov. '05	n.a.	48

November 25, 2005; the Japanese launch was on December 10. Microsoft also shifted its promotion to reflect a new market positioning. Compared with the original Xbox, which emphasized processing power and focused on hardcore gamers, Xbox 360's positioning has eschewed technology in favor of versatility, design, and coolness. The Xbox 360's marketing was led by Peter Moore, who was previously marketing head for Sega's Dreamcast. Sega's annihilation by Sony has provided added momentum to Moore's urge to defeat Sony in the new generation of consoles.

The Xbox 360 strategy emphasized the hardware's multifunctionality for home entertainment and Microsoft's strong online presence. Through Xbox Live, users could purchase and download video games, in-game extras such as weapons and costumes, and movies and TV shows – including high-definition TV shows. Table 11.5 compares the Xbox 360 with its leading rivals.

Sony Meanwhile, Sony's launch of its PS3 was dogged with multiple delays. Most of the problems related to the technological ambitiousness of the hardware. PS3's revolutionary multicore Cell processor, developed jointly with IBM and Toshiba, proved difficult and expensive to manufacture – it was estimated that each Cell processor cost Sony $230 per unit. Even more problematic was the delayed Blu-Ray DVD drive, whose initial production cost was estimated at $350. Merrill Lynch estimated that the total cost of the components for the PS3 could amount to $900 per unit in 2006.[5]

The Blu-Ray drive was a central element of Sony's strategy. It was engaged in a fierce standards battle with Toshiba over the technical format of the next generation of high definition DVDs. PS3 was to be a key product in gaining market acceptance of Blu-Ray.

Software was another problem for PS3. The complexity and power of the hardware extended the potential and the cost of games written for PS3. Software development costs were estimated at four or five times those of PS2. To encourage developers to write for PS3, Sony was obliged to cut its royalties. At its initial launch, Sony had 15 titles available for PS3, although few made full use of PS3's technical capabilities. The most popular of the new games was *Resistance: Fall of Man*.

TABLE 11.5 Comparison of seventh-generation games consoles

Console	Hardware	Connectivity	DVD	Games	Price (Dec. 2006)
Sony PS3	Cell Broadband Engine 550 MHz RSK GPU HDTV-capable	*20 GB version:* Bluetooth 2.0, an ethernet port and four USB docks *60 GB version:* Compact flash, SD and memory stick duo, WiFI	Integrated Blu-Ray player Backwards compatible with DVD	50 titles available at end of 2006	*20GB version:* $499 *60GB version:* $599
Microsoft Xbox 360	IBM Xenon Power-PC CPU 500MHz ATI custom GPU HDTV-capable	Option to purchase WiFI adapter *Core version:* Three USB docks, ethernet port *20GB version:* Wireless controllers	DVD player Additional HD-DVD drive available for $199	130 titles at end of 2006 (of which 65 allow interactive play through Xbox Live) Backwards compatible	*Core version:* $299 *20 GB version:* $399
Nintendo Wii	IBM Broadway Power-PC CPU GPU developed with ATI EDTV video output	Bluetooth, two USB docks, SD slot, internet via IEEE 802.11 or a Wii LAN adaptor	No current DVD playback Plans to launch integrated DVD version in Japan – c. 2007	c. 30 titles at time of launch Backwards compatible with GameCube	$250

PS3's launch in Japan on November 11, 2006 and in North America on November 17 was marred by lack of product. Following both launches, PS3s were selling on online auction sites in Japan and the US at a substantial premium to their retail list prices. The European and Australian launches were set for March 23, 2007. One of the results of product shortage was continuing strength of Sony's PS2. During the critical month of December 2006, Americans bought 1.4 million PS2s, outselling PS3 (491,000 units), Xbox 360 (1.1 million units), and Nintendo Wii (604,000 units).

Nintendo One of the biggest surprises of the new round of competition was the strong initial showing of Nintendo's Wii. Technologically, the Nintendo Wii lacked the advanced features of either the Xbox 360 or PS3; its primary innovative feature was its remote wand-like controller that was sensitive to a range of hand movements. As a result, Nintendo claimed that its Wii was more intuitive than other consoles and could be learned more easily. This linked with a marketing strategy that aimed to recruit new games players and targeted a very broad demographic – including older consumers. Wii was launched in North America on November 19, 2006, on December 2 in Japan and December 8 in Europe. The launch was accompanied by 16 new games for Wii – of which several were new versions of existing franchises (e.g. *Legend of Zelda: Twilight Princess*). Nintendo also mounted its biggest ever advertising compaign. (Table 11.6 shows the leading US video games advertisers.)

TABLE 11.6 Advertising expenditures for selected video game brands, 2003–2005

Brand	2003 ($m)	2004 ($m)	2005 ($m)
Microsoft Xbox	15.9	26.3	31.8
Sony PlayStation	95.9	99.6	127.9
Nintendo	84.7	76.9	80.6
Electronic Arts	–	55.5	105.0
Take-Two	n.a.	n.a.	28.7

n.a. = not available.

SOURCES: VARIOUS PRESS REPORTS.

Changing competitive dynamics The competitive situation at the beginning of 2007 was unusual in terms of the fluidity of market shares and market positioning. Despite its huge installed base of PlayStations (both the original version and the PS2), Sony was widely viewed as having mismanaged the launch of PS3. Most of the problems that had plagued PS3 – including delays and perceived high price – were the direct result of the technological ambitiousness of PS3, especially its incorporation of the Blu-Ray DVD drive. The one-year lead of Xbox 360 over the PS3 had given Microsoft its best opportunity to unseat Sony's position as market leader. Meanwhile the successful launch of Wii had indicated that Nintendo could not be written off as a serious contender.

In previous generations of video game consoles, there had been a strong tendency for one firm to dominate the market and scoop most of the industry profit pool. For instance, Nintendo had dominated the 8-bit generation and Sony had dominated the last two generations. Typically the winner was the firm that offered the most competing software titles, the most advanced technology, and did the most effective job of managing the complex tasks of coordination and logistics necessary for a successful product launch. A key issue for the new generation of consoles was whether the basis and dynamics of competitive advantage had changed. As technology had progressed, the contribution of advanced technology to user experience had become less and less perceptible. At the same time, the winner-take-all characteristics of the industry had changed, with more and more games becoming available for multiple platforms. Finally, video games consoles had become increasingly multifunctional. One reason for the intensity of the competitive battle between Xbox 360 and PS3 was that the market at stake was not just the market for video game consoles – what Sony and Microsoft were ultimately concerned with was control over the future of home entertainment. As video game consoles became general purpose devices, so their potential for differentiation increased. Some of the customers for PS3 were not even game players – for viewing movies, the PS3 was a cheaper alternative to a standalone Blu-Ray DVD player. As a result of these trends, together with the ever-increasing size of the total market and increased segmentation within it, it seemed possible that the market might lose some of its winner-take-all characteristics and might be capable of supporting two or even three profitable suppliers of consoles. Others suggested that the changing dynamics of competition might have caused a fundamental shift in

Appendix
Financial Data on the Console Manufacturers

NINTENDO
(Yen, billions)

	1996	1997	1998	1999	2000	2001	2002	2003	2004	2005	2006
Total sales	401	463	534	573	531	463	554	504	514	515	509
Operating income	133	115	172	156	145	85	119	100	110	113	91
Net income	60	65	84	86	56	97	106	67	33	87	98
Op. income/Av. total assets (%)	9.8	9.4	10.6	9.9	6.1	9.7	9.5	8.9	10.5	9.7	7.9
Return on av. equity (%)	12.3	12.1	14.0	12.9	7.7	12.2	12.0	7.4	3.7	9.6	10.4

SEGA
(Yen, billions)

	1996	1997	1998	1999	2000	2001	2002	2003	2004	2005	2006
Total sales	346	360	331	226	339	243	206	197	191	195	553
Operating income	30	31	7	4	(40)	(52)	14	9	14	6	113
Net income	5	6	(36)	(32)	(52)	(418)	(18)	3	9	2	66
Op. income/Av. total assets (%)	1.2	1.3	(9.7)	(8.1)	(15.7)	(115.2)	(7.5)	6.1	13.2	7.6	25.0
Return on av. equity (%)	3.0	3.1	(24.0)	(32.0)	(60.1)	(375.0)	(20.5)	3.6	11.0	2.3	23.0

Note: The data for 2006 relate to Sega Sammy Holdings (Sega merged with Sammy in October 2004).

SONY
(Yen, billions)

	1996	1997	1998	1999	2000	2001	2002	2003	2004	2005	2006
Sales	4,592	5,663	6,761	6,804	6,687	7,315	7,578	7,474	7,496	7,160	7,475
of which: Games	201	408	700	760	631	661	1,004	936	754	703	918
Operating income	235	370	526	348	241	225	135	185	99	114	191
of which: Games	n.a.	n.a.	117	137	77	(51)	84	113	68	45	9
Net income (loss)	54	139	222	179	122	17	15	116	89	164	124
Op. income/Av. total assets (%)	1.1	6.9	6.7	5.5	3.7	3.1	1.7	2.2	1.1	1.2	1.9
Return on av. equity (%)	4.6	10.7	13.2	9.8	6.1	0.1	0.1	4.8	3.6	5.3	4.1

MICROSOFT

($, millions)

	2000	2001	2002	2003	2004	2005	2006
Sales	22,956	25,296	28,365	32,187	36,835	39,788	44,282
of which:							
Home and entertainment	n.a.	n.a.	2,453	2,748	2,731	3,110	4,292
Operating income	11,006	11,720	11,910	13,217	9,034	14,561	16,472
of which:							
Games	n.a.	n.a.	(847)	(924)	(1,011)	(451)	(1,283)
Net income	9,421	7,346	7,829	9,993	8,168	12,254	12,599
Op. income/Av. total assets (%)	24.4	21.2	18.8	17.9	10.3	17.6	23.6
Return on av. equity (%)	26.9	16.6	15.7	17.6	11.7	19.9	28.6

n.a. = not available.

SOURCE: COMPANY ANNUAL REPORTS.

the balance of power between hardware and software companies and that the major games publishers – Electronic Arts, Activision, and Take-Two – would be the key players in the industry and the principal profit earners.

Notes

1 Successive generations of video game consoles have conventionally been designated according to processor bit size. In practice, bit size is a poor indicator of processing power. Beyond 32 bits, bit size has little to do with console performance – processor clock speed is much more important.

2 "Out of the box at last," *Financial Times*, Creative Business section, November 20, 2001.

3 Ibid.

4 "Console wars," *The Economist*, June 22, 2002, pp. 71–2.

5 "Delays likely for Sony's PlayStation 3," *Financial Times*, February 20, 2006.

Eni SpA: Building an International Energy Major

February 15, 2003 marked the 50th anniversary of the founding of Eni SpA – Italy's largest company and the world's seventh biggest public petroleum company[1] – and the beginning of Vittorio Mincato's fifth full year as chief executive officer. Under Mincato's leadership, Eni had experienced a period of continuous transition and development based on a strategy of "growth of the core energy business." The results were impressive. Between 1998 and 2003, Eni's revenues and hydrocarbon production had both grown by more than half, operating income had more than doubled, and Eni's share price appreciation had been greater than any other oil major.

The first two months of 2003 saw no slackening of pace for Mincato. During January and February 2003, Eni finalized its acquisitions of Fortum Petroleum (a Norwegian oil and gas company) for 1.1 billion euros and the 56% of Italgas (an Italian gas distribution company) that it did not already own. In January, Eni also purchased a service station network in Spain and four Hungarian gas distribution companies. However, Mincato's main preoccupation was Eni's corporate plan for the next four years. On January 29, Mincato and his senior executives presented Eni's strategic plans to the investment community in London. During the next two weeks, the roadshow visited the financial centers of Europe and America.

Mincato envisaged the next four years building on the achievements of the previous four. The centerpiece of Eni's strategy for 2004–7 was continued upstream growth. During 1999–2002, Eni's oil and gas production had grown faster than most other majors. The target for the next four years was production growth of 5% per annum. Increased upstream output would be supported by downstream

This case was prepared by Robert Grant and Michael Ritter. We are grateful for the support and cooperation of Eni SpA, in particular from Leonardo Maugeri and Renato Cibin.

expansion – especially in the European gas market. As a result, Eni would build its position as one of the world's leading vertically integrated natural gas companies. At the same time, Eni would continue to reduce its investment in chemicals and other non-core businesses.

Mincato was well aware that Eni's position as one of the world's most profitable and fastest growing energy majors was vulnerable to the challenges of a complex and turbulent business environment. High energy prices were a major contributor to Eni's stellar financial performance. The price of oil remained vulnerable to increased supplies from Iran, Iraq, and the former Soviet Union, while massive investments in liquefied natural gas (LNG) threatened to depress European gas prices. Any major slowdown in the world economy would also undermine energy prices. Longer term, environmental issues clouded the outlook for fossil fuels. Relative to its peers, Eni lacked massive size and the international scope of the new "supermajors" – Exxon Mobil, BP-Amoco, TotalFinaElf, and ChevronTexaco – created during the merger wave of 1996–2001. Mincato was determined to avoid large-scale mergers and acquisitions: "We've always preferred to grow organically and in an orderly manner. That's our history," he told investment analysts in London.[2] If Eni was to continue to outperform its larger rivals, it would need to continue to hone a strategy that exploited its distinctive differences, and execute that strategy with enhanced effectiveness and efficiency.

Mattei and the Creation of Ente Nazionale Idrocarburi, 1926–1962[3]

Eni traces its origins to 1926 when the Italian Prime Minister, Benito Mussolini, established Agip (Azienda Generali Italiana Petroli) as a state-owned oil refining company.[4] In 1945 Enrico Mattei, a former partisan, was appointed head of Agip and was instructed to dismantle this relic of fascist economic intervention. Contrary to instructions, Mattei renewed Agip's exploration efforts and, in 1948, discovered a substantial gas field in Northern Italy's Po Valley. In 1949, Mattei also took over the management of SNAM, the Italian gas distribution company. With the opportunity to create a national energy system based on the newly found gas reserves, pipelines were laid at a frantic rate. "Mattei built the pipelines first and negotiated afterwards . . . He simply ignored private and public rights and the law . . . Much of the work was done at night on the theory that by morning the work would be so far along that there would not be very much that anybody could do about it."[5] At San Donato, outside Milan, Mattei created Metanopoli, a small town comprising offices, gas plants, and employees' homes. On February 10, 1953, the government merged Agip, SNAM, and other state-owned energy activities to form Ente Nazionale Idrocarburi (Eni) with the task of "promoting and undertaking initiatives of national interest in the fields of hydrocarbons and natural gases." Mattei was appointed its first chairman and chief executive. In fact, Eni's 36 subsidiaries extended well beyond oil and gas to include engineering services, chemicals, soap, and real estate.

Under Mattei's leadership, Eni became committed to building an integrated, international oil and gas company that would ensure the independence of Italy's energy supplies and make a substantial contribution to Italy's post-war economic regeneration. Mattei soon established himself as a national hero: "He embodied great visions for post-war Italy – antifascism, the resurrection and rebuilding of the nation, and the emergence of the 'new man' who had made it himself, without the old boy network."[6] Mattei's daring and resourcefulness was especially evident in Eni's international growth. Post-war recovery was accompanied by a quest for new sources of oil – especially in the Middle East. Eni's problem was that most leading oil-producing countries had agreements with the existing oil majors: Standard Oil New Jersey (later Exxon), Mobil, Standard Oil of California (later Chevron), Texaco, Royal Dutch Shell, British Petroleum, and Gulf Oil. These "Seven Sisters" – as Mattei christened them – collaborated closely to tie-up oil supplies: the Arabian American Oil Company (Aramco) was jointly owned by Exxon, Chevron, Texaco, and Mobil; the Iranian Consortium involved all seven of the sisters together with Total of France.

The production agreement that Mattei signed with the Shah of Iran in 1957 marked the beginning of a fundamental shift of power from the oil majors to producer governments. It also established Eni as the *enfant terrible* of the international oil business. The Iranian agreement was revolutionary. It created a jointly owned exploration and production company headed by an Iranian chairman and with the proceeds shared between Eni and the Iranian National Oil Company. "This new approach opened the way to full control of energy resources for the producing countries and anticipated a trend that would become the basis of future agreements in the oil business."[7] The repercussions of the "Mattei formula" extended beyond the oil industry to international diplomacy. A 1957 US confidential progress report pointed to "the threat posed by Enrico Mattei to the political objectives of the United States." This "new deal" with producer countries allowed Eni to extend its upstream interests throughout North Africa. Between 1958 and 1960, Eni led the way in acquiring exploration and production rights in Libya, Egypt, Tunisia, and Algeria. Mattei continued to upset the status quo with deals to purchase crude oil from the Soviet Union. By the end of the 1950s, Italy had become the Soviet Union's biggest oil customer after China. Again, the deal was innovative and daring: Soviet oil was bartered for exports of synthetic rubber and other Italian products – in effect, Eni acquired Soviet oil at less than half of the prevailing world price.

Beyond Oil and Gas

Mattei's drive to build a corporate empire did not stop at hydrocarbons. By 1962, Eni was "engaged in industries as various as motels, highways, chemicals, soap, fertilizers, synthetic rubber, machinery, instruments, textiles, electrical generation and distribution, contract research, engineering and construction, publishing, nuclear power, steel pipe, cement, investment banking, and even education, to mention only a few."[8] This diversification resulted from Mattei's indefatigable deal making. As a state-owned enterprise dependent on political support, many of Mattei's acquisitions were politically motivated. For example, Eni's acquisition of Lanerossi, a wool textile company in Veneto, appears to have been motivated by Mattei's desire to influence a local Christian Democratic politician.[9]

Other business developments were designed to support Eni's oil and gas businesses. In 1955 Snamprogetti was created to design and construct chemical and petrochemical plants and pipeline transportation systems. Saipem was added, with operations focused on offshore construction, pipe laying and drilling. Pignone of Florence (later Nuovo Pignone) was acquired to produce equipment used in the oil and gas industry.

Eni after Mattei, 1962–1992

Adjustment, Rebalancing, and Political Intervention[10]

Mattei died in a mysterious plane crash on October 27, 1962. He was 56 years old. He left a sprawling corporate empire whose strategy had been Mattei's vision and opportunism, and whose integrating force had been Mattei's charisma and personal authority. At the time of his death, Mattei was president not just of Eni but also of its main operating companies – Agip Mineraria, Agip, Snam, Anic, Stanic, and Agip Nucleare.[11] Filling the void as Eni's new president was Marcello Boldrini, a 72-year-old professor of statistics with very little hands-on management experience. At the same time, Eni faced problems on multiple fronts. Despite Mattei's innovative deal making, the company remained tiny by international standards. It was also short of oil – in 1962 Eni was producing a mere 32,000 barrels per day of crude with only 18 active wells outside of Italy. Meanwhile, Eni was in a perilous financial situation. The profits generated by Eni's monopoly position in the Italian gas market were dissipated throughout the company's diverse business interests. Most serious was Eni's high level of debt. In 1960, the Italian Central Bank had forbidden Eni from issuing new debt.[12]

Financial weakness resulted in Eni becoming increasingly dependent on government. Increasing political control meant that Eni became an instrument of government economic, industrial, and employment policies. As a result, Eni continued to diversify into minerals and metals processing, chemicals, coal, and textile machinery – often to rescue failing companies. After 1975, the chairman of Eni lost direct control of the operating companies – their chief executives were appointed by government on the basis of political considerations. Nevertheless, during the 1960s and 1970s, Eni continued to expand its interests in oil and gas. Major initiatives included the purchase of natural gas from the Soviet Union (which involved Eni building a pipeline from the Austrian–Czechoslovak border to Italy), the Trans-Med Pipeline from Algeria and Tunisia to Italy, and the development of offshore projects in West Africa, Congo, and Angola.

1983–1992: Reform and Crisis

In 1983, Franco Reviglio was appointed chairman of Eni and quickly concluded that Eni could not continue down its present path. Its 335 operating companies spanned much of Italy's industrial sector. By 1982, losses totaled 1,501 billion lire ($1.28 billion) and debt had risen to over 19,000 billion lire ($14 billion). Reviglio's priorities were to reestablish Eni on solid financial ground, distance itself from political power, and to refocus on oil and gas. Between 1982 and 1989, Eni made considerable progress in reducing costs, eliminating losses, restructuring debt, and creating a more coherent and manageable business portfolio. Several businesses in nuclear power, minerals, and textiles were sold and Eni's chemical division, EniChem, was merged with Montedison's chemical division to create Enimont. By the time the chairmanship of Eni had passed from Reviglio to Gabriele Cagliari in 1989, Eni reported net income of 1,544 billion lire ($1.2 billion) on sales of 37,189 lire ($27.1 billion), and long-term debt was down to 9,850 billion lire ($7.9 billion). Table 12.1 shows Eni's growth and profitability since 1980.

TABLE 12.1 Eni's sales, profits, employment, and production, 1980–2003

	1980	1981	1982	1983	1984	1985	1986	1987	1988	1989	1990	1991
Sales (US$m)	31,440	32,532	30,677	29,221	29,542	24,328	22,557	24,464	25,220	27,105	41,764	34,594
Net income (US$m)	116	–232	–1,280	–922	–36	406	42	544	1,006	1,176	1,697	684
Employees ('000s)	n.a.	n.a.	140	136	n.a.	129	130	119	116	136	131	131
Oil and gas production ('000s boe/day)	320	322	307	335	371	371	384	443	490	538	590	618

	1992	1993	1994	1995	1996	1997	1998	1999	2000	2001	2002	2003*
Sales (US$m)	38,659	33,595	30,670	35,335	37,973	34,323	33,177	31,225	46,000	43,607	51,379	59,322
Net income (US$m)	–768	154	1,977	2,704	2,930	2,980	2,891	3,019	5,671	7,333	4,816	6,323
Employees ('000s)	126	109	92	86	83	80	79	72	70	71	81	77
Oil and gas production ('000s boe/day)	860	901	941	982	984	1,021	1,038	1,064	1,187	1,369	1,472	1,562

n.a. = not available.

Under Cagliari, Eni returned to an era of intense political interference, the result of which was to bring Eni to the verge of collapse. Between 1990 and 1992, Eni's capital investment and exploration expenditures were close to 150% of operating cash flow and long-term debt increased to 13,453 billion lire.

Meanwhile, the movement for far-reaching reforms of Italy's over-extended and inefficient public sector was gaining strength. Italy was facing increasing pressures from the European Commission and the new European Monetary Union to rein in public expenditures, reduce its public sector deficit, and free up industry from state intervention. In June 1992, a new government was formed under reformist Prime Minister Giuliano Amato. In July, the government announced the first steps in granting Eni greater autonomy: the Ministry for State Participation was dismantled, Eni and three other state-owned corporations were converted into joint-stock companies, and their relationships with the government were transferred to the Treasury.

The Bernabè Era: Privatization and Transformation, 1992–1998

The new legal structure had important governance implications for Eni. Henceforth, its board of directors was legally responsible to shareholders for the financial state of the company – even though the only shareholder was the Italian government. Top management responsibility was vested in a three-person board comprising Gabriele Cagliari as chairman, Giuseppe Ammassari as government representative, and Franco Bernabè as CEO. The 44-year-old Bernabè was a surprise choice – an economist who headed up Eni's planning department, he lacked line management experience. The significance of Bernabè's appointment was that he was a prominent advocate of privatization, having already drawn up plans for a privatized Eni.

As CEO, Bernabè moved quickly to position himself, rather than Chairman Cagliari, as the primary decision maker and center of executive power within Eni. In a directive to operating company presidents he announced that, henceforth, they would each report to him. He followed up with a series of visits to Eni's operating companies during which he met with managers, discussed their businesses, and laid out his ideas for Eni's future. Central to his thinking was the belief that Eni needed to be privatized as an integrated oil, gas, and chemical company – shorn of its various diversified businesses, but otherwise a vertically integrated upstream–downstream company similar to other international energy majors.[13]

During the fall of 1992, Bernabè launched his restructuring plan. Beginning with the sale of Nuovo Pignone (Eni's gas turbine business) to General Electric, several non-core businesses were sold and the proceeds used to reduce debt. Throughout the entire company, subsidiaries were pressured to cut costs, establish tighter capital expenditure discipline, and raise profit aspirations. However, in the early stages of Bernabè's restructuring, Eni was plunged into crisis.

In March 1993, Eni became caught up in the corruption scandal that had swept the country. Dozens of Eni executives became indicted on corruption charges, including Chairman Cagliari and the chief executives of several of Eni's main operating companies.[14] Between March 9 and 11, Cagliari and other top managers were arrested. The initial paralysis of Eni offered Bernabè the opportunity to clean house and restructure management. Later that March, Bernabè forced the resignation of the board and appointed a new, non-political board comprising technocrats and energy industry experts. In April, he demanded the resignation of all the board members of Eni's operating companies and embarked on a process of selection and reappointment. Within two months, 250 board members were substituted.[15]

Management changes paved the way for an intensified program of restructuring. Bernabè's corporate strategy was "to reduce Eni from being a loose conglomerate to concentrate on its core activity of energy."[16] In the troubled chemicals sector, five large plants were closed and capacity halved. During 1993, Bernabè's first whole year as chief executive, 73 Eni businesses were closed or sold worldwide, employment fell by 15,000, cost savings and asset sales amounted to 1.7 trillion lire, and net income went from a loss of 946 billion lire in 1992 to a 304 billion lire profit.[17] Commenting on Eni's financial recovery, Bernabè noted: "One of the reasons why we have been able to achieve better results is that we have been able to operate without political interference. We have been able to manage our business on commercial criteria."[18]

Eni's Initial Public Offering

Eni's initial public offering of 15% of its total equity on November 21, 1995 raised 3.3 billion euros for the Italian Treasury and on November 28 Eni shares commenced trading on the Milan, London, and New York stock exchanges. After more than 40 years of looking to political leaders in Rome for guidance, Eni's top management had to adjust to a new set of masters – the investment community in the world's financial capitals.

For Bernabè, the IPO marked a fundamental change in Eni's goals and responsibilities, but it was a starting point rather than an end in itself. "A government-owned, politically controlled monopoly could not be turned into a competitive global integrated oil company overnight," he observed.[19] Commitment to maximizing shareholder value provided the impetus for reconfiguring its portfolio of assets: "Eni's strategy is to focus on businesses and geographical areas where, through size, technology, or cost structure, it has a leading market position. To this end, Eni intends to implement dynamic management of its portfolio through acquisitions, joint ventures, and divestments. Eni also intends to outsource non-strategic activities."[20]

Capital investments became increasingly focused on upstream activities. In refining, marketing, and petrochemicals, costs were reduced and assets were sold. Organizationally, Bernabè combined centralization and decentralization. Subsidiary managers were given increased authority over human resource decisions and their authorization limits for capital expenditures were increased. At the same time, corporate planning systems were strengthened and financial discipline was increased. The merger of Agip into Eni in 1997 increased corporate control over Eni's most important subsidiary.

The results were striking. Between 1992 and 1998, Bernabè had halved Eni's debt, turned a loss into a substantial profit, and reduced the number of employees by some 46,000. However, 1998 was to be Bernabè's last year at Eni: his success at transforming Eni made him the obvious candidate to lead the turnaround of another newly privatized giant – Telecom Italia.

Eni under Mincato: From Restructuring to Growth

Vittorio Mincato brought a different background and a different style of management to Eni. Twelve years Bernabè's senior, Mincato had already spent 42 years at Eni. His career included both corporate and line management positions, including 15 years as chairman of EniChem where he cut chemical plants from over 40 to 20 and eliminated chronic losses. Mincato brought a powerful reputation and intimate knowledge of the Eni group to the chief executive suite, but little was known about the strategy or management style he would pursue.

Despite massive changes under Bernabè, the Eni that Mincato inherited faced sizable problems. During 1998, the world economy was hit by the financial contagion that had spread from south east Asia to Latin America and Russia, and oil prices fell to below $10 a barrel. At home, Eni's gas monopoly was threatened by EU initiatives to liberalize energy markets. Meanwhile, the petroleum arm's competitive landscape was being transformed by mergers – BP's acquisition of Amoco was followed by Exxon's merger with Mobil. Eni itself remained unsettled after the momentous internal changes of the previous five years. Mincato described Eni as strong but tired: "like an athlete at the end of an extremely long, grueling race."[21]

Developing a Corporate Strategy

In confronting Eni's external challenges, Mincato recognized that Eni "still lacked a clear and courageous vision of its future." This lack of strategic focus was reinforced by Eni's internal weaknesses. Despite Bernabè's efforts to establish control over Eni's operating companies, the group still retained the features of a holding company. During his first few months as chief executive, Mincato developed his thinking about Eni's future and throughout 1999 he shaped the group's strategic plan for 2000–3. The central theme of the strategy would be growth in Eni's core energy business. This would inevitably involve acquisition: "Our weakness is our size and our priority is to grow. The fastest way is through acquisition and we have ample financial means to do so."[22] Such growth would inevitably require further internationalization. In an interview with the Financial Times, Mincato spelled out the main thrusts of the strategy:

> The first phase of the company's strategy is complete. It involved refocusing the group on its core oil, gas and related activities and the disposal of all diversified lines. "We are now entering phase two: this will involve concentrating on growth and further rationalization of the core businesses," he says.
>
> The main target of rationalization is the group's chemical activities. Mr. Mincato, in charge of chemical operations before becoming CEO, said Eni was too small a player in the chemical sector. It needed alliances and joint ventures "even with a minority stake" to reduce the weight of the loss-making chemical business on the invested capital.
>
> The next issue, he says, is to deal with the liberalization of Italy's domestic gas market. "The impact of liberalization should be marginal because we are planning to offset lower direct sales in Italy with increased volumes sold abroad." The group plans to sell gas to Croatia and Greece and is negotiating with other European countries.
>
> Mr. Mincato is also keen to develop the group's presence in the electricity market. "Our interest is based on the possibility of a gas company becoming integrated downstream into power generation to stabilize or increase sales and revenues in the short term," he says.[23]

In Eni's annual report for 1999, Mincato explained Eni's strategy for 2000–3 in greater detail:

In 1999 the scenario in which Eni operates underwent deep changes . . . Two phenomena in particular affected the most important sectors of our core business: the consolidation of the oil industry globally and liberalization of the European and Italian gas markets. . . .

The four-year plan approved at the end of 1999 derives from a new strategic vision that features, on one side, an aggressive growth option in upstream activities and, on the other, a customer-oriented approach in the energy markets.

For the upstream sector we devised a plan calling for 50% growth in hydrocarbon production by 2003. Such an objective will be made up of two components. The first is represented by ordinary growth . . . the second component of growth is related to mergers and/or acquisitions . . .

In the natural gas sector, Eni has been active at three levels. First, it followed an internationalization strategy in downstream activities with the aim of selling at least 10 billion cubic meters of natural gas per year by 2003 in foreign growth markets . . . Second, with the creation of EniPower, Eni started to restructure its activities in the electricity sector, an area which represents a necessary step to strengthen its position in the gas chain, in view of the fact that most of the growth in demand for natural gas in Europe will come from the expansion of combined cycle electricity production.

To support the opening up of the natural gas market in Italy, we started to restructure our activities at Snam, separating . . . transport activities from supply and sale.

The scope of the changes affecting our industry will require on our part the achievement of strong efficiency improvements. For this reason, plans to cut costs have been revised, raising to 1 billion euro (an increase of 250 million euro) the amount of savings that Eni plans to achieve through cost cutting by 2003 . . . While costs will be cut across all sectors, strong measures will be taken in the Petrochemical sector – whose weight in terms of net capital will decline to 7% by 2003.[24]

Upstream Strategy

Mincato's boldest moves were in the upstream business. Once Eni had committed itself to a 50% increase in hydrocarbon output, acquisition became essential. Yet, Mincato was resolutely opposed to Eni participating in the wave of mega-mergers that was reshaping the global oil and gas industry. He saw large-scale mergers being driven by expectations of synergies and economies of scale that were seldom realized: "Eni carefully analyzed the history of major mergers of the last 30 years and was able to see that, in 80% of cases, these destroyed value, especially when they involved cultural problems."[25] Mincato also recognized Eni's limited experience in integrating acquired companies: Eni must be capable of "digesting" any acquisitions it made.[26] Furthermore, Eni's stock market valuation was relatively low compared with its peers; to avoid dilution, Eni's preferred medium of exchange was cash.

In May 2000, Eni made its first ever takeover bid for a listed company. It acquired British Borneo, a London-listed exploration and production company, for 1.3 billion euro (including debt). This was followed in December 2000 with the acquisition of another British-based upstream company, LASMO, for 4.1 billion euro (including

TABLE 12.2 Eni oil and gas production by area, 1997–2003 (thousands of barrels of oil equivalent per day)

	Italy	North Sea	North Africa	West Africa	Rest of World	World
Production						
2003	300	345	351	260	306	1,562
2002	316	308	354	238	256	1,472
2001	308	288	317	233	223	1,369
2000	333	168	306	225	155	1,187
1999	358	154	269	206	77	1,064
1998	394	156	236	196	56	1,038
1997	404	155	229	180	54	1,021
Reserves						
2003	996	912	2,024	1,324	2,016	7,272

debt). Mincato viewed these acquisitions as milestones for Eni: "We had never before bought foreign companies and the result has already helped internationalize our own internal culture."[27]

Eni also expanded its own exploration. In Kazakhstan, Eni took over the operatorship of the newly discovered Kashagan oilfield in the North Caspian Sea – the largest oil discovery of the past 30 years. Other major additions included reserves in Iran (South Pars and Baklal fields), in West Africa (notably Angola and Nigeria), in North Africa (mainly Libya and Algeria), and in the North Sea. By the end of 2002, Eni had already achieved its 2003 production targets. (Table 12.2 shows Eni's growth of production during 1997–2003.)

Eni also refocused its upstream portfolio. To exploit economies in infrastructure, Eni concentrated its exploration and production activities on a smaller number of countries, and to gain more effective control over its upstream investment it increasingly sought to be the operator of the oil and gas ventures in which it participated.

Vertical Integration in Natural Gas

If upstream (exploration and production) was to be the primary source of Eni's profit growth, natural gas was where the greatest opportunities lay. World demand for natural gas was expected to grow at twice the rate of that for oil. Moreover, Eni had the downstream market position essential for adding value to gas reserves. During 1999–2000, Eni embarked on two massive natural gas projects. The biggest and most ambitious, the Blue Stream project, involved a joint venture between Eni and the Russian gas giant, Gazprom, to invest over 2 billion euros in building a gas pipeline from Russia to Turkey that would pass under the Black Sea. Widely derided as "Blue Dream" for its technical and environmental complexities, by the end of 2002, Saipem had completed the two-line pipeline. The second major project was the Greenstream pipeline from Libya to Italy.

At the same time that Eni was investing heavily in natural gas reserves and long-distance pipelines, its downstream domestic business was under threat. In May 2000, the Italian government implemented the European directive on competition in natural gas. Eni's share of the Italian gas market was limited to 75% of primary transportation and 50% of the final market. In addition, primary transportation of natural gas and its marketing and local distribution had to be undertaken by separate companies. Eni's response was, first, to restructure its downstream gas company (Snam) and, second, to explore growth opportunities in other European gas markets.

Snam was split into two businesses. Its primary gas transmission network was vested in a new company, Snam Rete Gas, 40% of which was offered in an IPO in November 2001. Its marketing and supply business was merged into Eni to form the main component of Eni's Gas and Power division. The legislative decree of May 2000 also required the separation of gas storage from gas production and marketing. Hence, Eni's gas storage system in Italy was vested in a new regulated company, Stoccaggi Gas Italia, which was wholly owned by Eni. The new competitive structure of the Italian gas market also gave Eni the opportunity to sell natural gas to the new domestic competitors. In 2001 Eni signed seven multiyear contracts involving total sales of 15 million cubic meters each year. Eni also established EniPower SpA to develop combined-cycle power generation plants. Electricity production offered Eni a new market for its natural gas that did not count as part of Eni's share of the Italian gas market for regulatory purposes.

Outside of Italy, Eni acquired several gas distribution companies including major stakes in Spain's Union Fenosa Gas (50%), GVS in Germany (50%), and Galp Energia in Portugal (33%). Eni also entered the downstream gas markets of Hungary, Greece, and Croatia. In addition, the Blue Stream project would involve gas sales to Turkey of 8 billion cubic meters each year.

Figure 12.1 shows the vertical integrated structure of Eni's natural gas and its oil businesses while appendix 2 shows operating data over the period, including Eni's gas and power activities.

Refining and Marketing Strategy

Downstream, Eni pursued rationalization and cost reduction in both refining and distribution. Under Mincato's leadership refining capacity was reduced, and in 2002 Eni sold an equity stake in its refinery complex in Sicily. At the retail level, 1,900 service stations were closed between 1999 and 2001. Outside of Italy, Eni pursued selective expansion, acquiring service stations in France, Spain, Czech Republic, and Brazil while withdrawing from countries where Eni possessed neither the market share nor the supply infrastructure to permit profitability. Appendix 2 shows Eni's refining and marketing output and sales.

Rationalization in Chemicals

Under Mincato's leadership, Eni continued its strategy of reducing capital employed in petrochemicals. Eni's return on its chemicals investments was dismal and, given EniChem's limited presence outside Italy, it would always be at a competitive disadvantage to global players such as Exxon Mobil, Shell, BP, Dow, and Du Pont. In 2001, Eni agreed to sell its polyurethane business to Dow Chemical and it consolidated its olefins, aromatics, styrene, and elastomer production within a separate company, Polimeri Europa, in preparation for its sale.

FIGURE 12.1 Eni's vertical chains in oil and gas, 2003

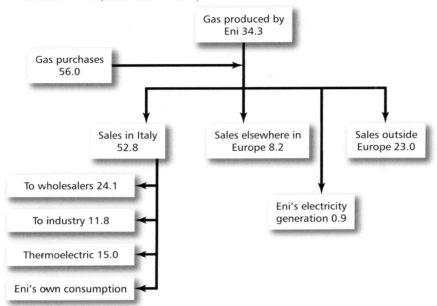

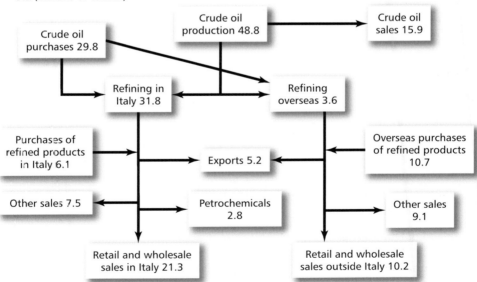

SOURCE: ENI FACT BOOK, 2003.

Internal Change

Some of Mincato's most important initiatives related to Eni's organization and management systems. While Bernabè had won the battle for Eni to be privatized as a single corporation and had initiated the merging of Agip into Eni, most of its principal businesses – Agip Petroli, Snam, Saipem, and Snamprogetti – were separate joint stock companies with their own boards of directors and a history of independence from corporate control. Between 2000 and 2003, Mincato transformed Eni from a holding company into a multidivisional corporation with the main operating companies reorganized into three divisions: exploration and production, gas and power, and refining and marketing. Appendix 3 describes Eni's main businesses.

Mincato recognized that reorganizing Eni as a single corporation would not cause Eni to act as a unified company. Hence, during 2000–3, Mincato introduced several initiatives to give Eni a clearer sense of identity and build a common culture. In May 2000, Eni announced major changes to its human resource policies. The "RES Program," introduced in June, 2001 inaugurated a new emphasis on human resources and their development:

> By means of the RES Program, Eni sets out to "capture" those who work in the group . . . trying to understand their abilities, their ambitions, how they can contribute to the success of the company, now and in the future. The approach is radically new: the policy of human resources management and development is centered on the person. Group employees will be considered not just as a collective entity (staff), but as individuals, each with his own merits and his own potential. This outlook means redefining methodologies, changing the model.[28]

The new HR policies included:

- Renewal of human resources through increased emphasis on professional and managerial development.
- Cost reduction through streamlining staff structures and developing greater flexibility in human resources management.
- Focusing Eni Corporation on its core functions of coordination and control and decentralizing human resource management and development.
- Internationalizing Eni's human resources.
- Establishing Eni Corporate University as a service company to provide human resource development.

In addition to increased internal dynamism, Eni also needed greater external recognition and clearer external identity – especially among international investors and host governments. In February, 2001 Mincato delivered a speech entitled "Eni's Way" in Houston Texas. The speech emphasized the role of technology and originality in Eni's development of new projects and its pursuit of new markets and reserves. During 2002, the term "Eni's Way" was adopted as the company's tag-line in a major campaign of corporate advertising. The meaning of "Eni's Way" remains vague, but the imagery used in the advertising suggested a commitment to technology, ethical and environmental responsibility, and a frontier spirit.

The Energy Sector in 2002

Since the first oil shock of the 1970s, the oil and gas industry had been transformed by the emergence of new competitors (especially the national oil companies), the development of international markets for trading oil and gas, the growing power of producer countries, the opening of more countries to inward direct investment, and the advent of new technologies. At the beginning of the 21st century, these forces of change continued to be sources of turbulence and unpredictability.

Industry Consolidation

Between 1998 and 2002, a wave of mergers and acquisitions resulted in the emergence of an elite group of "supermajors," comprising Exxon Mobil, BP, Royal Dutch Shell, ChevronTexaco, and TotalFinaElf (see table 12.3).

The stock markets responded favorably to most of these mergers and acquisitions – however, the extent to which they would generate real economic benefits was unclear. The primary motivation appeared to be the desire for growth – a particularly powerful motive when revenues and profits were depressed by low oil prices.[29] Once

TABLE 12.3 Major mergers and acquisitions in the oil and gas industry*

Leading oil and gas companies, 1995	Revenues in 1995 ($ bn)	Date merged	Leading oil and gas companies, 2002	Revenues in 2002 ($ bn)
Exxon	123.92		Exxon Mobil Corp.	182.47
Mobil	75.37	1999		
Royal Dutch Shell Group	109.87		Royal Dutch Shell Group	179.43
Enterprise Oil	1.18	2002		
British Petroleum	56.00		BP Amoco	178.72
Amoco	28.34	1998		
Arco	15.82	2000		
Chevron	31.32		ChevronTexaco	92.04
Texaco	35.55	2001		
Total	27.70		TotalFinaElf	96.94
PetroFina	n.a.	1999		
Elf Aquitaine	n.a.	2000		
Conoco	14.70		ConocoPhillips	58.38
Phillips Petroleum	13.37	2002		
Tosco	n.a.	2001		
Eni	35.92		Eni	46.33
Repsol	20.96		Repsol YPF	34.50
YPF	4.97	1999		

*Only includes acquisitions of companies with revenues exceeding $1 billion.

n.a. = not available.

TABLE 12.4 The majors' return on assets by business segment

	Exploration and production		Refining and marketing		Gas and power		Chemicals		Corporate and other	
	ROA 2000–2002	Share of total assets 2002	ROA 2000–2002	Share of total assets 2002	ROA 2000–2002	Share of total assets 2002	ROA 2000–2002	Share of total assets 2002	ROA 2000–2002	Share of total assets 2002
Exxon Mobil+	26.6%	48.8%	11.1%*	29.5%	n.a.	n.a.	5.8%	15.4%	(2.2%)	5.5%
Royal Dutch Shell	33.3%	36.1%	6.5%	37.8%	4.5%	12.1%	3.4%	11.6%	(5.0%)	3.3%
BP	19.8%	56.9%	10.7%	28.4%	32.2%	2.4%	1.8%	11.6%	(47.5%)	0.1%
ChevronTexaco	18.5%	66.6%	1.6%	28.6%	n.a.	n.a.	0.0%	1.7%	(146.8%)	3.3%
Eni	35.1%	58.9%	23.0%	9.2%	48.6%	21.3%	(15.4%)	4.9%	3.8%	0.4%
Total	25.0%	54.0%	16.3%	19.1%	n.a.	n.a.	7.3%	15.9%	16.4%	9.8%
Repsol	14.4%	41.0%	7.3%	32.3%	11.0%	6.8%	2.2%	7.4%	(1.8%)	12.5%

Notes: ROA is measured as segment operating earnings as a percentage of identifiable segment assets. Profit rates for Exxon Mobil and BP are return on capital employed (in the case of BP, profit is measured on a replacement cost basis). ChevronTexaco's return is net income as a percentage of net fixed capital. Eni's returns are operating income as a percentage of net fixed assets.

n.a. = not available.

*Includes gas and power.

the merger wave began, it was sustained by companies' fear of being relegated to "second division" status within the industry. The positive stock market reaction to the mergers was surprising given "study after study across [other] industries shows that only a small minority of mergers achieve measurable gains, such as higher productivity, profits, or share prices over the long term." An important motive was spreading risks through maintaining a portfolio of major upstream projects: "Only well-capitalized firms that are big enough to afford the time, money, and risk required to play in this poker game can hope to thrive. Because the stakes are so high, finding that 'elephant' of an oilfield has become the industry's obsession."[30]

Evidence of significant economies of scale associated with being a "supermajor" rather than a "major" is hard to find. Downstream there are substantial cost and market power advantages associated with market share in individual national and regional markets, but few scale economies at the global level. Upstream, size increases bargaining power, especially in dealing with host governments, but the main scale economies relate mainly to the utilization of infrastructure, which is specific to particular regions and hydrocarbon basins. The principal advantages of size in exploration and production may relate mainly to risk and learning. The huge costs and risks of developing oil and gas fields mean that there are risk spreading advantages from holding a large portfolio of projects. In terms of learning, the more projects of a similar type that a company undertakes (e.g. deep sea drilling in the North Sea, Gulf of Mexico, and offshore West Africa), the greater the scope for learning, innovation, and sharing of best practices.

The Economics of Exploration and Production

Upstream provides the primary source of profit for the energy industry. Indeed, the primary rationale for vertical integration was the companies' desire for secure market outlets for their production. In oil, such vertical integration is no longer essential – the development of international spot and futures markets for crude oil has all but eliminated the need for vertical integration. In the natural gas industry, however, difficulties in transporting natural gas (it requires either pipelines or expensive liquefaction facilities) mean that deriving value from gas reserves depends critically upon the availability of a nearby market or transportation infrastructure.

The superior profitability of upstream activities over refining and marketing and chemicals is evident in the sectoral financial performance of the majors (see table 12.4). Although upstream activities accounted for only one-fifth of revenues for large oil firms, they contributed over two-thirds of overall profits in 2002. The reasons for the disparity between upstream and downstream profit rates are not immediately obvious. Oil and gas are commodities supplied by many competing companies and in a global industry where production capacity typically exceeds demand. For most primary raw materials, including metal ores, coal, building materials, or agricultural products, these conditions typically result in miserable rates of profit. The world oil market differs in the existence of an effective cartel. Although the Organization of Petroleum Exporting Countries (OPEC) accounted for only 46% of world oil production in 2001, OPEC's commitment to maintaining price stability through production quotas for its individual member countries has had an important influence on oil prices since the early 1970s. When OPEC's discipline over its members' oil production disintegrates, prices drop – sometimes catastrophically. In the summer of 1986 and at the end of 1998, crude oil prices fell below $10 a barrel. Since summer

TABLE 12.5 Finding and development costs by company, 1998–2002

	$/barrel of oil equivalent
TotalFinaElf	4.20
BP	4.20
Exxon Mobil	4.40
Repsol YPF	4.50
ChevronTexaco	4.80
Royal Dutch/Shell	5.60
Eni	6.30
Occidental	6.70
Burlington	6.90
ConocoPhillips	7.20
Unocal	8.70
Anadarko	9.60

SOURCE: ENI, "UPSTREAM PERFORMANCE: ENI VERSUS BENCHMARK GROUP", 2003.

TABLE 12.6 US energy companies finding costs by region, 1993–2000 (dollars/barrel of oil equivalent)

	US onshore	US offshore	Canada	OECD Europe	Africa	Middle East	Other, Eastern hemisphere	Other, Western hemisphere	World wide
1993–1995	4.53	4.58	6.35	5.25	3.32	3.23	5.51	2.66	4.65
1998–2000	5.21	10.52	7.18	7.85	2.93	5.92	7.88	4.59	6.12
2001–2003	9.16	10.24	12.26	9.86	5.79	6.22	4.05	3.98	7.35

SOURCE: ENERGY INFORMATION AGENCY, US DEPARTMENT OF ENERGY.

1999, OPEC discipline together with disruptions to supplies in several key production areas has resulted in crude oil prices remaining, almost continuously, above $20 a barrel.

So long as crude oil prices remain at or above the mid-teens, most of the majors earn comfortable upstream profits. However, the extent of each company's profitability depends critically upon its costs. These vary between the companies (see table 12.5) and across geographical locations (see table 12.6). Eni's above average finding costs were primarily a result of the high cost of upstream activities in Italy.

Finding and development cost per barrel is the outcome of a chain of activities. Exploration begins with acquiring the legal rights to begin prospecting for reserves (typically allocated through a competitive bidding process). Geological and seismic analysis is then used to identify any "traps" (reservoirs of underground hydrocarbons). Drilling exploratory wells is extremely costly: hence, companies have invested heavily in new technologies to help identify potentially profitable traps prior to any drilling. However, until exploratory drilling confirms the presence of hydrocarbons, all prior analysis is scientifically informed guesswork. The main investment costs are incurred in bringing proven oil reserves into production through the construction and operation of drilling rigs, storage and loading facilities, and other infrastructure. As exploration has been forced into increasingly inhospitable locations – offshore locations in particular – the capital costs of exploration and production (E&P) have increased substantially. For natural gas fields, development costs are especially great due to the need for either pipelines or liquefaction plants. Yet, despite the industry's move to offshore locations, new technologies – 3D seismic analysis, directional drilling, lightweight platforms, semi-submersibles, enhanced recovery, reservoir modeling, to mention but a few – resulted in declining reserve replacement costs during most of the 1980s and 1990s.

New technology was not the only source of upstream cost reduction in E&P. The oil and gas companies outsourced more and more of their exploration and production activities. Drilling, seismic surveys, rig design, platform construction, and oilfield maintenance are increasingly undertaken by oilfield service companies. As these companies developed proprietary technologies, deepened their experience, and grew through mergers and acquisitions, so sector leaders such as Schlumberger, Baker Hughes, Halliburton, Diamond Offshore Drilling, Weatherford International, and Saipem emerged as powerful players within the international petroleum industry. Increasingly their status shifted from that of contractors to that of risk-bearing partners of the oil and gas majors.

The political changes of the 1990s greatly expanded upstream opportunities for the petroleum majors. The collapse of the Soviet Union and the global trend to economic liberalization offered access to oil and gas reserves previously reserved for national oil companies. During the 1990s, China and the former Soviet Union were major targets of attention. The immense, undeveloped, oil and gas reserves of the Caspian Sea were especially attractive to western oil companies. Among the leading OPEC members, Saudi Arabia, Venezuela, and Iran opened their doors to investment. In May 2001 Saudi Arabia welcomed eight major petroleum companies led by Exxon Mobil to build a $25 billion natural gas infrastructure in an effort to free up more oil for export. Venezuela auctioned 35-year leases to explore, pump, and sell natural gas.

Over time, major discoveries create new oil producing nations (Norway, Angola, and Colombia) while other countries gradually exhaust their reserves (USA, UK). In the future, the league table of leading producers will shift substantially. While Saudi Arabia, Iraq, Iran, Azerbaijan, Kazakhstan, and Venezuela have over 60 years of reserves at current rates of production, USA, Canada, Norway, UK, and Indonesia have 10 or fewer (see table 12.7).

The attractive rates of return earned in the upstream sector have meant that capital investment by the integrated majors has become increasingly focused on E&P. During 1998–2001, the leading majors invested between three and four times as much upstream as downstream (see table 12.8).

Refining and Marketing

In oil, downstream businesses include refining and the wholesale and retail marketing and distribution of refined oil products. The most important refined product is gasoline; other important products include diesel fuel, aviation fuel, heating oil, liquefied petroleum gas (LPG), bitumen, and petrochemical feedstocks (e.g, naphtha). For almost all the majors, profitability of downstream activities was dismal. Table 12.9 compares upstream and downstream profitability for US petroleum companies (see table 12.4 for the sectoral profitability of the individual majors). In both North America and Europe, the downstream sector was subject to intense competitive pressure. Low demand growth (due mainly to increased energy efficiency and competition from natural gas), combined with heavy investment in catalytic cracking

TABLE 12.7 Oil and gas production and reserves by country, 1991 and 2001

	Oil production (thousands of barrels/day)		Gas production (billions of cubic meters)		Oil reserves (billions of barrels)	Gas reserves (trillions cu. meters)
	2001	1991	2001	1991	2001	2001
Saudi Arabia	8,768	8,820	54	35	261.8	6.2
USA	7,717	9,076	555	510	30.4	5.0
Russia	7,056	9,326	542	600	48.6	47.6
Iran	3,688	3,500	61	26	89.7	23.0
Mexico	3,560	3,126	35	28	26.9	0.8
Venezuela	3,418	2,501	29	22	77.7	4.2
Norway	3,414	1,923	58	27	9.4	1.3
China	3,308	2,828	30	15	24.0	1.4
Canada	2,763	1,980	172	105	6.6	1.7
UK	2,503	1,919	106	51	4.9	0.7
UAE	2,422	2,639	41	24	97.8	6.0
Iraq	2,414	279	–	–	112.5	3.1
Kuwait	2,142	185	10	1	96.5	1.5
Nigeria	2,103	1,890	13	4	24.0	3.5
Algeria	1,563	1,351	78	53	9.2	4.5

SOURCE: BP STATISTICAL REVIEW OF WORLD ENERGY, 2001.

TABLE 12.8 Capital investment by business sector among the majors, 1998–2002

	Av. annual capital expenditure ($, million)	Upstream (%)	Downstream (%)	Chemicals (%)	Other (%)
Exxon Mobil	13,255	66.1	19.8	11.5	1.4
Royal Dutch/Shell	15,690	62.1	25.0	8.8	3.5
BP	19,711	50.6	25.1	10.7	14.6*
TotalFinaElf	9,071	66.4	13.5	16.8	3.3
ChevronTexaco	11,645	66.5	15.5	2.9	15.2
Eni	7,179	63.1	25.3	5.0	6.5

* "Other" includes acquisition expenditures.

SOURCE: COMPANY ANNUAL REPORTS.

and increased investment in refineries by the national oil companies, resulted in serious excess capacity in refining. At the marketing level, the chief problem was an excessive number of retail outlets. While the majors sought to consolidate their market position through asset exchanges, joint ventures, and outright mergers, their attempts to reduce price competition in downstream markets were thwarted by exit barriers and new

TABLE 12.9 Return on investment by line of business for US petroleum companies, 1980–99

	1980–4	1985–9	1990–4	1995–9	2000–3
US oil and gas production	15.4%	4.0%	5.8%	10.1%	14.4%
US refining and marketing	5.1%	8.0%	2.7%	5.7%	7.9%
Foreign oil and gas production	19.3%	12.2%	9.1%	12.4%	12.9%
Foreign refining and marketing	10.4%	6.8%	10.1%	7.0%	6.2%
Coal	5.5%	4.7%	2.9%	6.1%	3.7%

Note: Return on investment is measured as net income as a percentage of invested capital.

SOURCE: ENERGY INFORMATION ADMINISTRATION, US DEPARTMENT OF ENERGY

entry. Downstream markets in Europe were particularly depressed – demand had been stagnant for five years while excess capacity has remained stubbornly high. European refining margins fell below $2 a barrel in 2001, and continued to fall during 2002.

As refining capacity grew in the Middle East, European downstream markets came under increasing competitive pressure. At the retail level, the entry of supermarket chains into retail gasoline distribution was a key problem for the petroleum majors in several European countries (France and the UK especially). The majors responded by diversifying their retail activities. Increasingly, service stations added restaurants and convenience stores to their dispensing of gasoline.

Downstream Gas and Power

Among the petroleum majors, Eni was unusual in being established on natural gas rather than oil. For most of the majors, oil had been their dominant interest and, as a result, few had pursued the same strategy of vertical integration in gas that they had in oil. As the result, in most countries the gas chain was more fragmented than the oil chain, with exploration and production undertaken by the petroleum companies, and distribution traditionally undertaken by state-owned or state-regulated utilities. As demand for natural gas increased during the 1980s and 1990s, the petroleum majors reoriented their upstream activities towards gas. However, gas reserves were valueless unless they could be brought to market. Hence all the majors developed interests in the transportation and downstream distribution of gas. Deregulation of downstream gas markets and privatization of publicly owned gas utilities created the opportunities that the petroleum majors needed to increase their presence in gas marketing and distribution. Similar deregulation in electricity generation and marketing produced further opportunities for the majors – not only could they enter the electricity business directly, they could also seek to supply natural gas to the new independent power producers.

However, downstream gas and power typically did not offer rates of return comparable with their upstream businesses. The newly liberalized gas and electricity markets attracted entrants from a number of different sectors and were fiercely competitive. Fierce competition coupled with overinvestment could decimate profitability. During 2002, wholesale prices for electricity plunged in the US and UK, forcing a number of power producers into acute financial difficulty.

Chemicals

The petrochemical sector displayed many of the same structural features as oil refining: capital-intensive processes producing commodity products, many competitors, and a continual tendency for excess capacity (much of it resulting from investments in the Far East and in the oil-producing countries) to drive down prices and margins. In their approach to chemicals, the petroleum majors fell into two groups. Some, like Eni, viewed chemicals as a fundamentally unattractive industry and believed that chemical plants were better run by chemical companies. Others (including Exxon, Shell, and Total) viewed chemicals as part of their core business and considered that vertical integration between refining and petrochemicals offered them a cost advantage.

During the 1990s, all the majors repositioned and restructured their chemical businesses. The two trends were: first, withdrawal from fertilizers, agricultural chemicals, and many specialty chemicals in order to concentrate on bulk petrochemicals; second, within bulk petrochemicals, the companies engaged in a series of asset swaps and joint ventures in order to build positions of leadership within specific product categories. Such leadership was founded on two types of advantage: economies of scale and technological advantages through product or process innovations. By 2002, even the companies with the heaviest commitments to petrochemicals (Exxon, Shell, BP, and TotalFinaElf) were reducing their investments in chemicals as sluggish demand and continued new investment by Asian and Middle Eastern producers depressed profitability.

Eni in 2003

2003 was another year of sustained progress: operating income and net income were higher than 2002 and Eni comfortably exceeded its targets for oil and gas production and cost cutting.

Mincato was content that Eni had realized most of the goals that he had envisaged on becoming chief executive at the end of 1998. Eni was independent and financially and operationally robust. Its strong stock market performance would make it a difficult acquisition target, even without the protection of the Italian government's "golden share." Most important, Eni had a well-defined strategy and a clear identity as a company. Shorn of its various diversified businesses, Eni was purely an energy company. Within the industry, Eni had established a unique strategic position that fitted both its heritage and its capabilities. Through heavy capital investment in exploration and production and a series of acquisitions, Eni had greatly expanded its upstream position. Through its ambitious pipeline schemes and entry into the gas markets of Portugal, Spain, and Germany, Eni had built on its dominant position in the Italian gas market to create one of the world's biggest vertically integrated natural gas businesses. By resisting the trend towards outsourcing engineering and oilfield service requirements, Eni had built a powerful set of technical capabilities.

Yet, for all Eni's solid achievement and increasing respect from both its energy industry peers and investment analysts, Mincato believed that the next four years would be critical for Eni. After spending its first half century playing catch-up with leading oil majors, Eni had emerged as one of the most profitable and rapidly growing of the world's leading energy companies. (Table 12.4 shows financial performance of the leading majors.) However, increasing profits and creating value for shareholders was likely to be more difficult in the future than in the past. By 2003, Eni had divested most of its non-core businesses and eliminated most of the inefficiencies that it had inherited from its state-owned past. Increasing profits in the future would require pursuing profitable growth opportunities, more effective exploitation of existing competitive advantage, and building new sources of competitive advantage.

In many respects, Eni was well positioned with regard to the principal trends affecting the world's energy sector. Eni's traditional strength in gas had given it a vertically integrated presence that no other petroleum company could match. Italy's geographical position in terms of its proximity both to the huge gas reserves of North Africa, and to the markets of Europe, offered Eni a unique opportunity to link the two – particularly with its in-house engineering and construction capabilities.

But fulfilling Eni's potential would require developing the responsiveness and coordination that it needed to combine technology, physical assets, expertise, and human ingenuity to exploit the opportunities constantly emerging in the world's fast-changing energy markets. At the forefront of Mincato's mind were the internal challenges that Eni would have to overcome in order to successfully execute its strategy. Although major changes had taken place in organization (notably the creation of a divisionalized structure) and human resource management, further internal change was essential. The most obvious challenge was that of internationalization. Although Eni was internationally diversified upstream and in engineering and services, downstream – both in oil products and gas – Eni was heavily dependent on the Italian market. Overall, Italy accounted for almost half of Eni's sales and assets (see table 12.10). Internationalization was not just about increasing investment outside of Italy. The greatest challenges lay in internationalizing Eni's culture and personnel – including senior management ranks, where non-Italians and extensive overseas management experience were both scarce.

The second internal challenge was that of integration. Eni's large downstream gas business offered a market for its upstream gas production and its internal engineering and construction capabilities provided the means to link the two. Eni's ability to pursue vertical integration in gas represented a significant source of competitive advantage for the company. However, to realize this potential required effective collaboration between Eni's different divisions and subsidiaries. Although Mincato had created a more integrated divisional corporation, effective coordination required Eni's independently minded businesses to break down organizational barriers and share information, know-how, and opportunities.

Other challenges were likely to emerge from the external environment. The most troubling of these was whether Eni could find sufficient investment opportunities to achieve its growth targets without undermining its profitability. Eni had achieved its growth by a combination of organic growth and selective acquisitions. Organic growth was inevitably incremental – the key to maintaining upstream profitability was to develop new E&P activities in locations where Eni had an existing infrastructure. More rapid growth could be achieved through acquisition, but here Mincato was aware that reckless acquisition would cause earnings dilution.

The second external challenge related to the investment community's apparent lack of appreciation for Eni's solid operational and financial performance. Mincato and Chief Financial Officer Marco Mangiagalli had cultivated sound relationships with shareholders and investment analysts. Yet, they were continually dismayed by the stock market's lack of appreciation for Eni's investment qualities. Eni's valuation ratios remained considerably lower than those of its peers in the international petroleum industry (see table 12.11). Weakness in Eni's market valuation constrained

TABLE 12.10 Eni's sales and assets by geographic area ($, millions)

Revenues by area	1995	1996	1997	1998	1999	2000	2001	2002	2003
Italy	16,194.3	15,368.9	17,514.5	16,196.4	17,631.7	29,419.9	30,793.5	24,952.3	28,858
Other European Union	8,516.4	8,368.1	10,066.0	9,221.5	11,429.2	22,461.0	24,197.5	25,296.2	11,315
Other Europe	5,085.8	4,552.2	5,248.0	4,552.5	5,381.4	10,449.1	12,680.8	13,801.0	4,634
Africa	696.4	800.0	1,026.4	1,040.4	1,402.1	2,254.3	2,433.0	2,598.3	6,627
Americas	1,693.9	1,804.8	2,052.8	2,181.2	2,950.3	6,530.3	6,885.0	5,575.1	3,145
Asia	979.8	1,117.1	1,722.1	1,431.4	1,682.3	3,202.4	2,175.2	3,307.1	3,674

Assets by area	1995	1996	1997	1998	1999	2000	2001	2002	2003
Italy	41,994.0	43,713.0	34,750.1	19,383.0	20,767.6	26,573.6	26,242.2	25,714.6	34,459
Other European Union	14,036.0	15,592.5	14,609.9	10,422.4	14,359.0	20,688.3	30,626.1	29,729.5	8,427
Other Europe	7,573.0	8,901.3	6,754.1	4,231.4	5,256.8	7,606.1	11,458.7	11,187.0	5,045
Africa	5,755.0	5,985.5	6,017.0	4,209.9	5,777.9	7,198.1	9,657.4	9,564.9	13,238
Americas	708.0	705.7	1,838.9	1,034.1	2,170.6	4,176.4	5,080.4	3,598.6	3,680
Asia	–	–	–	930.9	1,149.0	1,699.1	4,417.4	4,597.9	6,048

SOURCE: ENI ANNUAL REPORTS.

TABLE 12.11 Valuation multiples for petroleum majors (9 May 2003)

	Price/earnings ratio	Price/book ratio	Price/sales ratio	Price/cash flow
Exxon Mobil Corp.	15.04	3.17	1 15	11.94
British Petroleum plc	15.08	2.13	0.72	8.58
ChevronTexaco Corp.	28.29	2.28	0.70	11.30
TotalFinaElf S.A.	17.25	2.94	1.02	n.a.
Royal Dutch Petroleum Co.	12.04	2.22	0.65	9.59
Eni SpA	9.55	2.45	1.34	n.a.
Repsol YPF, S.A.	31.40	1.51	0.53	5.40
ConocoPhillips	30.58	1.17	0.50	17.53
Industry average	15.13	2.37	0.94	7.70

SOURCE: HOOVER'S ONLINE.

Eni's ability to make acquisitions and put pressure on management to reallocate cash flows from capital investment to share repurchases.

The third external challenge was the uncertain outlook for the upstream sector. During recent years, upstream had accounted for the majority of Eni's operating profit and the attractiveness of the upstream had resulted in E&P accounting for an ever-growing proportion of Eni's capital expenditure. However, upstream returns were volatile; they depended critically upon the price of crude oil. When crude oil prices were low, as in 1998 and during the first half of 2002 (see figure 12.2), Eni's upstream profitability declined sharply. Could Eni continue to rely on the upstream sector as the fount of its profitability? If OPEC discipline was to break down, if major expansion occurred in production from the former Soviet Union, or if Iraq returned as a major supplier to the world market, then the current balance between supply and demand

FIGURE 12.2 Average world spot price of crude oil, 1997–2003

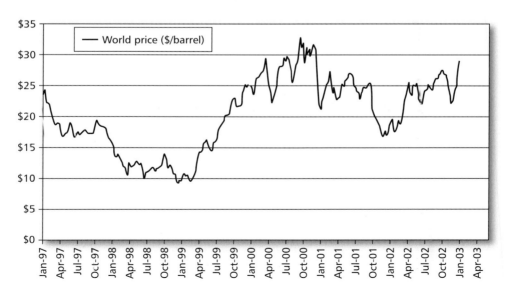

might tilt drastically towards excess supply. In a low oil price environment, Eni would be unfavorably positioned – not just in relation to some of the other majors, but also to some of the national oil companies with their massive reserves and low production costs.

Appendix 1

TABLE 12.A1 Eni SpA: selected financial data, 1997–2003

Income statement In millions of US$	1997	1998	1999	2000	2001	2002	2003
Revenue	34,323	33,177	31,225	45,854	44,368	51,379	59,322
Cost of goods sold	21,854	21,730	20,247	29,518	28,330	33,440	39,132
Gross profit	12,469	11,447	10,978	16,336	16,038	17,939	20,190
Gross profit margin	36.3%	34.5%	35.2%	35.6%	36.1%	34.9%	34.0%
SG&A expense	3,339	3,415	2,801	2,615	2,538	3,253	3,584
Depreciation and amortization	3,955	4,423	3,617	3,608	4,247	5,771	5,831
Operating income	5,175	3,609	4,560	10,113	9,253	8,915	10,774
Operating margin	15.1%	10.9%	14.6%	22.1%	20.9%	17.4%	18.2%
Nonoperating income	739	1,634	1,561	91	1,635	45	19
Nonoperating expenses	250	48	502	481	423	206	7
Income before taxes	5,447	4,589	5,087	9,723	10,465	8,664	10,58?
Income taxes	2,467	1,698	2,068	4,070	3,142	3,279	3,6??
Net income after taxes	2,980	2,891	3,019	5,653	7,324	4,816	6,32?
Net profit margin	8.4%	8.2%	9.2%	11.9%	15.6%	9.6%	0.0?%
ROACE	12.2%	10.7%	12.5%	21.5%	23.9%	13.7%	15.?%

Balance sheet	Dec 97	Dec 98	Dec 99	Dec 00	Dec 01	Dec 02	Dec 0?
Cash	1,736	912	1,220	1,168	1,162	3,423	4,11?3
Net receivables	11,067	10,733	10,838	12,566	12,219	14,186	17,C?3
Inventories	2,878	2,859	2,644	2,929	2,504	3,355	4,0?1
Other current assets	3,165	1,941	2,316	2,070	1,620	1,868	2,2?4
Total current assets	18,846	16,445	17,019	18,733	17,505	22,832	27,??1
Net fixed assets	22,593	24,434	23,236	25,157	29,653	35,327	42,??3
Other noncurrent assets	7,441	7,512	6,265	9,024	8,684	10,840	13,0?4
Total assets	48,880	48,391	46,520	52,914	55,842	69,000	82,8?8
Accounts payable	3,824	4,110	4,171	4,550	4,427	5,806	6,?75
Short-term debt	8,673	5,793	4,797	5,015	4,656	8,273	?,?39
Other current liabilities	6,413	6,294	6,292	9,440	7,341	8,560	1C,?85
Total current liabilities	18,910	16,197	15,260	19,005	16,424	22,639	2?,?99
Long-term debt	5,853	5,288	4,821	4,803	5,415	6,868	3,?51
Other noncurrent liabilities	4,443	4,835	4,768	6,506	8,021	9,766	1?,734
Total liabilities	32,107	29,478	27,993	30,314	29,860	39,274	4?,783
Minority interest	809	1,107	1,117	1,570	1,519	2,196	2,638
Total shareholders' equity	16,773	18,913	18,527	22,600	25,982	27,530	?5,714

Cash flow statement	1997	1998	1999	2000	2001	2002	2?03
Net operating cash flow	7,135	8,035	8,306	9,935	7,251	11,091	1?,257

Appendix 2

TABLE 12.A2 Eni's operating performance, 1993–2003

	Units	1993	1994	1995	1996	1997	1998	1999	2000	2001	2002	2003
Exploration and production												
Hydrocarbon production	boe/d (×10³)	901	941	982	984	1.021	1.038	1.064	1.187	1.369	1.472	1.562
Hydrocarbon reserves	boe (×10⁶)	4.175	4.224	4.318	4.675	5.073	5.255	5.534	6.008	6.929	7.030	7.272
Reserve life index	years	12.8	12.4	11.9	13.1	13.6	13.4	14.0	14.0	13.7	13.2	12.7
Gas and power												
Primary distribution natural gas sales in Italy	cm (×10⁹)	48.65	47.43	52.55	53.23	53.10	55.64	60.19	59.92	58.89	52.56	52.80
Primary distribution natural gas sales in Europe destined to Italy	cm (×10⁹)					0.04	0.05	0.05	1.30	3.10	7.70	9.30
Sales of natural gas in secondary distribution outside Italy	cm (×10⁹)				2.80	2.79	2.73	2.67	3.48	3.91	3.79	4.44
Natural gas volumes transported on behalf of third parties	cm (×10⁹)	4.93	5.34	6.01	6.64	8.07	9.97	11.29	14.70	16.76		
Electricity production sold	GWh								4,766	4,987	5,004	5,550
Refining and marketing												
Production available from processing	ton (×10⁶)	33.7	40.5	38.1	37.8	36.4	40.1	38.3	38.9	37.8	35.6	33.5
Refining capacity utilization rate of owned refineries	%	90	89	86	87	94	103	96	99	97	99	100
Sales	ton (×10⁶)	53.1	52.3	51.9	51.4	51.6	54.2	51.8	53.5	53.2	52.0	49.9
Service stations	units	13,705	13,699	13,574	13,150	12,756	12,984	12,489	12,085	11,707	10,762	10,647
Average throughput per service station	l/year (×10⁶)	1.399	1.402	1.431	1.448	1.463	1.512	1.543	1.555	1.621	1.674	1.771
Oilfield services and engineering												
Orders acquired	mil euro	1,586	2,710	2,616	2,937	3,849	3,242	2,588	4,709	3,716	7,852	5,876
Orders backlog at 12/31	mil euro	2,598	3,471	4,035	4,350	5,163	4,931	4,438	6,638	6,937	10,065	9,405
Employees	units	108,556	91,544	86,422	83,424	80,178	78,906	72,023	69,969	72,405	80,655	76,521

SOURCE: ENI FACT BOOKS.

Appendix 3
Eni's Business Operations, 2003

Eni is an integrated energy company operating in the oil, natural gas, electricity generation, petrochemicals, engineering, and oilfield services through its divisions or affiliated companies. Figure 12.A1 shows the divisional structure.

FIGURE 12.A1 Eni's organizational structure

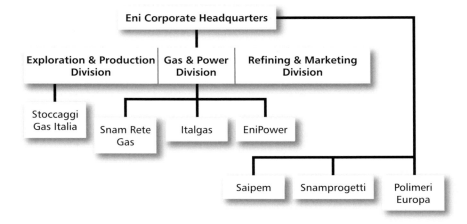

Exploration and Production

Eni operates in exploration and production of oil and natural gas in Italy, North Africa, West Africa, the North Sea and the Gulf of Mexico. It also operates in areas with great development potential such as Latin America, Australia, the Middle and Far East and the Caspian Sea.

Eni intends to maintain a strong production growth in the near future leveraging on internal development and targeting over 1.8 million boe/day in 2006 (a yearly average increase of approximately 6%). Eni's proved reserves reached over 7 billion boe in 2003.

Eni is pursuing a program for the rationalization of its portfolio of assets aimed at concentrating its activities in areas with significant growth potential where Eni is operator: in 2002 Eni sold 16 interests in fields in the North Sea, Italy, and Qatar, as well as exploration permits and other assets; Eni also acquired interests in operated or partially held assets in Kazakhstan, the United Kingdom, Norway, and Australia.

The importance of the Kashagan oilfield discovery in the Kazakh offshore of the Caspian Sea was confirmed by the appraisal activities performed and still underway in the area. The field's recoverable reserves, calculated according to the most recent estimates as 7–9 billion barrels, reaching 13 billion by employing the gas reinjection techniques, make Kashagan the most relevant discovery of the past 30 years.

E&P Strategies
Keep strong production growth rates
Rationalize and optimize asset portfolio
Select exploration areas
Intensify actions for efficiency improvement

Gas and Power

Gas Eni operates in natural gas supply, transmission, distribution, and sale. In 2002, sales of natural gas totaled 52.6 billion cubic meters in Italy, 8.2 billion cubic meters in Europe, and 3.8 billion cubic meters in secondary distribution outside Italy.

With the purchase in joint venture with German company EnBW of 97.81% of GVS, one of the largest regional operators in natural gas in Germany (where it transports and sells approximately 7 billion cubic meters of gas per year), Eni enters a large natural gas market and consolidates its European leadership in gas and power.

The agreement underway for the purchase of a 50% interest in Spanish natural gas company Unión Fenosa Gas, with an investment of euro 440 million, is an important step in Eni's strategy of international expansion of gas activities. . . .

Within its program of development of electricity generation capacity at Eni's industrial sites, work started for the construction of a new combined-cycle power plant at Ferrera Erbognone (Pavia) . . . and for the upgrade of the Ravenna power plant.

Gas and Power Strategies

Develop natural gas sales in Europe
Maintain market shares in Italy at the levels set by new laws leveraging on the gas power
Implement significant marketing actions
Obtain a significant competitive positioning in electricity generation by building new
    power stations

Refining and Marketing

Eni operates in refining and the sale of refined products mainly in Italy, Europe, and Latin America. In distribution, with its Agip and IP brands, Eni is market leader in Italy. In 2002, Eni's sales of refined products amounted to 52 million tonnes, of which 33 million tonnes was in Italy.

Eni is implementing a rebalancing of its retail distribution activities in Italy and outside Italy and will continue the upgrading of its network in Italy by selling and closing marginal service stations and developing the stronger part of its network (service stations with high throughput and high non-oil potential) and its non-oil retail activities. Eni's objective is to reach European standards in terms of average throughput, services to customers, and automation. Outside Italy, Eni intends to strengthen its position in selected areas in Europe where it can obtain logistical and operating synergies and exploit its well-known brand name. Eni also intends to increase the flexibility of its refining system [and] will intensify its efforts for efficiency improvements. . . .

Refining and Marketing Strategies

Continue the upgrading of the Italian distribution network and develop in selected areas
    outside
Increase refining complexity
Intensify actions for efficiency improvement

Oilfield Services and Engineering

Eni operates in oilfield services and engineering through Saipem and Snamprogetti. Saipem, a company listed on the Italian Stock Exchange (Eni's interest 43%), operates in oilfield services and is a world leader in the laying of underwater pipelines and the installation of offshore platforms, thanks to exclusive state-of-the-art technology and a world-class fleet of vessels, which has been upgraded with an investment plan amounting to over 1 billion euros, started in 1997. In the engineering and contracting area, Snamprogetti is one of the major international operators in the area of plants for hydrocarbon production, refining complexes, terminals for natural gas treatment, fertilizer and petrochemical plants, power stations, pipeline transport systems and infrastructure.

Major Projects

1 *Deep water.* Thanks to the experience gained in different areas of the world and the competence of its personnel, Eni has developed innovative technologies and methods for all phases of the activity: from exploration to drilling and production. Eni operates in several exploration projects in deep waters (more than 450 meters) and ultra-deep waters (more than 1,500 meters), including offshore Nigeria, Angola, Congo, and Gabon. Ultra-deep water offshore activities are also underway in the Gulf of Mexico and off the coast of Brazil.

2 *Transmed.* This 2,200 km gasline links Italy to one of the world's biggest natural gas reservoirs, located in the Algerian desert. Construction of the first pipeline was completed in 1983. In 1997, a second pipeline was laid.

3 *Blue Stream.* The Blue Stream is undoubtedly one of the most challenging projects of its type ever attempted because of the difficulties in terms of design, construction, organization, and logistics. The 1,250 km gasline links the gas distribution network of the Krasnodar region in southern Russia to the central Turkish grid at Ankara. Supplies of natural gas will start in 2003 and continue up to 2025, peaking at 16 billion cubic meters a year.

4 *Karachaganak project.* Eni works with British Gas to produce oil, gas, and condensates in Karachaganak field in the northwestern region of Kazakhstan. The project involves over 70 wells, collection and distribution networks, and constructing pipelines to connect Caspian Pipeline Consortium. Eni's production share will peak at around 72,000 barrels per day in 2009.

Source: "Eni SpA: Operations and Strategies" (www.eni.it).

Appendix 4

TABLE 12.A3 The world's top 20 petroleum companies, 2000

PIW Index*	Company	Ownership	Reserves Liquids (mil. BBL)	Reserves Gas (BFC)	Output Liquids (mil. BBL)	Output Gas (BFC)	Refinery capacity (thous. B/D)	Product sales (thous. B/D)
1. 100.0	Saudi Aramco	State	259,200	213,300	8,044	3,302	1,992	2,650
2. 98.8	Exxon Mobil	Public	11,260	56,796	2,444	11,378	6,400	8,887
2. 98.8	FDVSA	State	76,852	146,719	2,950	4,000	3,096	2,500
4. 98.0	NIOC	State	87,993	816,882	3,620	5,144	1,534	1,342
5. 97.4	Royal Dutch Shell	Public	9,775	58,541	2,268	8,218	3,212	6,795
5. 92.1	British Petroleum	Public	7,572	35,526	2,061	6,067	2,801	5,002
7. 91.8	Pemex	State	28,400	30,005	3,343	4,791	1,528	1,650
8. 85.4	Pertamina	State	7,860	118,702	973	6,300	1,050	1,190
9. 84.5	TotalFinaElf	Public	6,869	13,385	1,468	3,175	2,586	3,168
10. 81.6	KFC	State	96,500	52,700	2,025	936	1,075	1,165
11. 80.2	Sonatrach	State	8,830	136,303	1,480	7,587	485	750
12. 79.9	PetroChina	State**	10,999	24,603	2,124	674	2,066	1,367
13 77.8	Petrobras	State	8,100	10,663	1,191	1,235	1,953	1,818
14 77.0	Chevron	Public	4,784	9,056	1,127	2,513	1,524	2,384
15 73.2	Texaco	Public	3,480	8,108	885	1,999	1,417	3,221
16. 70.3	Adnoc	State	50,710	196,100	1,240	3,185	234	455
17. 67.1	Eni	Public	3,137	13,665	666	2,342	824	940
18. 63.0	Repsol YPF	Public	2,150	14,310	451	1,298	1,206	920
19. 62.7	INOC	State	112,500	109,800	2,528	320	348	520
20. 59.5	Libya NOC	State	23,600	46,243	1,211	600	380	400
20. 59.5	Petronas	State	2,952	64,469	636	5,097	290	425
	Totals		823,523	2,175,876	42,735	80,161	36,001	47,549

* Petroleum Intelligence Weekly's ranking based on reserves, output, capacity, and sales: ** IPO or ADR listed on NYSE April 2000 89% of shares held by state-owned parent company; BBL = barrels; BCF = billion cubic feet: B/D = barrels per day.

SOURCE: STANDARD AND POORS, OIL AND GAS: PRODUCTION AND MARKETING INDUSTRY SURVEY

Notes

1 After Exxon Mobil, Royal Dutch Shell, BP, TotalFinaElf, ChevronTexaco, and ConocoPhillips.

2 Fred Kapner, "Chief keeps it 'orderly' at Eni," FT.com, 30 January 2003.

3 We refer throughout the case to "Eni." For most of its history as a state-owned enterprise, the company's full name was Ente Nazionale Idrocarburi, but was known by its acronym, ENI. On becoming a joint stock company, its name was changed to ENI SpA. Under Mr Mincato's leadership the acronym ENI was replaced by the simple word Eni.

4 In common with other European governments, Italy recognized the growing strategic importance of oil and wished to avoid dependence on foreign-owned multinationals for its fuel supplies. The British government had purchased a controlling interest in BP in 1914 and France had established the Compagnie Française des Pétroles (Total) in 1924.

5 Don Votaw, *The Six-Legged Dog: Mattei and ENI – A Study in Power*, University of California Press, Berkeley, CA, 1964, p. 15.

6 Daniel Yergin, *The Prize*, Simon & Schuster, New York, 1992, p. 502.

7 www.Eni.it/english/panorama/storia/storia.html.

8 Don Votaw, *The Six-Legged Dog*, op. cit., p. 23.

9 Ibid.

10 Section sourced from "L'Eni di Fronte a un Bivio," Eni SpA, 2002.

11 Don Votaw, *The Six-Legged Dog*, op. cit., p. 71.

12 "L'Eni di Fronte a un Bivio," Eni SpA, 2002, p. 5.

13 *Franco Bernabè at Eni*, Harvard Business School Case No. 9-498-034, April 7, 1998.

14 Chairman Gabriele Cagliari later committed suicide in prison.

15 "L'Eni di Fronte a un Bivio," Eni SpA, 2002, p. 11.

16 "Eni savors the taste of freedom," *Financial Times*, June 9, 1994.

17 Securities and Exchange Commission, ENI SpA, Form 20-F, 1996.

18 "Eni savors the taste of freedom," *Financial Times*, June 9, 1994.

19 *Franco Bernabè at Eni*, Harvard Business School Case 9-498-034, April 7, 1998.

20 Securities and Exchange Commission, ENI SpA, Form 20-F, 1996, p. 3.

21 "Interview with Vittorio Mincato," *Financial Times*, October 12, 1999.

22 Ibid., p. 1.

23 Ibid.

24 "Letter to shareholders," Eni Annual Report 1999, pp. 4–5.

25 "L'Eni di Fronte a un Bivio," Eni SpA, 2002, p. 14.

26 "The important thing is that the target company should be rightly sized to be integrated easily," observed Mincato ("Eni, Thinking Big," *Petroleum Economist*, February 11, 2002).

27 "A quiet baritone on Italy's oil and gas stage: Vittorio Mincato," *Financial Times*, May 28, 2001.

28 Interview with Vittorio Mincato, *ECOS*, Vol. 30, No 6, 2001, p. 12.

29 In December 1998, crude prices fell below $10 per barrel.

30 Interview with Vittorio Mincato, *ECOS*, Vol. 30, No. 6, 2001, p. 12.

Birds Eye and the UK Frozen Food Industry

On February 12, 1946, George Muddiman arrived in Liverpool from Canada to take up the job as first chairman of Birds Eye Foods Ltd. "It was raining," he recalled. "There were no lights on the streets; it was seven o'clock at night and dark. As I looked out of the cab window my heart went into my boots and I thought, 'What have I done? Why have I left Canada to come to this?'"

By the early 1950s, after a host of problems with production, raw materials, and distribution, Birds Eye was firmly established. In 1952, it opened the "Empire's largest quick-frozen food factory" in Great Yarmouth and embarked upon a period of continuous expansion. By 1964 UK frozen food sales had grown to £75 million (from a mere £150,000 in 1946), with Birds Eye accounting for 70% of the total.

However, from the late 1960s both return on capital and market share declined as competition in the market intensified. By the retirement of Birds Eye's second chairman, James ("Mr Fish Fingers") Parratt in July 1972, the company's fortunes had passed their peak and by 1983, Birds Eye's share of retail frozen food sales had shrunk to 18.5%.

Beginnings[1]

Quick-freezing arrests the process of decay in perishable foods and enables fresh foods to be distributed to the consumer, wherever located and at any season. However, the freezing process must be quick to prevent the formation of large ice crystals that damage the cell structure of the food. By the late 1920s General Foods Corporation was successfully manufacturing and marketing "Birds Eye"

This case is based on an earlier case by Robert M. Grant, subsequently developed by David Collis and published by Harvard Business School (*Birds Eye and the Frozen Foods Industry [A]*, Case Number 9-792-074, 1994).

Copyright © 2008 Robert M. Grant

frozen foods in the United States using the multi-plate quick-freezers developed by Clarence Birdseye.

The establishment of Birds Eye frozen foods in the UK in 1938 was the initiative of a British businessman, Robert Ducas, with financial and technical support from General Foods Corp. and Chivers and Sons Ltd. (a British canner and jam-maker). Birds Eye was not alone in pioneering frozen foods in Britain. Smedley's (National Canning), Smethurst Ltd., Mudd and Son, and Associated Fisheries Ltd. (through Eskimo Foods Ltd.) all entered the frozen food business before World War II.

By 1942, Unilever had become strongly interested in the Birds Eye business. At a meeting of Unilever's management committee on February 4, 1942, the guidelines for a frozen food business were established.

> They expected to see the business develop in three main groups of produce – fruit and vegetables, fish, and meat. They hoped to see Birds Eye companies in operation all over the world, and they expected to get together a team of people who could go wherever they were needed to give help with setting up these new companies. They could see that some of their products were likely to be expensive, and they were not against running luxury lines, but in the true tradition of a business founded on the demand of the mass market for everyday products, they hoped that, in general, the business would be built on the large-scale development of certain main products.[2]

In March 1943, when World War II was at its height, Unilever acquired Birds Eye Foods. Its task of establishing a frozen food business in the UK was formidable:

> The costs of quick-freezing are high, and it does not pay to freeze any food except the best, that will sell for a price high enough to cover overhead and yield a profit worth having. . . . Next, food must be frozen at the top of its condition or most of the value of the process is lost. That means that something must be done to see that produce is gathered at precisely the right moment and processed, if possible, within hours. For fish, of course, and for some other foods there can be no control over production, but there must be a highly efficient buying organization.
>
> When the produce is frozen, there is the problem of keeping it frozen until it reaches the [consumer]. Since many of the products, such as peas, are seasonal, that means keeping them for months in cold storage. On the journey from factory to shop, there must be insulated vehicles. In the shops themselves, there must be cabinets; the shopkeepers must be persuaded to find room, and somebody must finance them – either the shopkeepers themselves or the freezing firms.[3]

Birds Eye's early history was directed towards establishing an organization that was fully integrated from controlling food production to stocking the retailer's frozen food cabinet. In the absence of a well-developed infrastructure for producing, storing, distributing, and retailing frozen foods, Birds Eye was forced to build its own system.

Building Market Leadership

Production and Raw Material Supplies

In production, the chief problems arose from the concentration of processing into a short time space, the unreliability of machinery, and the lack of skilled labor. Much of the machinery had to be imported from the US and Canada, and capital costs were high. Over two-thirds of processing costs were fixed, although each plate freezer could be used to freeze almost any food depending on seasonal availability. The location of frozen food processing factories was determined primarily by the source of raw materials. Prepared foods, like desserts or entrees, could be located anywhere. However, for vegetables and fish, production needed to be located on the eastern side of Great Britain, near the vegetable growing areas and the big fishing ports. Peas, for example, needed to be processed within 90 minutes of picking so processing plants were concentrated in Humberside, Lincolnshire, and East Anglia. By 1960, Birds Eye operated six factories and associated cold stores at Great Yarmouth, Lowestoft, Kirkby, Grimsby, Hull, and Eastbourne. Each factory produced a number of different products in order to utilize manpower and equipment efficiently in the face of seasonal availability of raw materials.

Once production facilities had been planned, the next task was to secure supplies of high-quality raw materials. For vegetables, this was usually achieved through annual contracts with farmers who committed a certain acreage to Birds Eye, in return for a fixed price per ton according to quality. Birds Eye exercised close control over the crops, supplying the seed, determining the planting times, and approving the fertilizer and insecticide used. Technicians monitored the moisture level in the produce to determine the optimal harvesting time and radioed the processing plants, which coordinated the movement of harvesting equipment from farm to farm and the transportation of produce from farm to factory.

Initially, Birds Eye owned most of the harvesting equipment that growers used. Equipment took the place of manual labor because of the speed with which the crop needed to be harvested before freezing. Over the years, growers bought their own machines under long-term contracts with Birds Eye, which agreed to repurchase the equipment if the parties could not agree on an annual acreage contract. Because of the high cost of pea harvesting equipment, farmer cooperatives became the main source of vegetables. By 1974 they were supplying 70% of the peas and 60% of the beans used for freezing. Many had been supplying Birds Eye continuously for 20 years. As the demand for frozen vegetables grew, the frozen food industry became the single most important customer for green vegetables. In 1975, half of all the peas were grown for freezing, as were three-quarters of green beans.

The fish used for quick-freezing was whitefish, mainly cod, haddock, halibut, plaice, sole, and coley. Most of it was either bought fresh from dockside auctions, or imported from Scandinavia in frozen blocks of fillets for use in fish fingers and other heavily processed items. Some fish, however, was frozen at sea and bought on contract. A typical contract guaranteed to buy a proportion of the catch, provided the catch exceeded a certain size, at a price up to 5% below the previous month's auction price. By the late 1960s, one-third of the total whitefish catch went to frozen food companies; as a result, contracts were tending to replace open auction at fish markets. Birds Eye also purchased fish at dockside auctions – mainly at Grimsby.

In some instances, Birds Eye sought direct ownership of its sources of raw material. It entered the broiler chicken industry in 1958 and within a few years had built a capacity for producing 6.5 million birds a year at about 20 farms. It sold the farms to Ross Poultry in 1972 in the face of overproduction in the broiler chicken industry and a belief that it was of suboptimal size. In 1965, Birds Eye acquired a majority stake in a fishing company to secure a regular supply of cod. Operating problems coincided with a drop in world fish prices, and Birds Eye sold the assets of the fishing company in 1969.

As Birds Eye developed a number of innovations in food processing and freezing techniques and developments in quality management it sought improvements in the production of its raw materials. In horticulture, Birds Eye was responsible for improvements in vegetable cultivation techniques, and harvesting equipment.

Distribution

Production problems were minor in comparison with those of establishing a national system of distribution. Distribution costs were estimated at between 15 and 25% of total costs for frozen food.[4] Only a limited capacity existed in public cold stores, which were used primarily for frozen meat, frozen fish, and ice cream. These were concentrated near big cities. Cold stores were also expensive. A minimum efficient scale cold store of 2.4 million cubic feet cost £0.6m in the mid-1960s. It was estimated that each doubling of capacity reduced operating expenses by 20%.

Birds Eye's investment in cold storage and refrigerated distribution was primarily through its sister company, SPD (Speedy Prompt Delivery) – also a wholly owned subsidiary of Unilever:

> SPD was increasingly drawn into the problem. They developed their cold storage capacity and added insulated vehicles to get the goods to shops. . . . Cold storage has increased steadily, with buildings that were more and more advanced in their design. Depots were run in close conjunction with SPD and increased to the point where Birds Eye could store about 50,000 tons of frozen food.[5]

By the end of the 1960s, SPD had built a national system of frozen food distribution for Birds Eye. It operated from 42 depots and enabled Birds Eye to directly serve some 93,000 outlets. Birds Eye treated it as an integral part of its own activities, paying for its services at cost and making an annual profit contribution to cover the capital employed by SPD on Birds Eye's behalf. In the few areas that it could not serve cost-effectively, Birds Eye franchised exclusive wholesalers to distribute its frozen foods to retailers. The coordination of investment between Birds Eye and SPD allowed Birds Eye's tonnage sales to increase at a remarkable 40% per annum during the 1950s.

Retailing

The biggest barrier to the development of the frozen foods industry was the state of retail distribution. During the 1940s and early 1950s retail distribution was highly fragmented, with many small shops and with counter service nearly universal. The structure of the retail trade virtually ossified in the early post-war period as a result of food rationing which continued until 1953 and almost eliminated competition among retailers. The chief short-term problem was persuading food retailers to install refrigerated cabinets:

> At an average cost of about £150, a QIF cabinet is a big enough outlay to cause the average retailer to think twice about installing one. However, it can be shown that an average-sized cabinet of 10 cu. ft. can be made – even without proper siting – to yield an annual turnover of anything between £500 and £1,500.
> On an average retail margin of 20%, a retailer with an annual turnover of, say, £1,000 can net a profit of £200 before servicing and maintenance charges are deducted. Over the 12–15-year life of the cabinet this represents a substantial return on investment.[6]

In the supply of ice cream, the major manufacturers lent cabinets to retailers. The problem of this approach was the enormous capital requirements (equivalent at least to the size of investment in production facilities). In 1953, Birds Eye decided that it would not rent cabinets to retailers. Instead, it persuaded two producers of industrial refrigerators and air-conditioning equipment, Prestcold and Frigidaire, to start the production of "open top" display cabinets suitable for frozen food storage and display. Birds Eye only sought new business with retailers that installed such cabinets.

Market Development and Product Innovation

With the infrastructure in place, demand for frozen foods expanded. In the beginning, frozen foods were regarded as a luxury preferred over canned or dried food for their retention of the appearance and flavor of the fresh product.

As the price of frozen foods fell, growth increased rapidly, though the price elasticity of demand remained very high and seasonal and annual fluctuations in the consumption of frozen foods were strongly influenced by the price and availability of fresh produce. Between 1956 and 1981, sales increased at an average annual rate of about 15%, although the rate of growth of tonnage sales tended to decline over time. From 1956 to 1961, average annual growth was 36%, falling to 10.5% per annum between 1962 and 1973, and 6.9% between 1974 and 1980. Table 13.1 shows the growth in UK spending on frozen food sales.

During the 1950s and 1960s, the number of retail outlets supplying frozen foods expanded rapidly. So too did the range of frozen foods available. Beginning with seasonal produce – green vegetables and fruit – a wide variety of processed foods and prepared meals soon appeared.

Once Birds Eye had established its integrated system of production and distribution during the 1950s, its strategy became more marketing oriented. With a national,

TABLE 13.1 UK frozen food expenditure 1967–1984

	Total constant 1975 prices (£ million)	Freezer owners (%)	Non-freezer owners (%)	Consumption	
				In-home (%)	Catering (%)
1967	322	–	–	84	16
1973	510	17	54	71	29
1974	527	20	50	70	30
1975	500	24	48	72	28
1976	515	30	46	76	24
1977	508	32	43	75	25
1978	514	37	40	77	23
1979	539	40	37	77	23
1980	570	47	32	79	21
1981	593	53	28	81	19
1982	621	59	24	84	16
1983	646	63	21	84	16
984	692	67	18	85	15

integrated organization in place, the company's principal task was to expand sales by introducing new products, promoting consumer awareness of the convenience and value for money of frozen foods, and developing consumer recognition of the quality associated with the Birds Eye brand. The introduction of fish fingers in 1955 was followed by beefburgers in 1960 and by a stream of new fish, meat, and dessert products. The five biggest-selling products – peas, beans, chips, fish fingers, and beefburgers – accounted for nearly 40% of revenue. The introduction of commercial television in 1955 was vitally important for its marketing strategy by allowing it to engage in mass-market advertising of its brand and new products. The medium also gave Birds Eye a big advantage over smaller producers – until 1958, Birds Eye was the sole industry advertiser.

Birds Eye pioneered frozen foods with a product quality higher than people were used to in processed food and with a personality that combined efficiency, hygiene, confidence, and completeness. Birds Eye added values beyond the physical and functional ones that contributed to a clear and likeable personality for the brand.[7]

Birds Eye's Market Dominance

The result of Birds Eye's pioneering efforts backed by massive investment by the Unilever Group was Birds Eye's dominance of the fast-growing UK frozen food market. Throughout the 1950s and 1960s, Birds Eye accounted for over 60% of UK frozen food sales on a tonnage basis. In terms of the retail market, the company estimated its brand market share at over 70% by value and around two-thirds by tonnage for most of the period. Among the outlets served by Birds Eye, its share of frozen food sales was 75%, and some 40,000 retail outlets were served exclusively by Birds Eye. Its top 20 retail customers accounted for nearly a third of total sales.

Birds Eye held a substantial competitive advantage over its closest competitors, Ross and Findus, and consistently achieved higher returns on capital employed (on an historic cost basis) than them. In 1974, for example, while Birds Eye's return on capital stood at 15.9%, Findus earned 8.9% (frozen food only) and Ross Foods earned 4.3% (all food businesses). Both Findus and Ross acted as followers to Birds Eye, while Birds Eye pioneered the development of the market. Findus and Ross followed with similar approaches to production, distribution, product development, and marketing. Because they imitated many of Birds Eye's product and marketing strategies, their advertising expenditures were limited. Ross Foods' parent company, Imperial Foods, told the Monopolies and Mergers Commission that it "considered massive brand support aimed at achieving dramatic increases in sales, to be far beyond the means of its frozen food companies and it never sought to answer Birds Eye's intensive advertising in kind. In 1973, Ross Foods virtually ceased advertising its retail packs since it was not making it more competitive."[8] Tables 13.2 and 13.3 show Birds Eye's brand leadership and superior profitability.

Neither of these leading competitors was prepared to undercut Birds Eye. Birds Eye's brand leadership was evident in the pattern of pricing behavior observed in the industry. Based on the evidence of published list prices, the Monopolies and Mergers Commission concluded: "The recommended retail prices of Birds Eye, Ross Foods, and Findus frozen food have until recently moved broadly in parallel, with Birds Eye more often than not, being the first to change its price."[9] The willingness of smaller producers to follow Birds Eye was explained by Imperial Foods:

TABLE 13.2 Brand shares of the UK retail market for frozen foods (% of total volume)

	1966	1970	1974	1978	1982
Birds Eye	62	60	45	29	20
Ross	5	8	6	6	8
Findus	13	13	11	8	4
Own-label	–	6	14	21	28
Other	20	13	21	35	40

TABLE 13.3 Comparative profitability (pre-tax return on capital employed %)

	1964	1967	1971	1972	1973	1974
Birds Eye	16.2	22.2	19.1	18.4	18.7	15.9
Findus	n.a.	n.a.	7.2	5.9	7.2	8.9
Ross	n.a.	n.a.	n.a.	7.6	5.5	4.3
UK manufacturing industry	14.6	12.0	12.5	14.9	17.4	17.4

n.a. = not available.

SOURCE: MONOPOLIES AND MERGERS COMMISSION

In supplying frozen foods to retailers for sale under the Ross name, Ross Foods sets its prices generally at the same level as Birds Eye. Since Ross Foods only advertises and promotes its products on a very limited scale, it cannot hope to win space in retailers' cabinets and charge prices above those charged by Birds Eye. On the other hand it cannot afford to undercut Birds Eye's prices to any significant extent.[10]

Birds Eye's retail dominance was assisted by a system of discounts that encouraged larger retailers to give Birds Eye the major part of their frozen foods business. The company offered discounts to a number of retailers. The size of discounts from its published trade prices depended on the annual turnover of the retailer, the cabinet space allocated to Birds Eye products, and the frequency and size of deliveries. Overall discounts averaged 6% of the gross revenues of all retailers. Its "criterion in discount negotiation was to achieve a consistent level of gross profitability from various customers"[11] and the discounts were intended to capture differences in the costs of serving different customers. As a result, "large retailers achieved the highest discount – over 10% of the gross value of their purchases – although these were said to exceed the cost savings in supplying them."[12]

The Growth of Competition

During the 1970s and into the 1980s, Birds Eye's market share, and its profitability, declined as competition grew in the frozen foods market.

Developments in Retailing

In the 1960s, developments in food retailing began to influence the frozen food industry. First was the move away from counter service towards self-service which increased vastly the marketing opportunities available to the frozen food processors, including introducing new and novel products and packaging. Second was the emergence of supermarkets and large supermarket chains. In 1960 there were only 367 supermarkets (self-service food shops with 2,000 square feet or more floor space). The ability of the supermarket chains to pass on their cost savings to consumers, together with consumers' demand for the wider variety of goods made available by supermarkets, were major factors behind increasing concentration in the grocery trade.

Many of the major supermarket chains operated central or regional warehouses from which they distributed grocery products to their individual supermarkets. They also began to supply their own brands of frozen foods. Following the introduction by Sainsbury of its own brand of frozen peas in 1967, retailers' brands took an increasing share of retail frozen food sales.

The impact of supermarkets in expanding the amount of retail cabinet space available was reinforced towards the end of the 1960s by the introduction of specialist frozen foods stores to serve the increasing number of home freezer owners. To serve this growing market, a new model of frozen food retailing emerged: home freezer centers that combined the sale of home freezers with the sale of large packs of frozen foods (packed for caterers). The retailing of frozen foods by these outlets was characterized by large pack sizes, wide product range, lack of brand consciousness, and low prices. Larger cabinet capacity, usually with backup storage, enabled freezer centers to require fewer deliveries with bigger drops. Their share of frozen food sales was 18% in 1978 and 23.5% in 1986. Table 13.4 shows the changing structure of UK grocery retailing.

New Entry

While the early development of the industry had seen a consolidation around three major, vertically integrated suppliers, there was a wave of new entries in the 1960s and 1970s. For companies already engaged in food processing, a new technology, blast freezers, could be purchased "off the shelf" for as little as a few thousand pounds for a small unit. These allowed freezing and packing to occur together and eliminated the need for two separate production processes. While large-scale processing and freezing offered opportunities for automation and greater division of labor, the cost savings from increased scale of production tended to be small.

TABLE 13.4 Shares of UK packaged grocery sales by type of retailer

	1970	1974	1978	1981
Multiples	49	53	64	70
Cooperatives	19	21	18	17
Voluntary groups	16	14	10	
Independents	18	13	8	6
Four-firm concentration ratio	0.26	0.27	0.34	0.42

SOURCE: C. BADEN FULLER, MINING CONCENTRATION: THE UK GROCERY TRADE 1970-80, LONDON: CONCENTRATION, 1984.

New entrants to the industry were a diverse group. The Monopolies and Mergers Commission observed in 1976 that:

A number of new companies have entered the frozen food processing industry during the past twenty years. They include Jus-Roll Ltd and Primecut Foods Ltd (then W. B. Wright Provision Ltd) in 1954, Northray Foods Ltd in 1956, Kraft Foods Ltd in 1963, McCain International Ltd and Potato and Allied Services Ltd in 1968, Frozen Quality Ltd in 1969, Country Range Ltd and King Harry Foods in 1970, White House Foods Ltd and Fife Growers Ltd in 1971, and Wold Growers Ltd in 1974.

Although some of the new entrants have been new enterprises, most have been either established companies or subsidiaries of established companies. In many cases companies already engaged in the production of food have extended production to include frozen foods. Many of the smaller processors of vegetables and fruit, for example, Northray Foods Ltd, Frozen Quality Ltd, Fife Growers Ltd and Wold Pea Growers Ltd originated as agricultural cooperatives. Among the meat companies which have entered frozen food processing are FMC Ltd, Dalgety Ltd (chiefly through Dalgety-Buswell Ltd and Dalgety Frozen Foods Ltd) and Thos Borthwick & Sons Ltd (through Freshbake Foods Ltd). Several fishing and fish merchanting companies have developed the processing of frozen food, notably Associated Fisheries Ltd, J. Marr (Fish Merchants) Ltd and Chaldur Frozen Fish Co. Ltd.

[Most] companies specialize in one or other of the broad categories of frozen food products, namely vegetables, fish, meat products and fruit and confectionery. Some companies specialize in a single product only – McCain's output is exclusively potato chips and King Harry Foods produces mainly pizzas.[13]

In addition, marketing-only companies, such as W. B. Pellew-Harvey & Co. Ltd. and J. Muirhead, emerged. These bought frozen food from other manufacturers and placed their own brand names, "Angelus," "Chef's Garden," and "4F," on the products. Independent companies such as Christian Salvesen handled their physical distribution needs.

Specialist storage, freezing, and transportation providers played a critical role in allowing the entry and viability of these smaller, specialist, frozen food suppliers. Public cold storage companies such as Christian Salvesen, Union Cold Storage, and Frigoscandia doubled their cold storage capacity between 1969 and 1973. These companies came to offer not only storage facilities but also a comprehensive range of processing, freezing, and distribution services. By 1974, Christian Salvesen's cold storage capacity was almost one-third of Birds Eye's. In 1978, Christian Salevesen processed three-quarters of the vegetables it stored, up from 20% in 1969. Services were made available on medium-term, multi-year contracts. Salvesen's fleet of refrigerated trucks operating out of its national network of cold stores was also available for rent, either on long-term contracts or as needed. Sainsbury and Marks & Spencer, two of Britain's largest food retailers each with a wide range of own-brand frozen foods, used Christian Salvesen for some of their refrigerated distribution needs. Other firms specialized in the importing, broking, and distribution of frozen foods. For example, Frionor and Bonduelle began marketing products imported from their overseas parents while companies such as Anglo European foods, Snowking, Frozen Foods, and Flying Goose specialized in distribution (mainly to the catering trade).

The rapid growth of eating away from the home by the British, and the rapid shift of the catering industry from fresh and canned foods to frozen foods, provided a particularly attractive opportunity for new entrants into frozen foods. Catering establishments were served by a separate segment of the market that was more concerned with price than with brand name recognition and sophisticated product packaging. Smaller processors could easily market their products to the catering trade without the need for investing in brands and distribution. From serving the catering industry it was easy to expand into supplies to retail home freezer centers and to supermarkets' own-label products.

Decline and Strategic Reappraisal

The retirement of Birds Eye's chairman, James Parratt, in July 1972 marked the highpoint of the company's fortunes. Under his successor, Kenneth Webb, Birds Eye was to face a new era of competitive pressure that led to a fundamental reassessment of its strategy.

Although still far and away the UK market leader in frozen foods, Birds Eye's market dominance existed primarily in sales of small retail packs to independent grocers and, to a lesser extent, supermarkets. Birds Eye was poorly represented in some areas: in home freezer centers its share was around 8% in 1974 and it had little involvement in retailers' own labels. In the catering sector Birds Eye's market share by value was about 10% in 1973. After the early 1970s, the company's share of tonnage sales fell continuously although the market as a whole continued to expand, albeit at a slower rate.

To respond to changes in the market – particularly the rise in bulk buying by consumers with home freezers – and to the competition of recent entrants in this sector, Birds Eye introduced bulk packs to the retail market in 1972 and followed this with the establishment in 1974 of a new business, County Fair Foods, to supply the home freezer centers and other purchasers willing to accept a minimum drop size. County Fair Foods shared production facilities with Birds Eye but had a separate distribution system using Christian Salvesen because of the different requirements of freezer centers with regard to quality, product types, distribution, prices, and promotion. In 1976, Birds Eye established Menumaster Ltd. to supply frozen prepared meals to caterers. In the traditional retail market, Birds Eye's main aim was to maintain sales growth, primarily by extending its product range through new product introductions. During the 1970s the company's dependence on its traditional products – vegetables, fish fingers, and beefburgers – was reduced by a constant flow of new product introductions – especially ready-to-eat meals, desserts, and ethnic dishes (e.g. Chinese, Indian, and Italian dishes).

The widening of Birds Eye's product range and increased range of market segments that it sought to serve posed major difficulties for Birds Eye's marketing strategy and the allocation of its advertising budget. The marketing effort necessary to promote Birds Eye's products in widely different sectors – promoting up-market prepared dishes while expanding into economy packs of commodity products – was difficult to orchestrate. "We will be walking a tightrope," explained marketing director Keith Jacobs, "the company's advertising will have two jobs to do: to maintain its image as a basic convenience foods company and to make it credible as a purveyor of, for example, pizzas." In relation to advertising, Birds Eye adopted a more targeted approach. It focused its national TV advertising on its lead lines, while new products were introduced with more regionally and segment-focused advertising. Advertising was largely withdrawn from "support products."

In response to the growing power of large supermarket chains, Birds Eye redirected its marketing efforts. During the 1960s, marketing had been focused almost exclusively on the consumer. During the 1970s, Birds Eye shifted its focus from consumer marketing to trade marketing, with particular emphasis on developing relationships with major supermarket chains, including joint promotion efforts.

On the production side, the mid-1970s witnessed a program of heavy investment in modernization and rationalization that was designed to exploit efficiency from volume production. Between 1977 and 1980 expenditure on this program amounted to some £20 million. A key feature of the program was focusing different product groups at specific factories – fish products at Hull and Grimsby, ready meals at Kirkby and Yarmouth, vegetables at Hull and Lowestoft, and cakes and desserts at Eastbourne – to permit much higher levels of automation.

The quest for lower costs was instrumental in the decision to merge Unilever's two principal frozen product operations, Birds Eye Foods and Walls Ice Cream, into a single company, Birds Eye Walls Ltd. Although the potential for cooperation and the elimination of duplicated functions between Birds Eye and Walls had been identified in the 1960s, the two Unilever subsidiaries had been almost entirely independent prior to the merger. During 1979–81, Birds Eye Walls worked on merging and rationalizing the two companies' distribution networks. On January 1, 1982, the combined refrigerated distribution company, Unicold-Walls, was transferred to Birds Eye Walls with the intention of speeding the reorganization of distribution and improving coordination. The goal was a streamlined national network of seven regional distribution centers in operation.

Despite Birds Eye's efforts to adjust to new market circumstances, its market and financial performance continued to deteriorate throughout the 1970s. Despite its claim that "few brands in the British grocery market can claim the sort of dominance which Birds Eye has in frozen foods," leadership was no guarantee of growth and prosperity. In the face of rising competition, Birds Eye maintained its advertising budget during the mid-1970s while cutting prices on some major-selling products. Though this approach raised sales volume, in July 1975 Chairman Kenneth Webb complained that profit margins had been halved over the previous two years and were currently one-third of the level consistent with the company's heavy investment in manufacturing and distribution facilities. In 1976, the company barely broke even and in 1977 it registered a post-tax loss. Table 13.5 shows Birds Eye's financial performance.

The appointment of Don Angel to the chairmanship of Birds Eye early in 1979 led to Birds Eye reappraising its strategy in the UK frozen foods market and considering a new phase of internal restructuring. Reflecting on the erosion of the company's dominant market position, Don Angel observed that the model that had served Birds Eye's development and growth during the 1950s and 1960s needed to be reconsidered and "choices must be made about what the company is best at." In particular, there was a widespread realization that the vertically integrated approach to the sourcing, processing, distribution, and marketing of frozen foods through which Birds Eye had developed the UK market for frozen foods may now be a weakness rather than a strength for Birds Eye.

TABLE 13.5 Birds Eye Foods Ltd: financial data for 1972–1979 (£ 000s)

	1972	1973	1974	1975	1976	1977	1978	1979
Sales	91,838	113,997	132,636	157,142	187,415	212,322	226,308	266,018
Operating profit	2,110	2,875	3,445	4,414	3,453	2,477	6,310	9,352
After-tax profit	1,223	1,465	1,468	1,925	249	(679)	1,094	1,094
Group service charge	n.a.	n.a.	n.a.	n.a.	n.a.	5,305	5,527	8,145
Net current assets	15,164	24,717	31,034	32,069	44,792	53,337	59,141	59,141
Stocks (Inventories)	17,479	26,012	29,263	30,983	40,356	52,431	54,317	54,317
Debtors	5,928	10,677	12,124	13,739	17,483	13,523	21,102	28,522
Creditors	4,863	7,484	8,768	9,481	10,592	14,563	15,350	24,573
Capital employed	33,893	42,947	48,993	52,199	90,383	100,004	122,352	132,801

SOURCE: ROBERT M. GRANT, "BIRDS EYE AND THE UK FROZEN FOOD INDUSTRY" CASE STUDY, JULY 1985, H 1-34.

Notes

1 Birds Eye's history is outlined in W. J. Reader, *Birds Eye Foods Ltd: The Early Days*, Birds Eye Foods Ltd, 1963.
2 Ibid., p. 9.
3 Ibid., p. 3.
4 K. McClaren, "The effect of range size on distribution costs," *International Journal of Physical Distribution and Materials Management*, vol. 10, 1980, pp. 445–56.
5 C. Wilson, *Unilever 1945–1965: Challenge and Response in the Post-War Industrial Revolution*, Cassell, London, 1968, pp. 172–3.
6 "Frozen food: market prospects," *Retail Business*, Special Report No. 14, April 1959, p. 83.
7 S. King, *Developing New Brands*, London: Pitman, 1973, p. 13.
8 *Report on the Supply of Frozen Foodstuffs*, Monopolies and Mergers Commission, HMSO, 1976, p. 44.
9 Ibid., p. 53.
10 Ibid., p. 42.
11 Ibid., p. 32.
12 Ibid., p. 32.
13 Ibid., p. 9.

Outback Steakhouse: Going International*

By 1995, Outback Steakhouse was one of the fastest growing and most acclaimed restaurant chains in North America. Astute positioning within the intensely-competitive US restaurant business, high quality of food and service, and a relaxed ambiance that echoed its Australian theme propelled the chain's spectacular growth (see table 14.1).

Chairman and co-founder Chris Sullivan believed that at the current rate of growth (around 70 new restaurants each year), Outback would be facing market saturation within five years. Outback's growth opportunities were either to diversify into alternative restaurant concepts (it had already started its Carrabba's Italian Grill restaurants) or to expand internationally:

> We can do 500–600 [Outback] restaurants, and possibly more over the next five years . . . [however] the world is becoming one big market, and we want to be in place so we don't miss that opportunity. There are some problems, some challenges with it, but at this point there have been some casual restaurant chains that have gone [outside the United States] and their average unit sales are way, way above the sales level they enjoyed in the United States. So the potential is there. Obviously, there are some distribution issues to work out, things like that, but we are real excited about the future internationally. That will give us some potential outside the United States to continue to grow as well.[1]

In late 1994, Hugh Connerty was appointed President of Outback International to lead the company's overseas expansion. Connerty had considerable experience in the restaurant business and had been Outback's most successful

---

* By Marilyn L. Taylor and Robert M. Grant. This case is an abridged version of an earlier case "Outback Steakhouse Goes International" by Marilyn L. Taylor, George M. Puia, Krishnan Ramaya, and Madelyn Genge back. It has been augmented with material from company reports and from "A Stake in the Business," by Chris T. Sullivan, *Harvard Business Review*, September 2005, pp. 57–64.

TABLE 14.1 Outback Steakhouses Inc.: growth and profitability, 1990–5

	Revenue ($m)	Net income ($m)	Return on average equity (%)	Company-owned restaurants	Franchised and JV restaurants	Total restaurants
1990	34	2.3	41.2	23	0	23
1991	91	6.1	34.4	49	0	49
1992	189	14.8	23.6	81	4	85
1993	310	25.2	22.2	124	24	148
1994	516	43.4	27.4	164	50	214
1995	734	61.3	27.0	262	58	320[a]

[a] Of these, 297 were Outback Steakhouses and 23 were Carrabba's Italian Grills.

franchisee, developing a number of Outback restaurants in northern Florida and southern Georgia. Connerty grasped the opportunity enthusiastically:

> We have had hundreds of franchise requests from all over the world. [So] it took about two seconds for me to make that decision [to become President of Outback International] . . . I've met with and talked to other executives who have international divisions. All of them have the same story. At some point in time a light goes on and they say, "Gee we have a great product. Where do we start?" I have traveled quite a bit on holiday. The world is not as big as you think it is. Most companies who have gone global have not used any set strategy.[2]

Connerty's challenges were to decide in which countries to locate; whether to franchise, directly manage, or joint venture; how the Outback restaurant concept should be adapted to overseas markets; and what pace of expansion to target.

Outback's Strategy

Outback was founded by Chris Sullivan, Bob Basham, and Tim Gannon. The three had met as management trainees at the Steak and Ale restaurant chain. Although red meat consumption was declining, they believed that this was primarily the result of less meat being consumed at home: steakhouses remained extremely popular. They saw an untapped opportunity for serving quality steaks at an affordable price – filling the gap between high-priced and budget steakhouses. Using an Australian theme associated with the outdoors and adventure, Outback positioned itself as a place providing not only excellent food but also a cheerful, fun, and comfortable experience. The company explained its strategy as follows:

> The Company believes that it differentiates its Outback Steakhouse restaurants by:
>
> - emphasizing consistently high-quality ingredients and preparation of a limited number of menu items that appeal to a broad array of tastes;
> - featuring generous portions at moderate prices;

- *attracting a diverse mix of customers through a casual dining atmosphere emphasizing highly attentive service;*
- *hiring and retaining experienced restaurant management by providing general managers the opportunity to purchase a 10% interest in the restaurants they manage; and*
- *limiting service to dinner (generally from 4:30 p.m. to 11.00 p.m.), which reduces the hours of restaurant management and employees.*[3]

Quality of food was central to the chain's differentiation. This began with the raw materials. Outback viewed suppliers as "partners" and was committed to work with them to ensure quality and develop long-term relationships. Outback's food costs were among the highest in the industry – not just in terms of ingredients but also in preparation, with most items prepared from scratch within each restaurant. For example, Outback's croutons were made daily on site with 17 different seasonings, and cut into irregular shapes to indicate that they were handmade.

The emphasis on quality extended to service. Among Outback's "Principles and Beliefs" was "No rules, just right" – employees will do whatever is needed to meet the needs and preferences of customers.

Inevitably, this emphasis on quality and service meant working practices that at other restaurant chains would be regarded as inefficient. Chairman Chris Sullivan explained that Outback had a different management model:

There are three kinds of turnover in the restaurant business – customer, employee and table. Most restaurant chains worry about the first, resign themselves to the second, and encourage the third. At Outback it's not as straightforward as that; we believe that all three are integrally related. Specifically, our management model and approach reflect the importance we place on fighting employee turnover. One of our catchphrases is "fully staffed, fully trained." You can't be either of those things if a restaurant is a revolving door. Besides, customers like to see a familiar face.

Restaurant work can be stressful. The better the staffers, the more intent they will be on doing things right – and the more frustrated they will become with the facilities and tools they've been given if they get in the way, whether the problem is dull knives or not enough burners . . . Bob Basham insisted on making all of our kitchens at least 2,500 square feet and keeping lots of cool air flowing through them. The kitchens occupy half of the typical Outback restaurant's floor plan – space that other restaurants allocate to revenue-producing tables. But we wanted to offer a bigger menu than the typical casual restaurant did in the 1980s, so we knew we would have to give the cooks and prep people the space to pull it off.

Likewise, we never assign our servers to cover more than three tables; the industry standard is five or six . . . A wide range of customers choose to dine with us on a variety of occasions . . . It has to be the customer who sets the pace for the meal, not the server or the kitchen staff. But for that to happen our servers need time to figure out the mood and expectations of a given table on a given evening, and the kitchen has to be well enough staffed and equipped to turn around orders without delay . . .

We think that employees who are not overstressed stay in their jobs longer than those who are; that employees who stay have time to master their jobs, become familiar with their regular customers' preferences, and learn to operate as teams;

that the combination of mastery, memory, and calm is more likely to afford customers themselves a relaxing, enjoyable experience; and that diners who are not hustled through their meals are more likely to come back. In short, low employee turnover leads to well-paced table turnover, which ultimately leads to low customer turnover.[4]

This model linked closely with two other distinctive features of Outback's strategy. First, Outback served only dinner. According to Sullivan, the conventional wisdom that restaurants needed to be open for lunch and dinner in order to make efficient use of capital ignored the hidden costs of longer hours of opening. These included the costs associated with extra hiring and employee turnover, the disruptive effects of shift changes, and the fact that employees who worked lunchtime would be tired in the evening – the time when they needed to be at their freshest. Similarly for the food, with preparation of food brought forward to the morning, it would lose its freshness by the evening.

Second, Outback located in residential areas rather than downtown. This reinforced the merits of evening-only opening, kept rents low, and encouraged customer and employee loyalty. As Sullivan explained: "The suburbs are our outback."

Outback's management and ownership structure was also unusual. Each of Outback's directly owned restaurants was a separate partnership where Outback Steakhouse Inc. was the general partner with an ownership of between 71% and 90%. Each restaurant was headed by a "managing partner" while between 10 and 20 restaurants within an area were overseen by a regional manager who is called a "joint venture partner" or "JVP." Sullivan explained the relationship as follows:

> *The terms "managing partner" and "joint venture partner" aren't symptoms of title inflation. They straightforwardly describe people's roles and relationships to the organization. All managing partners, most of whom start as hourly employees, must invest $25,000 of their own money – not because Outback needs the capital, but because their financial contributions make them committed investors in the business they'll be running. They must also sign a five-year contract, and they are granted roughly 1,000 shares of restricted stock, which vest only at the end of their contracts. In return, managing partners can keep 10% of the cash flow their restaurants generate each year. The idea is to ensure that at the end of five years each of them will have stock worth around $100,000 . . . At the end of five years, successful managers are encouraged to sign up with the same restaurant or to manage a different one . . .*
>
> *Outback's JVPs, who number around 60, must invest $50,000, which entitles them to 10% of cash flow of all the restaurants they oversee after the partners have received their 10%. Whereas the managing partners focus on operations and community relations, the Japes focus on monitoring performance, finding and developing new locations, and identifying and developing new managers, managing partners, and Japes like themselves. The Japes are the only management layer between the six operations executives at headquarters and the managing partners at the individual restaurants.*[5]

Initially, Outback intended its restaurants all to be directly owned and managed. However, in 1990, requests for franchising led to Outback agreeing to franchise to well-known acquaintances of the founders. Outback was very careful in its choice of franchisees to ensure that all were fully committed to Outback's principles and beliefs.

Management of hourly employees was very different from most other restaurant chains. One executive described Outback's approach as: "Tough on results, but kind with people." Employee selection was rigorous and included aptitude tests, psychological profiles, and interviews with at least two managers. The goal was to create an entrepreneurial climate that emphasized learning and personal growth. All employees were eligible for the company's stock ownership plan and health insurance was made available to all employees.

Part of the culture of "no rules" and commitment to quality and service is a constant drive for innovation and improvement:

> *Almost all our innovations bubble up from the individual restaurant, often originating with our servers or kitchen staffers. They'll suggest an idea to the restaurant manager who will try it on an experimental basis. If the recommended menu or process change clicks, the managing partner communicates the idea to his or her JVP. . . . If the suggested change meets company standards, videos and other materials showing how to implement it are distributed to other JVPs. Each is free to take it or not.[6]*

During 1993, Outback formed a joint venture with Houston-based Carrabba's Italian Grill. In January 1995, Outback acquired the rights to develop Carrabba's nationally. Carrabba's Grills were run with almost identical operating and management practices and ownership structure as Outback Steakhouses.

Preparing for International Expansion

Hugh Connerty, Outback's head of International, outlined his approach to international expansion as follows:

> *We have built Outback one restaurant at a time . . . There are some principles and beliefs we live by. It almost sounds cultish. We want International to be an opportunity for our suppliers. We feel strongly about the relationships with our suppliers. We have never changed suppliers. We have an undying commitment to them and in exchange we want them to have an undying commitment to us. They have to prove they can build plants [abroad].*
>
> *I think it would be foolish of us to think that we are going to go around the world buying property and understanding the laws in every country, the culture in every single country. So the approach that we are going to take is that we will franchise the international operation with company-owned stores here and franchises there so that will allow us to focus on what I believe is our pure strength, a support operation.[7]*

Connerty believed that his experience in developing Outback franchises in the US would provide the guidelines for overseas expansion:

> *Every one of the franchisees lives in their areas. I lived in the area I franchised. I had relationships that helped with getting permits. That isn't any different than the rest of the world. The loyalties of individuals that live in their respective areas [will be important]. We will do the franchises one by one. The biggest decision we have to make is how we pick that franchise partner. That is what we will concentrate on. We are going to select a person who has synergy with us, who thinks like us, who believes in the principles and beliefs.*

> *Trust is foremost and sacred. The trust between [Outback] and the individual franchisees is not to be violated. The company grants franchises one at a time. It takes a lot of trust to invest millions of dollars without any assurance that you will be able to build another one.*[8]

As for the geographical pattern of expansion, Connerty's initial thoughts were to begin close to home then tackle Latin America and the Far East:

> *The first year will be Canada. Then we'll go to Hawaii. Then we'll go to South America and then develop our relationships in the Far East, Korea, Japan . . . the Orient. The second year we'll begin a relationship in Great Britain and from there a natural progression throughout Europe. But we view it as a very long-term project. I have learned that people [in other countries] think very different than Americans.*[9]

Overseas Expansion by US Restaurant Chains

The international market offered substantial growth opportunities for US restaurant chains. For fast-food franchise chains – notably McDonald's, Burger King, and Kentucky Fried Chicken – international sales accounted for up to one-half of total sales, although for many "international" was limited to Canada and Puerto Rico. Among "casual dining" chains – such as Denny's, Applebee's, T. G. I. Friday's, and Tony Roma's – relatively few had ventured beyond North America. Table 14.2 shows the international presence of leading US restaurant franchise chains.

The attraction of overseas markets was that their restaurants markets were typically less saturated than those of the US and most of the local competition was independent, family owned restaurants rather than large chains. In overseas markets it was anticipated that market trends would follow those of the US: in particular, that greater affluence and a declining role of family life would result in increased eating away from home.

It was notable that, in overseas markets, not only had success been achieved principally by fast food chains, but most of the leaders were subsidiaries of large multi-

TABLE 14.2 The ten largest US restaurant franchise chains, 1994

	Total sales ($m)	International sales ($m)	Total outlets	International outlets
McDonald's	25,986	11,046	15,205	5,461
Burger King	7,500	1,400	7,684	1,357
KFC	7,100	3,600	9,407	4,258
Taco Bell	4,290	130	5,614	162
Wendy's	4,277	390	4,411	413
Hardee's	3,491	63	3,516	72
Dairy Queen	3,170	300	3,516	628
Domino's	2,500	415	5,079	840
Subway	2,500	265	179	8,450
Little Caesars	2,000	70	4,855	155

nationals with many decades of international experience. For example, KFC, Taco Bell, and Pizza Hut were subsidiaries of PepsiCo.; Burger King was a subsidiary of British conglomerate Grand Metropolitan.

A key impetus to overseas expansion was maturing of the US market. By 1994 there were over 3,000 franchisers in the United States, operating close to 600,000 franchised outlets. Not only was competition intense, but growth was slowing. Sales per store were growing at 3% during the early 1990s.

However, overseas markets also represented a substantial management challenge. Among the problems that other restaurant chains had encountered were the following:

- *Market demand*. The extent to which a market demand existed for a particular type of restaurant depended on levels of disposable income, urbanization, demographics, and a host of other social, economic, and life-style factors. Most critical to a specific company were national preferences with regard to cuisine and dining conventions. Even McDonald's whose name had become synonymous with global standardization adapted substantially to local differences: "Croque McDos" in France, rice burgers in Hong Kong, "McArabia Koftas" in Saudi Arabia, kosher outlets in Israel, no beef or pork products in India.

- *Cultural and social factors* are critical influences on customer preferences with regard to menus, restaurant facilities, and overall ambiance; they are also important with regard to employee management practices and entrepreneurial potential.

- *Infrastructure*. Proper means of transportation and communication, basic utilities such as power and water, and locally available supplies were important elements in the decision to introduce a particular restaurant concept. A restaurant must have the ability to get resources to its location. Easy access to the raw materials for food preparation, equipment for manufacture of food served, and mobility for employees and customers were essential.

- *Raw material supplies*. Overseas restaurant chains needed local supplies of food and drink. The US International Trade Commission noted that: "International franchisers frequently encounter problems finding supplies in sufficient quantity, of consistent quality, and at stable prices. Physical distance also can adversely affect a franchise concept and arrangement. Long distances create communication and transportation problems, which may complicate the process of sourcing supplies, overseeing operations, or providing quality management services to franchisees."[10] While a franchise chain could develop its own supply chain – for example, McDonald's when it entered the Soviet Union – the investment of management time and money could be substantial.

- *Regulations and trade restrictions*. Import restrictions are relatively unimportant in the restaurant business given that most food products are locally sourced. However, some countries have made the import of restaurant equipment difficult and expensive. Restrictions on foreign direct investment are of major significance only in emerging market countries. Far more challenging are national regulations relating to food standards, business licensing, and business contracts. Establishing new businesses in most countries involves far more regulation than within the US. Franchise agreements are an especially difficult area since they involve complex contractual agreements between franchisor and franchisee regarding trademark licensing, royalty payments, requirements for quality control and quality monitoring. Despite the provisions of the Uruguay Round's General Agreement on Trade in Services, most countries failed to make public their restrictions on franchising. In some countries some usual terms of franchise agreements have been viewed as restraints on commerce. Employment law was also important – particularly with regard to restrictions on employers' ability to dismiss or lay off employees and requirements for union recognition, and national collective bargaining arrangements over wages and work conditions.

Notes

1 M. L. Taylor, G. M. Puia, K. Ramaya, and M. Gengelback, "Outback Steakhouse Goes International," in A. A. Thompson and A. J. Strickland, Strategic Management: Concepts and Cases, 11th edn. (New York: McGraw-Hill, 1999), pp. C296–7.

2 Ibid., p. C291.

3 Outback Steakhouse, Inc. 10K, 1996.

4 Chris T. Sullivan, "A Stake in the Business," Harvard Business Review (September 2005), pp. 57–64.

5 Ibid., pp. 59–60.

6 Ibid., p. 58.

7 Taylor et al., "Outback Steakhouse Goes International," op. cit., p. C297.

8 Ibid., p. C297.

9 Ibid., p. C299.

10 US International Trade Commission, Industry and Trade Summary: Franchising (Washington, DC, 1995), pp. 15–16.

Euro Disney: From Dream to Nightmare

At the press conference announcing Euro Disneyland SCA's financial results for the year ended September 30, 1994, CEO Philippe Bourguignon summed up the year in succinct terms: "The best thing about 1994 is that it's over."

In fact, the results for the year were better than many of Euro Disneyland's long-suffering shareholders had predicted. Although revenues were down 15% – the result of falling visitor numbers caused by widespread expectations that the park would be closed down – costs had been cut by 12%, resulting in a similar operating profit to that of the previous year. The bottom line still showed a substantial loss (net after-tax loss was FF1.8bn); however, this was a big improvement on the previous year (FF5.33bn loss). Tables 15.1 and 15.2 show details of the financial performance.

Regarding the future, Bourguignon was decidedly upbeat. Following the FF13bn restructuring agreed with creditor banks in June, Euro Disney was now on a much firmer financial footing. As a result of the restructuring, Euro Disneyland SCA was left with equity of about FF5.5bn and total borrowings of FF15.9bn – down by a quarter from the previous year. With the threat of closure lifted, Euro Disney was now in a much better position to attract visitors and corporate partners.

Efforts to boost attendance figures included a new advertising campaign, a new FF600m attraction (Space Mountain), which was due to open in June 1996, and changing the park's name from Euro Disneyland to Disneyland Paris.

In addition, Euro Disney had made a number of operational improvements. Mr Bourguignon reported that queuing times had been cut by 45% during the year through new attractions and the redesign of existing ones; hotel occupancy rates had risen from 55% in the previous year to 60%; and managers were to be given greater incentives. The net result, claimed Bourguignon, was that the company would reach break-even during 1996.

TABLE 15.1 Euro Disneyland SCA: financial performance 1993–4. Operating revenue and expenditure (millions of French francs)

	1994	1993
Revenue:		
Theme park	2,212	2,594
Hotels	1,613	1,721
Other	322	559
Construction sales	114	851
Total revenue	4,261	5,725
Direct costs/expenses:		
Park & Hotels	(2,961)	(3,382)
Construction sales	(114)	(846)
Operating income	1,186	1,497
Depreciation	(291)	(227)
Lease rental expense	(889)	(1,712)
Royalties	–	(262)
General & Admin.	(854)	(1,113)
Financial income	538	719
Financial expenses	(972)	(615)
Loss	(1,282)	(1,713)
Exceptional loss, net	(515)	(3,624)
Net loss	(1,797)	(5,337)
Employees (cast members)		
Number	11,865	10,172
Annual Cost (FF, millions)	2,108	1,892

The stock market responded positively to the results. In London, the shares of Euro Disneyland SCA rose 13p to 96p. However, this did not take the shares much above their all-time low. On November 6, 1989, the first day of trading after the Euro Disneyland initial public offering, the shares had traded at 880p. Since then, Euro Disneyland stock had been on a near-continuous downward trend (see figure 15.1). The *Financial Times*' Lex column was also unenthusiastic:

> Still beset by high costs and low attendances, Euro Disney will find it hard to hit its target of break-even by the end of September 1996. Costs in the year were reduced by FF500m by introducing more flexible labor agreements (more part-timers, increased job sharing and the use of more students in the peak season) as well as outsourcing contracts in the hotel operation. But the company admits that the lion's share of cost reductions has now been realized. Now it hopes attendances are rising . . . Getting people to spend more once they are at the park might be more difficult. Euro Disney is pinning its hopes on economic recovery in Europe. It'll have to start paying interest, management fees and royalties again in five years' time. Management will not say whether it'll be able to cope then.[1]

Returning to his office at the end of the press conference, Bourguignon sighed. Since taking over from the previous chief executive, Robert Fitzpatrick, in 1993,

TABLE 15.2 Euro Disneyland SCA: financial statements 1992–4 (under US GAAP)

Balance sheet

	1994	1993	1992
Cash and investments	289	211	479
Receivables	227	268	459
Fixed assets, net	3,791	3,704	4,346
Other assets	137	214	873
Total assets	4,444	4,397	6,157
Accounts payable & other liabilities	560	647	797
Borrowings	3,051	3,683	3,960
Stockholders' equity	833	67	1,400
Total liabilities & stockholders' equity	4,444	4,397	6,157

Statement of operations

	1994	1993	1992
Revenues	751	873	738
Costs and expenses	1,198	1,114	808
Net interest expense	280	287	95
Loss before income taxes and cumulative effect of accounting change	(727)	(528)	(165)
Income tax benefit	–	–	30
Loss before cumulative effect of accounting change	(727)	(528)	(135)
Cumulative effect of change in accounting for pre-opening costs	–	(578)	–
Net loss	(727)	(1,106)	(135)

SOURCE: WALT DISNEY COMPANY, ANNUAL REPORT, 1994.

the 46-year-old had been engaged in a continuing battle to ensure the survival of Euro Disney. Now that survival was no longer an issue, Bourguignon now faced his next challenge: could Euro Disneyland ever become profitable – especially once Euro Disney had to resume paying licensing and management fees (amounting to some FF500 million a year) to Walt Disney Co. after 1998?

Disney Theme Parks

Walt Disney pioneered the theme park concept. His goal was to create a unique entertainment experience that combined fantasy and history, adventure, and learning in which the guest would be a participant, as well as a spectator. Current Disney-designed theme parks in California, Florida, Japan, and France are divided into distinct lands. All the parks include a number of similar lands with identical attractions. These include Main Street, Frontierland, Tomorrowland, Fantasyland, and Adventureland. The objective is to immerse the guest in the atmosphere of the particular land. The theme of each land is reflected in the types of rides and attractions, the costumes of

FIGURE 15.1 Euro Disneyland's share price in Paris, 1991–4 (in French francs)

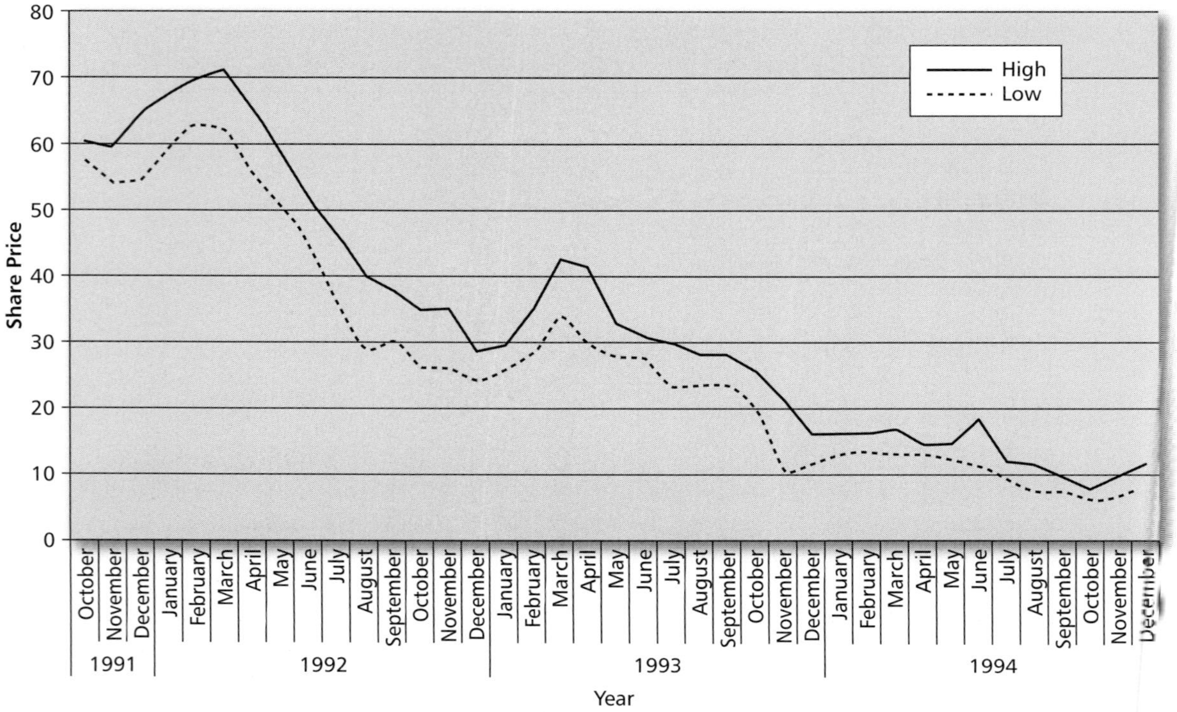

employees, the architectural style of the buildings, and even the food and souvenirs sold within the boundaries of the particular land. Rather than presenting a random collection of roller coasters, carousels, and other rides, the Disney parks create an all-embracing experience which envelops the guest in carefully designed, tightly managed fantasy experience such as space flight, a Caribbean pirate attack, a flying ride with Peter Pan, or a race down the Matterhorn in a bob-sleigh.

Disney theme parks benefit from the talent and expertise of the Walt Disney "family" of businesses. Parks are designed by the engineers and architects of a wholly owned subsidiary – WED Enterprises. The themes for the attractions and characters that are featured in them often have their origins in cartoons and live action movies produced by Disney's studios. The parks also benefit from management and merchandising techniques developed over many years at Disney. These techniques have led to tremendous successes. In merchandising, Disney retail stores achieved some of the highest sales per square foot in the United States.

Disney's success can be traced to the control of the environment to create a unique experience for the visitor. This control is achieved through highly systematized operations management and human resource management. Disney has sophisticated procedures for selecting and training employees to ensure the highest levels of service, safety, and maintenance in the industry. Disney's ability to reconcile a high level of occupancy with high levels of service and customer satisfaction is achieved through sophisticated methods of forecasting visitor levels on a daily basis, and careful design of parks to minimize the frustrations of crowds and waiting. Disney also emphasizes the continual renewal of its theme parks' appeal through investment in new attractions. It then supports these with heavy promotion.

Disney parks have historically had higher attendance levels than other theme and amusement parks throughout the world. During the late 1980s and early 1990s, Disney's theme parks in Anaheim, Orlando, and Tokyo together attracted over 50 million guest visits annually.

Disney's US Parks

The Los Angeles Disneyland theme park was finally opened in July of 1955 on 160 acres of land in Anaheim in California's Orange County. The success of Disneyland created a real estate boom in Anaheim, resulting in Disneyland being surrounded by a ring of hotels, motels, restaurants, and other businesses.

For his next theme park project, Walt Disney aimed for undiluted control over the business and its revenue stream. Walt Disney World Resort opened in 1971 on a huge tract of 29,000 acres that Walt acquired outside of Orlando, Florida. Walt Disney World eventually comprised three separate theme parks: the original Magic Kingdom, the Experimental Prototype Community of Tomorrow (EPCOT) Center that opened in 1982 which in itself hosted two themes: *Future World* and *World Showcase*, and Disney-MGM Studios which opened in 1989.

The experience of creating a theme park as a destination resort represented a major development in Disney's conception of a theme park and was influential in its expansion plans into Europe. The huge site allowed Disney to broaden the scope of its theme park activities to create themed hotels, golf courses and other sports, convention facilities, night clubs, a range of retail stores, even residential housing. The complementary coupling of a theme park with resort facilities that could even host commercial activities (conferences, a technology park) became central to Disney's theme park strategy.

By 1990, Walt Disney World had become the largest center of hotel capacity in the United States with approximately 70,000 rooms, of which almost 10% were owned and operated by Disney. Even though the room rates charged by Disney were considerably higher than other hotels in the vicinity, they achieved a remarkable occupancy rate of 94% during the late 1980s.

Tokyo Disneyland

Tokyo Disneyland, which opened in 1983, was a major departure for Walt Disney Company. The Oriental Land Company Limited (OLCL), a Japanese development company, had approached Disney with a proposal to open a Disneyland in Japan. Disney's top management regarded a Disney theme park in another country with a different climate and a different culture as a risky venture. Disney insisted on a deal that would leave OLCL with all the risk: the park would be owned and operated by OLCL while Disney would receive royalties of 10% on the admissions revenues and 5% on receipts from food, beverages, and souvenirs. These royalties represented licensing fees for Disney's trademarks and intellectual property, engineering designs for rides, and ongoing technical assistance. Despite the challenges of limited space and cold winter weather, Tokyo Disneyland was a huge success. By the late 1980s it was drawing 15 million visits a year – more than any other Disney park.[2] By 1989,

Disney's royalties from Tokyo Disneyland had risen to $573 million – greater than the operating income received from Disney's US theme parks.

Planning and Development

Beginnings of Euro Disneyland

The success of Tokyo Disneyland was clear evidence to Disney's top management of the international potential for Disney's theme parks. Europe was considered the obvious location for the next Disney park. Europe had always been a strong market for Disney movies, and there was a strong European demand for toys, books, and comics that featured Disney characters – European consumers generated about one-quarter of revenues from Disney licensed consumer products. The popularity of Disney theme parks with Europeans was evident from the 2 million European visitors to Disneyland and Walt Disney World each year. Moreover, Western Europe possessed a population and affluence capable of supporting a major Disney theme park.

In 1984, Disney management made the decision to commit to development of a European theme park and commenced feasibility planning and site selection. In assessing alternative locations, the following criteria were applied:

- proximity to a high-density population zone with a relatively high level of disposable income;
- ability to draw upon a substantial local tourist population, availability of qualified labor, and readily accessible transportation;
- availability of sufficient land to permit expansion of the project to meet increasing demand;
- provision of necessary infrastructure, such as water and electricity.

Two locations quickly emerged as front-runners: Barcelona and Paris. While Barcelona had the advantages of a better year-round climate, Paris offered key economic and infrastructure advantages, together with strong backing from the French government. Disney's interest in a European theme park corresponded with the French government's plans to develop the Marne-la-Vallée area east of Paris. The result was rapid progress of Disney's formal negotiations with the range of local government authorities and public bodies whose cooperation and agreement were essential for a project of this scale. The proposed site's demographic characteristics offered the right set of conditions for a successful theme park. The park rested on a 4,500 acre site 32 kilometers east of Paris, providing proximity to a metropolitan area and room for expansion; the high population of the greater Paris area (over 10 million) and Europe (over 330 million) provided a large consumer market; and existing and planned transportation equipped the park with access to vital infrastructure. Paris was already a major tourist destination with excellent air, road, and rail links with the rest of Europe.

On March 24, 1987, the Walt Disney Company entered into the Agreement on the Creation and the Operation of Euro Disneyland in France (the "Master Agreement") with the Republic of France, the Region of Ile-de-France, the Department of Seine-et-Marne, the Etablissement Public d'Aménagement de la Ville Nouvelle de Marne-la-Vallée, and the Régie Autonome des Transports Parisiens. This was followed by incorporation of Euro Disneyland SCA (the "Company") and the conclusion of an agreement with the SNCF (the French national railway company) to provide TGV (the French high-speed train) service to Euro Disneyland beginning in June 1994. The agreement involved commitments by Disney to establish Euro Disneyland as a French corporation, to develop a major international theme park, and to create 30,000 jobs in the process. The French authorities committed to provide land and infrastructure over the project's 30-year development period ending in 2017. The real estate deal involved Disney acquiring 1,700 hectares (approximately 4,300 acres[3]) of agricultural land at Marne-la-Vallée. In addition, a further 243 hectares were reserved for public facilities and infrastructure. The purchase price for the land included the raw land price (FF11.1 per square meter or approximately $8,360 per acre), direct and indirect secondary infrastructure costs, and certain financing and overhead expenses of the French authorities. The area of the total site was equivalent to one-fifth of the area of the city of Paris. The land for the first phase of the development was purchased outright by Euro Disneyland SCA, with purchase options on the remaining land. Euro Disneyland SCA also had the right to sell land to third parties, as long as the development plans of any purchasers were approved by the French planning authority.

The agreement provided for motorway links to Paris, Strasbourg, and the two international airports serving Paris – Charles de Gaulle and Orly, while the planned extension of the RER (the express commuter rail network) would allow visitors to reach the Magic Kingdom from the center of Paris within 40 minutes. Euro Disney[4] would also be linked to France's TGV system, with its own station serving the park. This would also give rail service from Britain through the Channel Tunnel. In addition to infrastructure, the French government's financial inducements included FF4.8 billion in loans and a favorable tax rate (34%). The total package of incentives added up to roughly FF6.0 billion.[5]

The Market: Demand and Competition

A key factor attracting Disney to Paris was market potential. The greater Paris metropolis has a population of over 10 million. Roughly 16 million people lived within a 160km radius of the proposed site; within a 320km radius were 41 million people; and within a 480km radius were 109 million people. Paris' transportation links facilitated access to this huge market. As a result, Euro Disneyland would be capable of achieving a high level of capacity utilization, even with much lower market penetration rates than those achieved by Disney's California and Florida theme parks. European vacation patterns were also seen as conducive to visits – Europeans received substantially more vacation time than US workers and in addition to their summer vacation, European families frequently took shorter vacations throughout the year. Estimates of numbers of visitors to Euro Disney and their expenditures were made by consultants Arthur D. Little as part of their financial projections for Euro Disneyland SCA (see Appendix 1).

The ability of Euro Disney to achieve its visitor targets would depend not only on the size of the market but also upon the relative attractiveness and number of competing tourist destinations. Although Disney viewed its theme parks as unique in terms of the quality and intensity of the entertainment experience that it offered, the company also recognized that, ultimately, a wide range of family vacation and entertainment experiences compete for household disposable income. Although there were very few large-scale theme parks in Europe to directly compete with Euro Disneyland (most of the world's major theme parks were located in the US), there were a

TABLE 15.3 Attendance at major theme parks

	Estimated attendance in 1988 (millions of guest visits)
Sea World – *Florida*	4.6
Tivoli Gardens – *Denmark*	4.5
Universal Studios Tour – *California*	4.2
Knott's Berry Farm – *California*	4.0
Busch Gardens – *Florida*	3.7
Sea World – *California*	3.4
Six Flags Magic Mountain – *California*	3.1
King's Island – *Ohio*	3.0
Liseberg – *Sweden*	2.8
Alton Towers – *United Kingdom*	2.3
De Efteling – *The Netherlands*	2.3
Phantasialand – *West Germany*	2.2

SOURCE: EURO DISNEYLAND SCA ABRIDGED OFFERING CIRCULAR.

number of family entertainment destinations within Europe that would be potential competitors (see table 15.3). In addition, European cities – such as London, Paris, Rome, Prague, Barcelona, and many others – offered a richness and variety of cultural and historical experiences that few US cities could match and represented an alternative to Euro Disney for short family vacations. Furthermore, there was a host of traditional forms of family entertainment in Europe, including fairs, carnivals, and festivals, some of which were small and local while others – such as the Munich Bierfest, the Pamplona bull-running festival, the Edinburgh cultural festival, and the Dutch tulip festivals – were major events attracting large numbers of international visitors.

In addition, Disney's plans for Euro Disneyland created its own competitors. Within two years of Disney's announcement to build Euro Disney, three French theme parks – Mirapolis, Futuroscope, and Zygofolis – had opened in an attempt to preempt Disney's entry into the market. By the summer of 1989, two more theme parks – Asterix and Big Bang Schtroumph – opened their gates. However, with aggregate annual losses of about $43 million on a total investment of over $600 million, these parks were considered financial disasters.[6]

The Development Plan

Euro Disney's Development Program provided for a theme park, based closely on the themes and concepts of Disney's US theme parks, that would be the largest theme park and resort development in Europe. The plan established two stages for the project.

Phase 1 Phase 1, the major part of the overall project, was subdivided into two sections. Phase 1A comprised the Magic Kingdom theme park, the Magic Kingdom Hotel (which would serve as the entrance area to the theme park), and a camping ground, which were to be completed at a budgeted cost of FF14.9 billion. Of the 570 acres allocated for Phase 1, Phase 1A would utilize 240 acres. The rest of the land would be developed in Phase 1B to accommodate five additional hotels; an entertainment, restaurant, and shopping complex; and sports facilities with an 18-hole championship golf course. Phase 1A also provided for the French government to construct two junctions with the nearby motorway, main access roads to the park, a drinking-water supply and distribution system, storm drainage, sewers, solid waste treatment, and telecommunications networks. The cost of the additional infrastructure, including links with the RER and the TGV, was to be financed by Euro Disneyland SCA.

The Magic Kingdom theme park was to include five themed lands: Main Street USA, the gateway to the park; Frontierland, a reproduction of wooden streets typical of a mid-nineteenth-century frontier town; tropical Adventure Land, the most exotic of the park settings; Fantasyland, with attractions drawn from well-known Disney stories; and Discoveryland, which, through the sophisticated use of technology, illustrates the past and the future. Each offers appropriately themed restaurants and shopping facilities.

To permit year-round operation, Euro Disney included adaptations designed to make attendance less dependent on the weather, with more interconnected covered areas than at other Disney parks. Many modifications to the themes, architecture, and dining facilities were made to tailor the park to the European market. For example, while French is the first language of the park, universal signposting is used wherever possible to aid non-French-speaking visitors, and many attractions are identified by visual cues.

Phase 2 Phase 2 of the Long Term Development Strategy extended to 2011. It envisioned a second theme park (Disney-MGM Studios) on a site adjacent to the Magic Kingdom; 15 additional hotels, which would increase the number of rooms available by 13,000; a water recreation area and second golf course; and residential and commercial development. This phase was left flexible to accommodate the policies of the French authorities, economic and market conditions, participant needs, and visitor preferences.

Construction Disney exercised close control over design and construction of Phase 1A of Euro Disney. Lehrer McGovern Bovis Inc. (LMB), an independent construction management firm with international experience in the management of large-scale construction projects, was the main contractor. LMB reported to Euro Disneyland Imagineering SARL (EDLI), a French subsidiary of Disney that had overall responsibility for designing and constructing Phases 1 and 2 of the theme park. Also reporting to EDLI were separate Disney companies responsible for design, conceptual and otherwise; engineering; and the development and equipping of attractions.

Participants As with other Disney theme parks, at Euro Disneyland Participants played an important role in financial and in marketing terms. Participants are companies or organizations that enter into long-term marketing agreements with the Company. Typically, these relationships represent a ten-year commitment and physically tie the Participant to the Magic Kingdom, where it hosts or presents one or more of the theme park's attractions, restaurants, or other facilities. Relationships with Participants may also involve marketing activities featuring the association between the Participant and the Company. Each Participant pays an individually negotiated annual fee, which may contribute to the financing of a particular attraction or facility.

FIGURE 15.2 The financial and management relationship between Walt Disney and Euro Disneyland

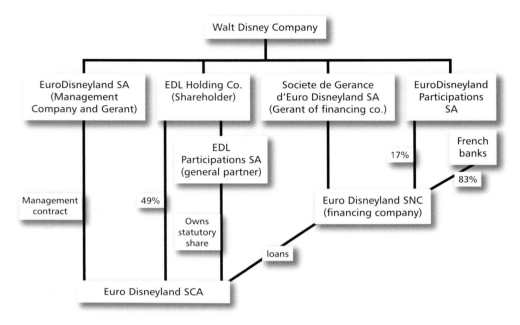

Initial Participants at Euro Disneyland included Kodak, Banque Nationale de Paris, Renault, and Europcar.

Financial and Management Structure

For Euro Disneyland, Disney chose a unique financial and management structure. Rather than a pure franchise operation similar to Tokyo Disneyland, Disney chose to retain management and operational control of the park while allowing European investors to take majority ownership and European banks to provide most of the debt financing. The relationship between Walt Disney Company and Euro Disneyland is depicted in figure 15.2.

Euro Disneyland SCA

Euro Disneyland SCA was formed to build and own Euro Disneyland. The company was a *société en commandite par actions* – the French equivalent of a limited partnership. The company was governed by a supervisory board elected by the shareholders and chaired by Jean Taittinger, the Chairman and Chief Executive of Société du Louvre and Banque du Louvre. Disney took a 49% stake in Euro Disneyland SCA; the remaining 51% of equity was floated through an initial public offering underwritten by three investment banks. The shares were listed on the Paris and London stock markets. Although Disney held 49% of Euro Disneyland SCA equity it contributed only 13% of its equity book value (FF273m net of incentives received). The difference was "granted" to the company, both as a goodwill "gesture" in recognition of Disney's reputation and credibility in the investment community and as compensation for Disney's assumed risk in the undertaking.

The Management Company

Euro Disneyland SCA was managed by a separate management company, Euro Disneyland SA (the "Management Company"), a wholly owned subsidiary of Disney. The Management Company, or *gerant*, was responsible under French law for managing Euro Disneyland SCA and its affairs in the company's best interests. In turn, the Management Company agreed that the provision of management services to the Company would be its exclusive business. Under the Articles of Association, the Management Company was entitled to annual fees consisting of a base fee and management incentive fees. The base fee in any year was set at 3% of the Company's total revenues, and increased to 6% after five years of operation, or after the Company had satisfied certain financial targets. On top of the base fee, the Management Company was entitled to incentive fees based on Euro Disneyland SCA's pre-tax cash flow. These incentives increased in stages up to a possible maximum of 50% of Euro Disneyland SCA's net profit. The Management Company also received 35% of pre-tax gains on the sales of hotels. In addition, Euro Disneyland SCA was obligated to reimburse the Management Company for all its direct and indirect expenses incurred in its management role. The management contract was for five years.

The Shareholding Company and General Partner

Disney's shareholding in Euro Disneyland SCA was held by EDL Holding, a wholly owned subsidiary of Disney. This shareholding company also owned EDL Participations SA, which held the key role of "general partner" in Euro Disneyland SCA – it assumed unlimited liability for the debts and liabilities of Euro Disneyland SCA. As general partner, EDL Participations SA was entitled to a distribution each year equal to 0.5% of Euro Disneyland SCA's net after-tax profits.

The Financing Company

Euro Disneyland SNC was formed to buy the park facilities from Euro Disneyland SCA at book value plus development costs, then lease them back to Euro Disneyland SCA. Euro Disneyland SNC was owned 17% by Disney and 83% by French corporations. The rationale was to allow French corporations to take advantage of the tax benefits of Euro Disneyland's early years of projected losses. Once again, Euro Disneyland SNC was to be managed by a Disney subsidiary and Disney would act as its general partner with full debt default liability.

The License Agreement

Under the License Agreement, Walt Disney Company granted to Euro Disneyland SCA a license to use any present or future Disney intellectual and industrial property rights incorporated in Disney's attractions and facilities and made available to the Company for Euro Disney. These included the Walt Disney name, the Disney characters, and the proprietary technology in theme park attractions. Disney was to receive royalties as follows:

- 10% of gross revenues (net of TVA, the French value-added tax, and similar taxes) from rides and admissions and certain related fees (such as parking, tour guide, and similar services) at all theme parks and other attractions (including the Magic Kingdom and any future theme park);

- 5% of gross revenues (net of TVA and similar taxes) from merchandise, food, and beverage sales in or adjacent to any theme park or other attraction or in any other facility (other than the Magic Kingdom Hotel) whose overall design concept is based predominantly on a Disney theme;

- 10% of all fees due from Participants;

- 5% of all gross revenues (net of TVA and similar taxes) from room rates and related charges at Disney themed accommodations (excluding the Magic Kingdom Hotel).

Cultural Issues

Euro Disneyland presented huge challenges for Disney. Climate was a major problem. The long gray winter of Northern France created complex design problems that were absent from Disney's sun-drenched California and Florida parks. However, the challenges posed by adverse weather conditions were mainly technical and amenable to careful analysis. The issues of culture were much less tractable.

While the success of Tokyo Disneyland was a major factor behind the decision to create Euro Disney, the cultural challenges of France were very different from those of Japan. Tokyo Disneyland had been conceived, built, and operated on a wave of popular Japanese acclaim. As a result, Tokyo Disneyland had made very few concessions to Japanese culture. Although, at first, Disney wanted to adapt some of the attractions to the Japanese context (for example, Samurai-Land instead of Frontierland), their Japanese partners strongly resisted efforts to "localize" Disneyland, arguing that the park would attract more Japanese people if it were built as a perfect replica of US Disneyland. They emphasized that Disney's cartoon characters were very familiar to the Japanese people and that visitors would want "the real thing." As a result, only minor changes were made, such as the addition of Cinderella's Castle and the Mickey Mouse Theater.

After the enthusiasm with which the Japanese greeted Disney's entry, the response of the French could not have been more different. France presented a very different situation. French intellectuals had long shown antagonism towards American popular culture, and they were supported by widespread nationalistic sentiment that saw the French language and French culture as threatened by the global hegemony of the English language. At the political level too, France had been the most independent of the Western European powers in terms of its independent foreign policy and unwillingness to accept US leadership in world affairs. The announcement of the Euro Disneyland project was greeted by howls of outrage from the French media and from the intelligentsia who viewed the park as "a cultural Chernobyl," "a dangerous step towards world homogenization," "a horror made of cardboard, plastic, and appalling colors, a construction of hardened chewing gum and idiotic folklore taken straight out of the comic books written for obese Americans."[7] Euro Disney quickly became a lightning rod for a variety of anti-American issues. For example, shortly after opening, Euro Disney was blockaded by farmers protesting US farm policies.

The design of the park incorporated many adaptations of French and European culture. Disney emphasized the European heritage of many of Disney's characters and storylines (referred to by Chairman Michael Eisner as "European folklore with a Kansas twist"). Some attractions featured European adaptations: Cinderella lived in a French inn and Snow White's home was in a Bavarian village. Other attractions were unique to Euro Disney: Discoveryland (which substituted for Tomorrowland at other Disney parks) was based on themes from Jules Verne and Leonardo da Vinci; "Visionarium" was a 360-degree movie theater showcasing French culture; an Alice-in-Wonderland attraction was surrounded by a 5,000sq. ft. hedge maze. Designing and constructing these European-themed attractions added substantially to the cost of Euro Disneyland.

Some "American" themed attractions were adapted on the basis of market research findings. For example, the finding that European visitors to Disney's US parks responded positively to themes embodying the American West encouraged Disney to redesign several attractions around a Wild West theme – including a mining town setting for one ride, a "Davy Crockett" themed campground, and hotels named the "Cheyenne," "Santa Fe," and "Sequoia Lodge."

Other adaptations were made to cater to European social behavior and culinary tastes. Concern over European aversion to queuing resulted in the provision of video screens, movies, and other entertainment for guests waiting in line. Disney's no-alcohol policy was adjusted by allowing wine and beer to be served at Feastival Disney, an entertainment complex just outside the theme park. In the restaurant facilities, greater emphasis was placed on sit-down dining and much less on fast food. At a seminar at UCLA in 1990, Robert Fitzpatrick placed a major emphasis on the Company's determination to provide the highest standards of quality at Euro Disney. This was evident both in the cuisine and in the furnishings and service standards of the hotels. In both areas, Fitzpatrick argued, quality was well in excess of the standards at Disney's US parks.

Human relations management posed further cultural challenges. Central to the Disney theme park experience was the way in which "cast members" interacted with the guests. Disney was famous for its meticulous approach to recruitment, its commitment to employee training, and the maintenance of rigorous standards of employee conduct. For example, Disney's employee handbook spelled out a strict code with respect to dress and appearance, including:

- Above average height and below average weight

- Pleasant appearance (straight teeth, no facial blemishes)

- Conservative grooming standards (facial hair and long hair is banned)

- Very modest make-up, very limited jewelry (for example, no more than one ring on each hand)

- Employees were required to wear specific types and colors of underwear; only neutral colors of pantyhose were allowed.[8]

Training embraced both general principles and specific knowledge and behaviors. For example, employees were instructed that their behavior on the job should be governed by three major rules: "First, we practice a friendly smile. Second, we use only friendly phrases. Third, we are not stuffy."

To what extent could locally recruited employees provide the level and quality and consistency of service at Euro Disney that would match that of other Disney theme parks, and to what extent could Disney simply transplant its US HRM practices? Euro Disney's selection and training were closely modeled on Disney's US approach. A Euro Disney branch of Disney University was opened and recruitment of 10,000 employees began in September 1991. Selection criteria were "applicant friendliness, warmth, and liking of people." The rules for job applicants were spelled out in a video presentation and in the employee handbook, "The Euro Disney Look." The rules went far beyond weight and height requirements, describing the length of the men's hair, beard and mustache requirements, tattoo coverage requirements, and hair color specifications (for example, hair had to be of a natural-looking color, without frosting or streaking). Only moderate use of cosmetics was allowed. Women could wear one earring in each ear with the earrings' diameter not to exceed three-quarters of an inch.[9] The goal was a nationality mix that would match that of Euro Disney's customers, about 45% of whom were French. However, in response to local pressure and the greater availability of local applicants, some 70% of employees were French. At the management level, Disney relied on importing about 200 managers from other Disney parks and training 270 locally recruited managers (this involved training at Disney's other theme parks).

Disney's recruiting practices and employee policies produced a storm of protest. French labor unions started protesting right from the moment that Euro Disney started interviewing applicants. Representatives of the General Confederation of Labor handed out leaflets in front of Euro Disney's HQ warning applicants that the Disney hiring practices represented "an attack on individual freedom." Many of Disney's normal US hiring and employment practices contravened French law. Workforce flexibility was limited by the restrictions on terminating employees with more than two years with the company and the high severance payments involved. There were also legal limits over the recruitment and dismissal of seasonal workers. As for Disney's dress and personal grooming codes, French law prohibited an employer from restricting "individual and collective freedoms" unless the restrictions could be justified by the "nature of the objective to be accomplished and were proportional to that end." Since Disney estimated that no more than 700 employees would be involved in "theatrical actions," dress code limitations could only be imposed on those employees, not on those who would only be "back stage."

The First Year

Euro Disney's opening on April 12, 1992 combined both fanfare and protest. An extravagant opening ceremony involved some of the world's leading entertainers and was televised in 22 countries. Michael Eisner proclaimed Euro Disney to be "one of the greatest man-made attractions in the world" while the French Prime Minister described the park as an "incredible achievement which transcends national frontiers . . . We are deeply attached to the links of friendship between our continent and yours. Euro Disney is one of the symbols of this transatlantic friendship." However, the opening was marred by a demonstration of local residents, a train strike affecting lines leading to the park, and a terrorist bomb threat. By the end of the first day, park attendance had been way below capacity and only one-half of the anticipated number.

The park ran into early teething problems. Design problems ranged from insufficient breakfast facilities to an absence of toilet facilities for bus drivers and a shortage of employee accommodation. During the first nine weeks of operation, 1,000 employees left Euro Disney, about one-half voluntarily. Long hours and hectic work pace were the main reasons given for leaving. Nevertheless, visitor reactions were mainly highly positive. Negative comments related to frustration with long periods of waiting in line and the high cost of admission, food, and souvenirs. Some voiced concern over the multinational, multicultural flavor of Euro Disney: "They haven't yet figured out whether it's going to be an American park, a French park, or a European park . . . Differences in waiting line behavior is striking. For instance, Scandinavians appear quite content to wait for rides, whereas some of the southern Europeans seem to have made an Olympic event out of getting to the ticker tape first." Some visitors had difficulty envisaging Disney within a European context: "Disney is very much an American culture. Florida is the true Disney World, the true feeling of Disney, what Disney is trying to project. Americans are part of that, the French aren't."[10]

Start-up difficulties were normal in the theme park business – all major theme parks, including those of Disney, experienced some teething problems during the period of initial operation. Universal Studios in Florida had a disastrous first few months, but subsequently rebounded. With 30,000 visitors daily during the summer of 1992, it seemed that Euro Disney might reach its projected target of 11 million visitors annually. However, it was soon clear that, despite good visitor numbers during the summer, Euro Disney's profitability would fall far below expectations. There were a larger number of day-visitors and fewer period-visits than had been anticipated. As a result, Euro Disney cut hotel rates by up to 25%. Moreover, average visitor expenditure on beverages, food, and gifts was 12% less than the $33 per day that had been anticipated. Part of the problem was the economic situation – during 1992, most of Western Europe was mired in one of the worst economic downturns since World War II. The depressed state of the French real estate market also prevented Euro Disney from boosting revenues through land sales.

By the end of Euro Disney's first full financial year, the extent of the financial underperformance was becoming clear. Even with exceptional items, the company lost over FF1.7 billion. In terms of US GAAP, Euro Disneyland's pre-tax loss was over half a billion dollars. Top-line performance was a key problem. Instead of the 11 million visitors forecast, Euro Disney attracted 9.8 million visitors during its first full year. Equally serious was the fact that average visitor spending was below target, and much lower than at Disney's US and Japanese parks. Fewer visitors than projected were staying in Disney theme hotels, deterred by room rates that were much higher than in comparable hotels in Paris. Hotel occupancy rates were below 50% in contrast to the 60% figure projected. On the cost side, Disney's emphasis on quality had boosted both construction and operating costs, while higher than anticipated debt together with rising interest rates caused interest charges to spiral upward. Labor costs amounted to a huge 24% of sales, rather than the forecasted level of 13% of sales. Much of the cost overruns could be attributed to Disney's belief that "Lacoste and Polo loving" Europeans would not tolerate anything unsophisticated or cheap. For example, in the US, "The Walt" restaurant had wallpaper but at Euro Disney the walls were covered in Moroccan leather. Yet, when it came to trading off sophistication for lower prices, most Euro Disney customers opted for the latter.

For Walt Disney Company, the financial returns were better than they were for Euro Disneyland's other shareholders. During 1992 and 1993, Disney's 49% share of

Euro Disneyland's losses was offset by royalties from its licensing agreement. These amounted to $36.3 million in 1993 and $32.9 million in 1992; however, Disney agreed to defer its management fees for 1992 and 1993.

Restructuring

During the winter of 1993/4, Euro Disney visitor numbers plummeted. Despite a fall of the French franc against the US dollar, many Europeans found that Disneyland Florida was not only a more attractive destination during the winter months, it was also cheaper. "It's cheaper to go on a two-week holiday in Florida than to come to Euro Disney for five days," remarked one British traveler with a family of four. With low transatlantic fares, European visitors to Walt Disney World in Orlando increased sharply during 1992 and 1993. By early 1994, Euro Disney was in crisis. Faced with mounting losses, rising debt, and doubts about the company's capacity to cover its interest payments, rumors were rife that the park would be forced to close.

The financial restructuring package agreed between Euro Disneyland and its creditors in June 1994 involved the following measures:

- A $1.1 billion rights offering of which Disney agreed to take up 41%.
- The provision by Disney of $255 million in lease financing at an interest rate of 1%.
- The cancellation by Disney of $210 million in receivables from Euro Disneyland.
- The agreement by Disney to waive royalties and management fees for five years.
- The agreement that Disney would receive warrants for the purchase of 28 million Euro Disneyland shares and would receive a development fee of $225 million once the second phase of the development project was launched. Euro Disneyland's lenders agreed to underwrite 51% of the Euro Disney rights offering, to forgive certain interest charges until September 2003, and to defer all principal payments for three years. In return, Euro Disneyland issued the lenders ten-year warrants for the purchase of up to 40 million shares of Euro Disneyland stock.

In a separate agreement, Disney agreed to sell 75 million shares, equivalent to 10% of Euro Disneyland's total shareholding, to Prince Alwaleed Bin Talal Bin Abdulaziz Al Saud. The sale reduced Disney's shareholding in Euro Disneyland to 39%.

Looking Ahead

While the restructuring package had staved off disaster for the time being, the traumas of the past year made Bourguignon cautious about the future. Despite heavy advertising, the addition of new attractions, and the fine-tuning of Disney's image, customer service, and offering of food, drinks, and souvenirs, Euro Disney had yet to reach the initial forecast of 11 million visitors annually. Significant cost reductions had been achieved; however, the scope for further cost reductions was limited if Euro Disney was to maintain Disney's standards of customer service excellence. While Bourguignon was convinced that the Company would be generating operating profits by 1995, such profits would be the result of Disney's agreement to forgo its royalties and management fees. Once these were reinstated, Euro Disney's costs would increase by about FF500 million annually.

Bourguignon believed that many of the problems that had dogged Euro Disney from the beginning had been resolved. In particular, the renaming of the park as Disneyland Paris had helped alleviate ambiguity and conflict over the park's identity. Disneyland Paris was to be a Disney theme park located close to Paris. Dropping the "Euro" prefix released the Company from the public's mistrust of all things Euro, and helped the park to avoid the debate over what European culture and European identity actually meant. Moreover, the new name firmly associated Euro Disney with the romantic connotations of the city of Paris. In terms of the need to differentiate Euro Disney from Disney's other theme parks, the experience of the past two years suggested that Euro Disney's expensive adaptations to meet European tastes and European culture were not greatly appreciated by customers. For the most part, visitors were delighted by the same rides as existed in Disney's US parks and generally preferred fast food over fine dining.

Over the next six months, Bourguignon recognized that key decisions needed to be taken:

- To what extent should Euro Disney cut admission prices in order to boost attendance? An internal study had estimated that a 20% reduction in admission prices would boost attendance by about 800,000 visitors; however, the net result would still be a reduction in total revenues of about 5%.

- The problems of insufficient demand related primarily to the winter months. In previous winters some senior managers had argued for the closure of the park. However, so long as most of Euro Disney's employees were permanent staff, such a closure would do little to reduce total costs.

- Bourguignon had already deferred Phase 2 of the development plan – construction of a Disney–MGM Studios theme park. The other members of his senior management team were urging him to go ahead with this phase of development. Only with a second theme park, they believed, would Euro Disney's goal of becoming a major destination resort become realized. However, Bourguignon was acutely aware of Euro Disney's still-precarious financial situation. With net equity of about FF5.5bn and total borrowings of FF15.9bn, Euro Disney was not well-placed to begin the large-scale capital expenditures that phase 2 would involve.

As Bourguignon arranged the papers on his desk at the end of a long day, he reflected on his success at pulling off the rescue plan and the continuing uphill struggle to realize the ambitions that had driven the project in the early days. The wartime words of Winston Churchill summed up the situation well: "This is not the end. It is not the beginning of the end. It is the end of the beginning."

Appendix 1
Euro Disneyland SCA's Financial Model

The Company has prepared a financial model, based on the principal assumptions described below, which projects revenues, expenses, profits, cash flows, and dividends of the Company

TABLE 15.A1 Euro Disneyland SCA: projected revenues and profits (FF millions)

1992–6					
12 months commencing April 1	**1992**	**1993**	**1994**	**1995**	**1996**
Revenues					
Magic Kingdom	4,246	4,657	5,384	5,835	6,415
Second theme park	0	0	0	0	3,128
Resort and property development	1,236	2,144	3,520	5,077	6,386
Total revenues	5,482	6,801	8,904	10,930	15,929
Profit before taxation	351	620	870	1,676	1,941
Net profit	204	360	504	972	1,121
Dividends payable	275	425	625	900	1,100
Tax credit or payment	0	138	213	313	450
Total return	275	563	838	1,213	1,550
Per share (FF)	1.6	3.3	4.9	7.1	9.1

Later years				
12 months commencing April 1	**2001**	**2006**	**2011**	**2016**
Revenues				
Magic Kingdom	9,730	13,055	18,181	24,118
Second theme park	4,565	6,656	9,313	12,954
Resort and property development	8,133	9,498	8,979	5,923
Total revenues	22,428	29,209	36,473	42,995
Profit before taxation	3,034	4,375	6,539	9,951
Net profit	1,760	2,538	3,793	5,771
Dividends payable	1,750	2,524	3,379	5,719
Tax credit or payment	536	865	1,908	2,373
Total return	2,286	3,389	5,287	8,092
Per share (FF)	13.4	19.9	31.1	47.6

for 12-month periods beginning 1 April, 1992 and ending 31 March, 2017 as summarized in table 15.A1. Although the Company's accounting year-end is 30 September, years beginning 1 April have been used for the projections in order to represent whole operating years from the projected date of opening of the Magic Kingdom. The projections contained in the model do not constitute a forecast of the actual revenues, expenses, profits, cash flows or dividends of the Company. The model assumes that the Company will complete Phase 1 as described in this document and will develop the remaining elements of Euro Disneyland according to the Long Term Development Strategy. As discussed above, the Company retains the flexibility to change the Long Term Development Strategy and the designs for Phase 1B in response to future conditions. Table 15.A2 summarizes the principal components of the development plan.

TABLE 15.A2 Planned development of Euro Disneyland

	Phase 1A	Phase 1B	Long-term development	Total
Theme parks	1	–	1	2
Hotel capacity (rooms)	500	4,700	13,000	18,200
Camping ground (campsite plots)	595	–	1,505	2,100
Entertainment center (sq. meters)	–	22,000	38,000	60,000
Offices (sq. meters)	–	30,000	670,000	700,000
Corporate park (sq. meters)	–	50,000	700,000	750,000
Golf courses		1	1	2
Single-family homes	–	570	1,930	2,500
Retail shopping center (sq. meters)	–	–	95,000	95,000
Water recreation area	–	–	1	1
Multi-family residence	–	–	3,000	3,000
Time-share units	–	–	2,400	2,400

SOURCE: EURO DISNEYLAND SCA ABRIDGED OFFERING CIRCULAR.

In addition, the model is based on other assumptions developed by the Company in light of Disney's experience with existing theme parks and resorts, after taking into account analyses of local market conditions and an assessment of likely future economic, market, and other factors. The major assumptions have been reviewed by Arthur D. Little International, Inc. ("ADL"), the independent consultancy firm retained by the Company to test and verify their reasonableness. Set out at the end of "The financial model" is a letter from ADL regarding its reports. While the Company believes that the assumptions underlying the model are reasonable, there is no certainty that the projected performance of the Company outlined below will be achieved.

Principal Assumptions and Rationale Underlying the Financial Model

Theme Park Attendance To project the number of visitors expected to visit the Euro Disneyland theme parks, several internal and external studies were commissioned. The most recent of these studies was undertaken by ADL in 1989 to verify and confirm the methods and assumptions used in the previous studies, and to make its own estimates of attendance.

The Magic Kingdom The model assumes that the Magic Kingdom will be constructed as described in this document, and that it will open and be fully operational by April 1992.

Summary figures for assumed attendance at the Magic Kingdom are shown in the table below. Attendance is measured in terms of the total numbers of daily guest visits per annum. For example, a visitor who enters a theme park on three separate days will count as three daily guest visits.

	1992	1996	2001	2011
Magic Kingdom (in millions of persons)	11.0	13.3	15.2	16.2

The assumed attendance of 11 million for the first full year of operation of the Magic Kingdom is in line with the average attendance achieved in the first year of operation of the Magic Kingdom theme parks in Florida and Japan, and is below the range of potential initial attendance estimated to be between 11.7 and 17.8 million in the attendance study conducted by ADL. Depending on its seasonal distribution, the higher end of the range could require acceleration of the attraction investment program. ADL concluded that the attendance target of 11 million could be achieved if the development program envisaged for Phase 1A is accomplished and a well-conceived marketing campaign tailored to European patterns is carried out to support the opening of the Magic Kingdom.

Attendance at the Magic Kingdom is assumed to grow over the period covered by the financial model at an average compound rate of 2% per annum. This growth rate compares with an average growth rate of 3.8% per annum for the three Magic Kingdom theme parks in California, Florida and Japan.

The assumed growth rate, which is higher in early years, consists of a basic growth rate, adjusted for the effect of the addition of new attractions every two to three years and for the effect of the opening of a second theme park. The overall assumed growth rate is broken down as follows:

Years	2–5	6–10	11–20	20+
Annual growth (%)	4.9	2.7	0.6	0.0

The method used by ADL involved three steps: first, individual target markets were identified by distance and population: second, penetration rates (the percentage of the total population in a target market which visits the theme park) were estimated for each target market; and third, the average number of annual visits per guest from each target market was estimated.

ADL noted that a number of factors, including the following, contribute to the high attendance levels at Disney-designed theme parks:

- The design and scope of a Magic Kingdom theme park are such that a complete visit requires more than one full day. This means that visitors are likely either to extend their stay or to return at a future date.
- The quality and capacity available at Disney hotels allow the demand for longer stays to be satisfied.
- The level of recognition of the Disney name and the quality of the experience make Disney theme parks popular holiday destination resorts.

In the opinion of ADL these factors distinguish Disney-designed theme parks from existing theme parks and amusement parks in Europe, which are much smaller and are basically designed for single-day visits. Accordingly, in determining potential penetration rates and the number of annual visits per guest to derive projected attendance levels at Euro Disneyland, ADL relied largely on the experience at Disney-designed theme parks.

ADL concluded that because of the large number of people living within a convenient traveling distance of Euro Disneyland, the assumed attendance figures in the model could be achieved with market penetration rates at or below those experienced at other Disney-designed theme parks.

The Company believes that these factors will exist at Euro Disneyland and will support the assumed penetration rates and attendance levels, which are consistent with those experienced at Disney-designed theme parks. The Company also believes that the location of the site at the center of an area of high population density with well-developed transport links will enable Euro Disneyland to draw visitors from both local and more distant markets.

Second Theme Park The model assumes that a second theme park will be completed and will open to the public in the spring of 1996. Summary figures for assumed attendance at the second theme park are as follows:

	1992	1996	2001	2011
Second theme park (in millions)	–	8.0	8.8	10.1

Attendance at the second theme park is assumed to grow at an average compound rate of 2% per annum over the first ten years, and 1% per annum for the next ten years until 2016. These assumptions are primarily based on Disney's experience of opening a second theme park at Walt Disney World, where EPCOT Center drew attendance of over 11 million guest visits in its first year of operation.

Per Capita Spending Theme parks derive their revenues principally from admission charges, sales of food and beverages consumed by visitors while at the park, and from sales of merchandise available at the park's shopping facilities. Revenues from these sources are measured in terms of *per capita* expenditure, which is the average sum spent per daily guest visit.

The Company has assumed *per capita* expenditure figures separately for the two theme parks under the four categories below:

	Magic Kingdom		Second theme park	
	Amount in 1988 FF[a]	Annual growth rate	Amount in 1988 FF[a]	Annual growth rate
Admissions	137.6	6.5%	137.6	6.5%
Food and beverage	56.7	5.0%	53.2	5.0%
Merchandise	74.9	5.0%	46.5	5.0%
Parking and other	5.2	5.0%	5.2	5.0%

[a] Excluding value-added tax.

The assumed real growth rate of admission prices of 1.5% per annum is less than the average 2.6% experienced at the Disney theme parks since 1972.

The *per capita* spending assumptions are based on experience in theme parks designed by Disney, adjusted for local conditions. A separate report on *per capita* spending was undertaken by ADL. To evaluate the reasonableness of the assumed admission prices, ADL reviewed the admission prices charged in Paris for major attractions which could be considered competitive in terms of entertainment value and also the prices charged by European theme and amusement parks. These reviews showed that the assumed admission prices for Euro Disneyland, although higher than those charged at other European theme and amusement parks, (i) could be considered low when related to prices charged in the Paris region for quality adult-oriented entertainment, and (ii) appeared in tune with prices charged for other family-oriented attractions. ADL concluded that the Company's assumed admission prices were justified, having regard for the destination resort features of Euro Disneyland and the high quality of its entertainment.

To evaluate the reasonableness of the assumed prices for food and beverages at Euro Disneyland, ADL analyzed the prices paid by residents of, and tourists to, Paris in those areas that were particularly attractive to visitors. ADL also examined food and beverage prices at other European theme and amusement parks and reviewed typical food and beverage expenditure patterns in France as compared with the United States. ADL concluded that Euro Disneyland's assumptions concerning food and beverage expenditure were reasonable.

ADL determined, in the case of assumed merchandise sales, that there was no comparable experience in the Paris region of small, high-intensity retail shops, exposed to a high volume of visitor traffic, as are found at Disney-designed theme parks. ADL accordingly concluded that it was reasonable to forecast Euro Disneyland's retail sales revenue on the basis of that at other Disney theme parks.

Revenues Total revenues projected in the financial model for the two theme parks are summarized in the table below (in FF millions):

	1992	1996	2001	2011
Magic Kingdom				
Admissions and parking	1,909	2,981	4,664	9,314
Food, beverage and merchandise	1,759	2,692	4,065	7,401
Participant fees and other	229	303	417	421
Second theme park				
Admissions and parking	–	1,788	2,697	5,794
Food, beverage and merchandise	–	1,178	1,660	3,107
Participant fees and other	–	162	208	412

The first two categories of projected revenues are based on the attendance and *per capita* spending assumptions described above. Projected Participant fees are based on the assumption that approximately ten Participant contracts will have been signed by the opening of the Magic Kingdom. Four contracts have been signed, each with a term of at least ten years.

Operating Expenses The principal operating expense assumptions are based on the following estimates:

Labor costs (including related taxes) have been estimated on the basis of experience at Disney parks, adjusted to the conditions of the French labor market. They include a premium on operating labor rates of approximately 10% over the market average, intended to attract high-quality personnel. On this basis, it has been assumed that gross operating labor costs will be FF424 million for the Magic Kingdom and FF232 million for the second theme park (measured in 1988 French francs) in the respective opening years of these parks and that they will increase at the rate of inflation, taking into account increased employment associated with higher attendance levels. Cost of sales has been estimated on the basis of experience at Disney parks, adjusted to reflect factors specific to Euro Disneyland. The assumptions are:

	Cost of sales (% of revenue)
Magic Kingdom	
Merchandise	40–43[a]
Food and beverage	31
Second theme park	
Merchandise	41.5
Food and beverage	31

[a] Declining from 43% in 1992 to 40% in 1996 and thereafter.

Other operating expenses have similarly been based on Disney experience, adjusted to reflect local market conditions. Individually they are assumed to be as follows:

- maintenance expenses:
  - Magic Kingdom: 6% of revenues
  - Second theme park: 6.5% of revenues
- general and administrative expenses (which include marketing, legal, finance and data processing):
  - Magic Kingdom: 14% of revenues
  - Second theme park: 16% of revenues
- property and business taxes, which have been estimated according to the French tax regime
- the base management fee.

Operating Income Operating income is the difference between revenues and operating expenses, but before royalties, financing costs and interest income, depreciation and amortization, lease expense, management incentive fees, and income taxes. The summary table below shows the operating income projected by the financial model for the two theme parks:

	1992	1996	2001	2011
Magic Kingdom (in FF millions)	1,603	2,773	4,226	8,006
Second theme park (in FF millions)	–	1,334	1,921	4,293
Total	1,603	4,107	6,147	12,299

Cost of Construction The cost of construction of the Magic Kingdom is assumed to be FF9.5 billion and the total cost of Phase 1A is assumed to be FF14.9 billion, in accordance with the estimated cost for Phase 1A. The construction cost of the second theme park has been assumed to be FF5.9 billion, with construction and related expenditures being incurred equally in 1994 and 1995. The construction cost of the second theme park has been estimated on the basis of Disney's direct experience of recent theme park construction, notably in completing the Disney–MGM Studios Theme Park within Walt Disney World. The construction cost of that theme park was then adjusted for capacity considerations, inflation, and the construction cost differential between Florida and the Paris region.

Table 15.A3 summarizes Walt Disney Company's financial results during 1984–8.

TABLE 15.A3 Summary of Walt Disney Company financial results, 1984–8 (US$ millions)

	1984	1985	1986	1987	1988
Revenue					
Theme parks and resorts	1,097.4	1,257.5	1,523.9	1,834.2	2,042.0
Filmed entertainment	244.5	320.0	511.7	875.6	1,149.2
Consumer products	109.7	122.6	130.2	167.0	247.0
Operating income					
Theme parks and resorts	185.7	255.7	403.7	548.9	564.8
Filmed entertainment	2.2	33.7	51.6	130.6	186.3
Consumer products	53.9	56.3	72.4	97.3	133.7
Net income	97.8	173.5	247.3	444.7	522.0

SOURCE: THE WALT DISNEY COMPANY ANNUAL REPORTS.

Appendix 2
Excerpt from Walt Disney 1994 Annual Report

Investment in Euro Disney

1994 vs. 1993 The Company's investment in Euro Disney resulted in a loss of $110.4 million in 1994. The loss consisted of a $52.8 million charge recognized in the third quarter as a result of the Company's participation in the Euro Disney financial restructuring, and the Company's equity share of fourth quarter operating results. The prior year's loss reflected the Company's equity share of Euro Disney's operating results and a $350.0 million charge to fully reserve receivables and a funding commitment to Euro Disney, partially offset by royalties and gain amortization related to the investment. The funding commitment was intended to help support Euro Disney for a limited period, while Euro Disney pursued a financial restructuring.

A proposed restructuring plan for Euro Disney was announced in March 1994. During the third quarter of 1994, the Company entered into agreements with Euro Disney and the Euro Disney lenders participating in the restructuring (the "Lenders") to provide certain debt, equity and lease financing to Euro Disney.

Under the restructuring agreements, which specify amounts denominated in French francs, the Company committed to increase its equity investment in Euro Disney by subscribing for 49% of a $1.1 billion rights offering of new shares; to provide long-term lease financing at a 1% interest rate for approximately $255 million of theme park assets; and to subscribe, in part through an offset against fully reserved advances previously made to Euro Disney under the Company's funding commitment, for securities reimbursable in shares with a face value of approximately $180 million and a 1% coupon. In addition, the Company agreed to cancel fully reserved receivables from Euro Disney of approximately $210 million, to waive royalties and base management fees for a period of five years and to reduce such amounts for specified periods thereafter, and to modify the method by which management incentive fees will be calculated. During the fourth quarter of 1994, the financial restructuring was completed and the Company funded its commitments.

In addition to the commitments described above, the Company agreed to arrange for the provision of a ten-year unsecured standby credit facility of approximately $210 million on request, bearing interest at PIBOR. As of September 30, 1994, Euro Disney had not requested that the Company establish this facility.

As part of the restructuring, the Company received ten-year warrants for the purchase of up to 27.8 million shares of Euro Disney at a price of FF40 per share. The terms of the restructuring also provide that, in the event that Euro Disney decides to launch the second phase of the development of its theme park and resort complex, and commitments for the necessary financing have been obtained, the Company will be entitled to a development fee of approximately $225 million. On receipt of the development fee, the Company's entitlement to purchase Euro Disney shares by exercise of the warrants described above will be reduced to 15 million shares.

In connection with the restructuring, Euro Disney Associes SNC ("Disney SNC"), an indirect wholly owned affiliate of the Company, entered into a lease arrangement (the "Lease") with the entity (the "Park Financing Company") which financed substantially all of the Disneyland Paris theme park assets, and then entered into a sublease agreement (the "Sublease") with Euro Disney. Under the Lease, which replaced an existing lease between Euro Disney and the Park Financing Company, Disney SNC leased the theme park assets of the Park Financing Company for a noncancelable term of 12 years. Aggregate lease rentals of FF10.5 billion ($2.0 billion) receivable from Euro Disney under the Sublease, which has a 12-year term, will approximate the amounts payable by Disney SNC under the Lease.

At the conclusion of the Sublease term, Euro Disney will have the option to assume Disney SNC's rights and obligations under the Lease. If Euro Disney does not exercise its option, Disney SNC may continue to lease the assets, with an ongoing option to purchase them for an amount approximating the balance of the Park Financing Company's outstanding debt. Alternatively, Disney SNC may terminate the Lease, in which case Disney SNC would pay the Park Financing Company an amount equal to 75% of its then-outstanding debt, estimated to be \$1.4 billion; Disney SNC could then sell or lease the assets on behalf of the Park Financing Company to satisfy the remaining debt, with any excess proceeds payable to Disney SNC.

As part of the overall restructuring, the Lenders agreed to underwrite 51% of the Euro Disney rights offering, to forgive certain interest charges for the period from April 1, 1994 to September 30, 2003, having a present value of approximately \$300 million, and to defer all principal payments until three years later than originally scheduled. As consideration for their participation in the financial restructuring, Euro Disney issued to the Lenders ten-year warrants for the purchase of up to 40 million shares of Euro Disney stock at a price of FF40 per share.

Euro Disney has reported that it expects to incur a loss in 1995, which will have a negative impact on the Company's results. The impact on the Company's earnings, however, will be reduced as a result of the sale by the Company in October 1994 of approximately 75 million shares, or 20% of its investment in Euro Disney, to Prince Alwaleed Bin Talal Bin Abdulaziz Al Saud. The sale will reduce the Company's ownership interest in Euro Disney to approximately 39%. Beginning in 1995, the Company will record its equity share of Euro Disney's operating results based on its reduced ownership interest. The Company has agreed, so long as any obligations to the Lenders are outstanding, to maintain ownership of at least 34% of the outstanding common stock of Euro Disney until June 1999, at least 25% for the subsequent five years, and at least 16.67% for an additional term thereafter.

1993 vs. 1992 The Company's investment in Euro Disney resulted in a loss of \$514.7 million in 1993, including the charge referred to below, after being partially offset by royalties and gain amortization related to the investment. The operating results of Euro Disney were lower than expected, due in part to the European recession which affected Euro Disney's largest markets.

During 1993, Euro Disney, its principal lenders, and the Company began exploring a financial restructuring for Euro Disney. The Company agreed to help fund Euro Disney for a limited period, to afford Euro Disney time to pursue the financial restructuring. The operating results for the fourth quarter and the year, and the need for a financial restructuring, created uncertainty regarding the Company's ability to collect its current receivables and to meet the funding commitment to Euro Disney. Consequently, the Company recorded a charge of \$350.0 million in the fourth quarter to fully reserve its current receivables and funding commitment.

In 1992, the Company's investment in Euro Disney contributed income of \$11.2 million. Although Euro Disney incurred a loss in 1992, the Company's 49% share of the net loss was offset by royalties and gain amortization related to the investment.

Source: Walt Disney Annual Report, 1994.

Notes

1 "Euro Disney," *Financial Times'* Lex column, October 30, 1996.

2 "Disney Goes to Tokyo," in D. Ancona, T. Kochan, M. Sculy, J. Van Maanen, and E. Westney, *Organizational Behavior and Processes*, Cincinnati, OH: Southwestern College Publishing, 1999, pp. M-10, 25.

3 The conversion factors used in the case are: 1 hectare = 2.47 acres, and 1 acre = 4,047 square meters. The US dollar/French franc exchange rates at the beginning of each year were: 1987 6.35, 1988 5.36, 1989 6.03, 1990 5.84, 1991 5.08, 1992 5.22, 1993 5.59, 1994 5.93.

4 "Euro Disney" is used to refer to the Euro Disneyland theme park: "Euro Disneyland SCA" or "the company" refers to the company that owns Euro Disney.

5 "The Euro Disneyland Project – Project Financing: Asset-Based Financial Engineering," Case Study: John D. Finnery, © 1996 by John D. Finnery, John Wiley & Sons.

6 "No magic in these kingdoms," *Los Angeles Times*, December 15, 1989.

7 "Disneyland goes to Europe," in Ancona, Kochan, Scully, Van Maanen, and Westney, *Organizational Behavior and Processes*, op. cit., pp. 38–9.

8 Ibid., p. 15.

9 From Jacques Neher, "France amazed, amused by Disney dress code," *The New York Times*, October 5, 1995.

10 *Euro Disney: the First 100 Days*, Harvard Business School Case No. 9-693-013, 1993, p. 14.

Richard Branson and the Virgin Group of Companies in 2007

Despite celebrating his 57th birthday at the beginning of 2007, Richard Branson showed no signs of flagging energy or entrepreneurial vigor. During the last two weeks of January 2007, Virgin announced a slew of new initiatives. These included the creation of Virgin Bioverda, a joint venture to develop ethanol plants in the US; a bid for vacation company First Choice; and a proposal to take over rail services between London and Edinburgh. At the same time, Branson was negotiating an alliance with Tata Group to establish Virgin Mobile in India and preparing to buy 50 acres of land in Macau to build a $3 billion casino and leisure complex. Meanwhile, Virgin America – Branson's San Francisco-based low-cost airline – was struggling to get approval from the US Department of Transportation. Some believed that Virgin Galactic – Branson's passenger spaceship service – might be first into the air.

Yet despite being lauded for his entrepreneurship, eccentricity, and embodiment of "the friendly face of capitalism," his Virgin group of companies remained a mystery to most outsiders – and to many insiders as well. At the beginning of 2007, there were 215 Virgin companies registered at Britain's Companies House, of which 20 are identified as recently dissolved. However, most operations are conducted through the 36 companies listed on the Virgin website (see the appendix). While a number are Virgin companies identified as "holding companies" – they exist only to own and manage other Virgin companies – there is no overall parent company for the group.

The opacity of Virgin's structure and finances encouraged frequent speculation about the overall performance of the group. During the late 1990s, there was consistent evidence that the group as a whole was not performing well. *The Economist* observed that: "Virgin Travel is the only one of Virgin's businesses to make a large profit . . . The rest of Mr. Branson's firms lost money in total."[1] The

Financial Times pointed to a net cash outflow and a negative economic value added for the group as a whole.[2] During recent years, overall financial performance was strengthened by profit growth at Virgin's wireless telecommunications businesses and the post-2002 recovery in the airline industry. Nevertheless, several Virgin companies continued to generate losses.

As ever, Branson was dismissive of outside criticism, claiming analysts and financial journalists misunderstood his business empire. Each Virgin company, he argued, was financed on a standalone basis; hence attempts to consolidate the income and assets of the companies were irrelevant and misleading. Moreover, Branson had little regard for accounting profits, preferring cash flow and capital value as the critical performance indicators. Thus, most of the Virgin companies were growing businesses that were increasing in their real value and long-term cash-generating potential, even if accounting profits were negative. "The approach to running a group of private companies is fundamentally different to that of running public companies. Short-term taxable profits with good dividends are a prerequisite of public life. Avoiding short-term taxable profits and seeking long-term capital growth is the best approach to growing private companies."[3]

Apart from questions about financial performance, outside observers also pondered the strategic direction of this motley collection of over 200 separate companies. The Virgin group covered a remarkable range of business, from airlines to bridal stores. In an era of corporate refocusing and the nurturing of core competences, what possible business rationale could explain the structure and composition of the Virgin group? It was not only Virgin's financial resources that risked being stretched. Was there a risk that the Virgin brand would become overextended and that its appeal and integrity would be damaged? With regard to Branson himself, should he attempt to involve himself personally in guiding the various Virgin companies? As the group expanded and Branson became more of a strategic and charismatic leader rather than a hands-on manager, did Virgin need to establish a more systematic approach to control, risk management, and strategy?

The Development of Virgin

Richard Branson's business career began while he was a student at Stowe, a private boarding school. His startup magazine, *Student*, was first published on January 26, 1968. The early success of the magazine encouraged Branson to leave school at 17 years old, before taking his final exams. Agreeing to the boy's request to leave, the headmaster offered the prophetic statement, "Richard, you will end up in prison or as a millionaire." Both predictions were to be fulfilled.[4]

This early publishing venture displayed features that would characterize many of Branson's subsequent entrepreneurial initiatives. The magazine was aimed at baby-boomers between 16 and 25 years old and was designed to appeal to the optimism, irreverence, antiauthoritarianism, and fashion consciousness of the new generation. It would also fill a "gaping hole in the market." *Student* was to be the "voice of youth" and would "put the world to rights." Its eclectic style reflected its founder's ability to commission articles by celebrities and to identify subjects not touched by many well-established magazines. Norman Mailer, Vanessa Redgrave, and Jean-Paul Sartre contributed pieces which appeared among articles on sex, rock music, interviews with terrorists, and proposals for educational reform.

Virgin Records

Branson's next venture was mail order records. Beginning with a single advertisement in the last issue of *Student* magazine, Branson found that he was able to establish a thriving business with almost no up-front investment and no working capital, and could easily undercut the established retail chains. The name "Virgin" was suggested by one of his associates who saw the name as proclaiming their commercial innocence, while possessing some novelty and modest shock-value. Virgin Records brought together Branson and his childhood friend Nik Powell, who took a 40% share in the company and complemented Branson's erratic flamboyance with careful operational and financial management. In 1971 Branson opened his first retail store – on London's busy Oxford Street.

Expansion into record publishing was the idea of Simon Draper – one of Virgin's record buyers. Draper introduced Branson to Mike Oldfield, who was soon installed at Branson's Oxfordshire home with a fully equipped recording studio. *Tubular Bells*, launched in 1973, was an instant hit, eventually selling over 5 million copies worldwide. The result was the Virgin record label, which went on to sign up bands whose music or lifestyles did not appeal to the major record companies. Among the most successful signings were the Sex Pistols.

The recession of 1979–82 was a struggle for Virgin. Several business ventures failed and several of Branson's close associates left, including Nik Powell, who sold his share-holding back to Branson for £1 million plus Virgin's cinema and video interests. Despite these setbacks, the 1980s saw rapid growth for Virgin Records, with the signing of Phil Collins, Human League, Simple Minds, and Boy George's Culture Club. By 1983, the Virgin group was earning pre-tax profits of £2.0 million on total revenues of just under £50 million.

Virgin Atlantic Airways

Virgin Atlantic began with a phone call from Randolph Fields, a Californian lawyer who proposed founding a transatlantic, cut-price airline. To the horror of Branson's executives at Virgin Records, Branson was enthralled with the idea. On June 24, 1984, Branson appeared in a World War I flying outfit to celebrate the inaugural flight of Virgin Atlantic in a second-hand 747 bought from Aerolinas Argentina. With the launch of Virgin Atlantic, Branson had embarked upon a perilous path strewn with the wreckage of earlier entrepreneurs of aviation, including Laker, Braniff, and People Express. Unlike Branson's other businesses, not only was the airline business highly capital intensive, it also required a completely new set of business skills, in particular the need to negotiate with governments, regulatory bodies, banks, and aircraft manufacturers.

Private to Public and Back

By 1985, a transatlantic airfares price war and the investment needs of Virgin Atlantic had created a cash squeeze for Virgin. Branson became convinced of the need to expand the equity base of the group. Don Cruikshank, a Scottish accountant with an MBA from Manchester and Branson's group managing director, was assigned the task of organizing an initial public offering for Virgin's music, retail, and vision businesses, which were combined into the Virgin Group plc, a public corporation with 35% of its equity listed on the London and NASDAQ stock markets.

Branson was not happy as chairman of a public corporation. He felt that investment analysts misunderstood his business and that the market undervalued his company. A clear conflict existed between the financial community's expectations of the chairman of a public corporation and Branson's personal style. With the October 1987 stock market crash, Branson took the opportunity to raise £200 million to buy out external shareholders.

As a private company, Virgin continued to expand, using both internal cash flows – mainly from Virgin Atlantic Airways – and external financing. The retailing group moved aggressively into new markets around the world. The Virgin Megastore concept provided the basis for new stores in Japan, the United States, Australia, the Netherlands, and Spain. This growth was facilitated by the formation of a joint venture with Blockbuster Corporation, the US video-store giant. New ventures launched during the early 1990s included Virgin Lightships, an airship advertiser; Vintage Airtours, an operator of restored DC-3 aircraft between Orlando and Key West; Virgin Games producing video games; West One Television, a TV production company; and Virgin Euromagnetics, a personal computer company. Meanwhile, Virgin Atlantic Airways expanded its network to 20 cities – including Tokyo and Hong Kong. It also won many awards for its customer service.

1990–2006: Continued Expansion, Selective Divestment

Expansion pressured cash flow and the Persian Gulf War of 1990–91 cut airline profits. Branson relied increasingly on joint ventures to finance new business development. The partnering arrangements were primarily in retailing and included one with Marui, a leading Japanese retailer, and another with W. H. Smith, a prominent UK retail chain.

Ultimately, the capital needs of Virgin Atlantic forced Branson to take drastic action. In March 1992, Branson sold his most profitable and successful business, Virgin Music, the world's biggest independent record label, to Thorn EMI for £560 million (close to $1.0 billion). Virgin Music's tangible assets had a balance sheet value of only £3 million. The sale marked a dramatic shift in focus for Virgin away from its core entertainment business towards airlines and travel, and provided the capital to support new business ventures.

In the meantime, Branson's long-standing rivalry with British Airways took a nasty turn. Evidence emerged that British Airways had pursued a "dirty tricks" campaign against Virgin. This included breaking into Virgin's computer system, diverting Virgin customers to BA flights, and spreading rumors about Virgin's financial state. The outcome was a UK court case which resulted in BA paying $1.5 million dollars in damages to Branson and Virgin.

The second half of the 1990s saw acceleration in Virgin's business development activities, with a host of new ventures in disparate markets. Virgin's new ventures were a response to three types of opportunity:

- *Privatization and deregulation.* The rolling back of the frontiers of state ownership and regulation in Britain (and elsewhere) created business opportunities that Richard Branson was only too eager to seize. Virgin's most important privatization initiative was its successful bids for two passenger rail franchises: the west coast and cross-country rail services. The resulting business – Virgin Rail – was a joint venture with transportation specialist,

Stagecoach. Deregulation in the world's airline sector also created opportunities for Virgin. In 1996, Euro-Belgian Airlines was acquired and re-launched as Virgin Express, and in Australia, Virgin Blue began operations during 2000. Branson's bid to operate the British National Lottery was unsuccessful, but in 2001, Virgin Atlantic was part of the consortium that acquired a stake in the British air traffic control system.

- *Direct selling of goods and services to consumers.* Branson was continually on the lookout for business opportunities offering a "new deal" to consumers. Most of these ventures involved direct sales to consumers and passing on the cost savings from bypassing traditional distribution channels. Virgin Direct, launched in 1995 as a joint venture with Norwich Union, offered telephone-based financial services to consumers. In subsequent years, Virgin Direct expanded the range of financial products it offered and moved to the internet. Virgin Car and Virgin Bike challenged the existing dealership system of the automobile and motorcycle manufacturers by offering direct sales of cars and motorbikes at discounted prices. Virgin Wine was also launched.

- *TMT.* The "TMT" (Technology, Media, Telecom) boom of 1998–2000 created a tremendous buzz within Virgin. Virgin's origins lay in media, while the internet offered a new channel for Virgin to reach consumers. In 1997 Virgin Net, an internet service provider and portal, was launched as a joint venture between Virgin and cable operator NTL. The next year Virgin Mobile, a joint venture with Deutsche Telecom's One-to-One wireless telephone service, began business in Britain. The success of Virgin Mobile in Britain – half a million subscribers were signed up within the first year and four million by 2004 – encouraged Virgin to expand into the US, Australia, South Africa, and southeast Asia. Virgin's increasing online presence was seen as offering important e-commerce opportunities to the Virgin group as a whole. TheTrain.com was set up as an online reservation service for train passengers. Virgin Direct offered music downloads. The Virgin.com portal became a shopfront for all of Virgin's consumer offerings.

Other new ventures appeared to be largely the result of Branson's whims and opportunism and defied any kind of categorization. These included a chain of health clubs (Virgin Active), space flight (Virgin Galactic), and biofuels (Virgin Fuels, Virgin Bioverda).

To fund so many new ventures, Branson sought to release equity from some of his established and growing businesses. Major divestments included:

- Virgin Atlantic: 49% was sold to Singapore Airlines for £600 million in 1999.
- Virgin Megastores, France: sold to Legardere Media in 2001 for £100 million.
- Virgin One: Virgin's home loan business was sold to Royal Bank of Scotland in 2001 for £100 million.
- Virgin Blue: 50% was sold to Patrick Corporation for £250 million in 2001; a further 25% of Virgin Blue was sold in that company's 2003 IPO, raising a similar amount.
- Virgin Mobile (UK): acquired by cable operator NTL for £962 million in 2006.

In addition, Virgin Express – Virgin's loss-making, Brussels-based airline – merged in 2005 with SN Brussels Airlines to form SN Airholdings, in which Virgin held a 30% stake.

The Virgin Group of Companies in 2007

Among the 200-plus companies forming the Virgin Group, the major businesses in terms of revenues and market presence are shown in table 16.1. The principal commonalities between this diverse range of enterprises are, first, their use of the Virgin brand name and, second, the role of Richard Branson as their instigator and, in most cases, their major investor.

The Virgin Brand

The Virgin brand was the group's greatest single asset. There are few brands that encompass so wide a range of products as Virgin. Can a brand that extends from train travel and financial services to night clubs and music downloads have any meaningful identity? The Virgin website explains the Virgin brand as follows:

> All the markets in which Virgin operates tend to have features in common: they are typically markets where the customer has been ripped off or under-served, where there is confusion and/or where the competition is complacent. In these markets, Virgin is able to break into the market and shake it up. Our role is to be the consumer champion, and we do this by delivering to our brand values, which are:–
>
> ● Value for Money: *Simple, honest and transparent pricing – not necessarily the cheapest on the market.*
> ● Good Quality: *High standards, attention to detail, being honest and delivering on promises.*
> ● Brilliant Customer Service: *Friendly, human and relaxed; professional but uncorporate.*
> ● Innovative: *Challenging convention with big and little product/service ideas; innovative, modern and stylish design.*
> ● Competitively Challenging: *Sticking two fingers up to the establishment and fighting the big boys – usually with a bit of humor.*
> ● Fun: *Every company in the world takes itself seriously so we think it's important that we provide the public and our customers with a bit of entertainment – as well as making Virgin a nice place for our people to work.*[5]

These attributes were communicated to customers in a variety of ways. Virgin Atlantic pioneered a range of innovative customer services (principally for its business class passengers). These included in-flight massages, hair stylists, aromatherapists, and limousine and motorcycle home-pick-up services. In 1998, it offered speedboat rides along the Thames from Heathrow to the City of London, allowing executives and bankers to dodge London traffic jams. British Airways – huge, stodgy, and bureaucratic – provided the ideal adversary against which Virgin Atlantic could position itself. When British Airways was experiencing problems erecting its giant Ferris

TABLE 16.1 Main businesses within the Virgin Group, 2006

Virgin Active	Chain of health and leisure clubs in the UK and South Africa
Virgin Atlantic	London-based airline serving 20 destinations in the US, Caribbean, South Africa, and Asia
Virgin Atlantic Cargo	Air freight using Virgin Atlantic's network
Virgin Balloon Flights	Passenger balloon flights in the UK, Holland, and Belgium
Virgin Blue	Low-fare airline flying in Australia
Virgin Books	Publishes books on music, sport, TV, movies, and comedy
Virgin Brides	Chain of bridal retail stores
Virgin Comics	Collaboration with writer Deepak Chopra, filmmaker Shekhar Kapur, and Sir Richard Branson
Virgin Cosmetics	Direct sales of specially formulated cosmetics
Virgin Credit Card	Credit card issued by Virgin Money
Virgin Digital	Online digital music collection
Virgin Drinks	Distributes Virgin-branded soft drinks
Virgin Experience Days	Offers innovative leisure experiences, from bungee jumping to Ferrari driving
Virgin Express	Brussels-based airline offering scheduled flights to UK and other European destinations
Virgin Galactic	Offers opportunities for space travel
Virgin Games	Online gaming
Virgin Holidays	UK-based tour operator specializing in long-haul holidays to America, the Far East, Australia, and South Africa, using Virgin Atlantic flights
Virgin Jewellery	Offers over 120 pieces of silver and fashion jewelry
Virgin Limited Edition	Offers vacation packages at exclusive hotels worldwide
Virgin Limobike	Motorcycle taxi service in London
Virgin Limousines	Limos serving Northern California
Virgin Megastores	80 Megastores in Europe, Japan, and N. America sell music, movies, computer games, and books
Virgin Mobile	Wireless telephone resellers offering easy-tariff service with no line rental or fixed-term contract
Virgin Money	Online financial services offering loans, mutual funds, and stock trading
Virgin.net	UK-based internet service provider
Virgin Play	Distributor, marketer, and promoter of computer and interactive games in Spain
Virgin Radio	UK digital radio broadcaster
Virgin Spa	Spa services in South Africa
Virgin Trains	Major UK operator of passenger train services and facilities and allows booking of Virgin Train tickets online
Virgin Unite	Charitable, volunteer organization supporting grassroots charities
Virgin Vacations	Vacation packages
Virgin Ware	Retail and online vendor of underwear
Virgin Wines	Direct seller of wines
V2 Music	Independent record label (artists include the Stereophonics, Tom Jones, Moby, and Underworld)
Pacific Blue	Airline operating daily services between Australia and New Zealand

SOURCE: WWW.VIRGIN.COM

wheel, the London Eye, Virgin positioned a blimp above the site bearing the message "BA Can't Get It Up!"

Some of Branson's ventures seemed to be inspired more by a sense of fun and eagerness to "stick it to the big boys" than by commercial logic. Virgin Cola was introduced in 1994 packaged in a "Pammy" bottle modeled on the body of *Baywatch* star Pamela Anderson. The goal, according to Branson, was to "drive Coke out of the States."[6] By 1997, Virgin Cola was losing £5 million on revenues of £30 million.

Virgin's ability to extend its brand so widely pointed to the broad appeal of Virgin's values and business principles. Much of this appeal was linked with Richard Branson's persona and style. The values and characteristics that the Virgin brand communicated are inseparable from Richard Branson as entrepreneur, joker, fair-playing Brit, and giant killer. The Virgin brand was identified too with the innovation and unconventional strategies and marketing that characterized most Virgin startups. Branson went to lengths to differentiate his new enterprises from established market leaders. Thus, the difference between Virgin Atlantic and BA, between Virgin Cola and Coke, and between Virgin Money and the leading banks was not primarily about products, it was more about the nature of the companies and how they related to their customers. As Virgin internationalized, a critical issue was whether Branson and the Virgin brand could achieve the same rapport with consumers in other countries as they did in Britain. Although Branson was well known in Europe and North America, in many respects he was a quintessentially British character who was a product of time and place.

A continual issue for Virgin was the risk that the brand might become over-extended. The head of brand identity at consultant Landor Associates commented: "He's still way too unfocused. He should get out of businesses that don't fit the Virgin/ Branson personality, such as beverages, cosmetics, certainly financial services, or come up with another brand name for them."[7] Widespread public dissatisfaction with rail services in Britain suggested that Virgin's vision of new standards of service for rail travelers might be unattainable given the structural problems of Britain's congested rail infrastructure.

Despite his renown, Branson, too, might be waning in market appeal. Was there a risk that, having seen Branson as flight attendant, Branson in a wedding dress, Branson with successive prime ministers, and Branson attempting to fly around the world in a hot-air balloon, the public might tire of his exploits?

During the late 1990s, Virgin had moved to consolidate around a number of core businesses, notably travel, entertainment, and retailing. However, this trend was short-lived: the telecom and internet revolution offered Branson a host of new entrepreneurial opportunities that were irresistible.

Branson as Entrepreneur

Almost all of the Virgin businesses were new startups. From the founding of *Student* magazine through to the formation of Virgin Galactic, Branson's primary strength as a businessman was in conceiving and implementing new business ideas – not that Branson was the source of all of Virgin's new business ideas. Branson acted as a magnet for would-be entrepreneurs and Virgin actively encouraged the submission of new business ideas to its corporate development offices in London, Sydney, and New York. Virgin employees, too, were encouraged to develop proposals for new businesses. The idea for Virgin Bride had originated with a Virgin Atlantic employee dismayed by the products and services offered by existing UK bridal stores. Nelson Mandela once offered a business idea to Branson, suggesting that Branson acquire a South African health club chain that had gone bankrupt putting thousands of jobs at risk. Virgin Active South Africa is now the country's biggest chain of health clubs.

Yet Branson's leadership of the Virgin Group extended beyond his role as a source of entrepreneurial ideas. As the creator of Virgin and its unique corporate culture, and the primary promoter of its image and entrepreneurial spirit, Richard Branson was synonymous with Virgin. To many of his generation he embodied the spirit of "New Britain." In a country where business leaders were members of "the establishment" and identified with the existing social structure, Branson was seen as a revolutionary. Despite a privileged family background (his father was a lawyer and Richard attended a private boarding school), Branson had the ability to transcend the social classes which traditionally divided British society and segmented consumer markets. As such, he was part of a movement in British culture and society that has sought to escape the Old Britain of fading empire, class antagonism, Victorian values, and stiff-upper-lip hypocrisy. Richard Branson symbolized the transition from "Rule Britannia" to "Cool Britannia."

Informality and disrespect for convention were central to Branson's way of business. Branson's woolly sweaters, beard, windswept hair, and toothy grin were practically a trademark of the Virgin companies. His dislike of office buildings and the usual symbols of corporate success was reflected in the absence of a corporate head office and his willingness to do business from his family homes, whether a houseboat in Maida Vale or Necker Island Caribbean retreat. This lack of separation between work, family, and leisure – indicated by the involvement of cousins, aunts, childhood friends, and dinner-party acquaintances in business relationships – reflected a view of business as part of life which, like life, should involve excitement, creativity, and fun.

An earlier case explains Branson's approach to new business startups:

> Much of the operating style was established not so much by design but by the exigencies of the time when Virgin was getting started. It has proved to be a successful model that Branson can replicate. His philosophy is to immerse himself in a new venture until he understands the ins and outs of the business, and then hand it over to a good managing director and financial controller, who are given a stake in it, and are then expected to make the company take off. He knows that expansion through the creation of additional discrete legal entities not only protects the Virgin Group, but also gives people a sense of involvement and loyalty, particularly if he trusts them with full authority and offers minority share holdings to the managers of subsidiaries. He is proud of the fact that Virgin has produced a considerable number of millionaires. He has said that he does not want his best people to leave the company to start a venture outside. He prefers to make millionaires within.[8]

His use of joint ventures was an extension of this model reinforced by his dealings with the Japanese. Branson was impressed by the Japanese approach to business, admiring their commitment to long-term development and focus on organic growth. His only major acquisition was the parts of British Rail that formed Virgin Rail. Prior to that, Branson had made only two significant acquisitions: Rushes Video for £6 million and the airline that became Virgin Express. He saw similarities between Virgin and the Japanese *keiretsu* system (multiple companies interlocking through managerial and equity linkages in a collaborative network). Virgin's network of small companies combined "small is beautiful" with "strength through unity." He explained this and other business maxims that he believed to be necessary for success in a speech to the Institute of Directors in 1993. "Staff first, then customers and shareholders" should be the chairman's priority if the goal is better performance. "Shape the business around the people," "Build don't buy," "Be best, not biggest," "Pioneer, don't follow the leader," "Capture every fleeting idea," and "Drive for change" were other guiding principles in the Branson philosophy.

Branson's values of innocence, innovation, and irreverence for authority were apparent in his choice of new ventures. He drew heavily on the ideas of others within his organization and was prepared to invest in new startups even in markets that were dominated by long-established incumbents. His business ventures, just like his sporting exploits, reflected a "just live life" attitude and a "bigger the challenge, greater the fun" belief. In identifying opportunity he was particularly keen to identify markets where the conservatism and lack of imagination of incumbent firms meant that they were failing to create value for customers. Branson entered markets with a "new" and "anti-establishment attitude" that sought to offer customers a better alternative. An example of this was Virgin's entry into financial services. Into a business that was long regarded as conservative and stuffy, Branson hoped to bring "a breath of fresh air."

At the same time, the affection of the British public for Branson reflected the fact that Branson's values and his sense of fair play were consistent with many traditional values that defined the British character. His competitive battles against huge corporations like British Airways and Coca-Cola linked well with the heroes of yesteryear who battled against tyranny and evil: King Arthur, Robin Hood, and St. George. Resisting British Airways' "dirty tricks" campaign and his other battles with corporate giants resonated well with the British sense of decency. Even his willingness to appear in outlandish attire reflected a British propensity for ludicrous dressing-up, whether for fancy-dress parties, morris dancing, or the House of Lords.

Virgin's Management Structure

Of Virgin's 200-plus companies, the majority are operating companies that own assets, employ people, and offer goods and services. These operating companies are owned and controlled by some 20 holding companies; most of these own several operating companies within the same line of business. For example, Virgin Travel (Holdings) Limited owns Virgin Group's investments in Virgin Atlantic, Virgin Blue, Virgin America, and SN Airholdings. Overall ownership of most of the Virgin Group lies in the hands of Virgin Group Investments Limited – a private company registered in the British Virgin Islands. Virgin Group Investments Limited is owned by Richard Branson and a series of trusts, the beneficiaries of which are Branson and his family members.

The most striking feature of the Virgin Group is its legal complexity. For example, Virgin's passenger train companies are Virgin West Coast Mainline and Virgin Cross Country. These are owned by Virgin Rail Group Holdings Ltd., 51% of which is owned by Ivanco (No. 1) Ltd., which is owned by Virgin Group Investments Ltd.

This financial and legal structure reflects Branson's unconventional ideas about business and his wariness of the financial community. The intricate structure involving offshore private companies cloaks the Virgin empire in a thick veil of secrecy. This is reinforced by the use of "bearer shares" by several of the Virgin holding companies through which minority shareholders (venture capitalists and other investors) could not be identified. However, Branson also views the loose-knit structure of the Group as consistent with his vision of people-oriented capitalism:

> We're structured as if we are 150 small companies. Each has to stand on its own two feet, as if they are their own companies. Employees have a stake in their success. They feel – and are – crucial to their company because they are one-in-fifty or one-in-a-hundred instead of one-in-tens-of-thousands. They indeed are all under the Virgin umbrella, but they are generally not subsidiaries. I'm over them to see if one company can't help another, but otherwise they are independent. Some people like the idea of growing fiefdoms – companies that brag about sales of over $5 billion a year – but there is no logical reason to think that there is anything good about huge companies. History in fact shows the opposite. Those huge corporations with tentacles and divisions and departments become unwieldy, slow growing, stagnant. Some chairmen want them like that so that one division's loss can make up for another's profit, but we'd rather have a lot of exciting companies that are all making profits – as are all of ours.[9]

The Virgin Group has been likened both to a brand franchising operation and to Japanese *keiretsu*, where member companies have financial and management links and share a common sense of identity. The reality, according to *Management Today*,[10] is somewhere between the two. Will Whitehorn, Branson's long-time strategist and business developer, describes Virgin as "a branded venture capital organization."

The formal linkages between the companies include:

- *Ownership*. Most of Branson's equity interests are owned by Virgin Group Investments Ltd.

- *The brand*. Virgin's trademarks – including the Virgin name and logos – are owned by Virgin Enterprises Ltd. Neil Hobbs, intellectual property lawyer for Virgin Enterprises, explains: "Our role is both to optimize and enhance the value of the brand and to protect that by ensuring that that value is not diminished through infringement by third parties. VEL licenses companies both within and outside the Virgin Group to use the Virgin brand."[11] One third-party licensee is EMI Records, which owns Virgin Records and is licensed to use the Virgin name.

- *Management*. Virgin Management Ltd. is the management arm of the Virgin Group. It manages the appointment of board members and senior executives to the different Virgin companies; it assists in coordination between the companies and is responsible for the development of new business enterprises. In 2005, Virgin Management Ltd. had 87 employees at Virgin's London headquarters at 120 Campden Hill Road.

However, the key to the management of the Virgin Group is the informal relations between Branson and a small core of long-term associates who form the senior management team of the Virgin Group and occupy key executive positions within individual operating companies. Among Branson's inner circle are:

- Will Whitehorn, originally Branson's press spokesman, who has been Virgin's director of brand development and corporate affairs for the past decade and is currently CEO of Virgin Galactic. He is widely viewed as Branson's second-in-command and key strategic thinker.[12]

- Gordon McCallum, who joined Virgin in 1997 as group strategy director from McKinsey & Company. He has pioneered Virgin's entry into mobile telecommunications and since September 2005 has been CEO of Virgin Management Ltd.
- Patrick McCall, who was formerly an investment banker at UBS Warburg. At Virgin he is a director of Virgin Management and has been a board member of a number of Virgin companies, including Virgin Rail and Virgin Blue.
- Stephen Murphy, who joined Virgin from Quaker Oats. He was Virgin Group finance director from 1994 to 2000 and, since 2001, has been a board member of Virgin Management as executive director, transportation.
- Rowan Gormley, who joined the Virgin Group as corporate development director after working as an accountant with Arthur Andersen & Co. He led Virgin's move into financial services in 1995 as chief executive of Virgin Direct. In January 2000, he became CEO of Virgin Wine.
- Frances Farrow, who joined Virgin Atlantic as commercial services director from the law firm Binder Hamlyn. She became CEO of Virgin USA Inc.

Figure 16.1 shows the structure of the Virgin Group of companies, including some major operating companies and the holding companies that own them.

Virgin's Organizational Culture

The ability of the Virgin Group to operate effectively with so little formal structure or management systems owes much to the Group's unique organizational culture. This is defined almost entirely by Branson's own values and management style. It reflects his eccentricity, sense of fun, disrespect for hierarchy and formal authority, commitment to employees and consumers, and belief in hard work and individual responsibility. The Group provides an environment in which talented, ambitious people are motivated to do their best and strive for a higher level of performance. While the working environment is informal, anticorporate, and defined by the popular culture of its era, expectations are high. Branson expects a high level of commitment, the acceptance of personal responsibility, and long hours of work when needed. Financial rewards for most employees are typically modest, but nonpecuniary benefits included social activities, company-sponsored weekend getaways, and impromptu parties.

The apparent chaos of the Virgin Group, with its casual style and absence of formal structure and control systems, belies its sharp business acumen and forceful determination. It is easy for more traditional business enterprises to underestimate Virgin – a key error of British Airways. Virgin possesses considerable financial and managerial talent, and what Virgin lacks in formal structure is made up for by commitment and close personal ties. The Virgin organizational structure involves very little hierarchy, offering short lines of communication and flexible response capability. Employees are given a great deal of responsibility and freedom in order to stimulate idea generation, initiative, commitment, and fun. The lack of formal controls is conducive to teamwork and entrepreneurial spirit.

Virgin's Financial Performance

Financial reporting by the Virgin companies was fragmented, hard to locate, and difficult to interpret. No consolidated accounts for the Group as a whole existed. Not

FIGURE 16.1 The Virgin Group of companies

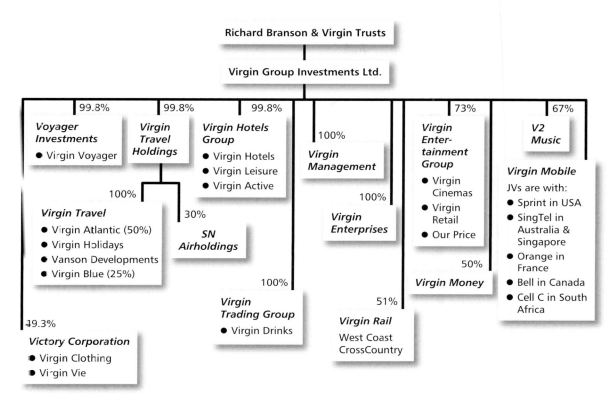

Note: This figure is intended to provide a general view of the structure of the Virgin Group, but it includes only some of Virgin's 200+ companies

only were there multiple operating companies, but ownership of these companies lay with a number of holding companies, some of which consolidated subsidiary accounts while others did not. Tracking financial results over time was difficult because investments in Virgin operating companies were frequently transferred within the Group. Individual Virgin companies (at least, those registered in the UK) submitted audited financial statements to Companies House (a government agency). Table 16.2 shows results for some of the Virgin's operating and holding companies.

The financial structure of the Virgin Group has changed substantially over the years. In particular, Virgin's near collapse during the 1990–2 recession has resulted in a more conservative approach to financing. During the past 15 years, Branson has relied increasingly on equity partners to finance his new business ventures. Typically, joint venture partners have taken 49% or 50% of the equity of the new venture despite supplying the majority of the equity capital. The power of the Virgin brand and Branson's celebrity status and promotional capabilities has meant that Branson has acquired equity stakes in new ventures that were disproportionate to the size of his financial investment – which was typically small. For example, Branson put up only £2,000 initially for minority stakes in Virgin Clothing and Virgin Vie; at Virgin Blue, Branson's initial investment was a mere A$12 million. Virgin's joint ventures include:

TABLE 16.2 Financial results for selected Virgin companies

Company	Revenue (£m)	Net profit (£m)	Total assets (£m)	Employees (incl. directors)	Financial year ending	Comments
Virgin Group Ltd.	0.2	(151.4)	69.9	4	03/31/05	Investment holding company. Owns Voyager Group Ltd. and Virgin USA Inc. Exceptional loss of £151m in 2005
Virgin Enterprises Ltd.	13.3	3.3	129.3	4	03/31/06	Owns and licenses Virgin brand
Virgin Management Ltd.	5.7	(13.3)	548.7	97	03/31/06	Management of other Virgin companies. Owns Virgin Bride Ltd., Virgin Mobile (Singapore), Vanson Group Ltd., and Virgin Life Care Investments Ltd.
Virgin Travel Group Ltd.	0	0.7	250.1	10	02/28/06	Holding company. Owns Virgin Atlantic Airlines Ltd. and Virgin Holidays Ltd.
Virgin Atlantic Ltd.	1,912.3	60.3	1,196.7	8,939	02/28/06	Airline
Virgin Leisure Ltd.	0	36.9	216.2	n.a.	03/31/06	Investment holding company that owns Virgin Active Group Ltd.
Virgin Mobile Holdings (UK) Ltd.	563.1	44.9	106.3	1,488	03/31/06	Telecommunications. Acquired by NTL on July 4, 2006
Virgin Mobile Group (UK) Ltd.	80.0	65.8	374.8	3	03/31/06	Holding company. Owns Virgin Mobile Telecoms Ltd.
Virgin Money Ltd.	51.1	12.8	20.0	4	12/31/05	Online financial services, primarily credit cards
Virgin Money Holdings (UK) Ltd.	258.2	8.5	40.3	376	12/31/05	Online financial services, primarily personal investment products
Virgin Rail Group Holdings Ltd.	717.1	(1.2)	372.6	4,456	03/04/06	Owns West Coast Trains Ltd. and CrossCountry Trains Ltd.
Virgin Retail Group Ltd.	0	(82.6)	39.2	4	03/31/04	Holding company. Owns Virgin Retail Ltd. and Vspace Ltd. (internet cafés).
Virgin Retail Ltd.	376.3	(74.7)	203.7	3,240	03/27/04	Holding company. Owns Virgin Atlantic Airways Ltd. and Virgin Holidays Ltd.
Virgin Trading Group Ltd.	0	(7.0)	7.6	4	03/31/05	Investment holding company. Owns Virgin Drinks Group Ltd

n.a. = not available.

SOURCE: COMPANY ANNUAL REPORTS SUBMITTED TO COMPANIES HOUSE.

- Virgin Atlantic was 49% owned by Singapore Airlines.
- Virgin Rail was 49% owned by Stagecoach.
- Virgin Retail had different partners and investors. These included Blockbuster and Marui.
- Virgin Trading drinks ventures had been launched with investments from William Grant and Cotts.
- Victory Corporation, the fashion and toiletries company, was pioneered by entrepreneur and investor Rory McCarthy. In addition, outside investors owned 25% of the equity. McCarthy also held one-third of V2 Music.
- Virgin Express was a subsidiary of SN Airholdings in which Virgin held a 30% equity stake.
- Virgin Blue was a publicly traded company where Virgin held 25%.
- In addition, private investors (including major equity and venture capital funds) held equity stakes in some Virgin businesses.

Looking Ahead

During early 2007, Virgin Group appeared to be relatively free of the cash flow and debt service problems that had plagued it in the past. While a number of Virgin businesses were making losses and others (e.g. Virgin Atlantic) were only marginally profitable, recent divestments had replenished the group's coffers. Longer term, however, there were fundamental strategic questions about the future shape and rationale for the Virgin Group. What kind of enterprise was Virgin? Was it a brand management and franchising company, an incubator of startup businesses, a vehicle for Richard Branson's personal ambitions, or a novel form of conglomerate? Was Virgin a unified, if diversified, business or a loose confederation of many independent businesses?

Whatever the identity and rationale of the Virgin Group, it was not apparent that the existing structure or organization fitted with any of these categories:

- If Virgin was a brand franchising organization, then the critical role for the Virgin Group was to develop and protect the brand and maximize the licensing revenues from its use by other companies. Clearly Branson would need to play a role in promoting the brand, but it was not necessary that he should have any strategic, operating, or ownership role in the companies using the brand.
- If Virgin was to be an incubator of new startups, then there needed to be a more systematic approach to evaluating new business opportunities and monitoring their progress and development.
- If Virgin was a conglomerate, then did this imply a stronger corporate role? What kind of strategic planning and financial controls were needed to ensure that value was not being dissipated? And could Virgin really perform across so wide a range of businesses?

Whichever path Virgin followed, it appeared that organizational changes would be needed in order to manage intercompany linkages. Although Branson liked to maintain that the different companies were independent and "stood on their own two feet," the reality was somewhat different. Some companies had been strong cash generators; others were heavy loss makers. Relationships between the companies were largely ad hoc, and Branson was proud of the fact that no consolidated financial statements were prepared, even for internal management purposes. Moreover, changes to Britain's capital-gains tax laws threatened to eliminate the advantages of multiple, offshore holding companies. Indeed, to obtain the tax benefits from Virgin's loss-making businesses, there were clear advantages in consolidation. Key questions also surrounded the management of the Virgin brand. To the extent that the brand was a common resource, how could it be best protected? The experiences of Virgin Rail suggested that adverse publicity from one company could negatively impact the overall status of the Virgin brand.

As always, the future of the Virgin Group could not be considered without taking account of Branson himself. What kind of role did he anticipate now that he had celebrated his 57th birthday? If Branson was to become less active as chief entrepreneur, public relations director, and strategic architect for the Virgin companies, who or what would take his place?

Appendix
The History of Virgin

1968	●	First issue of *Student* magazine, January 26.
1970	●	Start of Virgin mail order operation.
1971	●	First Virgin record shop opens in Oxford Street, London.
1972	●	Virgin recording studio opens at The Manor near Oxford, England.
1973	●	Virgin record label launched with Mike Oldfield's *Tubular Bells*.
1977	●	Virgin Records signs the Sex Pistols.
1978	●	Virgin opens The Venue night club in London.
1980–2	●	Virgin Records expands overseas. Signs Phil Collins and Boy George/Culture Club.
1983	●	Virgin Vision (forerunner of Virgin Communications) formed to enter broadcasting and produce and distribute films and videos.
	●	Vanson Developments formed as real-estate development company.
	●	Virgin Games (computer games software publisher) launched.
	●	Virgin Group earns pre-tax profit of £2.0 million on sales of £50 million.
1984	●	Virgin Atlantic Airways and Virgin Cargo launched.
	●	First hotel investment (Deya, Mallorca).
	●	Virgin Vision launches The Music Channel, a 24-hour satellite-delivered music station and releases its first feature film, *1984* with Richard Burton and John Hurt.
1985	●	Virgin wins Business Enterprise Award for company of the year.
	●	Virgin Vision extends film and video distribution internationally.
	●	Virgin Holidays formed.
1986	●	Virgin Group, comprising the Music, Retail & Property, and Communications divisions, floated on London Stock Exchange. Placement of 35% of equity raises $56 million.

- Airline, clubs, holidays, and aviation services remain part of the privately owned Voyager Group.

1987
- Virgin Records forms subsidiaries in US and Japan.
- British Satellite Broadcasting (Virgin a minority partner) awarded satellite broadcasting license. (Virgin sells its shareholding in 1988.)
- Virgin acquires Mastertronics Group, distributor of Sega video games in Europe.
- Virgin Airship & Balloon Company launched to provide aerial marketing services.

1988
- Recording studios opened in Barnes, London.
- New international record label, Virgin, launched.
- Virgin Broadcasting formed to further develop Virgin's radio and TV interests.
- Virgin Hotels formed.
- Virgin Megastores opened in Sydney, Paris, and Glasgow.
- Branson takes Virgin private with £248 million bid for outstanding shares.

1989
- Virgin Music Group sells 25% stake to Fujisankei Communications for $150 million.
- Virgin Vision (video distribution) sold to MCEG of Los Angeles for $83 million.

1990
- Virgin Retail Group and Marui form joint venture company to operate Megastores in Japan.
- Virgin Lightships formed to develop helium airships for advertising.

1991
- W. H. Allen plc acquired. Merged with Virgin Books to form Virgin Publishing.
- Sale of Virgin Mastertronic to Sega. Remaining part of the business becomes Virgin Games.
- Virgin Retail Group forms 50:50 joint venture with W. H. Smith to develop UK retail business.

1992
- Sale of Virgin Music Group to Thorn EMI plc.
- Joint venture with Blockbuster to develop Megastores in Europe, Australia, and US.
- Virgin Communications gains license for Britain's first national commercial rock station (Virgin 1215AM goes on the air in April 1993).
- Virgin acquires Euro-Magnetic Products, distributor of personal computer consumables.
- Vintage Airtours established to fly Orlando–Florida Keys in vintage DC-3s.

1993
- Virgin Games floated as Virgin Interactive Entertainment plc with Hasbro and Blockbuster taking minority equity stakes.
- Virgin Euromagnetics launches a range of personal computers.

1994
- Virgin Cola Company formed as joint venture with Cott Corp.
- Agreement with W. Grant to launch Virgin Vodka.
- Virgin acquires W. H. Smith's 75% stake in Our Price retail music stores.
- Virgin Retail Group forms joint ventures to develop Megastores in Hong Kong and S. Korea.
- Virgin City Jet service launched between Dublin and London City Airport.

1995
- Virgin Direct Personal Financial Service is launched as a joint venture with Norwich Union (whose stake is later acquired by Australian Mutual Provident).

- Acquisition of MGM Cinemas, UK's biggest movie theater chain, to create Virgin Cinemas.

1996
- Virgin Travel Group acquires Euro-Belgian Airlines to form Virgin Express.
- V2 record label and music publishing company launched.
- London & Continental Railways (in which Virgin a major shareholder) wins £3bn contract to build the Channel Tunnel Rail Link and operate Eurostar rail services.

1997
- Virgin Rail awarded franchise to operate the West Coast train services.
- Virgin Net, an internet service provider, formed with NTL.
- Branson acquires a 15% stake in the London Broncos rugby league team.
- Victory Corporation, a joint venture with Rory McCarthy, launches the Virgin Clothing and Virgin Vie toiletry products.
- Majority share in Virgin Radio sold to Chris Evans' Ginger Media Group.
- Virgin Bride retail chain formed.
- Virgin One telephone bank account and "one-stop integrated financial service" launched in collaboration with Royal Bank of Scotland.

1998
- Virgin Entertainment acquires W. H. Smith's 75% stake in Virgin/Our Price.
- Virgin Cola launches in the US.

1999
- Virgin sells its UK cinema chain to UGC for £215 million.
- Virgin launches mobile phone service in joint venture with Deutsche Telecom's One-to-One (November).
- 49% of Virgin Atlantic sold to Singapore Airlines for £600 million.
- Restructuring and relaunch of loss-making Our Price record stores.

2000
- Virgin Mobile launches US wireless phone service in joint venture with Sprint. Virgin Mobile Australia (a joint venture with Cable & Wireless) launched.
- Virgin Net, Virgin's portal and ISP venture, closes its content division.
- Virgin announces the closing of its clothing company (February).
- Virgin Cars, online sales of new cars, launched.
- Virgin and Bear Stearns form Lynx New Media, a $130 million venture capital fund.
- Inaugural flight of Virgin Blue, Virgin's low-cost Australian airline.
- Branson knighted by the Queen: becomes Sir Richard Branson.
- Virgin fails to win franchise to run Britain's government-owned National Lottery.

2001
- 50% of Virgin Blue sold to Patrick Corporation for A$138 million.
- Virgin expands into Singapore and SE Asia with joint ventures with local companies in radio stations, cosmetic retailing, and wireless phone services.
- Virgin.net merges its ISP and portal businesses.
- 16 French Virgin Megastores sold to Lagardere Media for 150 million euros.

2002
- Virgin Bikes (UK) begins direct sale of new motorcycles at discount prices.
- Virgin Mobile offers wireless telecom services in the US.

2003
- Virgin Blue initial public offering; Virgin retains 25% of equity.

2004
- 50% stake of Virgin Money repurchased from AMP for £90 million.

- Virgin Digital launched. Offers online music store and digital music download capabilities.
- Virgin Cars and Virgin Bikes sold to MotorSolutions Ltd. of the UK for an undisclosed amount.

2005
- Virgin Mobile launched in Canada.
- Virgin Atlantic increases services to Shanghai and begins flights to Beijing.
- Virgin Atlantic introduces self-service check-in for all passengers.

2006
- Launch of Virgin Atlantic credit card.
- NTL acquires Virgin Mobile.
- Virgin Mobile and Virgin Money launched in South Africa.

Source: www.virgin.com

Notes

1 "Behind Branson," *The Economist*, February 21, 1998, pp. 63–6.
2 "The future for Virgin," *Financial Times*, August 13, 1998, pp. 24–5.
3 Richard Branson, letter to *The Economist*, March 7, 1998, p. 6.
4 Branson is one of Britain's richest individuals, with a net worth exceeding $2 billion. Branson also spent a night in Dover police cells when arrested for tax offenses after he sold through his Virgin store a batch of Virgin records intended for export. The case was settled out of court.
5 "The Virgin Brand," www.virgin.com/aboutvirgin/howitallworks/

6 Peter Robison, "Briton hopes beverage will conquer Coke's monopoly," *Bloomberg News*, December 14, 1997.
7 Melanie Wells, "Red Baron," *Fortune*, July 3, 2000.
8 Robert Dick, "The house that Branson built: Virgin's entry into the new millennium," INSEAD, Fontainebleau, France, 2000.
9 Ibid.
10 Chris Blackhurst, "At the court of King Richard," *Management Today*, May 1998, pp. 40–5.
11 "Consolidating and Protecting the Licensed Virgin Brand," www.cscorporatedomains.com/downloads/IPScan_issue10_virgin.pdf
12 "Will Whitehorn: Galactico of the airways," *The Independent*, November 27, 2006.

Jack Welch and the General Electric Management System

On September 1, 2001 Jack Welch retired from the General Electric Company (GE) after almost 21 years as CEO. During this time GE's revenues had risen from $25 billion to $130 billion and its market capitalization from $13 billion to over $400 billion. This was not a case of corporate turnaround: Welch had inherited a highly successful company that had been led by Reg Jones – one of the most admired corporate executives of his generation. During his two decades at the helm of GE, Welch became the best-known CEO on the planet. His face graced the front covers of *Business Week* and *Fortune* 12 times. In 2001, *Fortune* magazine named GE as America's "most admired company" for the fifth year in succession, and the *Financial Times* identified GE as the "world's most respected company" for the fourth consecutive year. According to University of Michigan management professor Noel Tichy, "The two greatest corporate leaders of this century are Alfred Sloan of General Motors (GM) and Jack Welch of GE. And Welch would be the greater of the two because he set a new, contemporary paradigm for the corporation that is the model for the 21st century."

He also built a sizable personal fortune for himself. At the time of his retirement, his personal fortune was estimated to be in the vicinity of $1 billion. His retirement agreement provided an annual pension of more than $9 million a year and a host of benefits that included the use of GE's corporate jets, a box at the Metropolitan Opera, and prime tickets for the world's major tennis tournaments.

Does Jack Welch deserve either the acclaim he has received as one of the foremost business leaders of the 20th century, or the vast personal fortune that GE has bestowed upon him? And what can other companies and corporate CEOs learn from his example? To answer these questions we must investigate the way in which he managed GE during 1981–2001, and the extent to which GE's

TABLE 17.1 GE's profitability under different chief executives

CEO	Average annual pre-tax ROE (%)
Charles A. Coffin, 1913–22	14.52
Gerald Swope/Owen Young, 1922–39	12.63
Charles E. Wilson, 1940–50	46.72
Ralph J. Cordiner, 1950–63	40.49
Fred J. Borch, 1964–72	27.52
Reginald H. Jones, 1973–81	29.70
John F. Welch, 1981–2001	25.81

The dates given for each CEO are for the financial years that correspond most closely to each CEO's tenure.

SOURCE: WWW.GE.COM

outstanding growth and stock market performance over this period can be attributed to the management system he created.

General Electric Company

The GE in which Jack Welch spent his entire career from 1960 to 2001 was widely regarded as one of the world's most successful companies of the 20th century. It is the only company to have remained a member of the Dow Jones industrial index since the index was created in 1896. Throughout its history, it has been associated with near-continuous growth and above-average profitability. Table 17.1 shows GE's profitability under successive CEOs.

GE was founded in 1892 from the merger of Thomas Edison's Electric Light Company with the Thomas Houston Company. Its business was based on exploiting Edison's patents relating to electricity generation and distribution, light bulbs, and electric motors. Throughout the 20th century, GE was not only one of the world's biggest industrial corporations, it was also "a model of management – a laboratory studied by business schools and raided by other companies seeking skilled executives."[1] Under the leadership of Welch's predecessor, Reg Jones, GE had established a system of corporate management that had become a model for many of the world's leading companies.

As well as being one of the world's biggest companies, GE was also one of the world's most diverse. Its 33 business groups covered a vast spectrum of industry, from consumer appliances to coal mining. Figure 17.1 shows GE's organization and major sectors in 1981.

By 1981, such highly diversified industrial corporations were coming under increasing pressure from the stock market. The conglomerates that had flourished during the 1970s – Hanson, ITT, Seagrams, Philips, General Mills, and United Technologies – were being encouraged to spin-off parts of their empires, or even completely dismantle. The stock market's disdain for highly diversified companies was manifest in the "conglomerate discount," which resulted in their earnings being capitalized at lower multiples than for single-business companies.

FIGURE 17.1 GE's organization structure, 1981

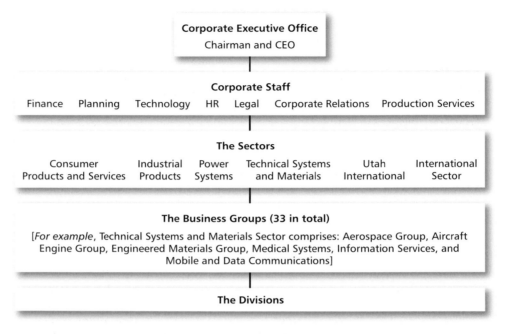

SOURCE: BASED ON INFORMATION IN GENERAL ELECTRIC 10-K REPORT, 1980.

Jack Welch and GE's Performance Culture

Welch had had a stellar career as head of GE Plastics, head of Components and Materials, head of Medical Systems, and finally head of the Consumer Products and Services sector. Yet, his selection for the top spot at GE was a surprise to most outsiders – he was viewed as a maverick with a short fuse and disdainful of GE's elaborate bureaucracy. John Cornell, a Paine Webber analyst, reported: "The word inside the company is that he's chomping at the bit to go crazy once he takes over."[2]

The fundamental feature of Welch's management style was his unremitting drive for performance. Welch's role in restructuring GE's business portfolio and redesigning its organizational structure and management systems will be described in subsequent sections, but underlying these contributions was his reshaping of GE's culture around his own values and beliefs. During his two decades at the top, Welch remade GE in his own image. The culture and management style that he had fostered were reflections of his own personality and belief system. Welch attributes these to two formative influences: his mother and ice hockey. Welch credits his mother with nurturing self-confidence, determination, and strong values:

> I was an only child. My parents were about 40 when they had me . . . It was my mother who trained me, taught me the facts of life. She wanted me to be independent. Control your own destiny – she always had that idea. Saw reality. No mincing words. Whenever I got out of line she would whack me one; but always positive, always constructive, always uplifting. And I was just nuts about her.

He credits ice hockey with developing competitive spirit, confrontation, and camaraderie. His ideas about the value of "constructive conflict" in management were informed by his experiences in ice hockey: "Hockey is the kind of game where people bang you up against the boards and then go out and have a drink with you."

From the outset, Welch set lofty goals for GE: in 1981, as the newly appointed chairman and chief executive, he outlined his vision:

> A decade from now, I would like General Electric to be perceived as a unique, high-spirited, entrepreneurial enterprise . . . a company known around the world for its unmatched level of excellence. I want General Electric to be the most profitable, highly diversified company on earth, with world-quality leadership in every one of its product lines.

For 20 years, Welch continually pushed his subordinates for more. In the early days he continually reiterated his goal of creating a company that was "better than the best." This meant not just imposing "stretch goals" on business-level managers, but encouraging GE's employees – at all levels – to embrace ambitious targets for themselves:

> Shun the incremental and go for the leap. Most bureaucracies – and ours is no exception – unfortunately think in incremental terms rather than in terms of fundamental change. They think incrementally primarily because they think internally. Changing the culture – opening it up to the quantum change – means constantly asking not how fast am I going, how well am I doing versus how well I did a year or two before, but rather, how fast and how well am I doing versus the world outside. Are we moving faster, are we doing better against that external standard?
>
> Stretch means using dreams to set business targets – with no real idea of how to get there . . . We certainly didn't have a clue how we were going to get to ten inventory turns [a year] when we set that target. But we're getting there, and as soon as we become sure we can do it – it's time for another stretch.[3]

Achieving superior performance required grappling with reality. Welch viewed corporate bureaucracy as cloaking the realities of business life. His career at GE was a continuing war on bureaucratic practices. Formality, elaborate PowerPoint presentations, complex strategic plans, were ways in which managers avoided reality and avoided coming to grips with painful decisions. Welch favored confronting reality, acknowledging disagreement, and reconciling conflict through open argument. "Constructive conflict" was his key tool. Welch would force his managers to defend their views, even if that meant getting into shouting-match arguments. "Jack will chase you around the room, throwing arguments and objections at you," said one executive. "Then you fight back until he lets you do what you want, and it's clear you'll do everything you can to make it work."

He spelled out his management philosophy in an interview with *Harvard Business Review*:

> Good business leaders create a vision, articulate the vision, passionately own the vision, and relentlessly drive it to completion. Above all else, though, good leaders are open. They go up, down, and around their organization to reach people. They don't stick to the established channels. They're informal. They're straight with people. They make a religion out of being accessible. They never get bored telling their story.

Real communication takes countless hours of eyeball to eyeball, back and forth. It means more listening than talking. It's not pronouncements on a videotape; it's not announcements in a newspaper. It is human beings coming to see and accept things through a constant interactive process aimed at consensus. And it must be absolutely relentless. That's a real challenge for us. There's still not enough candor in this company.

I mean facing reality, seeing the world as it is rather than as you wish it were. We've seen over and over again that businesses facing market downturns, tougher competition, and more demanding customers inevitably make forecasts that are much too optimistic. This means they don't take advantage of the opportunities change usually offers. Change in the marketplace isn't something to fear; it's an enormous opportunity to shuffle the deck, to replay the game. Candid managers – leaders – don't get paralyzed about the "fragility" of the organization. They tell people the truth. That doesn't scare them because they realize their people know the truth anyway.

We've had managers at GE who couldn't change, who kept telling us to leave them alone. They wanted to sit back, to keep things the way they were. And that's just what they did – until they and most of their staffs had to go. That's the lousy part of this job . . . The point is, what determines our destiny is not the hand you're dealt; it's how you play the hand. And the best way to play your hand is to face reality – see the world the way it is – and act accordingly.

For a large organization to be effective, it must be simple. For a large organization to be simple, its people must have self-confidence and intellectual self-assurance. Insecure managers create complexity. Frightened, nervous managers use thick, convoluted planning books and busy slides filled with everything they've known since childhood. Real leaders don't need clutter. People must have the self-confidence to be clear, precise, to be sure that every person in their organization – highest to lowest – understands what the business is trying to achieve. But it's not easy. You can't believe how hard it is for people to be simple, how much they fear being simple. They worry that if they're simple, people will think they're simpleminded. In reality, of course, it's just the reverse. Clear, tough-minded people are the most simple.[4]

By the end of the 1980s, Welch summarized his management beliefs in the slogan "Speed, Simplicity, Self-Confidence":

We found in the 1980s that becoming faster is tied to becoming simpler. Our businesses, with tens of thousands of employees, will not respond to visions that have sub-paragraphs and footnotes. If we're not simple, we can't be fast . . . and if we're not fast, we can't win. Simplicity, to an engineer, means clean, functional, winning designs; no bells or whistles. In marketing, it might manifest itself as clear, unencumbered proposals. For manufacturing people, it would produce a logical process that makes sense to every individual on the line. And on an individual, interpersonal level, it would take the form of plain-speaking directness, honesty.

But just as surely as speed flows from simplicity, simplicity is grounded in self-confidence. Self-confidence does not grow in someone who is just another appendage on the bureaucracy; whose authority rests on little more than a title. People who are freed from the confines of their box on the organization chart, whose status rests on real-world achievement – those are the people who develop the self-confidence to be simple, to share every bit of information available to them, to listen to those above, below and around them and then move boldly.

But a company can't distribute self-confidence. What it can do – what we must do – is to give each of our people an opportunity to win, to contribute, and hence earn self-confidence themselves. They don't get that opportunity, they can't taste winning, if they spend their days wandering in the muck of a self-absorbed bureaucracy.

Speed . . . simplicity . . . self-confidence. We have it in increasing measure. We know where it comes from . . . and we have plans to increase it in the 1990s.[5]

How successful was Welch in translating his performance culture into real financial performance? Tables 17.2 and 17.3 show key features of GE's performance under Welch.

TABLE 17.2 GE's performance 1981–2001

	2001	2000	1999	1998	1997	1996	1995	1994	1993	1992	1991
Revenues ($bn)	125.9	129.9	111.6	100.5	90.8	79.2	70.0	60.1	55.7	53.0	51.3
Net earnings ($bn)	13.7	12.7	10.7	9.3	8.2	7.3	6.6	4.7	4.3	4.7	2.6
Return on average shareholders' equity (%)	26.0	27.3	26.4	25.2	25.0	24.0	23.5	18.1	17.5	20.9	12.2
Total assets ($bn)	495.0	437.0	387.4	355.9	304.0	272.4	228.0	194.5	251.5	192.9	166.5
Long-term borrowings ($bn)	79.8	82.1	73.5	59.7	46.6	49.2	51.0	37.0	28.2	25.3	22.6
Employees at year end ('000s)											
United States	158	168	167	163	165	155	150	156	157	168	173
Other countries	152	145	143	130	111	84	72	60	59	58	62
Total employees	310	313	310	293	276	239	222	221	222	268	284

	1990	1989	1988	1987	1986	1985	1984	1983	1982	1981
Revenues ($bn)	49.7	54.6	50.1	48.2	42.0	28.3	27.3	26.8	26.5	27.2
Net earnings ($bn)	4.3	3.9	3.4	2.9	2.5	2.3	2.3	2.0	1.8	1.7
Return on average shareholders' equity (%)	20.2	20.0	19.4	18.5	17.3	17.6	19.1	18.9	18.8	19.1
Total assets ($bn)	152.0	128.3	110.9	95.4	84.8	26.4	24.7	23.3	21.6	20.9
Long-term borrowings ($bn)	20.9	16.1	15.1	12.5	10.0	0.8	0.8	0.9	1.0	1.1
Employees at year end ('000s)										
United States	236	243	255	277	302	236	248	246	n.a.	n.a.
Other countries	62	49	43	45	71	68	82	94	n.a.	n.a.
Total employees	298	292	298	322	373	304	330	340	367	404

n.a. = not available.

SOURCE: GENERAL ELECTRIC 10-K REPORTS.

TABLE 17.3 GE's divisional performance, 1997–2001

	Revenue 2001 ($bn)	Profit 2001 ($bn)	Average return on assets 1999–2001 (%)	Revenue growth 1997–2001 (%)	Profit growth 1997–2001 (%)
Aircraft Engines	11.4	2.6	24.2	46	91
Appliances	5.8	0.6	23.8	0	−17
Industrial Products and Systems	11.6	1.8	26.2	7	11
Materials	7.1	1.6	18.0	3	−2
NBC	5.8	1.6	31.6	12	31
Power Systems	20.2	5.2	28.3	153	305
Technical Products and Services	9.0	2.0	28.5	84	99
GE Capital	58.4	5.6	20.6	46	71

SOURCE: GE ANNUAL REPORT 2001.

Reconfiguring the Business Portfolio

Although Welch was resolutely determined to retain GE's identity as a broadly diversified corporation, he was clear that GE's business portfolio should, first, be focused around a limited number of sectors and, second, these sectors should be attractive in terms of their potential for profitability and growth. During the early part of his chairmanship, Welch announced his intention only to retain businesses that held number one or number two positions within their global markets. His intention was to focus GE's resources on its best opportunities: "My biggest challenge will be to put enough money on the right gambles and no money on the wrong ones. But I don't want to sprinkle money over everything." This involved increasing GE's emphasis on technology-based businesses and service businesses. Welch sold off its consumer electronics business, mining interests (notably Utah International), small household appliances division, semiconductors, and radio stations.

GE's acquisitions included a few major ones, such as RCA, NBC, Kidder Peabody, and CGR, plus a host of smaller companies. During 1997–2001, GE made over a hundred acquisitions in each year. By far the largest sector for acquisition was financial services. During the 1990s, GE Capital's phenomenal growth was built on continuous acquisition of businesses in leasing, consumer and commercial credit, insurance, and other areas of finance. The result was the emergence of GE Capital as one of the world's biggest and most diversified financial services companies.

For all GE's expertise in identifying acquisition targets and then integrating them into GE's structure and systems, not all were successful. Kidder Peabody was a disaster for GE, and the acquisition of Montgomery Ward was viewed by most outsiders as a mistake. Welch's final acquisition goal – Honeywell – finally had to be abandoned because of opposition from the European Commission on antitrust grounds.

Changing the Structure

The changes in the portfolio transformed the product-market face of GE and increased its growth potential. However, to realize this potential required revitalizing the management systems and management style to generate drive and ambition. Achieving this required changes to GE's structure. Under Welch, GE eliminated several layers of management and large numbers of administrative positions. In particular, Welch disbanded GE's sectors, requiring the leaders of GE's 13 businesses to report directly to the CEO. The office of the CEO was expanded, and a Corporate Executive Council (CEC) was created to provide a forum for GE's business-level chiefs and senior corporate officers. Further organizational layers were eliminated, both at headquarters and within the businesses. Decision making was pushed down to the operating units.

> We are now down in some businesses to four layers from the top to the bottom. That's the ultimate objective. We used to have things like department managers, section managers, subsection managers, unit managers, supervisors – we are driving those titles out . . . We used to go from the CEO to sectors to groups to businesses. We now go from the CEO . . . to businesses. Nothing else. There is nothing else there. Zero.
>
> When you take out layers, you change the exposure of the managers who remain. They sit right in the sun. Some of them blotch immediately – they can't stand the exposure of leadership. I firmly believe that an overburdened, overstretched executive is the best executive, because he or she doesn't have time to meddle, to deal in trivia, or to bother people. Remember the theory that a manager should have no more than six or seven direct reports? I say the right number is closer to 10 or 15. This way you have no choice but to let people flex their muscles, to let them grow and mature.[6]

Empowering line managers meant reducing the power – and number – of staff. Welch's goal was to "turn their role 180° from checker, inquisitor, and authority figure to facilitator, helper, and supporter of the businesses . . . Ideas, initiatives, and decisions could now move quickly. Often at the speed of sound – voices – where once they were muffled and garbled by the gauntlet of approvals and staff reviews."[7]

The result was massive reductions in numbers of employees. Between 1980 and 1990, GE's headcount fell from 402,000 to 298,000. The biggest cuts were at the upper levels of the organization: at corporate headquarters and within sectoral administration. In some areas employee numbers increased – particularly in overseas operations. Welch's ruthless attack on bureaucracy and administrative costs earned him the nickname "Neutron Jack" – the building remained, but the people had gone.

Figure 17.2 shows GE's overall structure in 2001.

Changing Management Systems and Processes

Strategic Planning

The changes in GE's structure were aimed at creating a more flexible and responsive corporation. This goal also necessitated changes in GE's highly developed management systems. In particular, Welch led a major overhaul of GE's much celebrated and

FIGURE 17.2 GE's organization structure, 2001

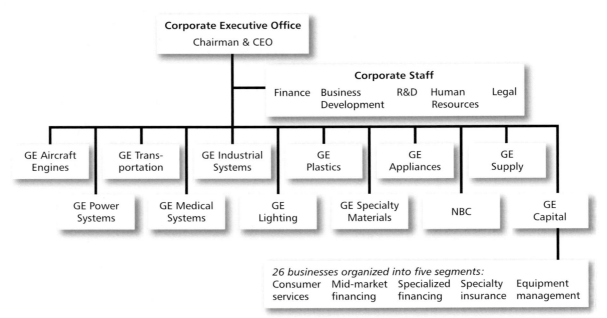

widely emulated strategic planning system. The framework of an annual planning cycle was retained, but the staff-led, document-driven process was replaced by a less formal, more personal process. Instead of the big planning reports, Welch asked each business head to prepare a slim "playbook" that summarized the key strategic issues that the business faced, and how it intended to address them. This document provided the basis for a half-day, shirtsleeves review in mid-summer when Welch and key corporate officers would engage in discussion and debate with the top management team of each businesses. On the 1986 meetings, Welch commented:

> We asked the 14 business leaders to present reports on the competitive dynamics in their businesses. How did we do it? We had them each prepare one-page answers to five questions: What are your market dynamics globally today, and where are they going over the next several years? What actions have your competitors taken in the last three years to upset those global dynamics? What have you done in the last three years to affect these dynamics? What are the most dangerous things your competitor could do in the next three days to upset those dynamics? What are the most effective things you could do to bring your desired impact on those dynamics?
>
> Five simple charts. After those initial reviews, which we update regularly, we could assume that everyone at the top knew the plays and had the same playbook. It doesn't take a genius. Fourteen businesses each with a playbook of five charts. So when Larry Bossidy is with a potential partner in Europe, or I'm with a company in the Far East, we're always there with a competitive understanding based upon our playbooks. We know exactly what makes sense; we don't need a big staff to do endless analysis. That means we should be able to act with speed.[8]

Financial Planning and Control

Supporting GE's strategic planning system was a sophisticated financial budgeting system, which centered on the annual budget. Budget preparation began in July and involved extensive negotiation between the operating units, the intervening groups and sectors, and the corporate headquarters. Once the budget was set, managers were locked in to meet it "at all costs" regardless of changes in the marketplace. It was generally agreed that the system had undesirable consequences, such as gaming to set low targets, and cutting long-term development to meet short-term targets. Because managers were locked in to figures established 18 months before, the budgeting system often inhibited adjustment to external changes and gave little information on management performance.

Welch's commitment to a performance-driven organization meant that financial targets were of critical importance. However, the key was to create shareholder value rather than accounting profits per se. In addition, it was essential that the system should permit the performance of divisional and business unit managers to be assessed. Two changes were made. First, the controller's office prepared a set of financial objectives for each operating unit to reflect more realistically each unit's prospects and to reduce gamesmanship in target-setting. Second, the budgets (now called operating plans) were subject to revision as economic or competitive conditions changed. Thus, line managers could propose changes to the plans once the original assumptions on which they had been based could be shown to have changed. Performance evaluation was then made against the revised targets.

Central to the changes in financial control was the idea that performance was not about "making the budget." It was about raising performance expectations to be "as good as possible": the primary task of the businesses, emphasized Welch, was to produce earnings. As a guideline, Welch proposed that GE's earnings should grow at between one-and-a-half and two times the growth of GDP.

Human Resource Management

The key to GE's long-term development and performance was the development of its management talent. GE had a well-established system of management appraisal and development, which Welch retained. He believed that giving managers greater profit-and-loss responsibility earlier in their careers would be conducive to an even greater flourishing of managerial talent. But to encourage risk taking and higher levels of performance aspiration required more powerful incentives. Welch believed in giving more recognition to individual contributors and higher rewards to those who produced superior results:

> A flat reward system is a big anchor to incrementalism. We want to give big rewards to those who do things but without going for the scalps of those who reach for the big win but fail. Punishing failure assures that no one dares.[9]

Welch redesigned the bonus system to reach deep into middle management. The bonuses became much more discriminating. The typical 10 to 15% bonuses for senior managers were replaced by 30 to 40% bonuses for far fewer managers. In addition, stock options were extended from the top echelon of management to a much wider range of managerial and technical employees. By 1996, Welch was able to report that the number of employees receiving stock options had increased from 400 in the early

1980s to 22,000 by the end of 1995: "Today, stock option compensation, based on total GE performance, is far more significant than the salary or bonus growth associated with the performance of any individual unit or business. This aligns the interests of the individual, the Company, and the share owner behind powerful, on-company results."[10]

Welch believed that a performance-driven organization would not only encourage GE's managers to perform up to the limits of their capabilities, it would also nurture those capabilities. Welch firmly believed that GE's ability to outperform its peers ultimately depended on having outstanding employees. GE could offer opportunities for career development and the acquisition of skills and expertise that no other company could match:

> Our true "core competency" today is not manufacturing or services, but the global recruiting and nurturing of the world's best people and the cultivation in them of an insatiable desire to learn, to stretch, and to do things better every day. By finding, challenging and rewarding these people, by freeing them from bureaucracy, by giving them all the resources they need – and by simply getting out of their way – we have seen them make us better and better every year.
>
> We have a Company more agile than others a fraction of our size, a high-spirited company where people are free to dream and encouraged to act and to take risks. In a culture where people act this way, every day, "big" will never mean slow.
>
> This is all about people – "soft stuff." But values and behaviors are what produce those performance numbers, and they are the bedrock upon which we will build our future.[11]

Maintaining a vigorous, performance-driven culture required putting managers under continual pressure, including ongoing weeding-out of weaker performers. GE's system of evaluation was renowned for its thoroughness and its ruthlessness:

> In every evaluation and reward system, we break our population down into three categories: the top 20%, the high-performance middle 70%, and the bottom 10%. The top 20% must be loved, nurtured and rewarded in the soul and wallet because they are the ones who make magic happen. Losing one of these people must be held up as a leadership sin – a real failing. The top 20% and middle 70% are not permanent labels. People move between them all the time. However, the bottom 10%, in our experience, tend to remain there. A Company that bets its future on its people must remove that lower 10%, and keep removing it every year – always raising the bar of performance and increasing the quality of its leadership. Not removing that bottom 10% early in their careers is not only a management failure, but false kindness as well – a form of cruelty – because inevitably a new leader will come into a business and take out that bottom 10% right away, leaving them – sometimes midway through a career – stranded and having to start over somewhere else. Removing marginal performers early in their careers is doing the right thing for them; leaving them in place to settle into a career that will inevitably be terminated is not. GE leaders must not only understand the necessity to encourage, inspire, and reward that top 20%, and be sure that the high-performance 70% is always energized to improve and move upward; they must develop the determination to change out, always humanely, that bottom 10%, and do it every year. That is how real meritocracies are created and thrive.[12]

GE's management development process in which managers were moved between businesses was a critical means of deepening organizational capabilities. Welch attributed the remarkable success of GE Capital to its ability to apply the principles and techniques of manufacturing management to financial services:

> At GE Capital, we combined ideas with manufacturing disciplines. When a loan went bad, we worked it out; we didn't put a line through it. One business of ours, Polar Air, came about because we had leased a bunch of 747s to Pan Am and the airline went out of business. We converted the planes to cargo carriers and started a shipping company. We got into the railcar business the same way, through a bankruptcy. That's what we could do at GE because we had the people with diverse operating experience, as well as capital, which gave us considerable staying power. Unlike most bankers, our people knew how to operate businesses . . . [W]e were able to bring manufacturing discipline to bear on credit decisions. Take commercial equipment finance, for example. The person running it today used to work in lighting and appliances. The experience in those businesses gave him rigor and operating discipline. He's worked with real hard assets; he understands them.[13]

Corporate Initiatives

One of the distinctive characteristics of Welch's system of management was his use of periodic new corporate initiatives as mechanisms to drive particular aspects of company-wide performance. Thus, while strategic planning, financial control, and human resource management provided the basic systems for managing GE, about every two years, Welch would announce a major new initiative designed to energize the company and drive its performance in a particular direction. Over time, these initiatives would become absorbed into the ongoing management systems of GE.

Work-Out

The idea for GE's "Work-Out" process began with the no-holds-barred discussion sessions that Welch held with different groups of managers at GE's Management Development Institute at Crotonville, New York. Impressed with the energy and impetus for change that these sessions generated, Welch initiated a company-wide process called "Work-Out."

The idea was to create a forum where a cross-section of employees could speak their minds about the management of their business without the fear of retribution by their superiors. Typically, the sessions assembled a cross-section of 50 to 100 of the business's employees for meetings that ran for two or three days. In an environment that Welch likened to an old New England town meeting, the group would be asked to openly and honestly review the management process and practices in their part of the operation. Initially they focused on unproductive or bureaucratic behaviors that had limited their personal effectiveness. At the end of each Work-Out, the group's manager returned to hear the findings and recommendations, and could either accept or reject them on the spot, or appoint a team to report back with more data by a given date. Welch believed that Work-Out could achieve fundamental changes in management:

> *Work-Out has a practical and an intellectual goal. The practical objective is to get rid of thousands of bad habits accumulated since the creation of General Electric . . . The second thing we want to achieve, the intellectual part, begins by putting the leaders of each business in front of 100 or so of their people, eight to ten times a year, to let them hear what their people think. Work-Out will expose the leaders to the vibrations of their business – opinions, feelings, emotions, resentments, not abstract theories of organization and management. Ultimately, we're talking about redefining the relationship between boss and subordinate.*
>
> *These Work-Out sessions create all kinds of personal dynamics. Some people go and hide. Some emerge as forceful advocates. As people meet over and over, though, more of them will develop the courage to speak out. The norm will become the person who says, "Damn it, we're not doing it. Let's get on with doing it." This process will create more fulfilling and rewarding jobs. The quality of work life will improve dramatically.*[14]

Initially, Work-Out focused on eliminating bureaucratic practices ("low-hanging fruit"). Over time, Work-Out sessions evolved to the evaluation and redesign of complex cross-functional processes – often involving suppliers and customers as well as GE employees.

The Boundary-less Organization

Welch reacted strongly to descriptions of GE as a conglomerate. But for GE to be greater than the sum of its parts required utilizing its product and geographical diversity to improve performance within each business. The key to transforming diversity into strength, believed Welch, was the frictionless transfer of best practices and other forms of learning within GE. But to achieve this required eliminating – or at least making permeable – GE's internal boundaries, as well as increasing openness to external learning. By 1990, Welch was developing the vision of a new GE organization that would be a truly "boundary-less" company. His boundary-less company was one in which both external barriers and internal barriers became blurred:

> *In a boundary-less company, suppliers aren't outsiders. They are drawn closer and become trusted partners in the total business process. Customers' vision of their needs and the company's view become identical and every effort of every man and woman in the company is focused on satisfying those needs. The boundary-less company blurs the divisions between internal functions; it recognizes no distinctions between "domestic" and "foreign" operations; and it ignores or erases group labels – such as "management," "salaried," and "hourly" – which get in the way of people working together.*[15]

Unbounding GE required changes in structures, attitudes, and behaviors that would permit the "integrated diversity" that Welch envisaged. Examples of boundary-less behavior were widely publicized and praised:

> *Two years ago, one of our people spotted a truly innovative method of compressing product cycle times in an appliance company in New Zealand. After testing it successfully in our Canadian affiliate, we transferred the methodology to our largest appliance complex in Louisville, KY. It has revolutionized processes, reduced cycle times, increased our customer responsiveness, and reduced our inventory levels by hundreds of millions of dollars. Teams from all of our*

manufacturing businesses are now living in Louisville so we can spread the New Zealand-to-Montreal-to-Louisville learning to every business in GE.[16]

Globalization

All of GE's businesses were given global responsibility, which meant exploiting international growth opportunities and exploiting the advantages of global reach in terms of exploiting global-level economies of scale and increased learning opportunities. Global diversity played an important role in allowing GE to cope with economic problems that affected particular countries or regions, and take advantage of the opportunities that such downturns offered. For example, as "financial contagion" affected much of Asia during 1997–8, GE was seeking acquisition opportunities:

We've been down this road before. In the early 1980s, we experienced a United States mired in recession, hand-wringing from the pundits, and dirges being sung over American manufacturing. We didn't buy this dismal scenario; instead, we invested in both a widespread restructuring and in new businesses . . . Europe looked a lot like the United States in the 1980s, and in need of the same remedies: restructuring, spinoffs, and the like. So, while many were "writing-off" Europe, we invested heavily, buying new companies and expanding our existing presence . . . "GE Europe" is now a $20.6 billion operation. Our revenues have more than doubled from 1994 to 1997; net income has tripled to more than $1.5 billion; and growth is accelerating as the European recovery progresses . . . Mexico in the mid-1990s was a similar story . . . GE moved, acquiring ten companies and investing more than $1 billion in new and existing operations. The result was revenue growth of 60% and a doubling of earnings in the two years following the crisis. Today we are determined, and poised, to do the same thing in Asia we have done in the United States, Europe, and Mexico: invest in the future.[17]

Six Sigma

From 1998 to 2000, Welch's Six Sigma program was its dominant corporate initiative and primary driver of organizational change and performance improvement. Welch described it as his next "soul-transforming cultural initiative." The methodology of defining, measuring, analyzing, improving, and then controlling every process that touches a company's customers until it reduces defects to 3.4 per million was borrowed from Motorola. However, at GE it was implemented with remarkable fervor across an unprecedentedly broad front. In four years, some 100,000 people were trained in its science and methodology, and, by 2001, GE was able to report: "Now Six Sigma is the way we work. We all speak a common language of CTQs (critical-to-quality), DPMOs (defects per million opportunities), FMEAs (failure mode effect analysis), and Needs Assessment Maps, to name just a few." Across every one of GE's businesses, major gains in performance, ranging from reduced waste and lower operating costs to faster customer service and improved financial management, were reported.

Digitization

Welch was a late convert to the electronic business. However, once converted, he became a raving evangelist, urging his line managers and launching his "destroy-your-business.com" initiative in 1999. Each organizational unit was encouraged to visualize how it might be crushed by the dotcom juggernaut. The result was widespread discovery of opportunities to use the internet to improve internal processes and better serve customers. By spring 2001, Welch reported:

> As we said in our 1999 letter, digitization is transforming everything we do, energizing every corner of the Company and making us faster, leaner, and smarter even as we become bigger. In 2000, these words began to turn into numbers, as we sold over $7 billion of goods and services over the net and conducted over $6 billion in online auctions. Digitization efforts across the Company will generate over $1.5 billion in operating margin improvements in 2001.[18]

GE's Operating System

By 2001, these different initiatives had been institutionalized to the point where GE referred to them as its "operating system." Thus, referring collectively to Work-Out, Boundarylessness, Globalization, Six Sigma, and Digitization, GE described an integrated system for performance improvement:

> The GE Operating System is GE's learning culture in action. It is a year-round series of intense learning sessions where business CEOs, role models, and initiative champions from GE, as well as outside companies, meet and share intellectual capital.
> The central focus is always on sharing, and putting into action, the best ideas and practices from across the Company and around the world.
> Meetings take place year-round, in an endless process of enrichment. Learning builds from previous meetings, expanding the scope and increasing the momentum of our Company-wide initiatives.
> Driven by the Company's values – trust, informality, simplicity, boundary-less behavior and the love of change – the Operating System allows GE businesses to reach speeds and performance levels unachievable were they on their own.
> The GE Operating System translates ideas into action across three dozen businesses so rapidly that all the initiatives have become operational across the Company within one month of launch, and have always produced positive financial results within their first cycle.[19]

Notes

1 "Can Jack Welch reinvent GE?" *Business Week*, June 29, 1986, pp. 40–5.
2 Ibid.
3 GE Annual Report, 1993, p. 5.
4 Noel Tichy and Ram Charan, "Speed, simplicity, and self-confidence: an interview with Jack Welch," *Harvard Business Review*, September–October 1989.
5 Ibid.
6 *GE 1984*, Harvard Business School Case No. 385–315.
7 Tichy and Charan, op cit.
8 Ibid.
9 Ibid.
10 Jack Welch, address to 1989 shareholders' meeting.
11 Chairman's letter, General Electric Annual Report, 2000.
12 Ibid.
13 H. Collingwood and D. Coutu, "Jack on Jack," *Harvard Business Review*, February 2002.
14 Tichy and Charan, op cit.
15 GE Annual Report, 1990.
16 Ibid.
17 Chairman's letter, General Electric Annual Report, 1997.
18 Chairman's letter, General Electric Annual Report, 2000.
19 The GE Operating System (www.ge.com).

Jeff Immelt at General Electric, 2001–2006

When Jeff Immelt took over as chairman and CEO of General Electric on September 7, 2001, he had no doubts that his predecessor, Jack Welch – "living legend," "best manager of the past half-century" – would be a tough act to follow. But little did he realize just how tough it would be.

A few days after occupying the chairman's suite, two hijacked airliners ploughed into New York's World Trade Center, setting off a train of events that would profoundly affect GE's business environment. A month later, Enron's collapse precipitated a crisis of confidence over corporate governance, executive morality, and financial reporting. The scandal at Tyco International – a company that had explicitly modeled itself on GE – reinforced suspicion of conglomerates and their management. It was not long before GE's own financial structure and financial reporting were under fire. After being lauded by analysts for its smooth earnings growth, rumors of earnings manipulation by GE circulated among the investment community. More specific criticisms were directed at GE's alleged disguising of the true risks of its businesses by consolidating the financial statements of its industrial businesses and its financial services business, GE Capital. In March 2002, Bill Gross, of the IPCO fund management group, argued that GE was primarily a financial services company but, with the support of GE's industrial businesses, GE Capital had been able to operate on a narrow capital base while maintaining a triple-A credit rating. Further problems for Immelt emerged with the September 2002 leaking of the details of Welch's remarkable retirement package from GE. Initial concerns as to whether Immelt could ever match the incredible 50-fold increase in GE's market value that Welch had achieved, were now refocusing around the question of how Immelt would halt GE's sliding share price. On the date that Immelt's selection as GE's next CEO was announced, GE's stock was trading at $53. Two years later it was trading at half that level.

By the end of 2006, Immelt had stabilized GE, established himself firmly at the helm, and had stamped his persona and style on the company. His first challenge had been to restore investor confidence in GE. This he had achieved through constant communication with investors and more detailed financial reporting. From February 2003 to January 2007, driven by strong underlying financial performance, GE's stock price followed a near-continuous upward trend – although never reaching the level of September 7, 2001 when Immelt took over.

A greater challenge was coming to terms with Welch's legacy at GE. Each of GE's CEOs had been associated with successfully adapting GE's strategy and management systems to the challenges of the particular era. Among these, Welch had been remarkable for the scale of his vision and his dedication to its implementation. Welch had unleashed top-to-bottom organizational change, and maintained the pace of change over two decades. He had swept away most of GE's carefully constructed structure and elaborate corporate planning system, instituting a system that relentlessly challenged GE managers for improved operational and financial results. The result was a corporation that combined massive corporate size with flexibility, entrepreneurial responsiveness, and a constant quest for superior performance.

Immelt recognized that Welch's strategy and style were ideal for the circumstances of the time and reflected Welch's own personality and beliefs. The challenge for Immelt was to develop an identity and strategy for GE that were suited to the challenges and opportunities that the corporation faced in the 21st century, together with a management style that was consistent with his own persona.

By the beginning of 2007, Immelt had made considerable progress in developing his vision for GE and articulating that vision through a number of key strategic themes. He had taken significant steps to communicate GE's new direction among GE's stakeholders and to enact it through acquisitions, capital investment allocations, changes in GE's organizational structure, and changes to GE's management systems. Immelt's strategic direction had received a strong endorsement from fellow managers, external analysts, and various GE watchers. In 2006, GE regained its status as "America's Most Admired Company," an award it had not received since 2002.[1] Growing confidence in Immelt was fueled by GE's strong growth in revenues and earnings (see table 18.1). However, as several analysts observed, this performance was attributable

TABLE 18.1 General Electric: selected financial data, 2001–2006

	(in $ millions unless otherwise indicated)					
	2006	2005	2004	2003	2002	2001
Revenues	163,391	149,702	134,481	112,886	113,856	107,558
Earnings before accounting changes	n.a.	16,353	16,819	15,823	15,182	14,078
Net earnings	20,829	16,353	16,819	15,236	14,167	13,791
Return on average share owners' equity (%)	18.8	17.6	17.6	19.6	27.2	24.7
Total assets	697,200	673,342	750,507	647,828	575,236	495,012
Long-term borrowings	n.a.	212,281	207,871	170,309	138,570	77,818
Employees at year end:						
United States	n.a.	161,000	165,000	155,000	161,000	158,000
Other countries	n.a.	155,000	142,000	150,000	154,000	152,000
Total employees	n.a.	316,000	307,000	305,000	315,000	310,000

primarily to the strength of the world economy after 2002. Whether Immelt's new strategy for GE would provide the basis for the long-term prosperity of GE had yet to be seen.

General Electric Company

The General Electric that Jeffrey Immelt inherited in 2001 was the world's most valuable company and was widely regarded as the world's most successful. The key to its success had been constant adaptation. This adaptation comprised both the business portfolio and its management systems. Under Jack Welch, GE's business portfolio had shifted substantially: by 2001 it was more of a service company than a manufacturing company – GE Capital contributed close to half of GE's revenues and technical and support services were important revenue generators for most of GE's industrial businesses. Figure 18.1 shows GE's structure in 2001.

GE's ability to generate superior financial and stock market returns during a period when corporate diversification was deeply unpopular among investors and management thinkers was a tribute to the management systems that GE had developed and the resulting capabilities that enhanced the performance of each of GE's businesses. No other company has been such a fertile source of management innovation and management technique. After World War II, Chairman Ralph Cordiner, assisted by Peter Drucker, pioneered new approaches to the systematization of corporate management. Under Fred Borch (CEO 1963–72), GE established a system of strategic management based on strategic business units and portfolio analysis that became a model for most diversified corporations. Reg Jones (CEO 1972–81) integrated strategic with financial

FIGURE 18.1 GE's organization structure, 2001

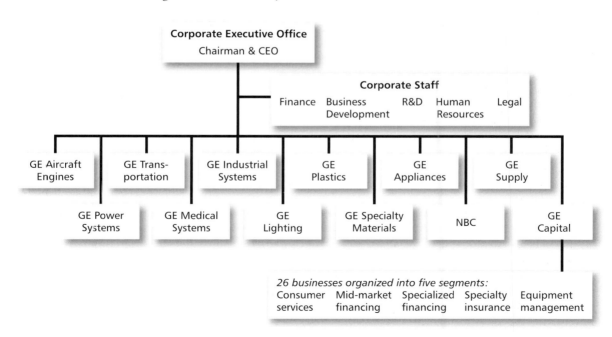

SOURCE: BASED ON INFORMATION IN GENERAL ELECTRIC 10-K REPORT, 2001.

planning and showed how decentralized decision making could be reconciled with corporate identity and discipline. During the early years of the 21st century, Jack Welch's innovations – "work-out," "boundarylessness," decentralization, and the use of management development as a vehicle for cultural change – were continuing to disseminate through other companies.

Ultimately, what all GE's CEOs had been able to achieve was the creation of value out of GE's diversity. This had involved both reshaping GE's business portfolio and managing the relationships between the businesses to ensure that each of GE's businesses were more valuable within GE than they could be outside. Thus, under Jack Welch, GE shed several of its resource-based businesses (including mining) and slow growth, low-margin businesses such as consumer electronics and small household appliances. In building cross-business linkages, Welch developed GE's systems of management development, strategy formulation, and financial control and drove company-wide initiatives such as six sigma and best practice transfer. Immelt viewed GE's diversity as fundamental to its stability and strength. Like Welch, Immelt acknowledged that GE was diversified, but rejected vehemently the label "conglomerate":

> *Our businesses are closely integrated. They share leading-edge business initiatives, excellent financial disciplines, a tradition of sharing talent and best practices, and a culture whose cornerstone is absolute unyielding integrity. Without these powerful ties, we could actually merit the label "conglomerate" that people often inaccurately apply to us. That word just does not apply to GE.[2]*

At the basis of GE's integration and its capacity to create value within each of its businesses was its management systems and its shared organizational culture:

> *GE is a multi-business growth company bound together by common operating systems and initiatives, and a common culture with strong values. Because of these shared systems, processes and values, the whole of GE is greater than the sum of its parts.[3]*

Jeff Immelt

Jeffrey R. Immelt was appointed CEO of GE at the age of 44. He had previously been head of GE's Plastics business and, most recently, head of Medical Systems. He had an economics and applied math degree from Dartmouth and an MBA from Harvard. He claimed that his own experience of GE extended beyond his two decades with the firm – his father spent his entire career at GE. On being recruited from Harvard by GE in 1982, Immelt was identified as a "young high potential" whose progress was tracked by senior executives at GE. In 1987, Immelt was invited to attend the Executive Development Course at Crotonville, GE's management development center. This course was considered the gateway to the executive ranks of GE. At GE Appliances, GE Plastics, and GE Medical Systems, Immelt acquired a reputation for turning around troubled units, driving customer service, and exploiting new technologies. He also demonstrated the ability to motivate others – an aptitude that he had revealed as an offensive tackler for Dartmouth's football team in the 1970s.[4]

In December 1994, the GE board began to consider possible candidates to replace Jack Welch. Immelt was one among a list of some 20 GE executives submitted by Welch for board consideration. After five years of careful monitoring and assessment, the list had shrunk to three: Jim McNerney, Bob Nardelli, and Immelt.

Immelt's emergence as front-runner was principally the result of his outstanding success at GE Medical Systems, which he was appointed to lead in 1997. In addition to rigorous cost cutting and exceeding his budget forecasts, Immelt showed the ability to pick good managers, motivate them, pioneer new technologies, and expand the business. His strength was in energizing and motivating others: "He brought the life and energy that drives major growth," commented GE's head of HR.

Immelt had developed a personality and leadership style that contrasted sharply with those of Welch. Yet, they seemed to be similarly effective in driving business performance. *Business Week* observed: "Where Welch ruled through intimidation and thrived as something of a cult figure, Immelt opts for the friendlier, regular-guy approach. He prefers to tease where Welch would taunt. Immelt likes to cheer people on rather than chew them out. That style has given him a very different aura within GE. He may not be a demigod, but it's his man-of-the-people nature that draws praise from the top ranks to the factory floor."[5] Immelt knew that his different style of leadership would have important implications for his role as CEO and the ways in which he would influence GE's strategy, structure, and systems. However, Immelt believed that the principal changes that he would initiate at GE would be a result of the changing environment and the shifting priorities that GE faced.

GE's Post-2001 Business Environment

The remarkable growth in profits and stock market valuation that Welch had achieved was against a backdrop of an economy effused by optimism, confidence, and growth. The period 2000 to 2002 was salutary for the entire world economy – and for the US in particular. "The exuberance of the late 1990s and the inevitable downturn have created difficult times. Entire industries have collapsed, poor business models have been exposed, large companies have filed for bankruptcy and corporate credibility has been called into question," observed Immelt in his first letter to shareholders.[6]

In these circumstances, Immelt recognized that managing risk would be central to GE's long-term stability and development. From the outset, Immelt saw the need to balance GE's business portfolio to ensure cyclical stability:

> We have four strong, powerful long cycle businesses: Power, Medical, Engines, and Transportation. These businesses are strong, number one, with multiple levers to grow earnings through technology and services. Our Power business has led the way through the past few years of gas turbine growth and, as that turbine market subsides, our Power business will thrive by servicing an installed base that has grown five-fold. Our Medical franchise has unlimited opportunities driven by world-class technology, favorable demographics, and global distribution. Our Aircraft Engines business gets even stronger every year as we continue to invest in new engine platforms and technology. The importance of these long-cycle businesses is that they give you steady earnings growth over time, with stable product cycles and rapid service growth.
>
> We also have a leadership franchise in our short-cycle businesses, like NBC, Plastics, Materials, Consumer, and Industrial businesses. These have been hardest hit by the downturn but so far in 2002 we are seeing encouraging signs of recovery . . .
>
> We have the world's most diversified financial services business, with consumer finance, mid-market financing, insurance, equipment management, and specialty

segments. We're growing assets at GE Capital by 15 percent . . . The importance of GE Capital is that it can use GE's financial and industrial strength to generate superior returns over time . . .

The GE portfolio was put together for a purpose – to deliver earnings growth through every economic cycle. We're constantly managing these cycles in a business where the sum exceeds the parts.[7]

Sensitivity to risk also implied balance sheet conservatism and a reduced dependence on financial services – especially in volatile sectors such as insurance.

The discrediting of the 1990s' obsession with shareholder value maximization also had a profound impact on Immelt's priorities for GE. In all his communications to shareholders, Immelt was emphatic that the job of the CEO was not to manage the stock price but to manage the company for the long-term earnings growth that would drive the stock price: "We all want the stock to go up. But to do that we have to manage the company. In fact, the only way you can run GE is to believe that performance will ultimately drive the stock."[8] Apart from providing the underlying earnings growth, the only other influence that management could play was to offer transparency to investors through detailed financial reporting. If the annual report had to be "the size of the New York City phone book, that's life," commented Immelt.

Immelt also saw the need to redefine GE's relationship with its external communities in a post-Enron, post-bubble world. Long-term stability and prosperity required forging relationships of confidence and trust not just with investors, but also with customers, suppliers, government, and society at large. Social and environmental responsibility would become central themes in GE's relationships with the outside world.

However, the most crucial issue for GE, believed Immelt, was to identify the likely sources of profit in the future. Under Welch, the potential for value creation through cost reduction and the elimination of underperforming assets had probably been fully realized. Immelt would need to look to new areas. Top-line growth would have to be the driver of bottom-line returns. Yet, opportunities for value creation were likely to be meager: "I looked at the world post-9/11 and realized that over the next 10 or 20 years, there was not going to be much tailwind." The primary driver of such growth, figured Immelt, was organic growth – given the level of M&A activity and the huge volume of funds flowing into private equity funds, acquisitions could easily destroy shareholder value.

Among the opportunities for profitable organic growth, Immelt was drawn to four global trends:

- *Demography.* The world's population was aging rapidly. This would create opportunities for goods and services required by older people – healthcare services in particular.

- *Energy and the environment.* The conflicting forces of growing demand for energy and global warming threatened to be a dominant feature of the global business environment in the 21st century. The growing demand for efficient, environmentally sound energy production offered interesting opportunities for GE.

- *Technology.* Developments in electronics, biosciences, materials technology, and nanotechnology would offer the basis for new products and new industries.

- *Overseas markets.* The major growth opportunities of the future were likely to be outside the mature industrialized countries, where GE was most strongly positioned. In the emerging market world, the so-called BRIC countries – Brazil, Russia, India, and China – offered the greatest opportunities.

Given the likelihood of modest growth in the world economy throughout the decade, Immelt recognized that the key to GE's ability to create value would be its success in generating organic growth. The central challenge was to identify where the most promising opportunities for profitable growth would lie. While Immelt's first priority during his first year at GE was shoring up confidence within the company and among customers and investors, and in the aftermath the various external factors that GE was forced to contend with, he also devoted considerable time to developing his thinking concerning GE's long-term strategy.

GE's Growth Strategy

The central theme of Immelt's new strategy for GE was growth. In 2002, he committed GE to an organic growth rate of 8% per annum – under Welch organic growth had averaged 5% a year – and to "double digit" earnings growth. Throughout his first five years as chairman and CEO, Immelt maintained these goals – with a particular emphasis on the 8% organic growth target. Profits would grow faster than revenues, explained Immelt, because of reductions in general and administrative expense as a percentage of sales and higher margins resulting from new products and services. While every business faced unique growth opportunities, Immelt believed that profitable growth would be the result of a number of common factors (see exhibit 18.1).

Reshaping the Business Portfolio

To position GE for stronger growth, the company would need to exit slow growth businesses, reallocate resources to businesses where growth prospects were strong, and enter new businesses. Despite Immelt's focus on organic growth, repositioning would require acquisition. Immelt stressed that GE's acquisitions would be selective and focused: "We don't acquire companies just because we can. We don't go for unrelated fields. We acquire companies that give us new growth platforms where GE capability can improve financial performance and build shareholder value."[9]

Immelt's first five years was a period of intense acquisition activity for GE. Between September 2001 and January 2007, GE's major acquisitions comprised:

- *Broadcasting and Entertainment:* Telemundo and Bravo TV networks and Vivendi's Universal entertainment business.
- *Healthcare:* Amersham (UK diagnostics and medical equipment company), HPSC (financial services for medical and dental practices), Abbott Diagnostics (the world's leading provider of *in vitro* diagnostics).
- *Energy:* Enron's wind energy business, BHA Group Holdings (emission reduction equipment), ChevronTexaco's coal gasification business, AstroPower (solar energy products).
- *Commercial Finance:* Bay4 Capital (IT equipment leasing), CrossCountry Energy (gas pipelines), CitiCapital's Transportation Financial Services Group

EXHIBIT 18.1

GE's Five Key Areas for Business Growth

GE is committed to achieving worldwide leadership in each of its businesses. To achieve that leadership, GE's ongoing business strategy centers on five key growth initiatives:

- Technical Leadership
- Services
- Customer Focus
- Growth Platforms
- Globalization

GE is committed to leadership in the "next generation" of **technology**. We are well-positioned to drive growth for the future with technical excellence in each business by developing a global technical capability, increasing new product growth, and investing in global research.

Services have grown from the traditional activities of parts replacement, overhauling and reconditioning machines to a larger and broader vision. Our new vision includes investing in our business and technology to improve the performance on our installed base and the way we actually service it. Through higher technology, we have the ability to go beyond servicing to reengineering the installed base. By doing so, we dramatically improve our customers' competitive positions. GE is in the midst of an incredible transformation brought on by the internet explosion. Our pursuit of digitization will rapidly change our dealings with our vendors, partners, and, most of all, our customers.

Customer focus is ensuring that everything we do provides value to our customers. It means creating a partnership that – combined with our expertise in financial, service, and technology industries – maximizes customer profitability and ensures quality.

A key GE strength is our ability to conceptualize the future, identify "unstoppable" trends, and develop new ways to grow. **Growth** is the initiative, the core competency we are building at GE.

Globalization is not only striving to grow revenues by selling goods and services in global markets. It also means globalizing every activity of the company, including the sourcing of raw materials, components, and products. Globalization especially means finding and attracting the unlimited pool of intellectual capital – the very best people – from all around the globe.

Source: www.ge.com

(Citigroup's commercial trucking lending business), IKON Office Systems (Transamerica Corporation's commercial finance business).

- *Consumer Finance:* DeltaBank (a Russian consumer bank), Wizard Home Loans (Australia), credit card operations of Dillard's.
- *Infrastructure:* InVision Technologies (explosives detections systems), Ionics (water purification and water treatment), Edwards Systems Technology (fire detection), Interlogix (security systems), BetzDearborn (water services), Smiths Aerospace (a leading supplier of integrated systems for aircraft and a subsidiary of UK company Smiths Industries).

TABLE 18.2 GE's business portfolio, 2004

Growth engines

COMMERCIAL FINANCE	A range of financial products and services for businesses, especially in the mid-market segment. Also capital asset leasing, real-estate finance, and commercial loans.
CONSUMER FINANCE	Credit services for consumers and retailers, including private label credit cards, personal loans, bank cards, real estate and home equity loans, purchasing cards, and credit insurance.
ENERGY	Comprehensive solutions for oil and gas, traditional, and renewable power generation, and energy management.
HEALTHCARE	Diagnostic and interventional medical imaging, information, and services technology.
INFRASTRUCTURE	Protection and productivity solutions for water, safety, plant automation, and sensing applications.
NBC	NBC TV network, 29 local US TV stations, cable channels (CNBC, Bravo, MSNBC), Telemundo; also Vivendi Universal Entertainment.
TRANSPORTATION	Comprises Aircraft Engines and Rail.

Cash generators

ADVANCED MATERIALS	Provides material solutions, including engineering thermoplastics, silicon-based products, fused quartz, and ceramics.
CONSUMER & INDUSTRIAL	Appliances, lighting products, industrial equipment, and systems and services.
EQUIPMENT SERVICES	Products and services that help medium and large businesses manage, operate, and finance business equipment, including: operating leases, loans, sales, and transportation and management services.
INSURANCE	Business insurance includes insurance and reinsurance products. Consumer insurance that helps consumers create and preserve wealth, protect assets, and enhance lifestyles.

SOURCE: GENERAL ELECTRIC 10-K REPORT, 2004.

In 2004, GE reorganized its 13 businesses into 11 and distinguished two types of business: "growth engines" and "cash generators" (see table 18.2).

At the same time, Immelt also saw value in a number of GE's slower growing businesses – the key was their potential to generate cash. For example, many analysts believed that appliances and lighting would be early candidates for divestment. However, while acknowledging that their growth was low, Immelt confirmed that, "We'll stay in those businesses. They both return their cost of capital."[10] GE's major divestment during this period was the major part of its insurance business. In addition, its plastics division was also slated for disposal.

A key theme in Immelt's reshaping of GE's business portfolio towards higher growth was the creation of new "growth platforms." Growth platforms could be extensions of existing businesses or they could be entirely new areas of business. For example, GE's expansion into Spanish language broadcasting (spearheaded by the acquisition of Telemundo) was an example of one of GE's businesses (NBC) expanding into a new, fast-growing market segment. Other growth platforms could be entirely new businesses that drew upon some of GE's existing strengths. For example, renewable energy and security services were entirely new areas of business for GE.

Identifying new growth platforms was established as a central strategic challenge for GE's businesses. The approach involved the analysis and segmentation of markets to identify high-growth segments that offered the potential for attractive returns, then to use a small acquisition as a basis for deploying GE's financial, technical and managerial resources to build a leading position.

Technology

Immelt remarked on the fact that he represented a different generation from Jack Welch, and that his generation had a much closer affinity for technology. He identified technology as a major driver of GE's future growth and emphasized the need to speed the diffusion of new technologies within GE and turn the corporate R&D center into an intellectual hothouse. His commitment to technology was signaled by expanding GE's R&D budgets. This began with a $100 million upgrade to GE's corporate R&D center in Niskayuna, NY, and was followed by the construction of new R&D facilities in Shanghai and Munich, Germany. By the end of 2006, GE Global Research had over 2,500 researchers working in GE research centers in New York, Bangalore, Shanghai, and Munich.

Immelt's emphasis on technology reflected his belief that the primary driver of sales was great products: "You can be six sigma, you can do great delivery, you can be great in China, you can do everything else well – but if you don't have a good product, you're not going to sell much."[11] Increasing product quality and product innovation became a critical performance indicator for all of GE's businesses.

Customer Focus

A key feature of Immelt's career at GE was the extent of his customer orientation and the amount of time he spent with customers, building relationships with them and working on their problems. Looking ahead, Immelt saw GE using IT and redesigned processes to become increasingly customer focused. Soon after taking over as CEO, Immelt emphasized the primacy of customer focus: "We're dramatically changing our resource base from providing support to creating value. Every business has functions that add high value by driving growth. These are the functions that deal with the customer, create new products, sell, manufacture, manage the money, and drive controllership. Call that the front room. Every business has back-room support functions that sometimes are so large and bureaucratic they create a drain on the system and keep us from meeting our customers' needs and keep us from growing. So we're going to take more of the back-room resources and put them in the front room – more sales people, more engineers, more product designers. We're changing the shape of this company and we're doing it during a recession."[12]

A key aspect of Immelt's creation of a customer-driven company was a revitalization of GE's marketing function. "Marketing was the place where washed-up salespeople went."[13] Upgrading GE's marketing was achieved through re-creation of GE's Advanced Marketing Seminar, establishing an Experienced Commercial Leadership

Program, and requiring that every business appoint a VP-level head of marketing. Most important was the creation of GE's Commercial Council that brought together GE's leading sales and marketing leaders to develop new business ideas, to transfer best practices, and instill a commercial culture within GE. A key initiative was "At the Customer, For the Customer," a program that deployed six sigma in marketing, sales, and customer relations activities, applied GE's six sigma methodologies to customers' own businesses, and used new metrics to track customer satisfaction and customer attitudes.

An important outcome of GE's enhanced customer focus would be the ability to better meet customer needs through bundling products with support services and combining product and service offerings from different businesses. Every business was encouraged to create customer value through bundling products with a variety of customer service offerings, including technical services, financial services, training, and the like. Across businesses, enterprise selling was given greater prominence. For example, in the case of a new hospital development, there might be opportunities not just for medical equipment, but also for lighting, turbines, and other GE businesses as well. To exploit new opportunities from that cut across GE's existing divisional structure, GE began to create cross-business, high-visibility marketing campaigns. "Ecomagination" emerged from GE's 2004 strategic planning process as a way for GE to better capitalize on greater environmental awareness through combining initiatives in emissions reduction, energy efficiency, water supply, and scarcity management. The ecomagination proposal then went to the Commercial Council, which planned an initiative involving 17 products.[14]

Increasing GE's capacity to better serve customers with integrated solutions was a key consideration in Immelt's 2005 reorganization – barely a year after the previous reorganization: "In 2005, we restructured the Company into six businesses focused on the broad markets we serve: Infrastructure, Commercial Finance, Consumer Finance, Healthcare, NBC Universal, and Industrial. Each business has scale, market leadership, and superior customer offerings."[15] Figure 18.2 shows GE's organizational structure at the beginning of 2007.

Immelt believed that some of the biggest payoffs from greater customer orientation would come from GE's increased success in international markets. This would involve more local product development and an increased emphasis on truly aligning products and services to meet local market needs rather than simply adapting product features. In terms of exploiting opportunities in major growth markets such as India and China, Immelt saw the need to go from a "defeaturing" mindset (i.e. providing a stripped-down American product) to "customer optimization" mindset.

Exploiting global opportunities would also involve globalizing GE's own talent base. Under Immelt's leadership, GE sought to internationalize its workforce – including core corporate functions. By 2006, among 400 younger members of GE's audit staff, about 60 were Indian.

Changing the GE Management Model

The management model that was in place throughout Immelt's years at GE had been developed and refined by his mentor, Jack Welch. Immelt respected GE's management systems and process and recognized that many of them were so deeply embedded within GE's culture they were parts of GE's identity and the way it viewed the

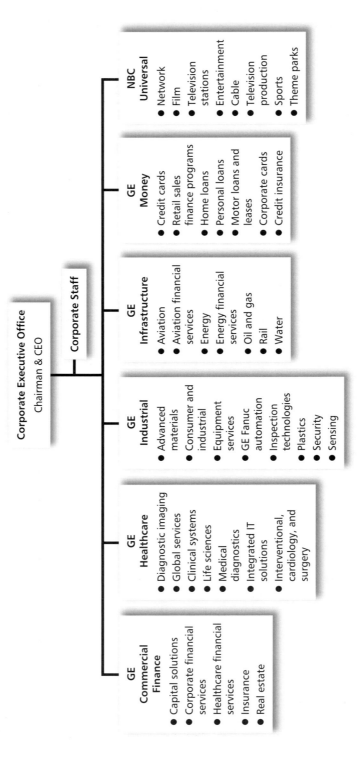

FIGURE 18.2 GE's organization structure: major businesses and divisions, 2007

world. For example, metrics are central to GE's management processes. GE was a performance-driven company and performance was driven by quantitative targets that allowed focus and accountability. "Nothing happens in this company without an output metric," observed Immelt. All of Immelt's strategic initiatives – from the 8% organic growth target to productivity improvements, reductions in overhead costs and six sigma – were linked to precise quantitative targets. In 2005 GE standardized its customer satisfaction metrics, focusing on "net promoter scores" (the percentage of customers who would recommend GE to a friend, minus the percentage who wouldn't).

There were also areas where the new growth strategy would require management change. As with Jack Welch, Immelt saw his most important task as helping to develop GE's managerial talent. To implement his growth strategy required that each of GE's employees internalized it as part of his or her personal mission. This required not only constant communication and reinforcement from the CEO, but also the skills and aptitudes to become "growth leaders." A benchmarking exercise on 15 companies with sustained records of revenue growth (e.g. Toyota and Dell) sought to identify the characteristics of their leading managers. The result was the categorization of five "growth traits." These included: external focus, imagination and creativity, decisiveness and clear thinking ability, inclusiveness, and deep domain expertise.

These growth traits became part of GE's annual HR review, with each of GE's top 5,000 people rated on each of the five traits and the results of the assessment built into their subsequent development plans. Career planning also changed: because of the importance of domain expertise, managers were being required to stay longer in each job.

A key challenge was to reconcile GE's famous obsession with profitability and cost control with the risk taking needed to exploit new growth opportunities. "Imagination breakthroughs" were promising projects for new business creation that had the potential to create $100 million in sales over a three-year period. By mid-2006, some 100 imagination breakthroughs had been identified and individually approved by Immelt. Once approved, these projects were protected from normal budget pressures. About half involved new products and the other half involved changing commercial structure. Immelt saw these imagination breakthroughs as a means of focusing attention on the goal of business creation and development. Given that some of these projects involved substantial levels of investment (GE's hybrid locomotive, for example, would require tens of millions of dollars), by lifting these projects from the business level to the corporate level, it took pressure off the business heads. One problem, observed Immelt, was that GE did not possess sufficient product managers and systems engineers to put in charge of high-visibility programs involving substantial risks and substantial possible returns.

Common to most of the organizational changes initiated by Immelt was the desire to create value through the many parts of GE working together more effectively to make major achievements. "Working at GE is the art of thinking and playing big; our managers have to work cross-function, cross-region, cross-company. And we have to be about big purposes."[16]

By 2005, Immelt developed his vision for growth and its attainment into a six-part process that was disseminated throughout the organization and became a key part of Immelt's communication to GE's external constituencies (see figure 18.3).

FIGURE 18.3 GE's six-part growth process

Customer Value
Use our process excellence to create customer value and drive growth

Growth Leaders
Inspire and develop people who know how to help customers and GE grow

Innovation
Generate new ideas and develop capabilities to make them a reality

Execute for Growth

Globalization
Create opportunities everywhere and expand in developing markets

Leadership in Technology
Have the best products, content, and services

Commercial Excellence
Create world-class marketing and sales capability to drive "One GE" in the marketplace

Growth is the GE initiative. After growing historically at an average of 5% revenue growth, in 2004 we launched this initiative to achieve 8% organic growth per year. This is about twice the rate of our industrial and financial peers. We want to make organic growth a process that is predictable and reliable.

SOURCE: GENERAL ELECTRIC 2005 ANNUAL REPORT, P. 8.

Looking Ahead

Immelt's strategy for GE required the development of new capabilities. At the most general level, this was the capacity to grow. This required the nurturing of capabilities in relation to commercially relevant technical research, customer relations, new product ideas, and the creation of novel bundles of products and services. Developing these capabilities meant reconciling GE's existing operational, financial, and strategic capabilities with the new priorities in relation to marketing, new product development, and business development. Using well-known GE tools of metrics management and management development, Immelt was demonstrating considerable progress in implementing the new strategy. Indeed, all of GE's major businesses – with the exception of NBC Universal, which was experiencing declining audience rankings – were reporting strong growth in both sales and profits (see table 18.3). A critical issue, however, was whether the new strategy would deliver the kind of long-run performance that Immelt had targeted. As Harvard Business School professor Clay Christensen observed:

TABLE 18.3 General Electric: segment performance, 2001–2006

	($ millions)					
	2006	**2005**	**2004**	**2003**	**2002**	**2001**
Revenues						
Infrastructure	47,429	41,803	37,373	36,569	40,119	36,419
Industrial	33,494	32,631	30,722	24,988	26,154	26,101
Healthcare	16,562	15,153	13,456	10,198	8,955	8,409
NBC Universal	16,188	14,689	12,886	6,871	7,149	5,769
Commercial Finance	23,792	20,646	19,524	16,927	15,688	14,610
Consumer Finance	21,759	19,416	15,734	12,845	10,266	9,508
Profit						
Infrastructure	9,040	7,769	6,797	7,362	9,178	7,869
Industrial	2,694	2,559	1,833	1,385	1,837	2,642
Healthcare	3,143	2,665	2,286	1,701	1,546	1,498
NBC Universal	2,919	3,092	2,558	1,998	1,658	1,408
Commercial Finance	5,028	4,290	3,570	2,907	2,170	1,784
Consumer Finance	3,507	3,050	2,520	2,161	1,799	1,602

	Fixed assets				Additions to fixed assets
	2006	**2005**	**2004**	**2003**	**2003–5**
Infrastructure	94,113	89,555	82,798	76,185	11,666
Industrial	43,216	41,556	42,040	40,359	10,683
Healthcare	28,561	24,661	24,871	10,816	2,339
NBC Universal	30,500	31,196	34,206	11,619	1,585
Commercial Finance	198,117	190,546	184,388	172,471	15,140
Consumer Finance	160,734	158,829	151,255	106,530	597

SOURCE: GENERAL ELECTRIC 10-K REPORTS.

> *The major growth engine at GE has been GE Capital . . . But the fact that it's been a great growth engine in the past means it likely won't be in the future. That's my biggest worry for GE. I don't see a new engine of growth that's comparable to what they had in the past. One challenge is that the bigger a business gets, the less and less interest it has in small opportunities. And all the big growth markets of tomorrow are small today.*[17]

Other concerns related to the ability of GE's organizational structure and management systems to effectively execute the growth strategy. Developing new products, businesses, and customer solutions required new and more complex cross-business and cross-functional coordination within GE. The new performance requirements were being built on top of GE's existing commitments to efficiency, quality, and financial performance. Could this added complexity be borne by a company that was steadily growing larger and encompassing a widening portfolio of businesses and products? Management research pointed to the fact that most companies pursuing the combination of innovation and efficiency in fast-moving business environments were forced to become less diverse in order to maintain outstanding performance. Among the other top-20 companies on *Fortune*'s "most admired" list in 2006, Procter & Gamble, Johnson & Johnson, Berkshire Hathaway, and 3M were widely diversified – the other 15 were much more specialized, with most being single business companies (FedEx, Southwest Airlines, Dell, Toyota, Wal-Mart, UPS, Home Depot, Costco). As Immelt made clear to his top managers, GE was entering uncharted waters: "The business book that can help you hasn't been written yet." While Immelt was extolling the benefits of GE's diversity as a source of strength and opportunity, other companies were moving in the opposite direction. At the beginning of 2007, Altria announced the sale of its Kraft food business and its refocusing around its core Philip Morris tobacco business, American Standard announced it was splitting into three separate companies, while Tyco was in the process of doing the same. As Chris Zook, head of global strategy at Bain, commented: "The conglomerates are dead. With some rare exceptions, the conglomerates' business model belongs to the past and is unlikely to reappear."[18]

Notes

1 "What Makes GE Great?" *Fortune*, March 6, 2006, pp. 90–6.
2 Jeff Immelt's 2002 Annual Report to Share Owners, Waukesha, Wisconsin, April 24, 2002, pp. 4–5.
3 Letter to Shareholders, General Electric Annual Report 2003.
4 "Running the house that Jack built," *Business Week*, October 2, 2000.
5 "The days of Welch and roses," *Business Week*, April 29, 2002.
6 Letter to Shareholders, General Electric Annual Report 2001.
7 Jeff Immelt, 2002 Annual Report to Share Owners, op. cit.
8 Jeff Immelt, Address to shareholders, Annual Share Owners' Meeting, Philadelphia, April 26, 2006.
9 Jeff Immelt, 2002 Annual Report to Share Owners, op. cit.
10 "This is just about the best gig you can have," *Business Week*, September 5, 2001.
11 "Growth as a process. An interview with Jeffrey R. Immelt," *Harvard Business Review*, June 2006.
12 Jeff Immelt, 2002 Annual Report to Share Owners, op. cit., p. 8.
13 "Growth as a process. An interview with Jeffrey R. Immelt," op. cit.
14 Ibid.
15 Letter to Shareholders, General Electric 2005 Annual Report.
16 "Growth as a process. An interview with Jeffrey R. Immelt," op. cit.
17 "The GE mystique," *Fortune*, March 6, 2006, p. 100.
18 "Less than the sum of the parts? Decline sets in at the conglomerate," *Financial Times*, February 5, 2007, p. 9.

AES Corporation: Rewriting the Rules of Management

God made us all a certain way. We're all creative, capable of making decisions, trustworthy, able to learn, and perhaps most important, fallible. We all want to be part of a community and to use our skills to make a difference in the world.

DENNIS BAKKE, CEO, AES

We broke all the rules. No overtime. No bosses. No time records. No shift schedules. No assigned responsibilities. No administration. And guess what? It worked!

OSCAR PRIETO, AES MANAGER AND DIRECTOR OF LIGHT
SERVICIOS DE ELECTRICIDADE, BRAZIL, OCTOBER 1998

Spring 2002 presented AES Corporation, the world's largest independent power generator, with the most difficult business circumstances in its 21-year history. After a decade of strong growth and a steeply rising market valuation that had taken AES into the S&P 500 in 1998, AES's world had been shaken to its foundations by four major shocks. The first was the Californian power crisis of 2001. Despite limited involvement in the Californian electricity market, AES was immersed in the recriminations, lawsuits, and regulatory investigations that had followed California's electricity debacle. Second, AES had been caught up in the wake of Enron's collapse at the end of December 2001. Although AES's direct losses resulting from Enron's bankruptcy amounted to a mere $15 million, Enron's collapse had a profound impact on investors' risk perception and upon the legitimacy of a range of previously accepted business practices, including off-balance-sheet financing. The third crisis having an impact on AES was Argentina. Argentina represented one of AES's largest overseas interests, with over $1 billion invested. The meltdown of the Argentine economy had rendered these investments all but worthless and had had knock-on effects on AES's power interests in Brazil. The gloom affecting AES's Latin American operations was further increased by the mounting crisis in Venezuela. Finally, the aftermath of the September 11, 2001 terrorist attacks on the US had created further uncertainties for AES's global interests. With investments in several Muslim countries – in particular Pakistan and Kazakhstan – AES was again subject to greatly increased financial, political, and physical risk.

These factors had combined to ensure AES's entry into the infamous "90% club" – those companies (mainly technology, media, and telecommunication companies) that had lost more than 90% of their stock market value. After touching $70 a share in September 2000, AES's share price had fallen below $4 in February 2002. The sharp decline in AES's market value had placed considerable strain on AES's finances, making it increasingly difficult for AES to access the capital markets. In February, ratings on AES's unsecured debt were cut to below investment grade.

These combined pressures had forced an abrupt reversal of strategy at AES. After two decades of continuous and rapid expansion, the company was forced to retrench. In a series of measures announced in February 2002, AES began the desperate task of shoring up its finances and protecting itself against an increasingly hostile external environment.

For co-founder and CEO Dennis Bakke the most troubling aspect of the sudden strategic shift was not the abandonment of AES's ambitious growth targets. He believed that AES possessed the financial and management strengths needed to survive the current financial pressures. His concerns related much more to his personal mission to build AES as a different kind of company. Under the leadership of its two co-founders, Roger Sant and Dennis Bakke, AES had rejected profit and shareholder wealth as its *raison d'être* and committed itself to the pursuit of integrity, fairness, fun, and social responsibility. These principles were embedded in a management system that was referred to by board member Robert Waterman (of *In Search of Excellence* fame) as an "adhocracy," and which the *Wall Street Journal* described as "empowerment gone mad."[1] There were no staff functions or corporate departments; almost all traditional management functions were devolved to workers at the plant level.

So long as AES was a darling of Wall Street, investors and analysts were happy to accept AES's lofty values and its founders' disdain for profit. But the events of 2001 and early 2002 had changed all that. AES's values and unique management system – which had been so effective in encouraging employees' loyalty and commitment, generating initiative and entrepreneurial drive, and promoting unmatched levels of operational efficiency – now had to come to terms with a very different environment.

AES had grown from an entrepreneurial startup to a public corporation with 38,000 employees and 179 plants in 31 countries. Could a management system based on trust, fun, openness, and decentralized decision making work in a large complex organization that embraced national cultures ranging from traditional Islamic societies (Pakistan), to post-communist systems (Hungary, Bulgaria, Ukraine, Kazakhstan) and the oligarchic societies of Latin America? AES's industry environment was also changing. During the 1990s, AES was one of a small number of independent power producers that was riding a wave of opportunity as governments throughout the world privatized their state-owned electricity sectors. During the 21st century the flow of privatization opportunities was slowing while competition was growing. New entrants into electricity production included not just the independent power producers but also traditional utilities (Duke Power, Consolidated Edison, Electricité de France), gas companies (Centrica, Gaz de France), and oil majors (BP, Shell, Exxon Mobil).

AES's Origins and Development

In January 1982, Roger Sant and Dennis Bakke founded Applied Energy Systems based in Arlington, Virginia. Their purpose was to take advantage of a 1978 Public Utility Regulatory Policy Act (PURPA) that required utilities to purchase power from independent energy producers. Sant and Bakke believed they could build a business in a niche segment of the enormous power-generation industry.

At first glance, Sant and Bakke seemed a rather unlikely pair to start what was to become a large international energy company. Although both held Harvard MBAs, their experience was primarily public sector. Sant headed the Ford Administration's energy conservation efforts and Bakke served as a chief aide. Following government service, they moved on to the Mellon Institute's Energy Productivity Center, where they researched energy conservation. It was during this time that the pair came up with the idea of starting their own company.

Sant and Bakke had a very difficult time raising money at first, because nobody took them very seriously. According to Bakke, "[we] had the worst possible background for raising money . . . first government and then academic experience. It looked to investors like a combination of inefficiency and ivory tower."[2] However, Sant and Bakke had one key advantage: as a result of their involvement in drafting PURPA, they were among the first to recognize the opportunity for independent generators to produce power at much lower costs than the established utilities.

After several joint ventures (notably with Arco) Sant and Bakke decided to go it alone and in 1985 built their first power plant adjacent to an oil refinery in Houston, Texas. The plant was not profitable; however, the second and third plants that AES built "weren't disastrous, and four, five, and six turned out to be superb. By 1989 it was clear that we had reached viability."[3]

In 1991, AES went public. With a stronger equity base it was ready to look at opportunities overseas. Because of the rapid growth in electricity demand in many emerging markets, inadequate generating capacity, and the trend towards privatization, Sant estimated that over 70% of AES's opportunities lay outside the US. The fast-growing Asian markets for electricity, especially the huge potential markets of India and China, were especially attractive. In the early 1990s, AES acquired two plants in Northern Ireland and one in Argentina. International expansion involved participating in the auctioning of state-owned power plants by governments, and bidding for long-term contracts to supply power to electricity utilities. During the mid-1990s, AES's biggest new investments in power generation were in Kazakhstan and China. The 1996 acquisition of Light Servicios de Electricidade, Brazil, was a major strategic departure for AES: this was its first entry into the distribution end of the power business. Deregulation was also creating opportunities in the US. Changes in utility regulations at the state level resulted in some utilities selling off their generating facilities – AES was among the most prominent bidders for these facilities.

Between 1998 and 2001, AES continued to expand rapidly both at home and overseas. Tables 19.1 and 19.2 show AES's plants and distribution facilities at the end of 2001.

TABLE 19.1 AES's generating plants, December 31, 2001

Country	Number of plants	Generating capacity (MW)	Date of entry	Notes
USA	30	38,729	1986	15 coal, 14 gas, 1 oil
Canada	1	110	1997	1 gas
Brazil	10	9,711	1996	8 hydro, 2 gas
Argentina	6	3,353	1993	2 gas, 3 hydro, 1 coal
Chile	4 (?)	1,716	2000	1 gas, 1 hydro, 1 coal
Venezuela	4	2,265	2000	4 gas
Colombia	2	1,090	2000	1 hydro, 1 gas
Panama	3	380	1999	3 hydro
Mexico	1	484	2000	1 gas
Puerto Rico	1	454	2002*	1 coal
Dominican Republic	3	1,107	1996	2 gas, 1 oil
UK	7	5,763	1992	3 gas, 4 coal
Netherlands	1	415	1998	1 gas
Italy	1	140	2001	1 oil
Hungary	3	1,331	1996	1 gas, 2 coal
Georgia	3	823	2000	2 hydro, 1 gas
Kazakhstan	8	8,414	1996	6 coal, 2 hydro
Pakistan	2	695	1997	2 oil
India	1	420	1998	1 coal
Bangladesh	2	810	2001	2 gas
Sri Lanka	1	165	2002*	1 gas
Oman	1	427	2003*	1 gas
Qatar	1	750	2004*	1 gas
China	4	1,665	1997	3 coal, 1 oil
Australia	3	1,247	1999	2 gas, 1 oil
Nigeria	1	290	2001	1 gas
Cameroon	1	800	2001	1 hydro
Tanzania	1	112	2003*	1 gas
South Africa	1	600	2001	1 coal

*AES to commence production.

SOURCE: AES 10-K REPORT FOR 2001.

The result of the years of expansion was not only a substantial growth in the size of AES between 1998 and 2001, but also increasing complexity of the business as AES diversified its activities within the power sector. During 2001, AES recognized four lines of business activity:

- *Contract generation* – producing electricity supplied on long-term contracts (5 to 30 years) to distribution companies.
- *Competitive supply* – generating facilities that sell electricity directly to wholesale and retail customers in competitive markets. Output is sold into power pools, into daily spot markets, and on short-term contracts.

TABLE 19.2 AES's electricity distribution businesses, December 31, 2001

Country	Gigawatt hours	Customers served (000s)	Date of entry
USA	22,999	626	1999
Brazil	86,949	12,137	1996
Argentina	4,822	698	1997
Venezuela	9,724	1,132	2000
El Salvador	669	226	2000
Dominican Republic	2,990	350	1999
Georgia	2,200	370	1998
Kazakhstan	2,572	469	1999
Ukraine	5,540	1,146	2001
India	2,102	600	1999
Cameroon	3,020	452	2001

SOURCE: AES 10-K REPORT FOR 2001.

TABLE 19.3 Revenues and gross profit by line of business, 2000 and 2001

	Revenue ($ billion)		Gross profit ($ billion)	
	2000	2001	2000	2001
Contract generation	1.7	2.5	0.77	0.83
Competitive supply	2.4	2.7	0.56	0.44
Large utilities	2.1	2.4	0.54	0.74
Growth distribution	1.3	1.7	0.13	0.30

SOURCE: AES 10-K REPORT FOR 2001.

- *Large utilities* – regulated monopolies supplying electricity within specific geographical areas. These utilities combine generation, transmission, and distribution capabilities.
- *Growth distribution* – distribution facilities that offer significant potential for growth because they are located in developing countries or regions where the demand for electricity is expected to grow at a higher rate than in more developed areas.

Table 19.3 shows revenues and gross profit earned by AES's four lines of business.

Performance

AES's financial and operating performance during the 1990s placed the company among the top-performing firms of the decade, not only in its sector, but across the stock market as a whole. During 1991–2000, AES's return on equity averaged 25%, while in the five years up to the end of 2000, returns to shareholders averaged 70% a year.

This performance amazed many observers, given the limited priority that AES accorded profits and shareholder return. In monitoring its own performance, AES emphasized four performance measures:

- *Shared values* – How did we do in having an organization that is fun, that is fair, that acts with integrity, and that is socially responsible?
- *Plant operations* – How safe, clean, reliable, and cost-effective were our facilities?
- *Assets* – What changes occurred in our assets, including AES people, during the year? This intends to measure the company's project development and construction progress as an indicator of future earnings potential.
- *Sales backlog* – What happened to our backlog of contract revenues during the year?

AES's performance targets combined operational efficiency, employee satisfaction, community development, project development, and growth. For example, AES's goals for 1998 were stated in "Our Wish List" published in the 1997 Annual Report. These included:

- Continuing progress in adapting to and living the AES principles and values.
- Creating the most fun workplace since the beginning of the industrial revolution, and eliminating hourly payment systems.
- Adding 10 to 15 new businesses to the AES portfolio.
- Engineering a breakthrough in slow development businesses such as Ib Valley (India), Puerto Rico, and Nile Power (Uganda).
- Maintaining 100 new business ideas in the development pipeline.
- Making our 1998 budgeted net income and cash flow.

Operationally, AES plants were among the best performers in their industry. AES's US plants typically operated at around 95% capacity, compared with an industry average of 83%. Nor was operational excellence restricted to new plants. AES's West Belfast power station has achieved 95% availability in some years, remarkable for a 43-year-old facility.

During 2001, AES's financial performance deteriorated sharply. Although revenues grew by a healthy 24%, this was mostly from acquiring new businesses and adding new plants. Revenue from existing operations grew by a more modest 5%. Net income fell by two-thirds as a result of lower market prices in the UK, decline in the Brazilian Real resulting in currency losses of $210 million, losses from closed telecom activities of $194 million, and higher expenses.

Table 19.4 summarizes some key indicators of AES's performance during 1991–2001.

Values and Principles

AES's unique organization and management systems were the direct result of the values upon which the company was established and which defined every aspect of its management. These values reflected the personal beliefs of the two founders, Roger Sant and Dennis Bakke. Both men were brought up in strongly religious families:

TABLE 19.4 AES's performance, 1991–2001

	1991	1992	1993	1994	1995	1996	1997	1998	1999	2000	2001
Revenue ($ million)	334	401	519	533	679	835	2,227	3,257	4,117	7,534	9,327
Sales backlog ($ billion)	n.a.	29	27	43	41	51	98	116	138	217	n.a.
Net income ($ million)	43	56	71	98	107	125	299	441	357	795	273
Earnings per share ($)	0.16	0.20	0.25	0.33	0.35	0.40	0.79	1.11	0.84	1.66	0.52
Total assets ($ billion)	1.4	1.6	1.7	1.9	2.3	3.6	11.1	12.9	23.2	33.0	36.7
Long-term debt:											
Non-recourse ($ billion)	n.a.	1.1	1.1	1.0	1.1	1.6	4.5	4.5	9.5	12.7	14.7
Recourse ($ billion)	n.a.	0.1	0.1	0.1	0.1	0.5	1.1	1.6	2.2	3.5	4.9
Stockholders' equity ($ billion)	n.a.	0.2	0.3	0.4	0.6	0.7	2.0	2.4	3.3	5.5	5.5
Equity generating capacity (thousands of MW)	0.7	1.2	1.5	1.5	2.1	3.4	4.6	n.a.	n.a.	n.a.	50.8
Return on average equity (%)	48.6	35.1	29.2	28.3	22.6	19.7	17.1	20.2	12.6	17.9	4.9

SOURCES: ANNUAL REPORTS, UBS SECURITIES EQUITY RESEARCH.

Bakke as a Baptist, Sant a Mormon. Bakke was raised on a farm in Washington State. From the age of five he had worked in the fields and by the time he was 18 he had built up a herd of 29 beef cattle. Bakke's attitude to enterprise and material possessions was strongly influenced by ideas of Christian stewardship, which emphasized responsibility, building for the future, and sharing good fortune with others. Sant attended Brigham Young University and spent two years as a missionary with Native Americans in Wisconsin. Over time, Sant became less committed to the church and increasingly active in the environmental movement.

From the outset, both men viewed AES as an opportunity for them to pursue their values and effect a fundamental change in business practices. In a section of its 10K report entitled "Principles, Values and Practices," AES stated:

> A core part of AES's corporate culture is a commitment to "shared principles or values." These principles describe how AES people endeavor to commit themselves to the Company's mission of serving the world by providing safe, clean, reliable and low-cost electricity. The principles are:
>
> ● Integrity – AES strives to act with integrity, or "wholeness." AES people seek to keep the same moral code at work as at home.
>
> ● Fairness – AES wants to treat fairly its people, its customers, its suppliers, its stockholders, governments, and the communities in which it operates.

- Fun – *AES desires that people employed by the Company and those people with whom the Company interacts have fun in their work. The Company believes that making decisions and being accountable is fun and has structured its organization to maximize the opportunity for fun for as many people as possible.*

- Social Responsibility – *Primarily, the Company believes that doing a good job at fulfilling its mission is socially responsible. But the Company also believes that it has a responsibility to be involved in projects that provide other social benefits, and consequently has instituted programs such as corporate matching of individual charitable gifts in addition to various local programs conducted by AES businesses.*

AES recognizes that most companies have standards and ethics by which they operate and that business decisions are based, at least in part, on such principles. The Company believes that an explicit commitment to a particular set of standards is a useful way to encourage ownership of those values among its people. While the people at AES acknowledge that they won't always live up to these standards, they believe that being held accountable to these shared values will help them behave more consistently with such principles.

AES makes an effort to support these principles in ways that acknowledge a strong corporate commitment and encourage people to act accordingly. For example, AES conducts annual surveys, both company-wide and at each business location, designed to measure how well its people are doing in supporting these principles through interactions within the Company and with people outside the Company. These surveys are perhaps most useful in revealing failures, and helping to deal with those failures. AES's principles are relevant because they help explain how AES people approach the Company's business. The Company seeks to adhere to these principles, not as a means to achieve economic success but because adherence is a worthwhile goal in and of itself.[4]

Sant and Bakke recognized that these values could not be easily reconciled with the concept of a shareholder-focused, profit-maximizing corporation, and both leaders made it very clear where their priorities lay:

Where do profits fit? Profits . . . are not any corporation's main goal. Profits are to a corporation much like breathing is to life. Breathing is not the goal, but without breath, life ends. Similarly, without turning a profit, a corporation too, will cease to exist . . . At AES we strive not to make profits the ultimate driver of the corporation. My desire is that the principles to which we strive would take preeminence.[5]

AES's commitment to its values, at the expense of shareholder gain where necessary, was indicated by the proviso that AES inserted in all of its prospectuses for new security offers which identified AES's values as a source of investor risk:

The Company seeks to adhere to these principles, not as a means to achieve economic success, but because adherence is a worthwhile goal in and of itself. However, if the Company perceives a conflict between these principles and profits, the Company will try to adhere to its principles – even though doing so might result in dominated or forgone opportunities or financial benefits.[6]

The AES principles and their implementation reflected a set of assumptions about human nature. Sant and Bakke believed in the ultimate goodness of people – "Man is made in the image of God," declared Bakke.[7] Hence, within organizations, people can and should be trusted to exercise responsibility, and at the same time should be held accountable. Critical to the ability to motivate people is the innate desire of people to make a contribution to society. This implies that, for an organization to be effective and to harness human effort and ingenuity, the organization must be committed to a wider social purpose. These views are at variance with many of the assumptions on which many traditional management systems and techniques are based and imply a different approach: "[t]he people in AES are not principally economic resources. We are not tools of the corporation. Rather we hope the corporation is structured to help individuals make a difference in the world that they could not otherwise make."[8] Table 19.5 summarizes some of the ways in which Bakke believed that AES was different from other companies.

Organizational Structure and Management Systems

AES's organizational structure and management systems were manifestations of its values and principles. AES described the key features of its organization in its statement of values:

> In order to create a fun working environment for its people and implement its strategy of operational excellence, AES has adopted decentralized organizational principles and practices. For example, AES works to minimize the number of supervisory layers in its organization. Most of the Company's plants operate without shift supervisors.
>
> The project subsidiaries are responsible for all major facility-specific business functions, including financing and capital expenditures. Criteria for hiring new AES people include a person's willingness to accept responsibility and AES's principles as well as a person's experience and expertise. Every AES person has been encouraged to participate in strategic planning and new plant design for the Company. The Company has generally organized itself into multi-skilled teams to develop projects, rather than forming "staff" groups (such as a human resources department or an engineering staff) to carry out specialized functions.
>
> Many people have asked us about our team structure and how it works. To begin with, there is no one person in charge of teams and there is no Human Resources department. Teams are the basis of our structure, and they encompass the four values of our company. They are fluid; many people are members of more than one team at one time. A team is somewhat autonomous; all decisions about a project are made within that team, with final say granted to that team. Decisions are made not from the top–down, but from the bottom–up. Furthermore, responsibility is pushed to the lowest level possible, encouraging everyone to be part of a decision. As a result, each team member views the project in terms of a whole. Colleagues and team members must trust each other to follow through to the best of their ability.
>
> Because people are what make up AES, we have decided not to resort to an organizational model. Instead, we give you the following comments from AES people regarding teamwork. In general, AES teams work extremely well in both

TABLE 19.5 What made AES different?

Conventional approach	Dennis Bakke's approach
More than 95% of important decisions are made by official leaders of the organization, officers and board members	Some 99% of all important decisions are made by non-leaders
Employees have established expenditure limits above which they must obtain prior approval	No approval by supervisors and higher-ups is required for spending company money; only obtaining advice is mandatory
Organization charts are published and job descriptions are determined for everyone by managers and HR dept.	No official organization charts; no job descriptions except those that say "Do whatever it takes" or ones written by the employee
Under "control" philosophy, the job of supervisors is to make decisions, hold people responsible, and perform a host of other tasks, making it impossible for more than a few people to report to any one leader. A large organization may require eight to 12 layers of management	No more than three to five supervisory layers between the CEO and an entry-level person. Each person is responsible for managing himself or herself
Leaders see their role as managing people and resources	Leaders see their role as serving other employees
Managers are responsible for closely monitoring employees and holding them accountable for performance	Leaders advocate self-accountability, self-initiative, self-control, and individual responsibility among employees
Many separate staff groups oversee operations. Members of each staff group have similar skills and educational backgrounds	Minimal number of specialist staff groups (strategy, finance, HR, etc.). These functions are assigned to local operating teams
Financial management, risk assessment, and new business development are set apart form general operations	Financial management, risk assessment, and new business development are important elements of each person's job
The principal purpose of the company is creating shareholder value, although other purposes or goals may be mentioned	The principal goal or purpose of the company is stewarding its resources to serve society in an economically strong manner
Shared values are promoted as a technique to achieve economic goals	Shared values are goals to which the company aspires in and of themselves
Board of directors sees primary role as representing the interests of shareholders	Board of directors sees role as representing the interests of all stakeholders (employees, suppliers, shareholders, customers)

SOURCE: DENNIS W. BAKKE, JOY AT WORK: A REVOLUTIONARY APPROACH TO FUN ON THE JOB (SEATTLE, WA: PVG, 2005), EXTRACTS FROM APPENDIX B PP 295–303.

achieving a common goal and having fun while doing so. The following ideas provide insight on what makes teams work well and what can stimulate true and productive teamwork.

"Teams imply friendship; not only the ability but the desire to work together. Starting with the wonderful example set by the original AES team, Roger and

Dennis, working together in small groups has been a natural way to get big things done while preserving the dignity of each person." Tom Tribone.

"There are two reasons why teams are successful at AES: the type of people we have here and the environment in which they work. People at AES tend to be independent and thrive in a loose environment where roles and responsibilities are not always clearly defined. The environment at AES is one where responsibility is pushed down to the lowest level possible, encouraging everyone to take ownership for not only their piece of the project, but for the project in its entirety." Michael Cranna.[9]

This is not to say that AES lacked formal structure altogether. The most striking feature of its organization was the few layers of hierarchy: until the mid-1990s there were only three organizational layers between the front-line employees and the CEO. AES was divided into regional organizations or "groups." These groups comprised the different plants, each of which was headed by a plant manager. Within each plant there were typically seven areas or "families," each of which was headed by a superintendent.

Figure 19.1 shows AES's formal structure at the beginning of 2002.

No Functional Departments

The company did not have a legal, human resources, or any other department. Decisions in such matters were made by teams at the plant level, which oftentimes had little or no experience in those decision areas. CFO Barry Sharp estimated that the company had raised $3.5 billion to finance ten new power plants, but he was personally responsible for raising only $300 million of that sum. The rest was secured by decentralized, empowered teams. When AES raised 200 million pounds sterling (about $350 million) to finance a joint venture in Northern Ireland, two control room operators led the team that raised the funds.[10] The same went for other areas of financial management. Treasury operations were decentralized to the individual plant level, where they were performed by teams of non-specialists:

His hands still blackened from coal he has just unloaded from a barge, Jeff Hatch picks up the phone and calls his favorite broker. "What kind of rate can you give me for $10 million at 30 days?" he asks the agent, who handles Treasury bills. "Only 6.09? But I just got a 6.13 quote from Chase."

In another room, Joe Oddo is working on J. P. Morgan & Co. "6.15 at 30 days?" confirms Oddo, a maintenance technician at AES Corp.'s power plant here. "I'll get right back to you."

Members of an ad hoc team that manage a $33 million plant investment fund, Messrs. Oddo and Hatch quickly confer with their associates, then close the deal. "It's like playing Monopoly," Mr. Oddo says as he heads off to fix a leaky valve in the boiler room, "Only the money's real."[11]

Similarly, there was no human resources department. At the corporate level there were no staff specialists dealing with salary ranges, or annual review procedures, or personnel policies, or contract negotiations with unions. There was a person whose responsibility was to track 401k retirement plan benefits and send out the necessary reports, but that was about it at the corporate level. Everything else was devolved to the individual divisions, and within these it was the teams within each plant that handled almost all the human resource functions.

FIGURE 19.1 AES's company structure

BOARD OF DIRECTORS
Chairman
(Roger Sant)

EXECUTIVE COMMITTEE
CEO
(Dennis Bakke)

COO	COO	COO	COO
Growth & Distribution Business	Contract Generation	Competitive Supply	Large Utilities
(Paul Hanrahan)	(John Ruggirello)	(Stuart Ryan)	(Barry Sharp)

CORPORATE OFFICERS

General Counsel	SVP & CFO	SVP, Investor Relations	SVP, Financial Forecasting and
(William Lurashi)	(Barry Sharp)	and Business Development	Corporate Issues
		(Kenneth Woodcock)	(Roger Naill)

OPERATING DIVISIONS

AES Americas (Brazil, Venezuela)
(Paul Hanrahan)
AES Andes (Argentina, Chile)
(Joe Brandt)
AES Aurora (Mexico, Central America, Caribbean)
(Sarah Susser)
AES Coral (Panama, El Salvador)
(Ned Hall)
AES Electric (England, Wales, France, Italy)
(Michael Armstrong)
AES Endeavor (N.E. USA, E. Canada)
(Dan Rothaupt)
AES Enterprise (Mid-Atlantic USA)
(Dan Rothaupt)
AES Great Plains (USA Midwest)
(Lenny Lee)

AES Horizons (Ireland, Low Countries, Scandinavia, Baltic States) (Ann Murthow)
AES Oasis (Middle East, South Asia)
(Shahzad Qasim)
AES Orient (China)
(Bill Rucius)
AES Pacific (Southern California)
(Mark Woodruff)
AES Sao Paulo (Brazil)
(Luiz Travesso)
AES Sirocco (Balkans, Turkey, North Africa)
(Mike Scholey)
AES Silk Road (former Soviet Union)
(Garry Levesley)
AES Transpower (Australia, N. Zealand, S.E. Asia)
(Haresh Jaisinghani)
Think AES (retail and telecom)
(Tom Tribone)

SOURCE: AES, 10-K REPORT, 2001.

The company operated without written policies or procedures. Issues such as hiring practices, leave periods, and promotion criteria, which in more conventional companies would be spelled out in a "Policies and Procedures" handbook, were left at the employees' discretion. When trying to find out how much time she could take off after the birth of her daughter, a Project Director for AES Puerto Rico discovered that the company did not have a policy about maternity leave. After investigating what other "AES people" had done, she decided to do what made sense for both herself and the business requirements of the project. In the end she decided to take three months, but she made herself available at critical points in the project's execution.[12]

Virtually all human resource decisions were made at plant level, and, within the plant, decision-making authority was located among the different teams. For example:

- *Recruiting.* The recruiting process was done at the plant level, without any support or guidelines from corporate headquarters. AES people at all levels were committed to the hiring process, and everyone could participate in it. The process generally involved an initial résumé review, and a phone interview followed by a group interview. Interviews usually did not include technical questions. Instead, they focused on characteristics that helped determine how the candidate would fit with the company's culture and values. There was little importance given to the candidates' educational background or experience, as greater emphasis was placed on the candidates' desire to learn, contribute, and grow, as well as their personal values and self-motivation.

- *Training and development.* In line with corporate values, AES employees were empowered to make decisions about their own development. Training was mostly done on-the-job, through open communication channels and embedded advice-seeking practices. However, AES people were free to take outside classes and they were reimbursed for them, as long as the courses were work-related.

- *Career paths.* Regarding development, there were no established career paths. Rather, the company encouraged flexibility, which was a necessary requirement in such a dynamic industry. Because one of the company's shared values was to "have fun," employees were encouraged to move within the company if they felt their current assignment was "boring." Job vacancies were always posted and promotion decisions were made at an area superintendent's meeting.

- *Compensation and benefits.* AES did not have a set salary schedule for any given job, and salaries were determined based on what others were being paid inside and outside the company. Raises were given every year and superintendents usually determined them in an annual meeting. Most AES people put their retirement savings in company stock, and the company matched up to 5% of the person's salary in the retirement plan.

This emphasis on multi-functionalism was central to AES's concept of making work fun. The key was to make people's work fulfilling by continually providing challenges and learning experiences. Moreover, argued Bakke, specialization did not promote efficiency or better decision making: "As soon as you have a specialist who's very good, then everyone else quits thinking," Bakke said. "The better that person is, the worse it is for the organization. The information goes through the specialist, so all the education is to the person who knows the most."[13]

Moreover, AES relied heavily on outside expertise. A key aspect of the system of empowerment was that individuals and teams were encouraged to seek out the best advice available, whether it was within the company or outside. In relation to finance, while AES's financial management and project management teams lacked great depth in financial expertise, they drew upon the knowledge of bankers and financiers. In any event, Bakke's view was that most management expertise, whether functionally specialized or general management skill, was not inherently difficult. Motivation, attitude, and a willingness to learn were more important determinants of ultimate performance.

Decentralized decision making and lack of functional expertise meant that AES frequently made mistakes – sometimes big ones. AES's experience in the former Soviet republic of Georgia displayed an inability to appreciate the implications of Georgia's political or criminal environment. The result was a $300 million loss for AES.[14] AES also experienced dire government relations in Hungary.

The "Honeycomb"

AES referred to its organizational structure as a "honeycomb." The idea was that each plant comprised a number of small, flexible, self-managed teams who were able to operate cooperatively and efficiently without any centralized direction. At the basis of this structure was the belief that organizations did not need to be managed. Thinking, motivated people could manage themselves and undertake the communication and mutual adjustment needed to coordinate complex tasks. According to Dennis Bakke, the key to effective decentralization was keeping the basic units of organization small:

> I think of AES as a conglomeration of small communities. And I don't think there's any company in the world that's so big that you can't organize this way. Even a plant with 400 people can be broken down into smaller groups. It's a small enough community that there is the ability to have an accountability structure within it, you know, a social structure as opposed to a military structure. We will break down the Kazakhstan plant into four units. How can we stay small and be big? By breaking the organization into groups with chief operating officers.[15]

The principle of self-organization imposed a very different role on managers from the conventional management model. Indeed, the term "manager" was seldom heard within AES; it was at odds with the principle of letting people decide for themselves. The example came from the top. "The most difficult thing for me as CEO," confided Bakke, "is not to make decisions." If individuals were to develop, they must be given responsibility and be allowed to learn:

> [T]he modern manager is supposed to ask his people for advice and then make a decision. But at AES, each decision is made by a person and a team. Their job is to get advice from me and from anybody else they think it's necessary to get advice from. And then they make the decision. We do that even with the budget. We make very few decisions here [indicating the headquarters office]. We affirm decisions.[16]

Sant made similar observations:

> If Dennis and I had to lead everything, we couldn't have grown as much as we have. People would bring deals for us to approve, and we would have a huge bottleneck. We've shifted to giving advice rather than giving approval. And we've moved ahead much faster than we would have otherwise."[17]

One consequence of this approach was the small size of AES's corporate headquarters. At any point in time there might be between 40 and 70 AES employees at the Arlington office, but in terms of actual corporate staff, these numbered only about 35.

In terms of performance, one of the most important advantages of the AES system was that it permitted speed in decision making, preparing bids, and completing projects. AES abounded with a folk history of teams and individuals given huge responsibilities or thrust into unique and unexpected situations. Consider the following:

- Oscar Prieto, a chemical engineer with two years' experience with AES, was visiting AES headquarters in May 1996 when he was asked by Thomas Tribone to join a meeting: "I've got 14 people from France and some guys from Houston coming to talk about buying a business in Rio de Janeiro. We've only got two AES people. Could one of you show up?" The meeting with Electricité de France and Houston Light & Power concerned a possible joint bid for one of Brazil's largest utilities, which was being privatized. Within a month, Tribone was on his way to Paris to negotiate an agreement with Electricité de France. The deal was concluded, and by 1997 Tribone had moved to Rio to become one of the utility's four directors and a key player in a succession of deals in which AES acquired a string of power plants and distribution facilities in Brazil and Argentina.

- The development of the $404 million Warrior Run power plant in Cumberland, Maryland was undertaken by an AES team of ten people who handled all the work necessary leading up to the plant's groundbreaking in October 1995. They secured 36 different permit approvals involving about 24 regulatory agencies and arranged financing that involved tax-exempt bonds and ten lenders. At other companies, such a project would typically involve well over a hundred employees.

- Scott Gardner joined AES in 1992 right after graduating from Dartmouth College. Gardner joined a team developing a $200 million cogeneration plant in San Francisco. "It involved a lot of work and few people to do it," he says. "I took on tasks that ranged from designing a water system to negotiating with the community to buying and selling pollution credits." Gardner also helped lead a bid for a $225 million cogeneration plant in Vancouver, British Columbia. When a comparable deal emerged in Australia, Gardner volunteered for that assignment. Two weeks later, he was on his way to Brisbane. "My task was to understand an unfamiliar regional power system, develop a design for the plant, and prepare a financial and technical bid document – all in six weeks," he says. When Gardner's proposal made the final round of competition, his division manager had him negotiate the terms of the $75 million deal. "The stress was incredible, but I was having fun," he says. His bid won. "I held a press conference and was interviewed by local TV stations," says Gardner, who has since left AES to attend business school. "I had to pinch myself to be sure this was happening."[18]

- Paul Burdick, a mechanical engineer, had only been at AES briefly when he was asked to purchase $1 billion in coal. "I'd never negotiated anything before, save for a used car," he said. Burdick spent three weeks asking questions of people both within and outside of the company on how to accomplish the task. At AES, he says, "You're given a lot of leeway and a lot of rope. You can use it to climb or you can hang yourself."[19]

- Ann Murtlow, a chemical engineer with no experience in pollution abatement, was given the job of buying air-pollution credits. She had already purchased the option to buy $1 million in credits when she discovered that the option she had bought was for the wrong kind of credit and useless to AES.

The Relationship with Employees

The AES principles and its concept of the honeycomb organization implied a different type of relationship between those employed and the corporation than that which characterized most companies. To begin with, the absence of functional specialists and the ideas about self-organization required a tremendous amount of information-sharing. According to the company, employees were given full access to the company's operating and financial information. Because of the extent of employee access to information that would normally be confidential at other companies, AES listed all its employees as "insiders" in its submissions to the SEC.

One of AES's crusades was to eliminate the distinction between salaried and hourly paid employees and to put all employees on a salaried basis. The 1997 Annual Report stated the goal of eliminating hourly payment systems. By the end of 1998 considerable progress had been made with more than half of AES's US employees salaried – despite the restrictions imposed by Federal health and safety legislation which perpetuated staff/worker distinctions. The primacy that AES accords its "people," as the company refers to its employees, was emphasized by its practice of listing every employee's name in the back of the AES Annual Report. However, once AES's total employment passed the 6,000 mark, this was no longer feasible.

AES and the Environment

AES's deep commitment to the environment extended well beyond Chairman Sant's personal involvement in environmentalist issues and his active roles in the World Wide Fund for Nature and as a member of the Environmental Defense Fund. AES used forestation to compensate for the emissions it generated. When the company constructed a coal-fired plant in Montville, Connecticut, it calculated that it would generate 15 million tons of carbon dioxide over its estimated life of 40 years. It devised a scheme to plant 52 million trees in Guatemala to offset these emissions. According to AES Executive Vice-President Robert F. Hemphill: "Making electric power historically has had a relatively high level of environmental assault. We are not planting trees as part of our strategy to make us a more valuable company, we're doing it because we think it's a responsible thing to do." AES's average company-wide emission levels were 40–60% of permitted rates.[20]

The Challenge of Multiculturalism

As more and more of AES's business became located outside the US, and non-US citizens far outnumbered US citizens among AES's employees, an increasingly important challenge was to retain AES's culture as the company grew. The company acknowledged that even the stated value of having fun was difficult to accomplish with so many people with many different backgrounds. By the end of the 1990s, fewer than 8% of AES people were native English speakers. The principles of equality, teamwork, empowerment, and individual initiative were also likely to be more difficult to implement in traditional Islamic societies such as Pakistan, and countries with a socialist heritage such as China, Kazakhstan, Ukraine, and Georgia.

Nevertheless, AES remained committed to its principles not just for its US concerns, but for all its worldwide operations. Bakke firmly believed that the AES principles were universal and were not culturally specific either to the US or to the West in general. AES's experience was that its own corporate culture could be transplanted in many different national cultures. The challenges presented in running one of the world's biggest (and once one of the most dilapidated) coal-fired power stations in Kazakhstan, and turning around heavily bureaucratized, former state-owned utilities in South America provided remarkable test-cases in AES's ability to export its company culture. The results were often amazing. Even though AES was unable to eliminate the distinction between salaried and hourly paid employees within the US, in England, Argentina, and Pakistan it moved to an all-salary workforce.

Instilling the AES culture into the 100-year-old Light Servicios de Electricidade involved, first, a generous severance package to cut the workforce by half, second, the careful selection of young, motivated engineers and supervisors to take key positions as facility supervisors, and finally, the devolving of decision-making power to them. At Light's Santa Branca facility, Oscar Prieto chose Carlos Baldi, a 34-year-old engineer, to lead the plant. "I knew he was the right person," says Prieto, "He was young, eager to do more." After agreeing to shared goals and expectations – zero accidents, thrifty construction budgets – Prieto turned Santa Branca and a $35 million upgrading project over to Baldi. After a short while, Baldi was managing in the same way with his project and team leaders.[21]

2002: Retrenchment and Restructuring

During the first quarter of 2002, CEO Dennis Bakke was forced to shift his attention from the issues that most interested him – AES's ability to maintain its values and live its principles – to address the fallout from Enron, Argentina, Venezuela, September 11, and the California power crisis that were devastating AES's share price. On February 20, AES announced a major shift of strategy. In the expectation that AES would be unable to access the capital markets in 2002 for additional borrowing, it would be forced to rely on its internally generated cash flows to fund operations and capital expenditures. Retrenchment measures included: reducing capital spending by $490 million in 2002, selling several existing businesses, and withdrawing from its merchant generation businesses.[22] However, several analysts were doubtful as to AES's ability to command a fair value for the assets it was putting up for sale. In a note to clients, Ronald Barone of UBS Warburg wrote: "The markets in which AES operates are depressed and there are a number of other companies that are already looking to dispose of similar assets."

Bakke recognized the seriousness of AES's situation: he opened his conference call to analysts with the simple statement: "Our world has changed." In the accompanying press release he stated: "We are taking aggressive action to restructure and de-leverage AES. Given today's market climate we are going to rely on the cash flows of our solid operating businesses. We have taken additional steps to provide a more substantial liquidity cushion. We believe the actions we have announced will provide for a more conservative business model."

Under pressure from the board of directors, Bakke was forced to make organizational changes. An executive office was created comprising Bakke as CEO together with four newly created chief operating officers – each with responsibility for one of

AES's four lines of business. The reorganization was intended to: "enhance operating performance, including further reductions of operating costs and revenue enhancements . . . Each COO is directly responsible for managing a portion of the Company's geographically dispersed businesses as well as coordinating Company-wide efforts associated with one of the Company's business segments. In addition, two special offices, the Cost Cutting Office and the Turnaround Office, have been created to bring improved focus and coordination to the management of expenses across the Company and to improve or dispose of businesses that AES believes to be under-performing businesses from a return on capital perspective, respectively. Each of these offices reports to the Executive Office.[23]

The new emphasis on financial control and centralization of decision making conflicted directly with AES values and management principles. But how far did it mean an irreversible rejection of the management model that Bakke and Sant had created at AES? The circumstances affecting AES in 2002 were a "perfect storm" of coincidental adversities: Enron, the California energy crisis, 9/11, the collapse of UK electricity prices, and instability in several of the countries where AES did business – Argentina, Venezuela, and Pakistan. Inevitably AES would have to downplay "integrity, fairness, fun, and social responsibility" while it weathered short-term turbulence. But what about the longer term? The pressure that the AES board had come under from investors and banks demonstrated that the financial community was tolerant of AES's radical approach to management only when its share price was buoyant. But even without this pressure, how realistic was it for AES to maintain its informal, principles-based approach to management in a company that was a multinational employing almost 40,000 people?

Moreover AES's industry environment had changed. Not only was competitive pressure intensifying, but the basis of competition was shifting. In a tougher competitive environment, operational efficiency and entrepreneurial zeal were no longer enough; sophisticated financial structuring, risk management, and government relations expertise were increasingly important. These capabilities tended to be associated with functional experts at head office rather than with task forces comprising front-line employees. AES's unique organizational structure, management systems, and corporate culture had shown themselves to be highly effective both in the efficient operation of power stations and in supporting the entrepreneurial capabilities required for winning power supply contracts all over the world. Moreover, because of its very low rate of employee turnover and open internal communication, it has been very effective in retaining this expertise and sharing it internally. Looking ahead, a critical question was whether AES's management philosophy and methods had reached the limits of their effectiveness and henceforth AES would need to replace its emphasis on fun and social responsibility with a more conventional approach.

Notes

1 "A power producer is intent on giving power to its people," *Wall Street Journal*, July 3, 1995, p. A1.
2 "Arlington's AES Corp. leads a battery of US energy companies overseas," *Washington Post*, May 22, 1995.
3 "The principles behind its power," *Washington Post*, November 2, 1998, p. F12.
4 AES Corporation, 10-K Report for 2001, p. 12.
5 Dennis W. Bakke, "Erecting a grid for ethical power," *The Marketplace*, May/June 1996, p. 5.
6 AES Corporation, 10-K Report for 2001.
7 Personal meeting, April 2000.
8 Dennis Bakke and Roger Sant, Annual Letter to Shareholders, *1997 AES Corporation Annual Report*.
9 AES Corporation, 10-K Report for 2001.

10 Alex Markels, "Power to people," *Fast Company*, 13 (March 1998), p. 155.

11 *Wall Street Journal*, July 3, 1995, op. cit.

12 Jeffrey Pfeffer, "Human resources at the AES Corporation: the case of the missing department," Graduate School of Business, Stanford University, 1997, p. 14.

13 *Wall Street Journal*, July 3, 1995, op. cit.

14 W. J. Henisz and B. A. Zelner, "AES-Telasi," Wharton case study, 2006.

15 Jeffrey Pfeffer, op. cit., p. 14.

16 "The power of a team: Arlington's AES Corporation," *The Washington Post*, February 12, 1996, p. F12.

17 Alex Markels, op. cit., p. 160.

18 *The Washington Post*, February 12, 1996, op. cit.

19 *Wall Street Journal*, July 3, 1995, op. cit.

20 "Power plant builder tries to reenergize environmental image," *The Washington Post*, July 6, 1992, p. F1.

21 Alex Markels, op. cit., p. 164.

22 AES Corporation, Press Release February 19, 2002.

23 AES Corporation, 10-K Report for 2001, p. 3.